Audrey

Audrey

HER REAL STORY

Alexander Walker

St. Martin's Griffin
New York

Library of Congress Cataloging-in-Publication Data
Walker, Alexander.
Audrey : her real story / Alexander Walker.
p. cm.
ISBN 978-0-312-18046-1
1. Hepburn, Audrey, 1929–1993. 2. Motion picture actors and actresses—
United States—Biography.
I. Title.
PN2287.H43W36 1995
791.43′028′092—dc20
[B] 94-33716 CIP

First published in Great Britain by Weidenfeld & Nicolson

D 20 19 18

CONTENTS

Contents

ILLUSTRATIONS

With William Holden in *Sabrina* (Katz Pictures)
With Mel Ferrer (Hulton/Bettmann)
Audrey (Scope)
In a ball dress for *Sabrina* (Weidenfeld Archive)
With Givenchy (British Film Institute)
At home in her Westwood apartment, 1954 (Syndication International)
Winning the Oscar (Katz Pictures)
Audrey and Mel in *Ondine* (Katz Pictures)
With Mel in Rome (Hulton Deutsch)
The wedding in Burgenstock (British Film Institute)

Photo Section III
Dancing practice for *War and Peace* (British Film Institute)
The ball in *War and Peace* (British Film Institute)
In *Funny Face* (British Film Institute)
With Fred Astaire in the darkroom scene in *Funny Face* (Katz Pictures)
Wearing white socks in *Funny Face* (British Film Institute)
Dancing with Fred Astaire in *Funny Face* (British Film Institute)
Having a picnic with Gary Cooper in *Love in the Afternoon* (British Film Institute)
As a cellist in *Love in the Afternoon* (British Film Institute)
In Paris, photographed by Bert Hardy (Hulton Deutsch)
Dancing the Twist with Mel (Rex Features)
Poster for *The Unforgiven* (British Film Institute)
With the horse Diablo in *The Unforgiven* (British Film Institute)
Poster for *Green Mansions* (Katz Pictures)
As Rima the bird girl in *Green Mansions* (Syndication International)
In *The Nun's Story* (British Film Institute)
On the set of *The Nun's Story* (British Film Institute)
With Peter Finch in *The Nun's Story* (British Film Institute)

Photo Section IV
With baby Sean (Katz Pictures)
With George Peppard in *Breakfast at Tiffany's* (British Film Institute)
In *Breakfast at Tiffany's* (British Film Institute)
Singing 'Moon River' in *Breakfast at Tiffany's* (British Film Institute)
Audrey's favourite photo of herself (Margaret Gardner)
In *My Fair Lady* (Weidenfeld Archive)
Wearing sixties fashions in *How to Steal a Million* (Syndication International)

With Albert Finney in *Two for the Road* (Rex Features)
Marrying Andrea Dotti (Rex Features)
As a blind woman in *Wait Until Dark* (British Film Institute)
With her son Luca in Rome (Rex Features)
With Ben Gazzara in *They All Laughed* (British Film Institute)
With Robert Wolders (Rex Features)
In Somalia as a Unicef ambassador (Unicef)
The villa at Tolochenaz (Camera Press)
Audrey's grave (Alexander Walker)

For Sheridan and Ruth——in friendship and gratitude

'The princess did become a queen—
not only on the screen.'

Gregory Peck

ACKNOWLEDGMENTS

As well as Audrey Hepburn herself, whom I met and talked to at intervals over a period of thirty-five years, many others contributed to the writing of this book. The following were specially interviewed for it and I thank them all for their time and trust.

Lindsay Anderson, the film director, covered Audrey's early film *The Secret People* in detail in his book *Making a Film,* and our talks refreshed his own memory and added to my knowledge of her extraordinary beginnings; Peter Bogdanovich, who directed Audrey in her last major role in *They All Laughed,* spoke to me for over an hour by telephone from Los Angeles; Doris Brynner, one of Audrey's closest friends and neighbours in Switzerland, answered my factual queries without breaching a lifelong confidence; Michael Burn, the writer and ex-PoW, recounted to me the extraordinary set of coincidences that had enabled him to help restore Audrey's health just after the war; Sidney Cole, who produced *The Secret People,* recalled her work in it; Stanley Donen, director of *Funny Face, Charade* and *Two for the Road,* knew his star in her every mood and at nearly all phases of her career; Dominick Dunne did some of the best interviews with her; Pauline Everts, a contemporary of Audrey's mother in the Netherlands before and during the war, gave me intimate knowledge of Baroness van Heemstra and her daughter, causing me to revise the hitherto accepted view of them and their family fortunes at this period; Robert Flemyng, the actor, co-starred with Audrey in *Funny Face.*

Margaret Gardner supervised Audrey's public relations at the height of her career; Maggi Goodman, former British editor of *Hello!,* assisted me with information on Audrey's funeral; Angela Hawke at Unicef's London offices, showed me many videos of Audrey's trips abroad for that charity as well as recordings of several of her major TV interviews; Peter King contributed early memories of the girl in the chorus line at Ciro's; Ernest Lehman, screenwriter of *Sabrina,* helped me place Audrey in her early

Hollywood setting with insights into her nature on and off screen; Princess Pignatelli, a friend of Audrey Hepburn's, guided me through the star's Italian background and second marriage; Frederic Raphael, screenwriter of *Two for the Road,* gave me valuable information about the change in Audrey's nature and talents which that watershed film role hastened; Henry Rogers, Audrey's public relations consultant, and his wife Roz Rogers recalled salient moments in their relationship with her; Christa Roth, at Unicef's Geneva offices, proved an invaluable source for the moving and tragic final years of the woman who was both star and friend to the world's destitute children; Walter R. Ruston, a cousin of Audrey and keeper of the Ruston family archives, supplied me with invaluable information on the true origins of Joseph Hepburn-Ruston and the tragic relationship between him and his wife and daughter; Professor Brian Simpson, professor of law at the University of Michigan and the leading authority on wartime internment in Britain, was another patient informant without whose generous sharing of knowledge I should not have discovered the bizarre history of Audrey's father; John van Eyssen recalled Audrey's early appearances in London cabaret; John Warburton, an authority on the British fascist movement, discovered relevant documents and made important contacts that confirmed the early allegiance of Audrey's parents to Sir Oswald Mosley's British Union of Fascists; Dana Wynter, the film actress and a friend of Audrey, recalled aspects of her first marriage.

All but three of the above were interviewed in person—the rest by telephone. The present tense ('he/she says') is used in the text to distinguish between quotations from these primary sources and those culled from elsewhere. Further relevant information, not easy to incorporate attractively in the text, can be found in the Notes on Sources at the end of this book.

In addition I owe a debt of gratitude to others who helped me make contact with major sources or, out of the blue, produced some fragment of information which finally unlocked a puzzling episode of the star's career or her family history. Among them, I gratefully acknowledge the following.

My fellow biographer and film critic Sheridan Morley most generously passed on to me much research material he had gathered for his own monograph on Audrey Hepburn, and Ruth Leon provided information about Audrey Hepburn's film retrospectives and memorial tributes.

Sandra Archer, in Los Angeles, located documents I asked for and most patiently transcribed studio memoranda in public collections; Keith Brace, former literary editor of the *Birmingham Post,* made many helpful research suggestions; Dr John Collee, the medical journalist, advised me on information sources concerning Audrey's possible 'compassion overload'; Ned Comstock, of the USC Cinema/TV Library, Los Angeles, pointed me to much collateral material when I was doing my main work in his archives; Brigid Crowley-Swaine, administrative secretary at the US Embassy in Dublin, assisted my inquiries about Audrey's father; Michael Dwyer, film critic of the *Irish Times,* helped me make contact with Dublin sources; Jeffrey Frost recalled a schoolboy memory of dining with Audrey's mother which helped clear up the mystery of her early post-war years in London; Bernard F. Gertenbach, a producer-presenter in Netherlands radio, found me a copy of Audrey's first film, the promotional short she made for KLM in 1947; Tony Moriarty, research officer at MSF, Ireland's union for skilled and professional people, supplied me with information useful in elucidating the later years of Audrey's father in Dublin; Diana, Lady Mosley, widow of Sir Oswald Mosley, helped me reach Professor Brian Simpson; Nicholas Mosley (Lord Ravensdale) helped me with my inquiries about his father, Sir Oswald Mosley, and possible connections with Audrey's father, Joseph Hepburn-Ruston; Phivos Petrou introduced me to Lois Watson who, in turn, trusted me enough to make contact with Pauline Everts, one of the surviving close friends of Audrey and her mother before the war; Stephen Walton and Nigel Steel, of the Imperial War Museum's reading room, found me many documents offering a fascinating glimpse into the internment experiences of Audrey's father; Gino Wimmers passed on to me contemporary documents throwing light on Audrey's wartime childhood in Arnhem and Amsterdam; Sir Peter Ustinov encouraged his friends at Unicef to see me and talk to me frankly and touchingly about their dearly loved goodwill ambassador; and Lord Weidenfeld opened his address book to offer me his huge range of contacts.

Researching a life involves much travel and paperwork, in addition to the combing of newspaper and magazine cuttings (which are acknowledged in the text where appropriate), and I am grateful to the following institutions in the various countries I visited which gave me access to their archives.

In Los Angeles: The University of Southern California, Cinema-Television Library: in particular the archives from Warner Bros. and King Vidor collections of interview transcripts, screenplays and studio memoranda, and also the Constance McCormick scrapbooks of Hepburniana; the Academy of Motion Pictures Arts and Sciences, Margaret Herrick Library: in particular the Hedda Hopper files and the John Huston collection, for access to which I thank Allegra Huston.

In New York: The New York Public Library at Lincoln Center: in particular the Billy Rose collection; the Museum of Television and Broadcasting.

In London: The Imperial War Museum: in particular the Wiseman Papers and collateral collections, autograph books, etc. relating to wartime internment in Britain; the Bank of England's Museum and Historical Research Section; the British Film Institute, Information Library; the National Film and Television Archives, Stills Library and Viewing Service which arranged for me to see Audrey Hepburn's films; St Catherine's House, the Register Office of Births and Deaths in England and Wales.

In the Netherlands: Airborne Museum, Arnhem: in particular the collection of photographs relating to the German wartime occupation of Arnhem.

In Dublin: Joyce House, the Office of the Register General of Births and Deaths.

I acknowledge the kindness of Mrs Valerie Eliot and the T.S. Eliot estate in allowing me to quote from *The Cocktail Party* (Faber & Faber, 1950).

Other works to which references are made, or from which brief quotations appear in the text, and for which I express gratitude to their authors and publishers, include: *Dangerous Friends* by Peter Viertel (Doubleday, 1992); *Fred Zinnemann: An Autobiography* (Bloomsbury, 1992); *Givenchy* (Exhibition catalogue, Paris-Musées, 1991); *In the Highest Degree Odious* by A. W. Brian Simpson (Clarendon Press, 1992); *Making a Film* by Lindsay Anderson (Allen & Unwin, 1952); *Million Dollar Movie* by Michael Powell (Heinemann, 1992); *Popcorn Venus* by Marjorie Rosen (Peter Owen, 1973).

I express my gratitude to Carol Smith, my agent, for her support and advice; and, at my publishers, to my patient and forgiving editor Allegra Huston.

A note on currency conversion rates used in the text: the pound sterling stood at $2.80 from 1950–67, when it was devalued to $2.40. Afterwards, it fluctuated, and towards the end of Audrey's screen career had dipped to well under $2.00: I have taken the median figure for this latter period to be $1.80. In retrospect, stars such as Audrey appear, at the start of their career, to have been paid an insulting pittance. This is a false impression caused by inflation. In 1950, for example, the equivalent sterling purchasing power of $100 was £68; in 1967, it was £42.

Alexander Walker
London, February 1994

PROLOGUE: THE ROAD
TO CHILDHOOD

*L*ATER, she was to recall the child touching her: it was as if she had stretched out her hand and a chicken had placed its leg and claw within her palm. It was thin and hard and she felt no skin caressing her own, none at all. 'But the worst thing', Audrey Hepburn remembered, 'was that this child's arm seemed to weigh nothing. I was afraid of breaking it. That's when it really hit me. Nothing in my own life, in my own childhood, had prepared me for this. If a child falls down, you pick it up. It's that simple. But there, in that terrible place, you half feared to hold a child in your arms to comfort it. You felt you had an armful of . . . nothing.'

The little convoy of Unicef vehicles—two Range Rovers and a medical truck—had halted for a rest stop near a grove of flat-topped thorn trees. In this part of Ethiopia winds had whisked the dust into writhing patterns as if a huge snake had wriggled over the landscape. It was dangerously easy to mistake such tracks for the road, and follow them into the unmarked wilderness. Even the local officials had had to verify the route by reference to their map. The land that Audrey could see, miles of it, looked as if it had caught jaundice: yellow with drought. Like the people themselves, it was isolated from everything except what was killing it. Audrey had been travelling nonstop for several hours, and she marvelled at how a few hours' flying time could change her view of the condition and destiny of people.

The year was 1988; the month, March. The day before, she had packed the two suitcases which was all the luggage she had been permitted to bring, kissed her Jack Russell terriers goodbye, and whispered 'Goodbye, little room: see you soon again' as she closed the doors of her manor house in the Swiss village of Tolochenaz-sur-Morges and walked into the snowy driveway. An hour or so later she was at Geneva Airport waiting to board the Swissair flight to Addis Ababa. And now this . . .

Five million people, half of them children, were on the point of dying from famine and drought. The refugee camp towards which the convoy was

1

heading contained 151,000 alone. She could not imagine what it would look like. With relief, she climbed out of the second Range Rover. The early years of training for the ballet stage had kept her limbs strong and cramp-free: it was the dehydration that was getting to her. She walked over to the shade of the thorn trees. It was then that she saw the children: a couple of dozen of them, squatting among the ganglion of exposed tree roots which curled around their hunched little bodies. 'The oddest thing was their silence,' she recalled. 'There wasn't a flicker of reaction to our arrival out of nowhere.'

She approached them carefully, fully expecting them to take flight like bats whose rest had been interrupted. 'But they simply hadn't the energy.' They might have been in their early teens—if they had been lucky enough to live so long—but malnutrition had given them the appearance of children half that age. Brown-black skin hung on their bones like tissue paper. Their legs were the thickness of two of Audrey's fingers. Their feet were like long narrow seed-pods. Scraps of blankets covered their ribs. Only their eyes moved, following her with the dulled stare of exhaustion.

Audrey said later that she realized suddenly how tall she must seem to them. And so, instinctively, she dropped on to her haunches, at eye-level with the children.

What did they see as they silently returned her gaze?

A woman just short of her sixties but still trim and springy as a wishbone. A face attuned to registering feeling easily and wonderfully. Tiny wrinkles now crisscrossed it, but they were like tributaries that could feed refreshment into a suddenly dazzling smile. The hair that had once set a worldwide fashion for the 'gamine' cut was still a natural chestnut, but streaked with grey and pulled sharply back into a tight worker's cap secured by a ponytail band. The backs of her hands were liver-spotted but they still suggested a busy temperament, as if they needed to be doing something every hour of the day. Those eyes that used to make love to the movie camera, so easily and naturally, now viewed the world through outsize spectacles that only seemed to magnify the concern of the wearer for what she saw. It was a face cleansed of vanity as completely as it was now cleansed of make-up. All Audrey allowed herself in the heat of Ethiopia was an hourly dab of moisturizing cream.

She moved a finger in front of the eyes of the child she was looking at, to make sure he was not blind. The little boy's pupils followed the movement but his face showed neither animation nor curiosity.

'It was such a shock to me.' She later likened it to stage fright. Only this time the anxiety was generated not by fear of forgetting her lines but by the helplessness that came from having no lines to speak that could break the terrible silence. 'I thought of all the years I'd spent at home in Switzerland and Italy, looking after my own children. And now I'd left home and here were all these children . . . and I could do so little.'

At a loss for words to give expression to her feelings, Audrey stretched out her hand towards the child. The gesture unleashed her emotions. 'I wept.' It was then that the child had placed his hand on hers.

She was still visibly affected as the party climbed back into their vehicles and resumed their journey. One of the Unicef field officers recalls thinking that if she felt so profoundly about one child, she would have a heavy burden of emotion to bear on the rest of this trip, and in the years ahead. There were thousands of children she would have to meet in the crisis spots of the world—territories so fraught with risk and strife, with disease, drought and civil war, that even local leaders hesitated to enter them. As the latest goodwill ambassador appointed by Unicef, Audrey had only her celebrity to protect her: the celebrity she had harnessed to charity in order to use her talent and fame on behalf of children everywhere. This first field trip had shown her the appalling dimensions of the task. 'To tell you the truth,' she confessed on her return, 'I wonder if I'll be strong enough to meet it.'

As they drove on, she had one consoling thought that almost made her feel ashamed. Unlike the doctors she was on her way to meet, she was not in Ethiopia to make people well. That she could not do. The only gift within her power was the one she had so often mistrusted, and even retreated from, in the years gone by: the aura of stardom. Her task was to draw attention to the United Nations' children's fund, to raise money for its work; in short, to use her own famous face to render the official face of international charity visible and compassionate. The special magic she had brought to the screen more than a generation earlier had at last found a purpose that was far more treasurable than self-advancement. The girl who had redefined a feminine ideal had become the woman who would undertake a far greater role than any she had ever been offered: giving the hope of life to many more millions than could ever have watched her films, recognized her face, or even known her name.

'There's one thing about children that makes them fortunate,' she was to tell herself in an effort to find some sort of sanity, some consoling feature in the nightmare whose extent she could never have imagined if she had not seen it with her own eyes. 'Children have only friends,' she would say. 'Children have no enemies.'

FAMILY SECRETS

'CHILDREN have no enemies . . .' Although her heart told her so, Audrey Hepburn's memories of her own childhood denied the truth of this. When the subject used to crop up in interviews many years later, she usually said as little as possible about it or found a means of diverting her interrogator's curiosity into other channels. Even with close friends she was reticent. There were things in her childhood that people might find it difficult to understand.

On her mother's side of the family, Audrey was Dutch and related to a long line of aristocratic landowners, high-ranking military officers, public servants and royal courtiers. The van Heemstras could trace their ancestry back to the early sixteenth century. Audrey's mother, Ella van Heemstra, was born in 1900 on the family estate at Velp not far from Arnhem, one of six children—five daughters and a son—each of whom automatically acquired the courtesy title of baroness or baron. Baroness Ella came from mixed Dutch-French-Hungarian stock and she had Jewish connections. She spent part of her childhood at what was then the family's other country estate in the province of Utrecht, the castle of Doorn. It became the property and sanctuary of the Kaiser when he abdicated and went into exile after Germany's defeat in the First World War. Ella's father, Baron Aarnoud van Heemstra, an eminent lawyer, a solicitor-general and deputy judge in the Arnhem judiciary as well as the town's first mayor, was also an active servant of the Netherlands' overseas empire. Queen Wilhelmina had appointed him governor of the South American colony of Surinam (Dutch Guiana). Baroness Ella was a high-spirited girl who married early, just short of her twentieth birthday. Her husband was a Dutch aristocrat, a royal equerry, the Hon. Jan van Ufford.

Ella's short-lived marriage had been stormy though not discouraging. She felt that things would turn out better 'next time'. This optimism was due in part to a romantic temperament that drew her to men of dashing appearance and impetuous disposition. Reality was further held at bay by the trust she placed in the Christian Science faith in which she had been raised, with the stress it laid on never looking back and regretting past misfortunes and on cultivating the conviction that whatever one wants can be obtained, provided it is pursued with sufficient determination.

Appropriately enough, quite a number of theatre and film people have shown an inclination to apply the tenets of this faith, in greater or lesser degree, to their own lives and careers: Vivien Leigh, Elizabeth Taylor, Doris Day, Marilyn Monroe, to name only a few. It can be dangerous, of course, in a profession already deeply in thrall to unreality; on the other hand it is a great source of comfort and resilience when things go wrong, which they often do in the lives of stars. Baron van Heemstra may well have had misgivings about Ella's temperament, for one family anecdote has him warning her against associating too freely with people of the theatrical world.

The man who was to become Ella's second husband, and Audrey's father, did not come from the theatre, but other warning signs should have been apparent. Joseph Victor Anthony Hepburn-Ruston is generally, and loosely, described as a British financial adviser. 'British' he was in part; 'finance' was something he practised intermittently; but 'adviser' is stretching it—perhaps 'adventurer' would be nearer the mark. His background and the tragedy that befell him were things that Audrey kept so determinedly out of view throughout her life that one almost suspects she had suppressed them from her own memory by a masterful effort of will. To be fair to her, she may never have known the full facts about her father. Even today it is not possible to establish them all, due to Hepburn-Ruston's understandable inclination to conceal the truth about himself as effectively as he was later to hide himself away from his wife and daughter.

One of the rare photographs of Audrey's father which has been released from the family album shows a tall man with a square jaw and a well-defined moustache. His hair is close to the skull and well-groomed. His well-cut jacket is pulled back by the hand resting in his trouser pocket: he looks very confident of the ground he stands on. At first glance he does not appear to be someone with whom it would be sensible to pick a quarrel. The photograph was taken in 1933 or thereabouts, to judge by the age of Audrey who stands holding her father's hand on the terrace of the family home in rue des Hetres, in Beersel, a suburb of Brussels. Hepburn-Ruston would then have been about forty-four, some ten or eleven years older than Ella van Heemstra. The date usually given in biographies of Audrey for her father's birth is 1889, and the place London. Audrey's own entry in *Who's Who* referred to him only as 'J. A. Hepburn'—and made no mention at all of her mother. *Who's Who in America* likewise dropped the 'Ruston'; in fact, he himself appeared to have had difficulty deciding what his name should be.

Ironically, the one name that he was not entitled to use is that which his daughter was to make world-famous. All her life, Audrey lived in the mistaken belief that her own lineage included a Hepburn ancestor. Not so. Audrey's father was descended from a shipwright and mechanical engineer called John Joseph Ruston, who was of Irish or Scottish origins, and who came to Vienna from Britain in 1832 at the invitation of one John Andrews in order to build steamships for the new Danube Shipping Co., of which Andrews was a founder. His success in bringing the steam engine to the European waterways is commemorated in the name Joseph Ruston-strasse, a thoroughfare in Vienna, and a similar street name in Gnunden, Upper Austria. John Andrews's wife Isabella had been born a Hepburn, and she claimed descent from John Hepburn, Earl of Bothwell, the second husband of Mary Stuart. On John Andrews's death, in 1847, Joseph Ruston promptly married his widow, who thus became Isabella Ruston. She died in 1857 in Vienna, without issue.

Ruston, who appears to have been very much the marrying kind, quickly became the husband of a rich Austrian, Barbara Victoria Belha, and they had four children in quick succession: two sons and two daughters. For reasons still unclear, Ruston divorced his wife after the birth of their last child and the family grew up having hardly known their mother at all. The children were wealthy and of a snobbish disposition, and preferred to stake a claim to a royal connection, however distant and tenuous, by making out that Isabella Hepburn had been their mother instead of Barbara Victoria Belha.

These facts have been established by a present-day cousin of Audrey Hepburn's, Walter Ruston, a successful and distinguished engineer living in retirement in Brussels, who has kept the family archives with great assiduity. 'As a result of all this,' he observes, 'Audrey's father probably really and truly believed that his grandmother was one Isabella Hepburn. Of course she wasn't. A short time before Audrey married her first husband, Mel Ferrer, she came to Vienna to visit her grandmother and on that occasion my father showed Audrey a painting of Isabella. But not wishing to hurt the feelings of this beautiful and tender-looking creature who had become a world-famous film star, he didn't have the heart to tell her that she had no real claim to the name Hepburn. I am convinced that, to her dying day, she believed she was a Hepburn.'

Audrey's father was indeed born in 1889, but in Austria, not in England: in a small town called Auschiz. Through his father's nationality, the child's claim to be British was admitted and registered with the embassy in Austria. The family were well-off, at least during Joseph's early childhood, for ownership of a sugar factory had come with his mother Anna's dowry. Pictures of little Joe Ruston show an elegantly tailored and groomed child in sailor suits, riding clothes, *lederhosen* and, in adolescence, the apparel of a young gentleman about town. His disposition to good living and the company of women can be easily imagined from his self-confident, almost cocky pose for the fashionable family photographers of the day. He was likely a very spoilt child. 'But he had a harder time when his mother divorced and remarried, and his stepfather turned out a bad lot and lost much of the family's money,' Walter Ruston recalls. Joseph was probably driven to live on his wits and his charm, of which he had a self-indulgent quantity. He had a gift for languages, which eased his way into various useful social circles and women's affections. His British nationality was clearly of great help in making advantageous connections and a head for figures— or at least an attraction to money—probably took him into international financial dealings of a more or less orthodox kind. His Scots-Irish and Austrian ancestry disposed him to take risks and use charm: a potent combination, though a perilous and unstable one, too, as it turned out. He married early, one Cornelia Wilhelmina Bisschop, and broke up with his wife not long after, perhaps predictably.

The business that took him to the South Pacific and the territory of the Dutch East Indies, as it then was, has not been clearly established, except that—like many of Joseph's later schemes—it involved finance. But photographs taken in Java in the early 1920s leave no doubt about the smart life he was leading. Several show him on the polo field, a beautifully accoutred young rider with dash and devilment written all over him; others show him clad in white tropical suits relaxing with other European acquaintances in elegant drawing rooms or gentlemen's clubs where only the tropical nature of the flowers and plants in the room distinguish the setting from its equivalent ambience of comfort and luxury in London, Paris or Vienna. Joseph Ruston, or Hepburn-Ruston as he may have begun calling himself, was clearly enjoying life.

The earliest record of him is in the official British Foreign Office list for 1923–4 where he features as J. V. A. Ruston, honorary consul in Sumarang, Java. Baroness Ella apparently made his acquaintance on a visit there—perhaps her honeymoon—in the early 1920s. Records indicate that his consulship was short-lived: his employment is listed as 'discontinued', a Foreign Office euphemism that, according to the law professor Brian Simpson, usually signifies that the office-holder left involuntarily, and under a cloud of a serious, though undisclosed, nature. When the baroness met him, he was either separated from his first wife or contemplating the divorce that shortly afterwards took place in San Francisco. He was soon back in Jakarta. Life in the Pacific Rim countries appealed to his pleasure-loving nature. In later years, Hepburn-Ruston acquired the nickname 'Java Joe' and was suspected of having mixed blood, because of his sallow complexion and somewhat alien attitude, though of course he always denied it.

It is a piquant coincidence—but only that—that Audrey Hepburn's own charming looks, her slim form, delicate yet strong body, high cheekbones, large serene eyes, wide smiling lips and, as Cecil Beaton was to put it in a pen sketch for *Vogue,* 'brows that already slanted towards the Orient', also carry suggestions of blood ties with the Far East. She shared many of the beautiful characteristics—not simply in looks, but in temperament too—of the Javanese. She remains to this day the star whose name arouses the most frequent and instantaneous recognition among the peoples of the Far East, particularly in Japan: it is as if they sense a special relationship that transcends her Western stardom.

The baroness met Hepburn-Ruston when she first visited her father in Surinam. She was immediately smitten by him. On her return to Arnhem, she soon found that her own marriage to the Hon. Jan van Ufford was foundering on the obstinate temperament of both parties. Despite having produced two sons, Ian (or Jan) and Alexander, the baroness sought a divorce. She then embarked for Indonesia, where she knew Hepburn-Ruston was now living, and married him in Jakarta on 7 September 1926. It was a love match devoid of fortune or property on the husband's side, quite out of keeping with the van Heemstra family history, and shows what a powerful attraction for women Joseph must have possessed. It went with his dark looks and devil-may-care nature.

Ella and her new husband returned to Europe and, rather oddly, settled in Brussels rather than in the baroness's own country. One senses a certain detachment from her family. What did Hepburn-Ruston do there? The answer generally given in biographies of his daughter is that he managed the Brussels branch of the Bank of England but there is no evidence to support this. Indeed the Bank of England has no 'branches' anywhere: it is not a commercial bank in the generally accepted sense. Moreover, its spokeswoman today firmly, if wearily, denies that the bank ever employed anyone with the surname 'Hepburn' or 'Ruston' or a combination of the two. An

individual named J. V. A. Ruston appears in a Netherlands business directory, listed as a financial adviser, but no other details are given.

It is possible, though extremely unlikely, that the Bank of England is
being a little disingenuous. One writer has asserted that Hepburn-Ruston
was employed on undercover financial work of a 'delicate' nature by Sir
Montagu Norman, Governor of the bank and a determined opponent of
Communism. Norman, it is said, may have used him to spread economic
disinformation about the Soviet Union while assisting the expansionist ambitions of Germany after 1932 and the rise to power of Hitler's National
Socialist Party. If this is true, the evidence has not yet been made public.
More likely, Hepburn-Ruston dabbled in investments and government
bonds as an independent broker. What is undeniable is his increasingly
strong support for right-wing politics. His alliance with Fascism would
eventually ruin his life.

On 4 May 1929, in a large and pleasantly secluded house in the outer
suburbs of Brussels, the baroness gave birth to a girl. She was baptized
Edda (after her mother's Dutch ancestors) Kathleen (after her father's pu-
tative Irish ones) Hepburn-Ruston. Audrey—as Edda would become
known—was a plump infant with a big head on a dumpy body. Nothing yet
suggested the paper-thin waif she would become. A photograph taken of
her around the age of four shows her hair cut in a 'Dutch-girl' style but with
a single thick lock dangling from the fringe over her left brow: a whisper
of the gamine. She was an active, inquisitive child.

Audrey's earliest memory of infancy has a strangely prophetic quality.
She recalled being cradled in her father's arms in a large room mesmerized
by what looked, in recollection, like glittering fragments of ice suspended
directly above her head. She later realized they must have been the crystal
lustres on a chandelier. Her parents' faces interposed themselves, looking
down on her, warm and smiling, but all the baby had eyes for were those
fascinating 'icicles'. Winter was always to be Audrey's preferred season;
white, her favourite colour; and the Swiss Alps, with their snowy peaks and
frozen rivulets, were the view that captivated her over the years when she
had no home of her own, and eventually called her back to spend her dying
days within sight of their pureness and serenity.

Her parents loved music and the sound of their gramophone often filled
the nursery. 'What's music used for?' Audrey later asked her mother, and
received the answer, 'To dance to.' When she was old enough she was taken
to England, and was one day toddling near her mother in a public park at
Folkestone. The baroness was alarmed to discover that her daughter had
disappeared. Seeing a small circle of nursemaids and prams near the band-

stand and going over to investigate it, Audrey's mother found her doing a lively if erratic dance to the popular tunes being played by the military band.

Other sounds filled the house, however, not so reassuring to a small girl: the sounds of parental quarrels. Ella and her husband were cut from much the same temperamental fabric: strong-minded and self-confident. The husband's Celtic wilfulness would never give way to his wife's Dutch stubbornness. Audrey recalled that she used to hide under the dining-room table when she heard the rising storm of her parents' voices. In later life, Audrey was never heard to raise her voice to anyone.

The frequent quarrels, however, had their compensations. After a time they fostered the development of a defensively placid disposition in the child. Her mother's way of dealing with unpleasant things was to ignore them: then they could be considered never to have happened. Audrey didn't take that pain-killing route to unreality. Instead she suppressed her own fears by never permitting herself to become involved in any parental dispute on one side or the other. She found her balance by instinct and, in time, a powerful self-reliance developed. Almost everyone who worked with Audrey in her early years of stardom refers to her total absence of 'temperament', her outward calm and a predisposition to make the best of everything and, if she possibly could, to see the best side of everybody. What began as self-protection grew into an abiding considerateness for other people: a most uncommon attribute in a film star.

Her childhood anxieties, however, took a physical toll on her. She developed mild symptoms of bulimia. She overate: 'It was either chocolate, bread—or my nails.' Still feeling confused and insecure about the attitude of her parents to each other and, consequently, to her, she rejected the dolls her parents bought her, preferring to play with small pet animals which didn't require her to mimic the way a parent behaved with a human baby. She was particularly fond of a Scots terrier and a Sealyham: 'my black and white mascots', she called them. They were the forerunners of Famous, the tiny, beribboned Yorkshire terrier that used to accompany Audrey wherever film-making took her.

But if her father and mother were temperamentally incompatible, they reared their daughter well. The baroness was the stricter parent. As if aware that one broken marriage already behind her and another under periodic strain did not reflect well on her capacity to organize her life, Ella van Heemstra laid emphasis on the Calvinist ethic of hard work, self-discipline and considerateness to others. And Christian Science was not forgotten. As soon as Audrey was old enough to understand and practise its principles she was encouraged to believe in the power of positive thinking. Later on she would see her mother's flaws only too clearly and claim that, although she always took care of her daughter's welfare, Ella had difficulty showing her child affection. But these early lessons in discipline, once learnt, proved enduring. They balanced desire and duty. They were an encouragement to strive, yet a brake on selfish ambition. They explain a great deal about the serenity with which Audrey Hepburn was able to withstand the pressures and temptations that came with fame.

Audrey liked reading and began early on the books which Jan and Alexander had finished with: Kipling's *Just So Stories* and *The Jungle Book* were her favourites. Charles Kingsley's *The Heroes,* about the gods of the Greek myths, was a close third. Her father was her favourite parent: a not uncommon preference of little girls at this stage in their lives. Hepburn-Ruston's impulsiveness, his willingness to 'break the rules' and indulge her, and the confidence which Audrey felt in the company of this handsome, imposing figure who knew his way around and delighted in introducing his daughter to new pleasures was a crucial influence of early childhood.

As the 1930s progressed, the Hepburn-Rustons, husband and wife, became increasingly involved in the right-wing politics of the time. It might have been expected that the baroness, having distant Jewish connections in Eastern Europe, possibly Hungary, would have repudiated any endorsement of the National Socialist movement which had come to power in Germany. But this is to disregard the appeal Hitler had for the financial and aristocratic classes to which her Dutch family belonged. Anti-Semitism, though present and explicit in *Mein Kampf,* was not at first a prominent part of the Nazi agenda; and even those who were aware of it, and apprehensive about it, still believed that the experience of governing Germany would moderate Hitler's views. The old nobility of Europe felt it could 'do business' with the Führer. The 1929 Wall Street crash had shaken some of its great fortunes: the baroness's own family had been hit. Perhaps her husband's financial advice had been to blame.

In any case it was natural for someone of Ella's temperament to support an evangelical call—not yet enshrined as the Nazi creed—to concentrate mind and body on the task of recharging the nation's energies. She was an impressionable woman with a romantic streak, drawn to strong men such as the Führer. As in her marriage, a time would come for repentance, but that time was not yet.

About her husband's support of Fascism much less excuse can be made. Perhaps his adventurous temperament pushed him naturally to extremes.

Perhaps his financial reverses had caused some innate anti-Semitism to germinate. The baroness would soon speak publicly, with approval, of 'the revolt against alien [Jewish] domination of banking and trade'; this sounds like an echo of her husband's prejudices, for none of her intimates can recall hearing her express such a view in casual conversation.

Whatever the extent of their commitment, there are well-attested reports of Ella and her husband attending various Nazi rallies in Germany along with other British and continental personalities of much the same patrician status. According to the biographer David Pryce-Jones, the Hepburn-Rustons figure in photographs of the mid-1930s taken on the steps of the 'Brown House' (the National Socialist headquarters) in Munich in the company of a jolly group of English supporters of Sir Oswald Mosley, who had recently become the leader of the British Union of Fascists. Among them was the Führer's camp follower and reputed lover, Unity Mitford.

Precisely what role Hepburn-Ruston saw for himself in fostering the Nazi cause is hard to determine. So far as is known, he never put his name to any Fascist manifesto, but in view of his subsequent fate this doesn't clear the air so much as add to the suspicions. It was as if he were biding his time, waiting to assume some undercover function. The baroness was not as prudent. She appears as an active supporter in the membership lists of the British Union of Fascists. Though foreigners were not permitted to join Mosley's party she was admitted as the wife of a British subject.

Ella contributed several articles to *Blackshirt,* the British Union of Fascists' publication, as 'Ella de Heemstra'—the French usage probably signifies that she was then living in Belgium. At least one of them was accompanied by a photograph of this determined yet feminine-looking woman, her hair in softly marcelled waves and a silk scarf knotted loosely around her neck in the fashion of an English county lady. Ella van Heemstra had always admired the English: she is said to have confessed on one occasion that her three ambitions were 'to be slim, to be an actress and to be English'.

This article, entitled 'The Call of Fascism' and published in *Blackshirt* on 26 April 1935, is a curious mishmash that does not condemn her so much as reflect her nature. It could have been written by many a so-called Fascist of the time, for it is essential to remember that the majority of Mosley's British supporters were motivated by nothing more sinister than the extremes of patriotism and national self-discipline. They were mainly drawn from the middle and upper-middle classes: professional people, hardworking, respectable and loyal subjects of King and country. The anti-

Semitism, street violence and thuggish intimidation for which the BUF became infamous was also a reality, but in fairness to the baroness, her thoughts were on a higher if rather more fuzzy plane.

The article is a blend of generalized Fascist ideology: dedication to 'King and Empire, the Corporate State, and the revolt against alien domination of banking and trade'. Then it plunges into what one charitably imagines were more congenial waters: her own conviction that salvation lay in bringing the mind to bear on freeing the spirit from 'the fetish of materialism'.

'Too long have we thought that matter paid for matter, and that earthly things could improve the earth. It is not so . . . We who have heard the call of Fascism, and have followed the light on the upward road to victory, have been taught to understand what dimly we knew, and now fully realize that only the spirit can cleanse the body, and only the soul of Britain can be the salvation of Britain . . .'

This adequately conveys the tone—and possibly the extent—of the baroness's commitment to Fascism. The terrible wartime experiences that lay ahead would certainly have purged her of it, had not the coming separation from her husband seemed to do so. But the article exemplifies the baroness's much more tenacious faith in willpower pure and simple. This she passed on to a daughter who otherwise escaped catching the slightest infection from her mother's ill-judged brush with Fascism—though concealing it, and what would be the much more tragic outcome of her father's commitment, was a necessity that Audrey never forgot.

This may help to account for the extraordinary self-control that everyone who ever worked with her recalls. Family secrets are heavy burdens for public people to carry. Audrey carried hers with grace and sweetness of spirit. Some of her closest friends sensed a guardedness about her without quite knowing the reason for it. Stanley Donen, who directed three of her films and came to love and admire her without reservation, wrote that, nevertheless, 'she, in some mysterious way, kept me from being totally intimate . . . I longed to get closer, to get behind what was the invisible, but decidedly present, barrier between her and the rest of us more mortal human beings. Something . . . was there, holding me back from getting as close as I wanted.'

At this time, of course, aged six or so, Audrey would have been unaware of her parents' 'political incorrectness'. Knowledge would come later. After the war it would be largely forgotten by those who knew the baroness and her family: there were much greater crimes to be reckoned with than the indiscretions of a woman with more idealism than good sense. But once Audrey began to become famous, the fact of her parents' allegiance to Fascism, however short-lived, was always present in her mind. Even though she herself was totally innocent, and her mother had long come to regret her misplaced sympathies, it remained a potential threat to both of them and, in particular, to Audrey's career. Any past liaison with the Nazis was a dangerous thing for a post-war celebrity; even a connection with Germany was concealed by the publicists of the time. For example, when Rex Harrison's second wife, Lilli Palmer, accompanied him to Hollywood in 1945 and embarked on her own film career at Warner Bros., the studio publicity machine took great pains to cover up her childhood in Germany by implying that she had been born in Austria, which was considered more acceptable. The care with which Audrey undertook each and every interview in later years is perfectly understandable in terms of her natural conscientiousness. But there was a cautiousness, too—as will be apparent—lest the embarrassing facts of her parents' political leanings be brought to the surface by some interviewer who dug deeper than the studio handout.

What the publicists did stress in Audrey's official biography was an episode so common in the life-stories of many film stars that it carried no stigma where Audrey was concerned, only well-merited sympathy: her parents' divorce. It was 1935, some time in the latter half of the year, when Hepburn-Ruston walked out on his wife and child. Audrey never gave a reason for the rupture of a marriage which was already under strain. It is known that the baroness's attachment to her husband's brand of Fascism was cooling. Perhaps the van Heemstras, with all the family's important connections in Dutch politics, the world of finance and the royal court itself, had prevailed upon Ella to see sense, or at least to be discreet.

But the immediate reason for the break-up of her parents' marriage was simpler and more commonplace, though no less brutal as far as Audrey was concerned. One day, coming home unexpectedly, Audrey's mother found her husband in bed with the nurse employed by the family to look after Audrey and her sons by her first marriage. Ella was terribly shocked. The romantic side of her nature, which had caused her to divorce her first husband at some cost to her family's reputation and financial standing, in order to marry this dashing man, recoiled violently from the suddenness of the disillusion. Strands of her hair turned grey overnight. After a row between husband and wife, loud and fierce in its intensity, Hepburn-Ruston left the house and never returned. He was gone when Audrey woke up.

'I was destroyed at the time,' she recalled some fifty years after the event, 'and cried for days and days. My parents' divorce was the first big blow I had as a child . . . I worshipped my father and missed him terribly from the day he disappeared. Having my father cut himself off from me when I was only six was desperately awful. If I could just have seen him regularly, I would have felt he loved me. But as it was, I always envied other people's fathers, came home with tears because they had a daddy. My mother had great love for me, but she was not always able to show it. I had no one to cuddle me.'

Like the circumstances of Hepburn-Ruston's 'disappearance', his whereabouts over the next few years is something that Audrey and her mother never alluded to: which supports the possibility that he went to Germany and continued his commitment to the Nazi Party. He was sighted there in 1938, by which time the baroness was divorced.

This visit to Nazi Germany may have been connected with Hepburn-Ruston's next appearance in public, which was in London in 1938 and under yet another variation of his name. A photograph taken at the time reveals a well-dressed individual stepping smartly along a city street with his gloves in hand, slightly balder and a shade haggard, but with the same darkly handsome looks that had captured the baroness's fancy. A caption on the photo identifies him as one 'Anthony Ruston', and describes him as 'Director of the European Press Agency'. He gives the photographer a sharp, somewhat suspicious glance—as well he might, for the European Press Agency was a 'front' for the diffusion of Nazi propaganda in Britain and the collecting of intelligence that might be useful to the Reich. It was being run from the German Embassy by Fritz Hesse, a party official who later organized the broadcasts from wartime Germany of the British traitors John Amery and William Joyce, a.k.a. 'Lord Haw Haw', both of whom were executed after the defeat of the Reich. Audrey's father was now playing a more active role on behalf of the Nazis.

Before he became director of the European Press Agency, Hepburn-Ruston had been a close associate of a Nazi sympathizer, Dr Arthur Tester, an Englishman who might have been created by Eric Ambler or Graham Greene in their novels of unease and pre-war conspiracy in Western Europe. Tester used a variety of business interests in London as cover for propaganda work on behalf of Fascism, in particular the Belgian Fascist party, the Rexists, and their leader Leon Degrelle. He was lavishly funded by the Axis, lived in luxury hotels and moved freely around the Netherlands and Belgium and across the Channel, where at one time he owned a huge yacht, registered at Lloyd's under the name *Lucinda* and kept on standby at Portsmouth, aboard which he and his associates would entertain prominent English people whose quisling propensities had been noted. Hepburn-

Ruston was included in some of these gatherings. In 1937, just after he had left his wife and child and made his visit to Berlin, he had been appointed to the board of one of Tester's English companies, British Glycerine Manufacturers Ltd, which had offices at 14 St James's Place, London. Despite its almost ostentatiously innocent name, the firm's manufacture of glycerine was negligible compared with some of its shadier dealings, which had to do with the transfer of moneys into and out of Fascist accounts around Europe. Jacques de Launay's well-researched account, *Histoires Secrètes de Belgique de 1935–1945*, contains details of its transactions and indicates the rich stew of right-wing aristocrats, disaffected military officers of high rank and extremely dubious financiers and their mistresses of which Audrey's father was now a willing and active part.

British Glycerine Manufacturers Ltd had a short life, being wound up in 1938; whereupon Tester, again with Axis money, set up the European Press Agency, appointing Hepburn-Ruston its director. His brief was to provide a flow of 'information', strongly anti-Communist and anti-Semitic, that European newspapers, particularly those in Belgium, could pick up and reprint in their own columns. For this purpose Dr Goebbels placed the sum of £100,000 in the agency's account for Hepburn-Ruston and his associates to draw on. The 'arrangement' was exposed in a debate in the Belgian Parliament on 23 March 1938, and Hepburn-Ruston suddenly found himself being interviewed on his doorstep by the British press, probably tipped off by the intelligence services. He admitted that his agency's aim had been to buy a Belgian newspaper and perhaps a cinema chain, though he refrained from adding the possibly enlightening comment that such media outlets would be used for diffusing pro-Nazi propaganda. On 7 April 1938, the British Home Office promised an investigation. Unsurprisingly, it failed to turn up any links with the German Embassy in London. Hepburn-Ruston retreated again to the shadows; but the whole operation sounds like a warning shot fired by the British authorities, and he must have known what a dangerous game he was playing.

He had in fact been marked out by MI5, the British security service, as a person associating with those who would soon become Britain's enemies. Once this is understood, it becomes clear why the fortunes of this strange man—a kind parent, a committed Fascist, the father of a girl who would become one of the best-known figures in the world—were, unknown to him, about to change so suddenly.

Almost immediately after her discovery of her husband's infidelity the baroness made plans to take herself and her children back to the Netherlands. She went straight to her family's small estate at Arnhem. As far as is known, Hepburn-Ruston never visited her there in any attempt to make things up.

Audrey's half-brothers, Jan and Alexander, continued to live with the baroness, though they spent frequent periods with their father in The Hague, and eventually became far more 'Dutch' in outlook than Audrey. The kinship was friendly, but not close.

Audrey's life changed again after her parents' divorce. It has always been assumed that her mother, coming from a wealthy family, had no financial worries. This was not the case. A friend and contemporary of the baroness, Mrs Pauline Everts, who remembers Ella's move from Brussels to Arnhem, smiles at the mention of the baroness's 'fortune'. 'What fortune?' she exclaims today. 'There was none to speak of. Although Ella came of good stock, and her father had been a colonial governor, don't forget he had six children to provide for. And he couldn't be extravagant even with two pensions, as an ex-judge and an ex-governor, which was largely an honorific appointment. Money had to be looked after. Audrey's family didn't live in a château, or anything approaching it. After a little while, Ella moved into a comfortable but small apartment in one of the main streets in Arnhem. She had enough money—but she wasn't rolling in it. She took part-time jobs. I remember her furnishing some show apartments for a German firm of property developers. She was lucky that Audrey was such a delightful, obedient child, always ready to assist her mother.'

'Audrey went to the Tamboers Basse school in Arnhem,' Mrs Everts recalls. 'Her father was British, so she spoke English fluently as well as French, from having been brought up in Brussels, and she also spoke Dutch very nicely. I believe she attended school in Amsterdam for a short time; perhaps Ella's work took her there. Ella was always a capable woman, a calculating one. She kept an eye open for any chance. She helped people: she was a good "manager". Audrey was an attentive student and well taught, even though she never went on to higher education. One thing my daughter recalls is that she had a very musical ear.'

But Audrey and her mother did not stay in Arnhem all the time. Some time in 1937, they moved across the Channel, to Kent, and Audrey began attending a small private school in Elham, a pretty inland village not far from Folkestone. It looks as if the baroness had decided that her daughter should have as English an education as possible, but it may have been necessary to make economies, too, for Audrey and her mother lodged with a Mr and Mrs Butcher in a comfortable cottage called Orchard Villa. Mr Butcher was the neighbourhood coal merchant. The relationship of the Butcher family to the titled van Heemstras is unknown, but was obviously cordial enough for the baroness to leave Audrey in their care on the occasions when she returned home to her father's estate at Rosendaal in the Netherlands. Audrey took lessons from the Misses Rigden, two spinster sisters who ran a school in the tiny village square for about fourteen local children, aged from five to thirteen. Among them was a girl of around Audrey's age, Joan Hawkins. 'I remember her well,' Joan (now Mrs Ford) says today. 'She called herself Audrey Ruston then, but one day she confided in me, "My name's not just Ruston. It's also Hepburn, too . . . like Katharine Hepburn, the film star." '

No mention was ever made of Audrey's father—'He was a bit of a mystery,' says Joan Hawkins. It seems clear that Ella took great care to impress on Audrey that the last thing her daughter must do was gossip about the divorce, her husband's sudden departure or indeed the right-wing politics of the Hepburn-Rustons. So at a highly impressionable age Audrey was taught the value of discretion, the need to be cautious, even with friends, in holding back protectively some small but vital part of yourself.

Curious evidence of this survives in a bit of verse written in Joan Hawkins's autograph book by Audrey in her irregular childish hand, very unlike the rather too perfect adult script that she later constructed for her rare correspondence. It is dated 8 September 1938, and reads: 'If you have a Friend / Then keep her / Let not that friend your secrets know / For if that friend becomes your foe / Then all the world your secrets know.' The guarded intimacy such sentiments express is disconcerting to find in a child of nine; it hints at a burden of conscience beyond her years, as well as the responsibility laid on her for preserving 'secrets' the nature of which—from what one knows of the Hepburn-Ruston family background—one may easily guess at. But it also speaks, touchingly, of the need to keep one's friends and thus emphasizes, at an early and decisive stage of growing up and recovering from the 'loss' of her father, the central place that the friendship of a few but valued people was to hold in the life of Audrey Hepburn. For whatever motive, friendship was a thing to be treasured. The same autograph book contains a contribution on the page facing Audrey's from Mrs Butcher, the English lady standing *in loco parentis* when the baroness was absent; and it, too, in view of what one knows of the break-up that cost Audrey the presence and companionship of her father, perhaps conveys an unconscious hint of the loneliness and sorrow that Audrey otherwise hid from her village playmates. Mrs Butcher wrote (apparently at the same time as Audrey): 'A little word in kindness spoken / A motion or a tear / Often heals a heart that's broken / And makes a friend sincere.'

Audrey lived the life of a typical English village child. 'She had a slight foreign accent,' says Joan Hawkins, 'but you hardly noticed it.' She joined the First Elham Brownie Pack, whose leader (known as 'Brown Owl') was Mrs Williams, the vicar's wife, and a surviving photograph of the Humpty Dumpty playlet staged by the pack at the village fête shows Audrey as one of the 'King's men' in a soldier outfit with a paper bearskin not quite hiding her distinctive 'Dutch boy' haircut. 'She was much like the rest of us at school,' says Joan Hawkins. 'If anything singled her out it was the ballet lessons she used to go to have in Folkestone. Her mother invited everyone to her ninth birthday party, in May 1938, which was held in the corrugated-iron village hall. What I chiefly remember is a tape that the mother stretched along the wall, to which were pinned little gifts; and the baroness led us up, one by one and blindfolded, to grope for our present . . . but I always felt she steered each child toward the gift she wanted him or her to have. She was quite manipulative that way. Later, we all went back to Orchard Villa and I think it was the baroness who took our group photo with Audrey. A very sharp, clear snapshot for those days, possibly with a German Leica. So far as I could judge, the family hadn't much money, or took care the way they spent it. The baroness bought Audrey my old red bike, second-hand, out of the cycle shop.'

But Audrey's stay among the English children of Elham ended abruptly and somewhat poignantly. Joan Hawkins cannot recall the exact date, but it was certainly in 1939, possibly just before Audrey's tenth birthday. The baroness was in the Netherlands at the time. Joan saw Audrey, with a small travel bag and wearing a white beret, getting into the local taxi. 'It went down the street, past the coal merchant's lorry, and turned out of sight going in the direction of Folkestone and I supposed the train for London. And that was the last I ever saw of Audrey Hepburn. Whatever the reason for her sudden departure, it must have been urgent. She had no time to say goodbye to us children who had been her friends and playmates. She had come to us unexpectedly—she left us just as mysteriously.'

2

THE GIRL WITH DEATH IN HER SHOES

THROUGHOUT her stay in Elham, a little under two years, Audrey apparently never once saw the man she loved most: her father. The marital break-up must indeed have been rancorous, for from 1938 on Hepburn-Ruston was living less than an hour's travelling time away, in London, where he had gone to work for the press agency that was a German 'front' organization. He was still an ardent, if unlisted supporter of the British Union of Fascists, though the gathering rumours of war and Germany's annexation of Austria had disposed of any lingering sympathies with the extreme right wing that his ex-wife had once cultivated.

Ella van Heemstra, who had relatives in the Dutch government, decided that the unsettled international situation was too threatening for her and Audrey to stay on in England. If war came, she preferred to have her family with her in Holland, which she thought a safer place since, after all, the Germans were the cultural cousins of the Dutch rather than the English. But she was in Arnhem when this need seemed urgent; so, allowing her anxiety to overcome the bitterness she still felt towards her ex-husband, Ella made contact with him in London and asked him to see their daughter safely onto an aircraft home. Thus it was that Audrey found herself wrenched away so abruptly from Elham that she did not have time to say goodbye to her friends or even explain where she was bound. Perhaps the baroness thought it more prudent not to intimate that England appeared to her to be a less safe bet than the Netherlands in the event of war.

Father and daughter met at Waterloo Station. It was the first time Audrey had laid eyes on her father since he had walked out of their house near Brussels. 'It was like that scene in *The Railway Children*,' she confided to friends many years later. In E. Nesbit's classic children's book, a father who has 'disappeared' for reasons that are kept hidden from his children because he has been sent to prison, is heart-rendingly reunited with his daughter as he descends from the train and she runs towards him through clouds of steam. In an ironic parallel, Hepburn-Ruston (although he could never have guessed it then) was about to make a journey that would take him away from his child in the opposite direction——into imprisonment for the duration of the war.

He dutifully saw Audrey onto a Dutch plane. Audrey remembered the journey back to the Netherlands as if it were part of a dream where everything was brighter and larger than life. 'It was a bright orange plane . . . it flew very low . . . That was the last time I saw my father.'

In retrospect, of course, bringing Audrey home to the Netherlands was the worst thing the baroness could have done. Much personal suffering would have been avoided if she had taken the rest of the family across the Channel to England. But that was not how things appeared at the time. The Netherlands remained officially neutral when the United Kingdom and Germany went to war, and hoped to stay that way. The sympathies of the majority of Dutch people were with those resisting Hitler, and in the opening months of the offensive it was hard to believe that war would lap over into their country with its long-established ties of trade and blood with the older, pre-Hitlerite Germany. The baroness was one of those who thought so. Audrey would be safer with her, she reasoned.

Audrey showed an early liking for dancing and in 1939, just before her tenth birthday, her mother enrolled her in the ballet class at the Arnhem Conservatory of Music and Dance. She was growing fast. Her puppy fat had dropped away and the regular athletic exercises toughened her muscles, accelerated the slimming process and brought into sight that famous flat-chested figure, the oval face with its high cheekbones and the unusually long yet graceful neck which lessons in posture taught her to hold as gravely and naturally as a flower stem. Although much of the early training for ballet involves looking at oneself in mirrors, it is not necessarily a narcissistic pursuit. Ballet students are taught to search for imperfections, not gratify their vanity. Audrey, as she later confessed, did not much like what she saw of herself in the reflections of the wall mirrors. She always fancied she was awkwardly put together. Individually, the parts of her body may indeed have been imperfect——but so were Greta Garbo's. Yet, as with Garbo, the total effect, in movement or at rest, suggested someone in complete and natural command of herself.

Daily life in Arnhem was calm, though increasingly tense the following year, during the period known officially as 'the phoney war'. In May 1940 the Sadler's Wells ballet company arrived as part of a morale-boosting tour of the Netherlands. They were led by Ninette de Valois; Margot Fonteyn and Robert Helpmann were the principal dancers. In an atmosphere of mounting apprehension they performed the ballet *Façade*. Audrey was chosen by the Arnhem Conservatory to present bouquets to de Valois and Fonteyn, who was her particular favourite. She had seen Fonteyn dance on one of her pre-war visits to London, and had gone backstage afterwards and talked to the charming and welcoming young woman in her dressing room. Later, those who knew both Audrey and Dame Margot Fonteyn, as she became, saw a strong resemblance: not only because of Audrey's early ballet training but also in the serenity of manner that each possessed, the calm and disciplined approach to work, and, above all, in the way they spoke. Both had soft and lyrical intonations that seemed to carry their words to the listener on a thermal current of sincerity and charm. Fonteyn was certainly one of Audrey's earliest role models, in personal style as well as in ballet.

A reception and supper followed the performance of *Façade*. Now the mood of the evening, which had been nervous but kept under control by good manners and the pleasure of watching such artistry, became downright ominous. The sounds of distant gunfire could be heard from over the Dutch border with Germany. The baroness's speech of thanks was endured with tense politeness by the members of the company. The minute she finished, they rounded up their personal belongings, leaving behind their stage costumes and the scenery, and hurried into the waiting bus which left immediately for a Channel port. The next day Arnhem was occupied by German troops. The Dutch queen left for London, followed, a few days later, by her government ministers. The war had arrived on Audrey's doorstep.

'The second worst memory I have after my father's disappearance,' she said, 'was my mother coming into my bedroom one morning, pulling back the curtains and saying "Wake up, the war's on." '

As the Occupation began to clamp down on town and country, everyday life became oppressively unpredictable for Audrey and her family. More than ever she wished that her father were with them.

It is unlikely, given the circumstances of his arrest, that Audrey would have been aware of the fate that had befallen Hepburn-Ruston back in England. Fear of a 'Fifth Column' of Nazi sympathizers, and perhaps saboteurs, among the population led the British Parliament to pass a series of emergency defence regulations even before the outbreak of war. These gave the government powers of summary arrest and detention without trial for an indefinite period. The culmination of these measures, Regulation 18b, as it was known, was passed on 23 May 1940 as a secret law expressly directed against the British Union of Fascists. Mosley's party was proscribed a month later. Several thousand people, including British Union members, were eventually taken into custody under this totalitarian power. Sir Oswald Mosley was imprisoned in Brixton Prison and Diana, Lady Mosley in Holloway. For the most part, the detainees comprised middle-class men and women from all trades and professions: teachers, clerics, civil servants, serving officers (some of whom were arrested in their quarters or even on the barracks square), local government officials (a large group), small tradesmen and high-class store owners, journalists, a sprinkling of Members of Parliament and parliamentary candidates of the extreme right. The sick or hospitalized were not excused, along with one or two terminally ill patients who were forcibly removed from the wards and carted off to prison. Italians and Germans, often long established in Britain and constituting no reasonable risk to the nation's security, were rounded up. Children were included, as well as a few pathetic cases of mentally unstable individuals who had found the Blackshirt cause a focus for their various manias. Most of those interned were simply misguided zealots and super-patriots, right-wingers or so-called gentlefolk impelled by the entrenched class system to support the cause that seemed likeliest to shore up their social privileges and sense of 'English' identity. It is a chapter of British wartime history that has been largely ignored or forgotten, out of a sense of shame, perhaps, but also from a lack of easily available evidence. The bulk of the files relating to 18b detainees, including Audrey's father, either is still withheld from the public archives by the Home Office, or has been destroyed. Professor Brian Simpson's painstaking and horrifying study of the greatest invasion of civil liberties to have occurred in Britain this century was published in 1992 under a title that condemns as well as categorizes it: *In the Highest Degree Odious*.

This, then, was the political pogrom—no other word is more apt for the swiftness, inhumanity and frequently blundering inefficiency with which the police and MI5, the secret services, acted—in which Hepburn-Ruston now found himself caught up. He was arrested, some time after July 1940, and charged at first with membership of the British Union of Fascists. However, his name still did not appear on the official membership list. The charge was changed to one of 'hostile association'. This was much more serious. It implied that the person named—on the charge sheet he was referred to as 'John [*sic:* not Joseph] Victor Anthony Hepburn-Ruston', an error typical of those made by Regulation 18b's harassed officials—was effectively, if not legally, suspected of being an enemy of the state or of being a security risk by virtue of associating with others who were known enemies. Apart from Hepburn-Ruston's unswerving allegiance to Fascism, the basis for this charge must have been his post as director of a Nazi-controlled news agency based in London which was used as a 'front' for the Reich. Had Hepburn-Ruston chosen to go to Germany at the outbreak of war, the fate that was now about to befall him could have been even more grievous; for from what one knows of his nature, there is little doubt he would have found his way into the same network of foreign nationals whom the Nazis used to make propaganda against the Allies. As he was a British subject, the consequences could have been a charge of treason and the penalty the same as that paid at the end of the war by other turncoat Britons like John Amery and William Joyce: namely, execution. Hepburn-Ruston was luckier, though he probably didn't view it that way at the time of his arrest. The papers relating to his case have not been made public, if they exist at all at this date. Consequently all information about the incarceration he was to endure for the next five years is anecdotal, or based on his fellow detainees' mention of him in letters, diaries or present-day interviews.

Hepburn-Ruston was first held in Brixton Prison, then, according to one eyewitness, transferred at the time of the early air raids on London to the concentration camp that had been built on Ascot racecourse, complete with barbed wire, watchtowers and machine guns. When this holding pen became overcrowded he was moved north to liverpool, to endure the Dickensian conditions of Walton gaol.

It is a strange irony that while Audrey, who had been summoned back to what her mother regarded as 'safety', began to suffer the privations of enemy Occupation, her father, who had stayed safely, as he thought, in England was now subjected to years of detention, degradation and the loss of civil rights. Hepburn-Ruston's hope of early release gradually drained away—Herbert Morrison, the Home Secretary, turned down his appeal in the summer of 1941 on the grounds that *habeas corpus,* which protects citizens against imprisonment without charge or trial, had been superseded by Regulation 18b. Audrey and her family back in the Netherlands were also suffering physical hardship and daily danger, and learning how ruthlessly and quickly life could change.

What remained of the van Heemstra family's old estate was seized by the German forces of occupation. The few valuables Audrey's mother and her uncle had been able to rescue they buried in the countryside under cover of darkness. They were just in time. Soon all gold and precious metals in private hands were confiscated. German troops, who at first had been on their best behaviour towards the Dutch population, changed their tactics as the underground Resistance was formed and began to hit back with acts of sabotage. If the baroness had counted on her German connections to ease her family's hardship she was disappointed; more likely and prudently, she decided not to put them to the test. Throughout these years Ella van Heemstra appears to have conducted herself with every patriotic propriety although no evidence exists to confirm the story that she was ever an active member of the Resistance. As for Audrey, having already been deprived of her father, she now lost another relative, when one of her half-brothers was taken off to a labour camp in Germany, and would not be seen or heard of again until the end of the war. Audrey herself took precautions which would have been unthinkable in her old life. In public, she never permitted herself to utter a word of English. She warned her schoolmates never to call her Audrey, only Edda, although before the war she had preferred to use the English version of her Dutch name. German instead of English became the foreign language taught in schools. And although Audrey could speak Dutch, her knowledge of it was basic, having been acquired in early childhood before the move to Brussels. She now felt way behind girls of her age. 'I didn't even speak the way other youngsters did. I was all stilted and shy.' It was more pleasurable to use her feet than her tongue to express herself.

Next to her father and mother, Audrey's best-loved relative was her paternal grandmother, Frau Anna von Foregger (as she had become through her second marriage), who was now living in Vienna. Throughout the war, even though her own circumstances were harsh, this doughty old lady corresponded with the child and sent her presents, usually clothes; and Audrey replied, sometimes with a poignant footnote expressing how much she missed her father. 'Dearest Grandmother,' she wrote on 24 April 1940, telling the far-off old lady how spotless the house was now that she and her mother had finished the spring-cleaning, and adding that she had got a pitch-black dog she was calling Pluto. In a PS, whose very brevity has the concentrated ache of the lonely child, she asks: 'Have you heard anything from Papa?'

The letters make it clear that Audrey filled the space left in her life by her father's 'disappearance' with her growing dedication to ballet. She wrote to her grandmother on 12 March 1943 (noting on the envelope, for the convenience of the wartime censors, that it was written 'in Engels') thanking her for the presents of a 'sweet little blouse. Having quite a lot of brown clothes, I can wear it often' and a hat and muff, and added that she was leading a very busy life: no fewer than three dance evenings with overflow audiences in the town theatre. She had had her first crisis when, just a few days before the last rehearsal, one of the four dancers, who included Audrey and the ballet teacher, had telephoned to say that she could not possibly dance on the evening. Audrey proudly reported that she and another girl had had to work 'like niggers' to learn three dances in as many days. Her letters simmer with just this kind of surplus energy and certainly don't give the impression that wartime life (at this stage anyhow) was physically draining. Even in her teens, Audrey already had a strongly developed impulse to rise above disasters.

She kept up her ballet lessons at the Arnhem Conservatory, but soon the unheated rooms and wartime restrictions on lighting and assembly spelled the end of them. The baroness, realizing that her child's passionate dedication needed an outlet, set up an exercise barre in a friend's house and engaged a part-time teacher to come and give ballet lessons to her daughter and a few other girls. Mrs Everts remembers Audrey's mother earning extra money by giving bridge tuition and assumes this paid for Audrey's dance instruction. Eventually the teacher had to stop coming. Then Audrey stepped into her shoes and started giving lessons to the younger children. 'There was no room for a barre in the little flat they occupied, but I remember Audrey encouraging the children to put their toes on the windowsill and use it as a barre,' says Mrs Everts. Audrey was always an ingenious child.

'I wanted to dance solo roles,' she recalled later, adding in words that suggested how even her childhood loneliness was a spur to ambition, 'I desperately wanted to do these roles because they would allow me to express myself. I couldn't express myself while conforming to a line of twelve girls. I didn't want to conform. I was going to hit my mark.'

Ballet wasn't only what Audrey preferred to do; it was virtually the only form of entertainment available to her. 'I'd never gone very much to the cinema. Now I never went. The only films shown were German ones.' Driven in on herself, she danced. Behind the blackout curtains of neighbours' houses, wearing felt slippers when her ballet shoes wore out and she couldn't get another pair, Audrey performed classic excerpts to piano accompaniment or sometimes, if German patrols were likely to pass by and might notice that more people were assembled in one place than martial law permitted, in a tense but appreciative silence. The money raised by passing the hat round at the end of these solo performances went into the Resistance purse, after Audrey had deducted a little for her family's needs.

'I had very little real youth,' was her verdict on this time, 'few friends, little fun in the usual teenage way and no security. Is it any wonder I became an interior sort of person?' It was in this grim period that she learned the value of living from day to day. 'I think I was older in those days than I am now.' Chance encounters—one in particular—gave her a devastating glimpse of other people not so 'lucky' as herself.

'I found myself several times at the railway station. It was one way of picking up news of what was happening elsewhere in Holland, from people you'd snatch a few words with as they leant out of the windows while the train halted.' One day, she recalled, a goods train pulled in. She could hear noises inside the wagon, the sound of shuffling and bodies scraping against the wooden sides. 'Then I saw faces squinting over . . . where a plank had been taken out to let air in.' They were Dutch Jews being transported eastward to slave-labour camps, or worse. As she watched, additional Jews were ordered out of closed trucks and pushed into the already crammed wagons. 'I remember very sharply one little boy standing with his parents on the platform, very blond, wearing a coat that was much too big for him, and he stepped onto the train. I was a child observing a child.'

From contemplating the fate of other people, it was a small step to feeling implicated in it. Later, when Audrey was given Anne Frank's diary to read, those years flooded back. Only now she found herself humbled by a child of her own age who had been transformed by her experience of hiding, until discovery had doomed her. She felt that Anne Frank's endurance surpassed human understanding. Years later, when pressed to play her in a film version of the book, Audrey refused with the words, 'I don't want to profit from a saint.'

Yet her common sense told her that even Anne Frank had enjoyed 'good days', resisting despair by recording her joys and her hopes of survival. Audrey's resistance to the enemy found more practical expression. She helped distribute anti-Nazi propaganda leaflets and copies of clandestine broadcasts by the BBC or secret Dutch radio stations. She carried them concealed in her shoes.

A small mythology of Audrey's wartime work has accreted over the years, and should be viewed with caution. Successive waves of magazine writers—particularly those who found it difficult to set up interviews with her and turned instead to inventing them—have grafted a layer of Hollywood-style suspense on to the genuine risks that Audrey ran. But at least one incident is well established, for its source is Audrey herself and she never boasted, or lied, about what she did. In 1943, an English parachutist landed and went into hiding in the wooded hills of the Klarenbeeksche, not far from Arnhem. Audrey agreed to carry a message to this contact from the Resistance. A child in the woods would be less suspicious than an adult Hollander.

She made contact with the man by singing a song in English near his hiding place, relayed the message, then turned for home. She had the wit to start picking woodland flowers which, if she were challenged, would explain why she was in the woods and might even enhance her appearance of innocence. And challenged she was. An armed German on foot patrol appeared over a hill and barred her way. She stopped, curtseyed and proffered her posy to him. It was as if she were taking a bow at the ballet. The man smiled at what he took to be timorous good manners though in fact she was trembling in fear of arrest, and let her pass with a fatherly smile and an officious wave of his gloved hand.

It would seem that Audrey's health kept up reasonably well until 1944. Mrs Everts remains somewhat sceptical about biographers' stories that the family suffered dire privations. 'That was certainly the case in the west of Holland, but many of us in the east put on waders, walked through the flooded meadows and reached some of the outlying farms in small boats and were able to buy eggs and milk from the peasants. I can't remember if the van Heemstras did that, but Audrey was certainly well enough to give a ballet performance in the theatre at Arnhem, and that was in the spring of 1944.'

Letters from her grandmother were a highlight of these war years, and parcels even more so. Clothes continued to delight Audrey, even when they were second-hand garments, passed on perhaps from the children of her grandmother's own family, and in need of alteration to fit a rapidly growing girl—growing, perhaps, too much for her ambitions as a ballet dancer. She didn't mind having to let down the hems of the topcoats her granny sent her—presents that the baroness kept secret until it was time to put them under the Christmas tree that had been dressed in tinsel and the occasional fairy light to help them ignore the wartime power cuts. She had good news about her half-brother: he was quite safe and 'very busy' in the German work camp to which he had been deported from the Netherlands. Even when being 'busy' meant forced labour, it seemed to Audrey to be preferable to doing nothing. Work was a redemptive virtue. Her adolescent correspondence suggests that the resilience which served Audrey so well all her own working life, right up to the hours before her death, was cultivated during these years until it became a natural reflex.

But eventually the war began to tell on even her resilient constitution. With her family, who now included a grandmother, uncle and aunt under the same roof, she now lived a one-meal-a-day regime that hardly ever varied: watery soup made from wild cress and herbs, with 'bread' consisting of mashed pea-pods allowed to set in a jelly-mould. There was no fuel, no soap, no candles, no safe drinking water. There was never enough fruit or root crops to go round. Audrey shot up to over 5 feet 6 inches on a diet that was insufficient to sustain such accelerated development, and her slow descent into malnutrition began. She became anaemic and her sluggish bloodstream, failing to disperse impurities, silted them up in her lower limbs so that her legs and feet became painfully swollen with edema. Dancing was a thing of the past. It is not entirely true to say that the privations she suffered in the last year of the war shaped the waif-like body that was so much a part of Audrey Hepburn's screen appearance: other factors, like genes, were probably more influential. But deprivation did do temporary harm to her metabolism, and she was not helped by shocks to her emotional system. One day she witnessed her uncle, who had been a well-known judge, being escorted away by the Gestapo. He was shot in a wave of reprisals following attacks on the German military.

'In those days I used to say to myself, "If only this comes to an end, I will never grumble about anything again," ' Audrey recalled.

She was as good as her word. The defensive air of serenity which she had cultivated as a child when family rows erupted around her was reinforced by the wartime knowledge that someone, somewhere, was likely to be worse off than she.

By September 1944, it was clear that the Allies were winning the war. German positions in France had been overrun and the enemy was pulling back to its bunkers in the east. A quick thrust was planned by Eisenhower and Montgomery, a grand offensive which would shorten the war dramatically by dropping 35,000 combatants by glider and parachute to capture and hold the bridge over the Rhine at Arnhem, thus allowing Allied armies to drive deep into the heartland of the Ruhr. The ambitious plan misfired with frightful casualties: 17,000 men were killed or wounded, and some 5000 citizens of Arnhem lost their lives. The German revenge was swift and terrible. That night every surviving man, woman and child, including Audrey, her mother, half-brother and friends who had hidden with them in a cellar throughout the bombardment, was told to be out of Arnhem by 8 a.m. the next day. Those who refused (or were simply too late) would be summarily executed.

Audrey helped fill the suitcases, backpacks and any other containers that could hold the maximum of clothing and other necessities, without impeding the bearer too much. Then they joined the snaking column of nearly 100,000 townsfolk—the hale or sick, sturdy or lame—left to fend for themselves in the devastated countryside. At least 3000 died from exposure, exhaustion or disease.

The van Heemstras were again lucky. They found refuge at the mansion in Velp, a village not far from Arnhem, which belonged to Audrey's grandfather. It soon became an appallingly overcrowded refuge for others in all stages of wretchedness, who had been driven out of their homes and had nowhere else to go. 'Food was nonexistent,' Audrey remembered. With the younger refugees she grubbed up the remains of turnips from the frozen ground; even flower bulbs were found and eaten raw. Years later, when she saw *Gone with the Wind* in London, she pulled her mother close to her as she watched Vivien Leigh as Scarlett scrape with her bare hands in the once-rich soil of the devastated estate to find food for herself and her family. It brought back to Audrey those desperate days when her own stomach had been almost empty.

It must have been around this time, in the closing months of the war, that she was nearly caught by German troops rounding up every man and boy as well as able-bodied women and girls to work on the fortifications being hastily thrown up in an effort to halt the advance of the Allied armour and allow for the evacuation of what remained of the German army of occupation. Audrey had gone back into Arnhem to look for food, and saw a patrol. She disappeared into the cellar of a ruined house. The myth has it that she stayed hidden for a whole month, but this is clearly apocryphal. Still, she remained in hiding long enough for her mother to imagine that the child had been caught in 'the trawl'. The shock and rejoicing when she eventually limped home were quickly overtaken by alarm at her condition. In hiding Audrey had developed jaundice in addition to her anaemia and edema. If the war had not ended when it did, it might have been the end for Audrey Hepburn.

3

DANCE LITTLE LADY

*A*UDREY was spared a long and possibly crippling illness, perhaps even death, by an extraordinary coincidence that, looking back over her life, has a strange and touching symmetry.

A 'very dear friend' of Ella van Heemstra in pre-war days was a young Englishman called Michael Burn. When Audrey was staying with friends on a farm near Feltham on that last visit to England in 1939, Burn, in the army, was stationed nearby. Ella asked him to visit and see how her child was keeping and soon afterwards Audrey was rushed back to Holland by her anxious mother. 'With the outbreak of war they seemed to have gone out of all reach,' says Burn.

Michael Burn was captured in the naval commando raid on St Nazaire at the end of March 1942 and sent to a concentration camp. One day, to his great surprise, long before he had received any message from his parents, or they from him, 'I received a Red Cross parcel. No donor was indicated.' Not until his repatriation at the end of the war did he learn that Ella van Heemstra had been in Haarlem one day where she had gone to the cinema and seen, in a German newsreel, a propaganda version of the St Nazaire raid which depicted that daring and successful operation as an apparent fiasco for the Allies.

Suddenly Burn appeared on screen 'being marched through the streets into captivity with a bayonet in my back and my hands up (in the V sign, for the benefit of British Intelligence). Ella recognized me, and in her excitement seized the arm of the person next to her, a German officer, and said in English, "It's Mickey." ' The baroness knew the Jewish cinema owner, a woman, and together they sneaked back into the requisitioned movie house at midnight, ran the newsreel again and cut out the frames showing Burn before splicing the film together again. With the blown-up picture of Burn, Ella contacted the Red Cross—hence the food parcel.

Flash forward to the liberation. Audrey is critically ill. Burn has been repatriated. 'Ella wrote to me in desperation, saying she needed the new wonder drug, penicillin, but it was next to impossible to come by in the Netherlands except for more money than she was able to spare at that time. Could I send her some cartons of cigarettes?—which then fetched a staggeringly high price on the black market. I sent hundreds and hundreds, thousands of cigarettes.' Ella sold them on the black market in Amsterdam, where Audrey was in hospital and where the baroness was living with her reunited family in a small apartment. She wrote to tell Michael Burn that the penicillin which the cigarettes had bought had saved Audrey's life.

When asked about the war years in press interviews in later life Audrey would sometimes speak of liberation possessing 'the smell of English cigarettes'. It was generally assumed that she was referring to the Allied soldiers on the streets of her home town. Perhaps so: but those gifts of English cigarettes from Michael Burn purchased for her a more precious kind of liberation. In its small way the incident was one more link in the chain of events that would later impel Audrey to take up her mission of aid to children with whom she had only one thing in common: like them, she knew what it was like to be at death's door.

Audrey's recuperation was assisted by the parcels of food and medicine she received from the United Nations Relief and Rehabilitation Administration, the forerunner of Unicef.

Though not subjected to the same risks and privations as his daughter, Audrey's father finished the war in low spirits, too. At one point early in the war, he came near to being transported to the South Atlantic island of St Helena, which was being considered as a detention centre for the 'Fifth Column', as the hard core of internees in Britain were popularly known. But with the passing of the Isle of Man (Detention) Act in 1941, which brought the island's legal system into line with mainland law, Hepburn-Ruston was shipped off some time after May and deposited in Peveril Camp near Peel, with several hundred other male prisoners. (Women and aliens went to a camp at Port Erin.) Daily routine was not harsh. The camp comprised several large lodging houses by the seawall and a number of terrace houses, all surrounded by barbed wire. In the course of time, sporting and educational activities were organized, and considering most of the inmates were well educated, some even distinguished academics, they did not do too badly; but survivors recall that Hepburn-Ruston kept himself unsociably apart from them. It was there that he was given the nickname of 'Java Joe'. He also, in the words of one detainee, 'behaved like a man who had been used to handling a lot of money, and now had very little of it'. Clearly his nature had been soured by his treatment as an internee, which may have included tough interrogation. Hepburn-Ruston spent most of his time reading and nursing an increasingly bitter hatred of Britain and the British.

Hepburn-Ruston did not join in the nightly rendering of 'God Save the King' which some internees accompanied by arms raised in the Fascist salute. His name does not appear in any of the surviving autograph books with their morale-boosting inscriptions such as 'Meekness is weakness', 'In wartime, reason is treason' or 'Force rules the earth'. He ate his meals in the dining hall—in silence for the most part—alongside the shabby and the unshaven who, despite sitting at bare board tables, eating off tin plates and drinking tea out of mugs made from condensed-milk tins, nevertheless managed to sustain a mood of middle-class gentility and even, on special occasions, the atmosphere of a City dinner. An empty chair was kept at the top table for the 'lost leader', Sir Oswald Mosley, who was still in gaol on mainland Britain.

Hepburn-Ruston was kept in internment until April 1945, an exceptionally long period, testifying to the extreme opinions he held or to the serious view taken of his actions during the time he had 'fronted' the Nazi-backed propaganda agency. He was one of thirty-nine in the last but one batch of detainees, all with strong pro-Nazi sympathies, to be released only a month before the war officially ended. In the unlikely event that he had applied for any form of compensation he would certainly have been denied it. Restrictions may well have been placed on what jobs he could subsequently apply for or hold. He would then have been a man entering his sixties.

At this point Audrey's father vanishes from the few official records that might have disclosed his fate. He also vanished, following his divorce from her mother, from her published recollections of him. Eventually she would catch up with him in strange and saddening circumstances and discover what had happened to the once handsome and dashing man, such a 'cuddlesome' father, in the years following his release from prison. But for the moment, she and her mother had their own lives to reconstruct.

Once Audrey was out of danger, her health began to improve with reasonable speed. Pauline Everts remembers the liberation parties that took place in Arnhem. 'Audrey's mother rather enjoyed the fun with the English officers. So did Audrey. I remember there was a club in the woods called the Brass Hat and we were invited to go to the dances. Audrey was asked, too. Ella allowed her to go and I chaperoned her. She was between fifteen and sixteen at the time. The food that the officers served helped her recovery.'

Funds were short. Ella van Heemstra used her name and connections to get a job in Amsterdam, first buying market produce for the high-class restaurants that were now reopening, then as a caterer for foreign firms beginning to rebuild their businesses and in need of a knowledgeable, well-connected person to organize menus and guest lists. The money she earned went to pay for Audrey's medicines, then, once her daughter's health allowed, for more dancing lessons. From Amsterdam, Audrey wrote to her grandmother on 8 May 1945 to say she had now started at a Russian dancing school in the city and thought it much better run than her old school in Arnhem. Her teacher, Sonia Gaskell, a Russian emigrée, was 'charming'.

'Ella did other little things to earn money for herself and Audrey,' says Mrs Everts. 'A friend of mine in Amsterdam, who was a dressmaker and wanted to show her clothes, used me as a mannequin, then got Audrey to model the children's clothes. We also gave "fashion shows" in Arnhem. I thought of this many years later, when Audrey was famous and living near Lausanne. My own daughter was at a nearby finishing school and used to come over to Audrey and there was always a beautiful couture dress, or something else Audrey had finished with, for her to take back to school with her.'

Sonia Gaskell, to whose studio Audrey now went daily, was the leading dance teacher in Amsterdam. Her avant-garde methods incorporated jazz rhythms and *musique concrète* as well as the classical repertoire. Soon her leg and thigh muscles regained their strength and elasticity; her body, the grace of movement that became second nature to her.

But dancing was not her only gift. Wartime necessity had made her a handy jack of all trades. Her life throws up small but telling instances of how good she was with things as well as with people. At this time she accepted a lift on a fellow dance student's ancient motorbike, which broke down when an oil-feed tube dropped off. Audrey ran into a cafe, asked for a drinking straw and, using this and her hair ribbon, in a quick bit of make-do-and-mend by the kerb, got the machine going again at least as far as a repair shop. Many years later, when she was one of the world's best-known film stars, she performed a similar impromptu repair on the car belonging to a photographer doing a picture-spread with her on the Côte d'Azur.

Audrey brought all her considerable concentration to bear on her ballet lessons. Her tutor believed she drove herself so hard because, having just had a brush with death, she knew the value of living. But it went back earlier than that. Her Calvinist upbringing had instilled in her the obligation to work hard, and her Christian Science training had insisted that anything was possible if the mind (and God) willed it so. The only thing her willpower could not influence was her height. At nearly 5 feet 7 inches she was inconveniently tall for the ballet. Male dancers would have had to be at least an inch taller in order to make a pleasing physical partnership in the classical repertoire, and in those days dancers tended to be even smaller than they are today.

Audrey's dancing lessons were brought to an end when the school's municipal subsidy was drastically cut and Sonia Gaskell decided to move to Paris. The baroness refused to follow, feeling that she would be unable to support her family as well in a city and country where she was a total stranger. Perhaps she had already decided to take advantage of her British citizenship, acquired through marriage, by taking Audrey to London and continuing her tuition there. This decision was taken at the end of 1946, for Audrey wrote to her grandmother on 4 January 1947 and expressed the delight she felt at a recent visit she had paid to England. She told her that she and her mother hoped to go and live there 'soon'. Her eagerness to make dancing her career had been whetted by the two ballets she had seen at Covent Garden. This enthusiasm for moving across the Channel seems to have been assisted by the imminent closure of Sonia Gaskell's dance school in Amsterdam, even though Audrey, in common with the other pupils, had applied for admission to the New Opera Ballet which was being re-formed as part of the Netherlands Opera. Audrey had to pass a stiff test for this—dancing in front of a jury—and was happy to find she had passed it. But a second and maybe harder examination awaited her, just as soon as the new *maître de ballet* was appointed, and it is possible that she felt apprehensive about her abilities. Whether or not she passed this second test is unrecorded. But if not, then it was an additional reason for leaving Amsterdam and trying her luck and talent in London.

Audrey had been recommended to the Ballet Rambert, the most important school in the English capital, for a scholarship by her Amsterdam teacher who had maintained links with Marie Rambert, the founder of the school and a former dancer. Madame Rambert had some sympathy with a girl who had grown too fast and too far for her professional good. Her own aspiration to be a prima ballerina had been frustrated by a similarly inconvenient number of inches.

The career-in-waiting for Audrey appeared just before she left Holland and it was not in ballet. The national airline, KLM, newly anxious to promote itself and revive tourism in the Netherlands, was financing a forty-minute travel documentary. A girl was needed, proficient in both Dutch and English, to play the stewardess who would open and close the movie. Strings were pulled: the baroness knew a KLM director. Audrey landed her first part—and her first notice. 'She was cheerful, charming, lovely . . . a little sun shone out of her,' one of the producers, H. M. Josephson, was quoted as saying years later. These are indeed the essential qualities Audrey radiates the minute she appears, although the role presents a somewhat un-expected image of her. The KLM stewardess's uniform, with its military-style tunic and skirt falling well below the knee, makes Audrey appear older than her actual seventeen or eighteen years: almost a young woman, in fact. On her head she wears a stewardess's long cap, which emphasizes her wide brow; and instead of the later gamine fringe, her hair falls in loose waves on each side. In a wordless cameo, she mimes a brisk greeting to one of the airline's test pilots, a famous figure of the time, and then sees a male visitor, whom she is introducing to the delights of Holland, up the plane's steps for an aerial view of the country. This (unseen) young man—called George by the commentator—says goodbye to her with a flattering remark clearly referring to the beauty of his escort, rather than the country. From the 'grace' angle, the camera looks down on Audrey standing at the foot of the steps: for a second or two, her face considers the compliment; then, as in *Roman Holiday* when she introduces herself to Gregory Peck after spending the night (alone) in his bed, a charming smile of acceptance breaks across her face—the first of many, on screen and off.

She gave people the feeling that they had made a sudden and very fortunate discovery the moment they laid eyes on her, heard that voice with its distinctive up-tilt. To those who knew her, like Pauline Everts, she radiated an almost palpable air of optimism and good humour. She had an honest trust in her eyes that flattered the recipient of her gaze and made him or her resolve to be worthy of it. Her self-confidence was fragile at this moment of 'discovery', and would remain so for many films with far less justification, but this was not apparent to the camera.

The often repeated version of events that has Audrey and her mother arriving in Britain in 1947 with a suitcase apiece and only £35 between them omits most of the real story. In fact, the two of them did not arrive in England together. Audrey's admission to the Ballet Rambert was held up by what seems to have been bureaucratic confusion over her status as a minor and her nationality. The baroness's passport had expired: she needed to renew it. Though she could readily prove British citizenship by reference to her marriage certificate, the same document would have revealed to the British authorities the name of a man who had only recently been set at liberty after five years' internment as a Fascist sympathizer. The upshot was that Madame Rambert vouched for Audrey, who arrived safely in London and moved into a room in her teacher's own house. The baroness followed a month or so later, having obtained a new passport, probably Dutch, but no doubt crossing her fingers that the articles in praise of Fascism which she had imprudently contributed to *Blackshirt* had either been forgotten or would not compromise her. Her daughter was not the only lucky member of the family.

Within a few months of their arrival mother and daughter were installed in an apartment at 65 South Audley Street, Mayfair, one of the most fashionable and expensive neighbourhoods in London. How did they make ends meet? According to one account, the baroness worked for a florist. No, says another, she worked as housekeeper in the South Audley Street building. She may well have done. But the money to support her and Audrey in some comfort, and to pay for Audrey's dance tuition, came from a long-time friend and admirer of Ella van Heemstra. He was Paul Rykens, a Dutchman who had headed the huge Anglo-Dutch Unilever conglomerate since before the war, and who had patriotically followed his queen to England and placed all the services of his business empire at the disposal of the British and their allies.

Paul Rykens was a man of immense courage and energy, and had overcome a crippling attack of polio as a child. He now became the baroness's benefactor. Audrey was devoted to him: if any man replaced her father at this stage in her life, it was he. He had an apartment in Berkeley Square, in the same part of central London as the baroness's residence. Thus, for the first time in years, Audrey felt she had security.

Work filled Audrey's days and nights. The eighteen-year-old girl had no time for boyfriends or parties or going to the theatre or the cinema. The ballet, yes, following the progress of Margot Fonteyn and the rest. That was work, though. Her pleasures were the simple ones of 'being there'. London was still austerity-ridden, with food, clothes and fuel rationed, and the rubble-strewn bomb sites uncleared. There was a pervasive atmosphere of exhausted and dowdy English grimness, now that the galvanizing currents of wartime endurance and a polyglot population of governments in exile had been switched off. But to Audrey it seemed full of opportunity. For the moment she was bent on making up for a lost childhood by exploring the new world of peacetime. Only a very few years later—incredibly—she would be starring in a Hollywood film as a princess who has almost as little experience of the world as Audrey herself had in the late 1940s. The simple things of life that Audrey learnt to enjoy in these years were of the same order as those that the princess discovers on her own naive and briefer sortie into the streets of a capital city.

Men, however, were not part of Audrey's discoveries. No boyfriend, much less suitor, has ever emerged to claim that he dated the future Audrey Hepburn. Surely vanity could not be so self-effacing! Audrey was not innocent of the facts of life: no more than the fictional Princess Ann of *Roman Holiday* was. But she was immature, even by the conventions of the time. And her mother's two broken marriages, along with the grief that had lapped around her childhood, made her in no hurry to test that dangerous tide for herself.

For all the effort Audrey put into her classes at the Ballet Rambert it was soon evident to her and her teacher that she was not going to be another Ninette de Valois or Margot Fonteyn. In any art, the gap between having talent and being gifted with exceptional brilliance may be narrow; but it is crucial. Dedication alone cannot succeed in bridging it. Audrey made the depressing discovery that hard work did not always bring the wished-for reward. If star quality wasn't there, one might seek it for a lifetime in vain.

'If she had wanted to persevere in ballet,' Madame Rambert said later, 'she might have become an outstanding dancer.' This is surely politeness. The key word here is 'might'. Even when she became a movie star and won every award going, Audrey made the point in almost every interview that she was not a 'natural' actor. She conceded that nothing came easily to her: she had to work damn hard at it. During her days at the Ballet Rambert her self-critical faculties were at their sharpest; for ballet is a more precise and unforgiving art than cinema. One cannot 'cheat' at it. She probably measured her own worth against the finest of her contemporaries and reached a sad but realistic conclusion: she was unlikely ever to reach the top. Lack of money to pay for tuition was not what made her drop out: Paul Rykens's generosity would have seen to that. While continuing to attend movement classes, Audrey began looking for other outlets.

She modelled hats for a trade catalogue; put her languages to use as a filing clerk with a travel company; then landed a job dancing at Ciro's, the smart nightclub in Orange Street, just off the Haymarket, where the jazz rhythms that had been part of her practice steps in Amsterdam came into their own. Those who remember seeing her perform swear that they are not exercising hindsight when they report that she was the girl who caught the eye. 'It was her personality,' says Peter King, then a young lawyer and now a magazine publisher. 'Her smile had a particular radiance. Enjoyment was all over her face.' And John van Eyssen, who was to become chief executive of Columbia Pictures in Britain, recalls nights at Ciro's wondering who 'the girl with the big eyes was. You couldn't take your own off them.' She was gradually being pulled into show business, and liking it. 'We would finish around two in the morning and I'd walk home, through Piccadilly,' Audrey recalled. 'It was so lovely: so safe.'

In fact, at that time Piccadilly and the area around the baroness's apartment was a notorious beat for London prostitutes. But if they saluted another nightclubber, Marlene Dietrich, for the camaraderie that the star had established with them in her films, the trade appears to have let Audrey Hepburn pass unnoticed. Her future image would not depend on erotic allure: quite the reverse.

Audrey always said she did not look far into the future—wartime had shown her the vanity of doing that—yet when she had to choose between a student tour of the provinces with the Ballet Rambert and a part in a musical comedy, she made the decision with brutal finality. She put ballet behind her, forever.

The producer Jack Hylton was auditioning for the chorus line on the London production of the hit Broadway musical, *High Button Shoes*. Audrey was one of ten girls who survived out of three thousand applicants. One of her front-line companions was Kay Kendall, and Audrey later acknowledged how the memories of Kay's 'kookiness'—though the word wasn't then invented—helped overcome her initial hesitation about accepting the role of a high-class hooker called Holly Golightly in *Breakfast at Tiffany's*. 'Kay had a craziness even then that made it absolutely impossible to hold anything against her.'

Both of them had high spirits, long limbs, a sense of fun and enough professionalism to execute the quite tricky Jerome Robbins choreography. They were required to look like Mack Sennett-type bathing beauties forever chasing their own tails in and out of beach tents and tea pavilions. It was a comedy routine that required the same vigour, timing and discipline as ballet. The pay was around eight pounds a week: very good for a beginner. Part of it went to pay for elocution lessons.

The English accent that Audrey Hepburn now acquired has always been a matter of debate. She did not sound at all like most of the London stage stars from Vivien Leigh to Deborah Kerr, whose South Kensington tones stamped (and dated) them as upper-middle-class ladies (they became much better actresses once they got into American movies and lost their English daintiness). Audrey's continental upbringing had given her an intonation that connoted 'quality' without confining her to any niche in the

English class system. To American ears she was, well, 'different'—English-speaking, but with a voice that went with her nature not her class background.

What seems clear at this time is that her smallish voice needed enlarging for the stage. So she took lessons from Felix Aylmer who possessed one of the most precisely cadenced voices in the West End theatre. He sharpened Audrey's diction without impairing its charm. However, elocution lessons were not the same thing as going to acting school and acquiring a vocal range. Audrey remained a 'limited' performer though for a long time it did not matter in her career. She had the personality: others could supply the technique.

Before *High Button Shoes* ended its successful run Audrey had won a place in a musical revue, *Sauce Tartare*. She was promoted to being one of six girls and six boys whose dance numbers formed a link between satirical sketches starring light comedians such as Moira Lister, Claude Hulbert and Ronald Frankau. Her wages improved, too: to ten pounds (fifty dollars) a week.

In this role her lack of the usual curves and protuberances gave rise to concern for the first—and possibly the last—time. A pair of ankle socks offered a stopgap solution. Rolled into two balls and strategically positioned, they simulated a bosom. Later on, Audrey would win Billy Wilder's laconic approval as 'the girl most likely to make bosoms a thing of the past'.

Cecil Landeau, the impresario who was producing *Sauce Tartare,* had a flair for finding beautiful women. He took to Audrey, with or without the ankle socks, and this was a cause of some anxiety to her. She was now about nineteen, but it was possibly the first time she had had to cope with a man's flattering attentions. She did not take to the dressy and flamboyant showman, but she was enough of a realist to know that staying in the show would be easier if she didn't give way to her feelings. Landeau was a martinet at rehearsals, drilling his girls hard, and then revelled in their company when he went on the town. 'Put yourself around,' he ordered Audrey, which meant that he put himself around with her. They lunched together at the Ivy or the Savoy. Such show-business self-advertisement was not to Audrey's taste: yet Landeau's patronage, however much vanity had to do with it, helped draw the professional scrutiny of agents as well as other diners. He sent her to Anthony Beauchamp, the society photographer, who took her picture for *Tatler* and *Bystander*. That was useful, but the next photo-session Landeau arranged for her was even better. Angus McBean, then winning his reputation for the surrealist effects in his photographs, had spotted Audrey's possibilities as soon as *Sauce Tartare* opened in May 1949. Landeau readily agreed to her posing for an advertisement promoting Lacto-Calamine, a moisturizer that encouraged 'skin-response'. He was paid £25 ($70). Audrey was paid £4 ($11.20) for half a day's work.

'What shall I wear?' Audrey asked McBean.

'Nothing,' was the answer. She recoiled.

'Oh, I'm not taking my clothes off.'

'So I stuck her in the sand,' the photographer explained. She gazes out at us, bare-shouldered, sand piled round her and usefully concealing her absence of bosom, hair worn in a low fringe, but the large and tranquil eyes, strong brows and high cheekbones of the star-to-be already fully formed. Two obelisks positioned near her in the sand cleverly distort perspective and endow Audrey with the faintly Middle Eastern aura of a perfectly preserved sphinx.

Landeau kept Audrey hard at work even while *Sauce Tartare* was running. She recalled: 'He said one day that anyone who'd like to make an extra shilling could be in cabaret. So after *Sauce Tartare,* at eleven thirty at night, I'd be at Ciro's again at midnight, make up and do two shows. All dancing. I made £11 ($31) for the first show and £20 ($56) for the second. So I was doing eighteen shows weekly and earning over £150 ($420) a week. I was completely nuts.' But she was also in the money. At Christmas Landeau decided to put on a show for children. 'I got home at 2 a.m. [from Ciro's], slept and was up and in rehearsal at 10 a.m. I was very ambitious and took every opportunity. I wanted to learn and I wanted to be seen.' Audrey opened the Christmas show dressed as a fairy with a wand and did eight matinees a week. 'My voice was pitched so high that my mother said I sounded as though I were about to take off.' This continued for five weeks, until the New Year of 1950 mercifully released her from such entertainment.

At this time, at least when out with Landeau, Audrey appears to have cultivated an air of attractive but scatty helplessness, rather similar to Kay Kendall's. Perhaps she assumed it to protect herself from a more intimate involvement with her employer.

Sauce Piquante, the successor to *Sauce Tartare,* opened midway through 1950. Bob Monkhouse, the comedian, appeared in it with Audrey. His memory is of a girl whose dancing was nothing special. In typical self-deprecatory mood about her talents, Audrey agreed: 'All I really did was throw up my arms and smile, but somehow I was the one who got mentioned in the papers. It really was most unfair to the others.' On the strength of these mentions she was given a small sketch in which she played a saucy French waitress. Like Kay Kendall, her personality projected her across the footlights. To Milton Shulman, the *Evening Standard*'s theatre critic, 'she looked as if she were enjoying herself'. She made others enjoy her, too. Professionalism could wait for a while. For the moment, personality was sufficient.

She also fell in love. Not with Landeau but with a young French singer in the show, Marcel le Bon. This showed a new confidence—or rashness—on Audrey's part. Landeau, in pique, informed the girls that he had entered a 'no marriage' clause in their terms of employment. Audrey was too valuable to be dismissed from the show—which was in trouble, anyhow, due to a summer heatwave—but Landeau's attitude to her now changed abruptly. Some fourteen years later Hedda Hopper, the Hollywood columnist, received a letter from one Jack Oliphant of Monterey, who had been brought in to inject a little American 'pizzazz' into 'a fading London show called *Sauce Piquante*'. His account suggests an abrupt rupture in Audrey's relations with the impresario.

The letter read:

I arrived at the theater during a rehearsal and in the line of girls going thru their routine under the critical eye and tongue of Cecil [Landeau], I spotted a beauty of outstanding attraction. Without taking my gaze off the patrician belle, I said to the producer, 'That third girl from the left—if ever I saw a cover picture for the snob magazines, she's it!' Cecil, unfortunately, did not react with any enthusiasm. He leant towards me, shook his head and dryly replied, 'Yes, she's pretty but dumb.' That girl was Audrey Hepburn.

By now, however, Audrey did not need the good favours of Cecil Landeau. She was developing a second career: in films.

4

THE BEST ADVICE IN THE WORLD

*T*HE part was small; the film, fortunately for her later career, was even easier for critics to ignore. *One Wild Oat* was the first movie Audrey made in Britain, and it was to be one of the last.

British filmgoers have always thought of Audrey as one of their stars. But beginning with *One Wild Oat* in 1950 and continuing through *Laughter in Paradise* and *Young Wives' Tale* to *The Secret People* in 1952, her British screen career had run its course within two years: she never worked in Britain again, was never domiciled in Britain and, although she continued to hold a British passport which gave her the right to citizenship, she never really thought of herself as 'British'—or, indeed, as any particular nationality.

A passing remark she made to Bob Monkhouse, while playing in the doomed *Sauce Piquante* revue, illuminates Audrey's attitude on the matter. Significantly, she didn't refer to herself as British. 'I'm half-Irish, half-Dutch and I was born in Belgium. If I was a dog, I'd be a hell of a mess.' 'Half-Irish': an allusion to her father's country of origin. At the time of Joseph Hepburn-Ruston's birth, in the 1880s, Ireland was not yet the independent republic of Eire but still an integral part of Britain. In view of the harsh treatment which Audrey's father had endured at the hands of the British authorities for most of the war, which Audrey must by now have discovered, it is understandable that his daughter associated herself with the Irish, and not the British, side of him. The Republic of Ireland was the country to which Hepburn-Ruston migrated the minute his captivity in Britain was over. What he did there, how he occupied himself, even where he lived are things that Audrey probably did not know at this time. There is no evidence that he communicated with his ex-wife Ella van Heemstra, or even with the child who was soon to make at least one half of his name world-famous. Audrey would one day find out these things, but that day was still a long way off.

Meanwhile she was offered bit parts in a variety of films. Having tasted the insecurity of stage work she was grateful for them. Googie Withers, herself half-Dutch and already a well-established actress married to John McCallum, had seen *Sauce Piquante* and now persuaded the leading theatrical agency of Linnet and Dunfee to represent Audrey. This led to her role as a hotel desk clerk in *One Wild Oat,* a self-consciously 'naughty' farce which nevertheless proved too blatant for the prudish British film censor of the time. Audrey's scenes, already brief, were even shorter when a spurious virtue was imposed on the piece by censorship cuts.

She attracted the attention of John Redway, a casting director for John and Roy Boulting, who were re-establishing the post-war momentum of their careers with films like *Fame Is the Spur* and *Brighton Rock.* 'We tested her,' John Boulting later recalled ruefully, 'and found something wrong for the camera in every angle and feature of her face—eyes too big, mouth too wide, nose too small. As we described Audrey to a very disappointed Redway, she sounded a proper freak.' (The penitent Boultings paid more attention when, some years later, they tested another Redway 'find' called Peter Sellers.)

Audrey didn't give up her toehold on the stage. Cecil Landeau, still trying to recoup his losses on *Sauce Piquante,* was assembling some of the numbers and sketches and planning to send a 'cabaret version' of the show on tour at the end of the summer of 1950. To safeguard his investment, he was even reconciled to retaining Audrey's lover Marcel le Bon as part of the revamped entertainment. The romance between le Bon and Audrey, and the prospect of their touring together, led her to say no to a more substantial part in a new film: a leading role in *Laughter in Paradise.* Again there is an odd connection with the past: the film's Anglo-Italian director, Mario Zampi, had been interned on the Isle of Man with Hepburn-Ruston although there is no evidence that they ever met. Zampi's stay behind barbed wire was quite short: he had been rounded up simply because he was Italian and therefore officially an enemy alien, and had relatives in Fascist Italy.

Then Landeau's planned tour collapsed. Marcel le Bon went back to Paris and Audrey went back to Zampi to ask for the part she had turned down. The film-maker was despondent: he had seen her in *Sauce Piquante* and knew that his comedy, about the beneficiaries of a will attempting to fulfil the conditions of their bequests, was perfect for someone with her stylish sense of fun. But it was too late: the leading role had been filled. Then Zampi brightened: there was another part he could offer Audrey, not a big one, but he liked her so much he would double its screen time. It was that of a cigarette girl and it lasted all of twenty seconds. She did not rate even a mention in the reviews. But Zampi had the last laugh. 'She will be a big star some day,' he is quoted as saying in the trade weekly *Cinema* in January 1951.

From this inauspicious beginning she went into *Young Wives' Tale,* a lame and witless comedy set in post-war Britain during the housing shortage. Audrey played a single girl in a household consisting of two married couples who constantly got in each other's way and behaved as if they would like to get into each other's beds. To Audrey's embarrassment, *Young Wives' Tale* was released in America after she had become famous. 'That pretty Audrey Hepburn' was the kindest oblivion to which the critics consigned her.

Other parts she had the good fortune to miss. They included the title role in *Lady Godiva Rides Again:* girl wins beauty contest, girl becomes charm-school starlet, girl ends up as striptease lady—a natural for Audrey Hepburn! Her old voice coach, Felix Aylmer, was responsible for securing her an audition for a role in *Quo Vadis,* which MGM was making in Rome: it went to Deborah Kerr. The director, Mervyn Leroy, would later find it tedious explaining how he had come to turn down Audrey Hepburn. 'But she had no experience then,' Leroy used to protest. To which William Wyler once responded: 'No more than she had when we put her into *Roman Holiday.*'

At least the casting agents were well aware of her potential: all she lacked was the break. At the start of 1951 she did a day's work in *The Lavender Hill Mob*—again as a cigarette girl, who approaches Alec Guinness seductively ('Who wants a ciggy?') in what appears to be a smart restaurant abroad and is surreptitiously slipped a *pourboire* for some service she has rendered him. Only at the end of the film does it emerge that Guinness, a bullion robber, is in handcuffs and the 'restaurant' is the airport lounge where he is awaiting deportation. Michael Balcon, the producer of this Ealing comedy, had wanted 'a dishy-looking girl' whose affection for Guinness could suggest the extent to which stealing a fortune had changed the quiet little pinstriped man. Audrey's 'doe-like looks' caught Balcon's eye. Later, he too would publicly kick himself for not signing her up to a film contract. That, however, had already been done by someone with a sharper eye.

Robert Lennard, casting director for the Associated British Picture Corporation, one of the major studios in England, whose parent company both distributed films and owned the cinemas that showed them, had caught Audrey's act at Ciro's and also in *Sauce Piquante.* Finally, after seeing her sidle in and out of *The Lavender Hill Mob* in the rushes in a studio screening room, he signed her for an Anglo-French film, *We Go to Monte*

Carlo, which was due to go into production that summer in Monaco and on the Côte d'Azur. Audrey's fluent French would be a help in shooting two versions of the film simultaneously. For Audrey, the bait lay in the non-linguistic attractions of unrationed food and sunshine.

Then Lennard took a longer-term gamble. He persuaded Associated British to sign Audrey for a three-year contract, starting at £12 ($33.60) a week, one film a year guaranteed, with the right to continue her stage work. Agreeing to these terms, which were standard for starlets at the time, was to turn out to be the most expensive mistake Audrey Hepburn ever made.

What impelled Lennard to sign her up at that moment, besides her obvious potential, was the prospect of employing her very shortly in a film that his company was about to make as a prestige production. *The Secret People* had actually been conceived four years earlier, around 1947, by its director Thorold Dickinson and his co-author, the British novelist Joyce Cary. It was a political thriller about European refugees in post-war England being drawn into a plot to assassinate a Balkan dictator. Ever since Dickinson and his producer, Sidney Cole, had gone to see Audrey in *Sauce Piquante* after spotting a press agent's photograph of her in a London evening newspaper, they had considered her for the role of the younger sister of the woman who is in love with the chief conspirator and is destroyed by him. However, at the last minute the timid, stingy and narrow-minded Scottish executives who ran Associated British decided that the subject was a bad box-office bet—too political, too intellectual, too foreign—and withdrew from the project. Even then Audrey might have seen the trap into which she had fallen. The men who now had her under contract were not star-builders; they were basically cautious accountants. They liked others to take the risks, leaving them free to take any profits. For years to come Audrey would be the golden windfall that enriched Associated British's balance sheet without their having to lift a finger to employ her.

The Secret People only got off the ground when Michael Balcon welcomed it, an unwanted orphan, to his Ealing Studios, hoping that its 'serious' theme would be an invigorating transfusion for the rather inbred comedies which Ealing was turning out. It was scheduled to start shooting in the spring of 1951. On 30 October 1950 Thorold Dickinson interviewed Audrey for the part of Nora, the young refugee sister. She already knew all about it, for *The Secret People*'s production offices were next to the set on which she had made her fleeting appearance in *The Lavender Hill Mob.* She had sounded out Balcon's staff to see if there was 'anything in it for me'. 'She was very ambitious,' recalls Lindsay Anderson, the future director of films like *This Sporting Life* and *If . . .*, who was currently writing a book about the making of *The Secret People*. To meet her, you would never have imagined it. But the determination which had powered her long years of ballet training now drove her acting career. She wanted above all to succeed.

'She didn't even strike one as an "actress" either,' Anderson says. 'The bit parts she'd had up to then gave little indication of her immense talent. Anyhow, what Thorold was after was her dancing talent—what he called her "vivacity".' The trouble was Audrey's height. Dickinson felt she was a tiny bit too tall to make Nora a plausible match for her elder sister, who was to be played by the Italian actress Lea Padovani. The first thing they did to her at the interview was stand her against the office wall and measure her. Definitely too tall. By December, though, Padovani had withdrawn from the movie due to conflicting commitments. Audrey's excess inches were more in line with Valentina Cortese, who was signed in early February 1951. (Twenty-five years later Audrey found the pencil marks recording her height still on the office wall at Ealing Studios. The place had not been repainted since her trial measurement. Frugality of that kind was in keeping with Balcon's ethos and this film's budget.)

Camera tests for the role of Nora began at Ealing Studios on 15 February 1951. Audrey and another actress were in competition for the part; they each had to dance and do a dialogue scene. Audrey had luck on her side for the woman responsible for the ballet scenes was an ex-colleague of Madame Rambert. But in her keen desire to see her former pupil succeed she overdid things, 'cuing' and 'encouraging' Audrey by hand signals during the dialogue test, to the irritation of Spike Priggen, the first assistant director, who spoke ominously of reporting her to the all-powerful film union. ('She'll be moving the lamps next.') Audrey did a bad test.

What gave Audrey the decision on points was an attribute that would become her strongest attraction. Her rival's acting was 'satisfactory' but, according to Anderson's diary notes at the time, 'her eyes, strangely enough, are too expressive: experience shows in them'. Audrey's eyes, on the contrary, had the desirable quality of innocence. She was called back to the studios on 23 February although the part still wasn't definitely hers. She and another actress, a professional dancer, again ran through a dance test and then the dialogue scene.

This time Audrey's luck held. There must have been excited talk about her for although Valentina Cortese was due to fly back to Italy that evening on a brief visit before starting work on the film, the Italian star volunteered to do the scene with Audrey. The moment she saw this slim and vibrant girl she said, 'Why haven't they already cast you?'

'They think I'm too tall,' said Audrey.

'How silly! Step out of your shoes and I'll play the test standing on tiptoe.'

The short scene was the one where an excited Nora rushes in and reports that she's been asked to dance at the garden party where the attempt on the visiting dictator's life will be made. She has to audition for it, she adds. Thus the thrill as well as the nerves which Audrey had to simulate in her test exactly matched the way she was feeling at this crucial moment. 'After . . . the runthrough,' Anderson noted, 'people start eyeing each other meaningfully; Audrey has the quality all right. After another rehearsal it seems almost a waste of time to shoot the test.'

Sidney Cole confirms this. 'Thorold said to me, "Why did we shoot the test? It's obvious." ' Three days later the matter was settled. 'Audrey Hepburn is Nora', was Anderson's entry in the film logbook on 26 February 1951. She was on her way.

Part of Audrey's screen test had been to dance a snippet of ballet. No difficulty: she was clearly superior to the male dancer who partnered her. But in the weeks before the actual shooting, scheduled for 15 March, Audrey met the dancer who would partner her in the film. John Field was in a class well above Audrey, and she now found that the choreography tested her to the limit. The repetition necessary for the lighting photographer tired her quickly. What became a well-concealed characteristic of her later career was worrisomely apparent at the start of it. If she had to sustain a fairly complex emotional mood or series of movements, repetition tended to take the edge off her wonderfully natural early responses. The difference was minute, to be sure, though noticeable when the later takes were printed and screened. 'At that stage,' Lindsay Anderson says, 'she had to rely on her looks and whatever emotions she could set throbbing. But it was enough to see her through, especially under Thorold's painstaking instruction. Just as well, though, that her role wasn't larger.'

The dance sequences were unexpectedly onerous when filming began. Audrey found herself looking forward more than ever to shooting *We Go to Monte Carlo* in the Riviera sunshine. The month of March 1951 was freezing cold in England. Heating in the old Bedford Theatre, London—which was doubling for the opera house in Dublin where the ballet scene was set—was a stop-start affair. In both senses of the word Audrey had to perform cold over four days of rehearsal and two days of filming. Her muscles and ankles ached at the end of the day. Though only three or four minutes' dancing were needed—and fewer were eventually used in the film—work took longer and was far harder than dancing a conventional ballet. The orchestra repeated the same snatches of music at every take, and Dickinson demanded many takes. 'I could have screamed,' Audrey said, 'at hearing the same half-dozen bars again and again.'

Anderson's book records how Audrey's introduction to making a major film stripped away any illusions of glamour she might have harboured. 'The camera crane mistimed its movement in the first take; in the second, John Field's wig flew off as he pirouetted; the third one saw the corps de ballet spread too widely across the stage; the fourth was satisfactory; but a fifth was taken as reinsurance and the camera moved too slowly; the sixth was a "possible"; and it was only at the seventh and eighth takes that Dickinson called "Print—both." ' The next day Thorold Dickinson appeared on the set in a bad temper, with the beginnings of flu and declared himself dissatisfied with all the ballet takes of Audrey and Field up to then. They would have to be redone. Audrey was philosophical. It was no good complaining that these things were sent to try her. She took a different line: they were sent to toughen her.

Between takes, Anderson remembers, she would rush back and forth to warm her hands and feet at a two-bar electric fire in her dressing room and then, at the end of the day and if the water tank was still hot, she would run the shower over her body until the goose bumps had been smoothed away.

Though Thorold Dickinson, then in his forties, was a hard task-master, he tempered perfectionism with a regard for Audrey that Sidney Cole described as 'almost paternal'. She came to depend on him. 'He was very solicitous over any scene that gave her trouble,' says Cole. One traumatic moment for Nora comes after the bungled assassination attempt which has killed an innocent waitress. 'Something horrible happened,' Nora begins, as she and her sister return in a state of shock. 'There was an explosion . . . Oh, it was terrible.' Audrey had difficulty hitting the right emotion. Dickinson said, 'But you must have seen or heard something like this during the war.' He didn't know what an understatement this was. 'Forget the words,' he told her. Emotion, pure emotion would help her to find the feeling in the scene. Anderson noted how she retired to a corner of the set, remained alone for several minutes of concentrated communion with herself and then, summoned back by Spike Priggen, the assistant director, reactivated feelings dredged up from the wartime years of fear and privation. Some time later Audrey spoke of a Dutch drawing teacher who had told her, 'There are two sides to every line.' A metaphysical conceit, perhaps. Yet Audrey's directness in giving every mood its visible feelings demonstrated how well she learnt to follow the line of character through a screenplay and find the motive on one side of the line that she turned into human impact on the other.

On the set of *The Secret People* she also received what she was to call 'the best advice in the world'. She overheard Valentina Cortese protesting about the demands for interviews with herself and Serge Reggiani, the Italian star who was playing the chief conspirator, 'to help the film'. Cortese had already experienced the Hollywood publicity machine when making *Black Magic* and *Thieves' Highway* there a year or so earlier and she knew how it chewed up one's personality, then spat it out in a new and sometimes unrecognizable shape. 'Of course, I realize that if an actress is popular, it is more than just acting . . . it is her personality, too, and people want to know about her, to feel they are in touch with her. And sometimes that can be very touching. But we must be allowed to have our own lives. In Hollywood, it is terrible; they expect you to be their slave; you have to be ready to do anything for them, at any time, not just when you are making a picture.' Turning to Audrey with a shudder she added: 'Think hard before you sign a long-term contract. Liberty is the most wonderful thing of all.'

From this time until the end of her days, Audrey Hepburn measured out her life, public and private, with steel-willed resolution. Yes, she had an obligation to promote the work she did. She acknowledged it fully and performed it scrupulously, if not over-generously. But her life off-screen was a totally different matter, to be lived her way and protected from invasive curiosity, yielding as little as possible to inquisitors who asked how she spent her time between films. Audrey was among the earliest stars to insist, in a way that is commonplace today, on the right to a private life. There is, for example, hardly any record of her ever consenting to an interview that would take place in her own home: a public life was kept for public places.

The naturalness and simplicity she radiated in later films are already visible the minute she appears on screen in *The Secret People*: in the check suit and flat hat with a floating ribbon that Nora wears with such vivacity; in the guileless pleasure she demonstrates at exchanging her refugee status for British nationality. Even when her character has nothing particular to do—which is most of the time—one notices Audrey. She stays alert, poised like a bird ready to flit off a branch. In her audition scene for the ballet, she appears totally aroused, taut with expectation. Her actual dancing, while proficient enough, reveals something that may have led to her leaving the

Ballet Rambert. She does not dance 'on points' (on her toes), only on 'half-points' (on the balls of her feet). This was due to the return of the edema, or ankle swelling, caused by sluggish circulation. What compensates for any physical shortcomings, however, is her personality. When Valentina Cortese says in the film, 'They're right, [Nora] would be very good in cabaret', it is a comment that applies to Audrey, too. She has the liveliness associated with cabaret rather than the concentrated self-absorption of the ballet dancer.

Audrey's first significant film did not live up to all the hopes—and money—invested in it. Though carefully directed, and valuable for the detail it offers of domestic life and street-scene in post-war Britain, *The Secret People* is a badly flawed film. It fatally forfeits the audience's sympathy with Valentina Cortese once she turns police informant and betrays the patriots who have involved her in the bomb plot. The defect has to be attributed to Dickinson, a very morally minded man and a committed pacifist. The movie's message may be that 'Resistance to tyrants is obedience to God' but the dramatic morality becomes muddled when that obedience involves selling out on one's lover and friends. And as sympathy is withdrawn from Cortese's character, so the credibility of Audrey's Nora suffers, too: she appears downright ingenuous when she permits those responsible for what she believes to have been her sister's death to go on involving her in their conspiracy. The scene that is needed to bring Nora to political consciousness was never written. A pity; it would be interesting to see how Audrey would have handled it.

Yet she benefits from comparison with well-trained and experienced stars like Cortese and Reggiani. While they play in the mood of doomed romanticism then fashionable in European cinema, Audrey's style is altogether looser, fresher, more natural.

Already the media Audrey was to come to mistrust were talking about her. Thorold Dickinson tried to persuade Balcon to buy her out of her Associated British contract but Balcon was a poor businessman where female stars-to-be were concerned. The fact that virtually all the Ealing comedies, and most of the other films he produced, have a masculine bias suggests that he felt on surer ground with the male players he put under contract. Yet, even before Audrey had finished shooting her role she was being booked for interviews and photoshoots. The mass-circulation weekly magazine, *Illustrated,* whisked her off to the South Downs countryside and photographed her feeding ducks on a village pond, paddling in the sea and stretching her arms lyrically against the skyline. She hated it. 'What's this got to do with the film?' she asked. But she did it.

Even so early in her career, she expressed misgivings, though not the usual ones of incipient stardom, to do with looks, lighting, comforts and convenience. These would come later. Audrey's main concern was of another kind: whether she had actually earned such attention. Was she worthy of it? 'I'd much rather wait until I have something to show [the public]—instead of risking a momentous anticlimax when people finally do start seeing the first little bit I've done in films,' she told Dickinson. This over-concern with duty, and the fear that 'the public will get sick of me' if advance publicity oversold her performance, was to be a continuous refrain in the years ahead. 'She even called me "sir",' one reporter from a daily newspaper wrote in his column. It was a most unusual mode of address for a star in the making; yet it fitted exactly into Audrey's upbringing.

The reporters were certainly impatient to probe her 'private' life and already she had something to be reticent about: a boyfriend. What was her relationship with the handsome young man seen escorting her around town? they asked.

James—or 'Jimmy' as the future Lord Hanson was then known—was approaching thirty, the polished and sophisticated son and heir of a north-country family that had made its money building trucks. In appearance he resembled Michael Wilding, Britain's top box-office star at the time—good tailoring, long English face, smooth manner, easy smile. His background was reassuring: wartime officer in a crack regiment, lover of field sports, frequenter of nightclubs, escort of attractive women of the kind who caught the photographers' lenses but, in those days, with consistently flattering results for both parties. Hanson had already been photographed escorting Jean Simmons and at one time had even had to deny that he and Jean were engaged. Audrey met him at a party after he had seen her dancing at Ciro's. 'Part of Jimmy Hanson was a hard-headed businessman,' says a former associate of the millionaire boss of Hanson Trust, 'but in those days, show business had a strong pull for him. His family all thought he should get married, settle down, raise a family, expand the transport business into North America. Jimmy was a late starter. He showed no signs of settling down until he met Audrey.'

Had they met a little earlier, before she signed her film contract with Associated British, it is likely that Audrey Hepburn's life would have been radically different. As Mrs Hanson, and later Lady Hanson, she would have been 'one of those film people' who appear in a few movies, show promise, then have the sense to marry money and/or the aristocracy, dedicating themselves to furthering the commercial or parliamentary ambitions of their husbands, working for charities, featuring in the gossip columns of the daily newspapers, and living a busy life divided between the country estate, the house or apartment in London's Belgravia or on New York's Upper East Side and perhaps a third home in the South of France or the New England states. Audrey would have been an adornment in anything her husband chose to do, anywhere he took her. Children would have arrived. She would have supported him in business setbacks and been firm but forgiving if he occasionally made a fool of himself with some other woman.

But none of this was to be Audrey's lot. Though neither she nor Jimmy Hanson knew it then, the time for their alliance was past. A new suitor would soon arrive for Audrey Hepburn in the shape of international stardom. Few men could fight that rival.

5

'Voilà ma Gigi!'

*A*CCOMPANIED by her mother, Audrey set off for the South of France and her new film on 31 May 1951, the day after finishing work on *The Secret People*. They stopped in Paris to approve the Dior dress that Audrey was to wear for her role: she was to play a film star involved in a plot about a missing baby that becomes the property of the American band-leader, Ray Ventura, and his players. Ventura was producing the film. It was not a reassuring combination. Audrey was glad that the Dior dress would be hers once the film was shot: she might see very little additional profit from it.

Indeed, *We Go to Monte Carlo*—a title that was changed to *Monte Carlo Baby* in America to suggest a female who wasn't of the diapered variety—was harder work than Audrey had expected. Its French writer-director, Jean Boyer, fussed around between takes and Audrey soon grew tired of summoning up the right bilingual emotions for the separate English and French-speaking versions. The schedule was based on French hours, which meant filming began after lunch—good—and continued until well into the evening—bad. Mornings at least were free to explore Monaco.

It is a myth which refuses to die that the French novelist Colette first spotted Audrey filming in the Hotel de Paris where she was staying as a guest of Prince Rainier and instantly chose her to play the precocious child-woman of her novel *Gigi*. In fact, Audrey had caught the fierce eye of this frail-looking but imperious old woman, then in her seventies and a semi-invalid confined to a wheelchair, much earlier. As Colette was being pushed along the seafront by her husband, the writer Maurice Goudeket, she saw a skinny girl wearing a one-piece black swimsuit that enhanced the androgyny of her flat-chested form. She was amusing herself with a lively air. She looked impertinent, yet curiously innocent. 'Voilà ma Gigi!' Colette said to Goudeket. 'Ah, oui,' he replied, somewhat wearily.

The two of them had spotted quite a few Gigis in recent months, in the parks, boulevards and department stores of Paris. Ever since the American writer Anita Loos had adapted the novel for the stage, Colette had become a compulsive Gigi-spotter. She saw the type everywhere—the kind of girl whose simple good nature conquers all avarice despite the tutoring given by her grandmother and aunt, both great courtesans of their day, in how to hook the young millionaire who is the catch of the season. The trouble was, none of Colette's Gigis was a professional actress. It was strange, she had reflected with some irony, how this of all professions refused to throw up the ideal candidate for such a demimondaine role.

Gilbert Miller, the New York impresario who had bought the adaptation rights in the book, was impatient to stage the play and threatening to exercise his option clause and designate his own choice, should Colette find it impossible to make hers.

Colette and her husband were about to enter the main dining room of the Hôtel de Paris later that day when they found it temporarily closed. A film unit was preparing to shoot a scene there so dinner would be served in the breakfast room. Undeterred, indeed irritated by this interruption to her routine, Colette insisted on complaining to the management and was promptly wheeled into the room—only to be half-blinded by arc lights which emphasized the contrast between the baroque magnificence of the hotel and the tawdry little comedy being filmed there. Intolerable! she thought, shading her eyes from the lights. But lo! there was surely 'her Gigi' again.

The movement of the wheelchair across her eyeline temporarily distracted Audrey from the scene she was shooting. She fluffed her dialogue. 'Coupez!' called Jean Boyer, following the look Audrey directed at the interloper. A few minutes later Boyer was scattering crumbs of information about his film before this tiny, hunched and insatiably curious woman whose rouged cheeks and red hair made her look like a Daumier caricature of tyrannous aristocracy. She ignored him: her eyes were still fixed on Audrey. Marcel Dalio, the distinguished French character actor who had been persuaded to appear briefly in the film as 'Himself' in the hope that his celebrity would enhance the production, knew Colette well and introduced her to Audrey. Soon the two of them were making small talk in French. Jean Boyer later confessed that he wished he had had the nerve to ask Colette to pass through the scene as 'Herself'.

Both elated and covetous, Colette finally went on her way. Like an art collector who has seen a painting in a gallery that she simply must have (particularly as someone else was paying for it), Colette knew that she *must* have *this* Gigi.

Audrey's mother was next approached, and introduced to Colette in the hotel foyer. A conference was arranged, and an invitation issued to Audrey by Colette, like a royal command, to play Gigi. Her instinctive reaction was to say, 'I can't. I have never acted before. I am a dancer and have never spoken onstage.' Acting? That could be taught, she was assured by the old woman whose heroine, based on Colette herself, had been taught much trickier attainments, such as the advice, 'Wait for the first-class jewels: hold on to your ideals.'

Gilbert Miller and Anita Loos, over in New York, were cabled with the command not to cast their Gigi until Colette's letter arrived nominating the only possible candidate: a girl they had never heard of and who had no stage experience in a major production. The letter explained that Audrey would be in London at the beginning of July, free of film commitments, and was desperately eager to play the part on Broadway. This was somewhat stretching the truth. Audrey still flinched from an undertaking which she thought absurdly beyond her talents. Moreover, she wanted to get married to Jimmy Hanson as soon as possible. But the decisive factor was her contract with Associated British which committed her to make movies for them for the next three years and gave them approval over any stage appearances. If they had a role ready for her, she would find herself on a sound stage at Elstree and not a theatre stage on Broadway. She should have been over the moon at Colette's offer. Instead, she was oddly confused and depressed. She felt the power of deciding her own life was being taken from her.

In this mood Audrey did what she would do frequently in the future: she turned for advice to an older man, the fifty-one-year-old fatherly figure of Marcel Dalio. Life even then was anticipating art, for it is Honoré, the spry roué and honorary 'uncle', to whom Gigi turns for comfort and counsel about marriage and life. Dalio's advice offered Audrey reassurance, if not exactly direction. 'Follow your instincts,' this impromptu 'agony uncle' recalls telling her. 'If it feels right, it will be right.' Not much use, though, if it means being sued for breaking your contract. Yet the words entered Audrey's consciousness and, by all accounts, lodged there for good. It was the 'philosophy' that she trotted out in years to come when an interviewer's questions came a little too close for comfort. It sounded wise but had a useful vagueness. And the words had another advantage too: she came to believe them.

She was undecided, however, when she entered Gilbert Miller's suite at the Savoy Hotel soon after returning from France. Her agents had been busy in the interval. Whatever Audrey's own hesitations, the chance of having a client in a starring role on Broadway was like collecting the interest on someone else's investments. Such things happened more frequently in fairy tales than in the experience of theatrical agents. Audrey was sent along for her crucial interview in a costume that looked suspiciously as though she were already rehearsing for the role of Gigi. A man's shirt, several sizes too large, enhanced her waifishness. White bobbysocks emphasized a schoolgirlish length of leg. Flat shoes reduced her height to the minimum. She was twenty-three but this get-up created the impression of a girl ten years younger—of a tomboyish child.

Despite his determination to size up Colette's candidate like the hardheaded businessman he was, Gilbert Miller was charmed. A much-travelled man and a connoisseur of art—the kind he hung on the walls of his New York apartment as well as the kind he created on stage—he had enriched himself by his own enterprise and possessed the additional collateral of the fortune inherited by his wife Kitty. In other words, Gilbert Miller could tell 'quality' when he met it. Without delay he escorted Audrey along the corridor to Anita Loos's suite where the writer was awaiting her with Paulette Goddard, the actress and former wife of Charlie Chaplin.

The two women had arrived in London the week before to be met at Victoria Station by Miller's chauffeur, Glynn, a man in whom his employer placed an almost superstitious amount of trust. The chauffeur immediately handed them a large portfolio of photographs and said, 'Miss Loos, here's the star of *Gigi*.' 'So Mr Miller has already signed someone?' Anita Loos asked with a slight air of pique. 'No,' Glynn replied with grim satisfaction, 'not yet. He's holding out against me.' And he indicated that the girl in the photos had his full, unqualified approval. While being driven to the Savoy the women leafed through the pictures. As Anita Loos was later to express it, Audrey Hepburn had 'everything that is important in a female'. Then Paulette Goddard said, 'There must be something radically the matter with this girl, because if there weren't she would have been famous at the age of ten.'

Now these two shrewd women, familiar almost to the point of being jaded with the talents of the people they served, satirized or (briefly) married, sat and surveyed the girl herself. What struck them at once was Audrey's 'freshness'. 'She seemed to have a line drawn around her,' Anita Loos said, 'the way some only children have. Whatever she did, she stood out.'

Gilbert Miller saw Audrey to the door. Then, with the sigh of someone baffled at not recognizing the obvious, yet gratified to have others reveal it to him, he said: 'I should have listened to Glynn in the first place.'

A test followed: to be accurate, two tests. In the first, Audrey read Gigi's most dramatic scene in which she sets her heart against marrying the millionaire selected for her. She did not do it any too well, stumbling over the words, losing the 'feeling'. In retrospect, she may have been troubled at having to put off her own impatient suitor, Jimmy Hanson, now that the prospect of playing Gigi would take her far away from him. She did little better when her voice was tested against the acoustics of a London theatre auditorium. Cathleen Nesbitt, who had already been cast as Gigi's poker-backed grandmother, monitored Audrey's thin, strained tones from the back of the stalls. She could scarcely hear her. Audrey had never had voice-projection lessons, such as a drama school would have given her, and it was clear that she would require extensive coaching. The situation was slightly unreal. Although nominated as a star-in-waiting, Audrey possessed little more in the way of technique than a raw beginner. Whatever the reward might be, the burden she had to assume was awesome.

As a child, Audrey had suffered mild attacks of asthma which tended to occur as relations between her parents deteriorated and she felt insecure. These attacks now recurred. Everything was happening far too fast. She felt isolated and vulnerable. Surprisingly, her mother seems to have had little influence in determining Audrey's priorities: stage, screen or marriage. Ella van Heemstra was a woman who believed in the benign effect of letting things come about of their own accord, with perhaps just the gentlest of pushes. Despite her own early aspirations to be an actress, she was the very opposite of the 'stage mother'. This was the pattern of the relation-ship between mother and daughter in the years ahead: it would be Audrey who had to make the decisions and take the responsibility. She put her trust in her own instinct and did not look to her mother for counsel.

Cathleen Nesbitt undertook to coach the nerve-ridden Audrey as soon as she arrived in New York. Reassured by this, Gilbert Miller formally opened negotiations with Associated British to borrow Audrey, on 'loan-out', for the title role in *Gigi*. The idea of having someone else take the risks and allow them to make a profit greatly appealed to the film studio.

If star-making was not among the talents of the frugal executives at Associated British, it was very much part of the daily agenda at the Hollywood studios of Paramount Pictures. It was from this quarter that, a week later, in July 1951, the request arrived for the services of a girl whose only sub-stantial role, in *The Secret People,* had not yet been seen on the screen. Be-fore Audrey had even set foot on Broadway, she was in demand for the film Paramount were casting: *Roman Holiday.* No wonder Audrey felt she scarcely had time to breathe. ·

The director William Wyler was already in Europe lining up possibilities for the role of the young princess who slips off the constraints of royalty in Rome to go on the town with an American newspaperman. 'Is French actress Colette Ripert a practical possibility?' New York cabled Richard Mealand, Paramount's production chief in London, obviously taking their cue from an inquiry by Wyler.

'I have another candidate for *Roman Holiday*,' Mealand replied to his New York office on 9 July. 'I was much struck by her playing a bit part in *Laughter in Paradise*.' New York requested: 'Please airmail report and photographs . . .' In retrospect, Audrey Hepburn seems so absolutely right for the role, surely the one and only candidate, that it is salutary to remember the part that luck played in her selection, and how nearly she missed the chance of a lifetime.

Roman Holiday was by no means a hot new project. The script had been written by Dalton Trumbo and Ian McLellan Hunter as long ago as the mid-1940s. It had been intended for the director Frank Capra, who had difficulty casting it; so it lay gathering dust in the archives or was passed around other directors, coming to nothing. When Wyler read it he had just finished shooting *Carrie,* with Laurence Olivier and Jennifer Jones, which was to turn out to be a commercial disappointment, and was awaiting the release of *Detective Story,* with Kirk Douglas. Rightly guessing that it would be a critical and box-office hit, Paramount allowed Wyler to pick *Roman Holiday* as his next film and go off to Rome to scout locations. However, he had run into the same difficulty as Capra—casting the role of the princess. Unless the actress were absolutely right the story would not work. 'I wanted a girl without an American accent,' Wyler recalled, 'someone you could believe was brought up to be a princess.' He thought he had found her in Elizabeth Taylor who had been born in England. Her new film, *A Place in the Sun,* for which Paramount had borrowed her from MGM, had revealed a full, yet delicate beauty, a tenderness and vulnerability, too, that Wyler thought would be perfect. But MGM would not agree to 'their' star adding further to Paramount's profits. Wyler had to forget about Elizabeth Taylor.

Richard Mealand's report on Audrey was promising. 'She is twenty-two years old, 5'5 1/2" in height [*sic*], darkish brown hair . . . She is a little on the thin side . . . but very appealing. There is no question of her ability and she dances very well. Her speaking voice is clear and youthful with no extremes of accent. She looks more Continental than English.'

The reply read, 'Studio very interested Hepburn. Anxious see her soonest on film.' Almost on the heels of this cable, another arrived: 'Ask Hepburn if OK change her last name avoid conflict Katharine Hepburn.'

Others might have immediately acceded to a request that was not un-usual in Hollywood at this time. But Audrey showed her mettle right from the start. 'If you want me, you'll have to take my name, too,' she replied.

All this was going on at the same time as Audrey was being considered for the leading role in Colette's play on Broadway. To be offered either of the two parts, Gigi or Princess Ann, would lead a beginner to believe that the gods took a very special interest in her. To have both roles virtually thrust on her simultaneously suggests that the gods were nothing less than head over heels in love with Audrey Hepburn.

Paramount, however interested, would not decide definitely until they saw a screen test. An inter-office memo went from London to New York saying, 'Test arranged Pinewood Studios, September 18, 1951. Thorold Dickinson directing. Other players Lionel Murton and Cathleen Nesbitt. Two scenes from *Roman Holiday* script and an interview.' The first thing this prosaic memo reveals is how well protected Audrey was. Thorold Dickinson, who had just finished working with her on *The Secret People,* liked her and she felt confident with him. The Canadian actor Lionel Murton had be-friended Audrey while they were making *We Go to Monte Carlo.* Cathleen Nesbitt, who was already cast for *Gigi,* had undertaken to coach Audrey for the play—so there is a strong presumption that she also coached her in the test scenes for *Roman Holiday.* Everything suggests that Mealand had agreed to give Audrey and her agents final approval of the people making the screen test. Wyler himself could not be there; he was still in Rome. But he knew how unreliable such tests could be. They might present a flattering illusion of the actress, or else, because of her nervousness, fail to do her jus-tice. What the memo does not reveal is the confidential arrangement he en-tered into with Dickinson and Paramount's representative, Paul Stein. They were instructed to keep the camera running at the end of the scene, without telling Audrey, so that her natural personality could be judged when she was not consciously acting.

The test exists still. Contrary to Mealand's description it shows a sur-prisingly podgy Audrey Hepburn—all that French food, perhaps, during the recent filming on the Côte d'Azur—awakening in the American re-porter's (otherwise empty) bed, stretching in a delightfully kittenish way, throwing out her arms with all the youthful innocence and freshness of a newcomer to this wonderful world of ordinary folk, engaging in conver-sation with the newsman (Lionel Murton), and then moving to the door with all the easy grace of her ballet training and, as she opens it, turning round and winking like a mischievous elf.

'That's it,' Paul Stein's voice is heard saying. Audrey hesitates ever so slightly, looks full at the camera and then an expression of amusement lights up her face as she guesses the deception that is being practised on her. She is equal to it. 'Only one man has the right to say "Cut",' she says, obviously addressing Thorold Dickinson, 'and I won't move until I hear him.' The camera goes on turning until, suddenly, she doubles up in helpless laughter. It's a response that's totally unaffected and appealing. 'Absolutely charming,' Wyler said when he viewed the test in Rome. New York shared that view. 'Congratulations. Fine test Hepburn,' ran the cable. 'All here think her great.'

A letter from New York a few days later made it official. Below the words 'Audrey Hepburn', underlined and in red ink, it said: 'Exercise the option on this lady. The test is certainly one of the best ever made in Hollywood, New York or London . . . Hearty congratulations . . . This includes Barney, Frank and Don.' Barney Balaban, Frank Freeman and Don Hartman were Paramount's top executive troika. No blessing could have been given with more authority. Only one person did not share the general elation. The Paramount files still hold a personal note to Richard Mealand written in the round, schoolgirlish hand of Audrey Hepburn. 'Heaven help me live up to all this,' she ended.

Sorting out her commitments, to appear on stage in *Gigi* and on screen in *Roman Holiday,* must have taxed even the cajolery, ingenuity, patience and profit-conscious acumen of Gilbert Miller and Paramount Pictures. Associated British, who had seen the value of their artist immeasurably increased, without so much as lifting a finger, had only to rub their hands. As part of the deal for *Roman Holiday* Paramount attempted to buy Audrey out of her British contract, believing, with some justification, that if they took the risk of starring this unknown quantity, they should be granted the right to benefit from it. They offered Associated British £100,000—then equal to half a million dollars and by today's values worth over £5 million. A deal was struck. The British studio held on to Audrey's contractual obligations—insisting she would make at least two more films for them—but granted Paramount the right to sign her to a seven-picture contract, one film a year, to be made for Paramount or on loan-out to another studio. The right to do television and stage work remained hers. Associated British would be paid a fee for every film she made under the Paramount contract or else would acquire the rights to distribute it in Britain, an even more valuable prospect. As for Audrey, she was to be paid £2,500 ($7,000)—which at the time seemed a fortune to her. One wonders if she appreciated what a pitiful bargain for her all this represented. An option clause in her American contact permitted Paramount to drop her if the promise she so abundantly displayed in the screen test failed to materialize in the film of *Roman Holiday*.

The impending production of *Gigi* was now fraught with even greater risk for Audrey. If she was a success in it, well and good. As she had not yet signed Gilbert Miller's contract, Paramount was able to force the impresario to agree to release her from the play when William Wyler had completed pre-production in Rome and was ready to start shooting the following summer. In compensation to Miller, Audrey had to agree to do an American tour with *Gigi* immediately after finishing *Roman Holiday*. But supposing *Gigi* turned out to be a disaster on Broadway? Then Audrey would have to start filming a major movie knowing that the shine was off her personality. The responsibilities she was bearing were an intolerable burden on a girl with a conscience, at this age and stage of her career.

Jimmy Hanson followed all these negotiations ruefully. It must have been clear to him that Audrey was now so solidly locked into work for the next year or so that prospects of their marrying had to take second place. Still, they swore their affection for each other was strong enough to meet the test. And besides, Hanson's family business interests would take him to North America while Audrey was there doing *Gigi*. She sailed alone on a slow boat to New York so that she would have plenty of time to learn her role. The baroness stayed behind in London, in the South Audley Street apartment whose door now carried a brass nameplate: 'Baroness van Heemstra' and, below it, 'Audrey Hepburn'.

Audrey got out of bed in her cabin in the early hours of the morning to see the famous skyline of New York as the boat approached Manhattan. So many dreams had already come true that it was perhaps inevitable that one romantic urge would be denied her. 'We arrived at 3 a.m. in pitch dark,' she recalled. 'I stood freezing in my nightie in front of the porthole—and saw nothing.'

6

HER ROYAL HIGHNESS

WITHIN two hours of landing in New York, Audrey was whisked away by an aide of Gilbert Miller to watch a World Series baseball game. She sat in the stadium, elated after two weeks at sea to feel the great open space of America around her and eating a hot dog. 'The food,' she wrote back to her mother in England where meat was still rationed— 'all those steaks!'

When Gilbert Miller saw her he realized that he had another, unexpected problem with Audrey: her weight. He had said goodbye in London to a gawky, adolescent-looking young woman, for after signing her for the future, Paramount had put her on a diet. Confronting him now in New York was a person who verged on plumpness. On her slow boat to America Audrey had gorged herself at every meal and snacked liberally in between: understandable considering the worry, responsibilities, hard work and loneliness that were to be her daily lot over the next six weeks or so. Miller immediately put her back on a diet and gave strict instructions to the maître d' and chefs at Dinty Moore's, the show-business restaurant where Audrey took her meals, that she was to be served only steak tartare and green salads. Her work schedule was as strict as her diet sheet. Every day she was coached by Cathleen Nesbitt, and during weekends, too, at Nesbitt's rented home outside New York.

This stage production of *Gigi* was not, of course, the musical version which was filmed a few years later. Nevertheless Audrey had taken singing lessons to improve her voice production. Now she applied herself to the dialogue of the play in which she was already word perfect. 'During my first days of rehearsal, I couldn't be heard beyond the front row,' she said. 'I worked day and night. Every night I would go home and speak each word clearly and loudly.' She succeeded. 'I could be heard at last.' Even Cathleen Nesbitt approved her. Yet Gilbert Miller took no chances. Audrey still showed a lack of self-confidence, possibly due to the demands she made on herself. To build her up, Miller had publicity photographs taken of her by

Irving Penn and Richard Avedon. It was during the sessions with Avedon that Audrey learned to mask what she regarded as defects. Her jawline looked too determinedly set, her face too square when viewed full on. Avedon showed her how these things were corrected for the camera lens. Thus the three-quarter profile, head ever so slightly angled so that her high cheekbones slimmed the lower part of her face, became a characteristic pose of Audrey's. The session with Avedon strangely anticipated the scene she would play five years later in *Funny Face,* when Fred Astaire, as a fashion photographer named Richard Avery and clearly inspired by Avedon, reassures a reticent Audrey about her 'funny, funny face'. The inner girl, of course, had a self-correcting effect on any real or imaginary flaw in her features. Another great photographer for whom Audrey would subsequently sit, Philippe Halsman, said: 'Her face has such facets, such changes of expression, you're always afraid you'll be too late. She keeps escaping the camera.'

The French director Raymond Rouleau was to guarantee the Gallic flavour of the New York production of *Gigi*. He was not happy with Audrey. She had Gigi's energy: no doubt about that. But her phrasing of the dialogue was variable, her tempo over-animated, she often gabbled her lines and she still gave a reading of the part instead of playing it on feeling. The speech that repeatedly tripped her up in rehearsal was the same one that had bedevilled her audition, in which Gigi rejects Gaston, the man whom her grandmother and aunt have selected to be her husband. Audrey and James Hanson were still seeing each other when he was in New York, but she seemed reluctant to settle on a date for their engagement, much less marriage. 'I want to get married,' she insisted. 'I think it a great waste of time not to get married to James.' She blamed lack of time for not getting round to it but, perhaps, like Gigi, she was discovering that marriage was not the first priority when life itself was still waiting to be celebrated.

According to Raymond Rouleau's widow, 'The first eight days of work [in New York] with Audrey were truly terrible. She was acting extremely badly, totally failing to understand the meaning of the text, going out late at night and arriving very tired at the theatre in the mornings. Finally . . . [Rouleau] told her quite firmly she must improve, or else.' Her late nights were due to her going out on the town with Hanson whose family, rather surprisingly, had interests in the El Morocco nightclub, where he and Audrey would see midnight come and go. Rouleau's fatherly sternness seems to have had the desired effect. 'Next day,' Madame Rouleau recalled, 'a new Audrey emerged.' James Hanson saw much less of her.

Even so she appeared strained and nervous, and the playbill for *Gigi* reveals, inexplicably, a girl with bags under her eyes from worry and sleep-lessness. David Niven, who was appearing with Gloria Swanson at the same time, in an ill-fated Broadway production of a play called *Nina,* was one witness to the trauma Audrey was undergoing. In his memoir, *The Moon's a Balloon,* he recalls the 'doe-eyed waif' in the next room of the hotel in Philadelphia, where the play's out-of-town try-outs were taking place, who like him was making her stage debut. 'We shook with terror as our opening nights drew inexorably nearer.'

The Philadelphia reviews of *Gigi* were cool, except in one respect. The critics took Audrey to their hearts. Their ecstatic comments suggest that her very inexperience translated into Gigi's almost palpable vulnerability, and made reviewers and audiences want to embrace her protectively. The critics could no more have given this girl a cruel notice than they could have raised their fists to a child. It was the first sign of the Hepburn phenome-non—and it was repeated on Broadway when the play opened on 24 No-vember 1951.

'Her quality is so winning and so right that she is the success of the evening,' wrote Richard Watts Jr, and Walter Kerr in the *New York Times* wrote: 'She brings a candid innocence and a tomboy intelligence to a part that might have gone sticky.' The renunciation-of-Gaston scene appears at last to have gone right. Brooks Atkinson commented in the *New York Times:* 'She develops a full-length character from artless gaucheries in the first act to a stirring climax in the last scene. It is a fine piece of sustained acting that is spontaneous, lucid and captivating.' The review in *Esquire* comes nearest to giving us a picture of what she actually did, suggesting a vitamin-packed performance like a child bowling a hoop with excess but pardonable brio. 'She shouts, slams doors and runs deftly round the furniture. In surefooted confusion, she never knocks over a lamp. She is able to put on an athletic show that would shame a track meet.' Offstage the same writer found her 'smoothly wholesome-looking . . . she has an untrammelled expression and a long stride. She looks like a kid who has been fed on milk and vegetables and never allowed to cross the street alone.' That the 'kid' was in her twenty-third year was overlooked in the youthfulness she radiated, 'as fresh and frisky', to quote Richard Watts again, 'as a puppy out of a tub'. The photographs of a serious-looking young miss in the playbill are the only in-dication of the worry Audrey had been through and suggest that at this stage of her career she needed the invigoration of performing to bring her up to pitch. Even then she probably overdid things. Noël Coward, passing through New York in April 1952 when, admittedly, *Gigi* was about to close after a most successful run, records in his diary that he had witnessed 'an orgy of over-acting and a vulgar script. Cathleen Nesbitt good and digni-fied, and the sets lovely. Audrey Hepburn inexperienced and rather too noisy, and the whole thing badly directed.'

How to reconcile these two views? Possibly by acknowledging that the production left a lot to be remedied—it was put together in a hurry, per-haps due to the long time taken in casting Gigi. Audrey's performance would have deteriorated in the months before Coward caught up with it: she was not suited to sustaining the repetition of a long run. But on open-ing night, her personality-playing was so sharp and vivid that it dimmed the play's shortcomings. Within days of the first night the neon sign, which had ordained the order of things as:

GIGI
with
Audrey Hepburn

was changed to:

AUDREY HEPBURN
in
Gigi

Even in her moment of triumph Audrey did not forget her manners. To Richard Mealand, Paramount's man in London, she wrote: 'my knees are shaking, only with happiness now, not fright!' Sidney Cole, producer of *The Secret People,* had sent her flowers on the opening night. (Cole, a man not usually given to poetic feelings about film stars, always described Audrey as having 'the serenity of a single white rose'.) In a touchingly modest thank-you letter she added in brackets after her signature the name 'Nora', lest he should have forgotten her among the more distinguished members of the cast of the film.

After such a build-up and release of emotion came the inevitable let-down. The novelty of sudden stardom palled quickly. 'I thought it would be heady and fun seeing my name in lights. But it was not like being a suc-cess in the chorus. The rest of the show can help you there. When you are the lead, it is no longer happy-go-lucky. You feel everything depends on you. Another thing about being called a star: you can never feel tired any more, ever. I thought that being "The Toast of Broadway" might mean peo-ple standing up and raising champagne glasses. But no one has ever done that. I thought it might mean sailing into restaurants when they were full and getting a table with just a smile at the head waiter . . .' Significantly considering the efforts that James Hanson was making to bring her to the point of engagement, she added: 'But Jimmy didn't risk it——he booked in advance.'

The thing never to be forgotten about Audrey Hepburn is that despite her basic good sense she remained at heart an incorrigible romantic: sometimes even a childish one. When quizzed about her favourite childhood reading she always mentioned the classic fairy tales——'Cinderella', 'Sleeping Beauty', 'Hansel and Gretel'——because of their happy endings. Most children allow experience of the world to rewrite the last paragraph, but Audrey never did——or, more accurately, didn't care to do so. This is an important element in her allure. Her upbringing played its part, too: the baroness instilled in her daughter the conviction that setbacks and disappointments were merely temporary delays, and everything would turn out all right in the end.

In seeking to understand why her love affair with James Hanson left her with nothing but a nostalgic memory, one has to take account of Audrey's ingrained romanticism. The young and handsome millionaire began to fade as a Prince Charming when stardom came courting Audrey Hepburn. A man who has to book in advance for a fashionable restaurant loses his lustre compared to a man who simply smiles at the head waiter and is ushered with his companion to the best table in the room. A few nights after *Gigi* opened, reporters noticed that the silver-framed photograph of James Hanson was no longer in its place in Audrey's dressing room. Audrey had an unconvincing explanation. 'So many people ask me what his name is . . . My private life is my own. How am I going to laugh off these questions without appearing rude?' It looked as if the bloom was off the affair. And yet . . .

On 4 December 1951, the London *Times* carried the long-delayed announcement of the engagement between 'James, son of Mr and Mrs Robert Hanson, of Norwood Grange, Huddersfield, Yorkshire, and Audrey Hepburn, daughter of Baroness Ella van Heemstra, of 65 South Audley Street, London, W1.'

That seemed to be it, then? Officially, yes; but behind the scenes a lot was happening, or, rather, not happening. Anecdotal testimony from one or two of those who were closest to Audrey raises the question of who inserted the engagement notice in *The Times*. Traditionally, this is the responsibility of the bridegroom's family——but did the Hansons do so with the concurrence of Audrey's mother? Earlier biographers have supposed that Ella opposed, or, at any rate, did not encourage Audrey's marriage into the Hanson family, that she felt Jimmy was not ready to settle down and, although this was hardly marrying in haste, she wished her daughter to avoid the same mistake as she had made twice. This view is not supported by those who knew Ella van Heemstra. Her friends say that she was fully behind a Hanson-van Heemstra alliance. James was an appealing match—rich and likely to become even richer, and to a woman as vulnerable as Ella to handsome men, an attractive proposition for a son-in-law. In short, Audrey's mother is most likely to have been the person whose persuasiveness resulted in the overdue announcement of the engagement. Certainly James Hanson was not opposed to making it official. Audrey, although she went along with it in everything she said for the record, is a less certain quantity.

Indecisiveness appears to have been her mood at that time. Understandably so. 'I'm halfway to being a dancer and an actress,' she told a magazine interviewer soon after the opening of *Gigi*. 'I've got to learn.' Ballet was not abandoned: she still attended body-movement classes at a Manhattan dance academy. But she was now under the very strict orders of Paramount Pictures, who were preparing *Roman Holiday* for production and guarding one of their main assets as if she were indeed a royal princess. Audrey dutifully followed the studio's instructions about diet and beauty which arrived by mail from California and were supervised by a Paramount executive in New York. She now had her nervous appetite under control; success had at least achieved that. The Hepburn figure of a flat chest, ultra-slim waist—for many years it did not exceed 20 inches—slender hips, strong upper thighs that powered her like battery cells, and long flexible legs, was shaped for life at this time.

During the run of *Gigi* Audrey met Edith Head, one of the leading costume designers in Hollywood, to decide what Princess Ann should wear. A couple of formal ensembles were agreed on: a sumptuous ballgown for the opening scene where the princess chafes at the restrictions of protocol and surrenders herself resignedly to the ageing courtier with whom she opens the dancing; and an 'official' day dress for the press conference when the looks that pass between the princess and the newspaperman underline the romantic divide between love and duty, royalty and commoner, which gives *Roman Holiday*'s ending such a powerfully affecting tension between loss and fulfilment.

Heavy brocade, a royal sash and a hint of beribboned insignia, a tiara and white gloves—regulation wear for European royalty at this time—contrasted vividly with Audrey's youth and innocence. Such Zenda-like regalia would be a perfect foil for the comic and wholly understandable reflex that causes the young princess to ease her high-heeled shoe off her tired foot and then probe around under her ballgown in order to retrieve the elusive slipper—a nice inversion of the Cinderella touch. Audrey accepted that such finery was part of the role but told Edith Head that she doubted she could ever feel comfortable in it. 'That's the idea, darling,' the designer said, amused at her professional innocence. In other matters, she discovered that Audrey knew her mind very well indeed.

Audrey's own everyday clothes were anything but fashionable. She felt most at home in a man's shirt whose front tails she pulled back round her waist and tied together very tightly. 'Shirts are so wonderful,' she was to say in one of her early Hollywood interviews, 'all you do is wash and iron them.' 'Yourself?' asked the journalist, clearly not familiar with stars who did their own laundry. 'Myself.'

For Princess Ann's city escapade, Edith Head adapted this casual look, adding a flared skirt of the kind that was then found on every American campus, white bobby socks worn over stockings, which was also the uniform of youth across America, and flat shoes. The princess's 'plainclothes' outfit was an inspired bit of mix'n'match for its simplicity served a double purpose. It defined Audrey's style as well as her character's; and it created a fashion that could be easily copied by any girl with pin money the world over. Audrey herself suggested the broad leather belt that cinched her narrow waist even more tightly: it suggested the fantasy proportions conjured up by Disney animators and thus lent her a fairy-tale aura. (This was somewhat harder for the fans to copy.) It is on such special and elusive elements of figure, looks and personality that stardom is built. Edith Head set the style for Princess Ann but Audrey's instinct transfigured it.

Gigi ran for 217 performances, closing on 31 May 1952. But for the agreement which Gilbert Miller had made with Paramount to release Audrey as soon as *Roman Holiday* was ready to go, it could have run indefinitely.

Audrey had no time to rest between play and film—only a few hours in her hotel between the final curtain and the scheduled flight time of her TWA Constellation to Rome. She arrived showing the strain of what lay ahead and was hustled through an airport press conference that provided her with her first experience of how intrusive the media could be (the Broadway press had been gentlefolk compared to Rome's predators). She was twenty-three, wasn't she? (Yes.) Then why wasn't she married? (She was going to be married.) Would Signor 'Anson and she get married before the film or after it? (After it, she had told him.) Why did they wait? (No reply.) Did they not love each other enough? (No reply.)

In fact, Audrey had suggested to her fiancé that they should postpone the wedding until she had finished filming and before she started the tour of *Gigi*. This decision was now weighing on her conscience. With each step she took into the world of stardom, it seemed, she took two (or more) back from the altar. She was learning about the incompatibility of fame and personal happiness but not yet wanting to admit it.

That same evening Audrey met the star of the film, Gregory Peck. Like her, he had not been William Wyler's first choice. Cary Grant had been sent the script originally and had turned it down, as he so frequently did—often on irrational grounds, or none at all that he would admit to. So self-possessed and relaxed on screen, Grant was in reality extremely pernickety, and though the list of the films he made is distinguished, an alternative list of great movies he did not make, or pulled out of, would be nearly as long. He rejected *Roman Holiday* because he knew the centre of attention would be the girl.

Gregory Peck was then thirty-six. A star since Hitchcock's *Spellbound*, in 1945, his six-foot physique and forthright manner radiated moral and physical strength. Any role he played collected around it an air of reliability and integrity. He was perfect casting for many Hollywood genres: Westerns *(The Gunfighter)*, suspense mysteries *(Spellbound)*, romantic dramas *(The Macomber Affair)*, social melodramas *(Gentleman's Agreement)*, war sagas *(Twelve O'Clock High)*, even religious epics *(David and Bathsheba)*. He was almost too good to be true: popular with fellow stars, generous to newcomers. Audrey could not have found a better 'godfather'. He was also unhappily married: a fact he was trying to live with, as stars used to do in the days before the phenomenon of celebrity killed the fear of scandal.

Like Cary Grant he had been initially reluctant to play the role of the reporter, and for much the same reason. William Wyler skilfully overcame his reluctance by delivering a reproach that was itself a compliment: 'I didn't think you needed to measure the length of a part.' Peck recognized the quality of the script, and when he met Audrey at an introductory party at the Excelsior Hotel, he recognized hers just as quickly. He took her small hand in his large one, felt shyness in her modest grasp and said in playful rehearsal for their roles, 'Your Royal Highness.' She replied, 'I hope I don't let you down.'

Unknown to anyone else, William Wyler had had to quieten Audrey's nerves, which were in a poor state on her arrival in Rome. She had learned that Wyler's heart had been set on Jean Simmons, who was already a star of the first rank, but Simmons was under exclusive contract to Howard Hughes, the reclusive millionaire, who refused to release her or even to discuss a loan-out. This disappointment had almost made Wyler decide to cancel the film. Thus Audrey was well aware she was stepping into shoes that some other 'princess' might have filled.

It had been decided to shoot the entire film in Rome. Location filming was not yet commonplace even in major Hollywood films and the rarity of this event was thought important enough to be stated explicitly in the credits. But Wyler had not reckoned on the very special hell that Rome became in the summer. The summer of 1952 was one of the hottest on record, and humidity turned the city into a steam bath. The excitement of seeing a movie being shot in the streets at the height of the tourist season made it a stop-start-stop event and a personal ordeal for Peck in particular, the only high-visibility star in the cast. Filming frequently had to be halted as Romans and visitors closed in on the very tourist sites that the newsman and the absconding princess were supposed to be enjoying at leisure and unrecognized.

The script deftly projected the princess's discovery of the joys of life. The freshness Audrey brought to it made it seem as if she too were tasting them for the first time. She conveyed royalty's delight in the novelty of not being recognized, the freedom felt by a sheltered girl suddenly able to go wherever she wants, the exhilarating disobedience of nibbling an ice-cream cone on the street and, most happily for Audrey's own future image, the sinful fun of having the hairdo that was intended to support a tiara chopped down by a barber to the length and raggedness of a happy-go-lucky gamine.

When Audrey wanders the streets as the incognita princess, swinging her body and tasting the simple pleasures of the people, one realizes that this is a star taking her first outing, too. Neither she nor Princess Ann would ever again be so innocently happy. There is a complete identity between the role and the performer. What Ann does is very simple, but because one is aware of her true identity, her smallest action, her least reflex of joy is charged with interest. And the fact that Peck's cameraman, played by Eddie Albert, is secretly sneaking candid shots of Her Royal Highness imparts suspense to the most routine event.

All this depends on the realism of the setting, the weather, the time of day or night, the noises of the passing world: all things hard enough to control anywhere but next to impossible in Rome. Making *Roman Holiday* was no holiday for anyone. The city seemed to have been designed to test a filmmaker's patience to destruction point. Streets had to be closed off, traffic diverted, public monuments roped off to the irritation of tourists, and bribes liberally distributed to anyone in so-called authority—which usually waned as the day wore on. Because all these arrangements were so troublesome, Wyler was limited to a small number of takes for each scene. For Audrey that was a godsend. Wyler was well-known to be demanding, insisting that actors repeat their scenes over and over again. Had *Roman Holiday* been shot in a studio, his demands could have been devastating to the morale and even the art of a performer like Audrey, who was at her best in the first few takes. As it was, Wyler had to snatch the effect he wanted on the run, so to speak, which suited Audrey perfectly.

Moreover, the film was being shot in black and white. Colour would have been too costly in those days, when film stock needed the controlled conditions not available on every street corner or piazza in Rome. Again, this was an advantage. It avoids the sense of travelogue prettiness that colour might have imparted. As it is, one can stop the film at any point and the frame looks like a magazine layout—candid, immediate, realistic. To the mass of American filmgoers, the landmarks visited by Audrey Hepburn and Gregory Peck were still unfamiliar in the 1950s: De Sica's *Bicycle Thieves* was almost the only 'location' picture to have been shown in the United States before the release of *Roman Holiday*. Those Americans who did recognize Rome were the US servicemen who had marched into the 'open city' at the end of the war. For them, it was a return trip, with nostalgia in their eyes now, not victory.

These were perhaps unpremeditated elements contributing to the film's freshness. But Audrey Hepburn was undoubtedly its greatest asset. Remembering the lessons of *The Secret People,* she conserved her energy, spoke to barely a soul, sipped only a single glass of champagne at lunch, and retreated into herself before going in front of the camera so as to touch the real emotion and forget the need to act, trusting all the while that the camera would catch 'the truth'. Invariably it did. The motor-scooter ride with Peck that lasts only a few minutes actually took six days to shoot, yet no sign of the endless disruptions appears on screen. Everything is easy, natural, joyful and touching. One feels a bodyguard's protectiveness towards Audrey, wanting life to be kind to her as one would want a child to share the untrammelled pleasures of a day's outing.

Only one curious but potent moment breaks the spell of the princess's innocence—and Audrey's, too. It occurs just before the princess parts from the newsman in the back of a taxi, at night, outside the gates of her country's embassy through which she will soon vanish, once more (and forever this time) beyond reach of a commoner. Just before she leaves him, Audrey plants a very carnal kiss on Peck's lips. The way the shot is photographed, in semi-silhouette and with the highlights of desire visible in the two faces, suddenly adds years to Audrey and suggests the range of roles that ought to become available to this debutante star. That she would choose not to exercise the power that comes from stardom, and remained within a narrow range of roles, could not be known at the time.

The ending of *Roman Holiday* is part of its secret. Because the princess knows so little of the outside world—and because Audrey is so successful in convincing one of this—the feeling that most of the film generates is one of liberation. But self-sacrifice is the keynote of the closing moments. Though love unconsummated preserves the logic, as well as the purity, of a story in which duty wins over the promptings of the heart, the ending has a transcendent feeling of loneliness very rare in Hollywood of that time— and virtually extinct today. Death has not separated the lovers, as in *Romeo and Juliet;* duty has done so. The princess retires behind her palace walls. She only meets her lover once more, at the formal press conference, when protocol separates them more efficiently than prison bars. Then the newsman makes his way alone through marble halls towards the street that is his beat. Looking back, one sees it as a *Nun's Story* in reverse. Instead of walking out on her vows, Audrey's character preserves them—and seals up the spell of the tale along with herself.

7

M E N I N H E R L I F E

*R*OMAN *HOLIDAY* was due to finish filming in September 1952. Several times during the shooting James Hanson flew to Rome in the hope of persuading Audrey to commit herself to a wedding date. A photo-spread in *Look* magazine had Hanson exclaiming 'By George!' as he watched her having her gamine hair-cut elevated with a false hairpiece to hold a tiara for the 'poor little princess' scene at the embassy ball. Anticipating events, *Look*'s caption-writer added (in brackets that suggest a certain stop-press anxiety): 'They were married last month.' Only they weren't.

Audrey and her fiancé finally set the wedding date for 30 September 1952. Two hundred guests were invited to the ceremony in a parish church: it was to be the event of the year in Huddersfield. Sharon Douglas, daughter of the then American ambassador, Lewis Douglas, agreed to be a bridesmaid. The presents had already begun to arrive when the ceremony had to be abruptly cancelled: *Roman Holiday* was overrunning its shooting schedule. On the morning of what should have been his wedding day Hanson found himself at Northolt Airport, London, waiting for his fiancée to arrive from Rome. They had four hours together in town before flying on to New York. The wedding dress, which Audrey had had made in Rome, travelled with them. She hardly had time to try it on, and reflect how she might look as Mrs James Hanson, before Gilbert Miller whisked her off in a limousine to a West Side rehearsal room for a refresher course as Gigi. Before the week was out she left on tour with the play. No new date was fixed for the wedding. Hanson left to attend to family business in Toronto.

If the couple were as much in love as they professed to be, it seems strange that they did not get married on American or Canadian soil. Before leaving London they had emphasized to the press that there was 'no tiff between us. We expect to be married within the next three months.' Hanson added, 'We shall make our home in New York, London and Ontario, where I have business interests.' It didn't seem to occur to him that this added up to three homes. Here was a symptom of something far more serious than a lovers' tiff. Whether or not either was willing to acknowledge it publicly or privately, a rift had begun to open between them, caused by Audrey's reluctant recognition that if this was what life was like when they were not married, it was unlikely to get much better when they were. Putting it another way, she was now rather more in love with her career than she was with her fiancé and appears to have had no wish to sacrifice it for him.

In Rome she had worked with celebrities and been the focus of everyone's attention. She had finished the film with Wyler's assurance that she herself could be 'one of the biggest stars in the world'. The romantic obligation to Hanson—for that is what love had dwindled to in the waiting period—now looked less and less attractive. 'I shall only feel married when I am well and truly married,' she had said early in 1952. 'I won't have anyone ask me "Have you ever been married before?" ' Increasingly, she felt that, with a career still being established, she could not feel 'well and truly' married. Sensibly she and Hanson decided to part as friends.

The announcement to that effect was made on 18 November 1952 while Audrey was playing in *Gigi* in Chicago. Hanson had come down from Toronto and they talked it over: 'When we've [both] made our careers, we might talk again,' said Audrey. Her subsequent statements showed as much concern for logic as for love, perhaps more: 'As we were not going to get married, it seemed sensible not to stay engaged . . . We saw as much of each other as we would have had we been married—it was bitter little'—perhaps the word she used was 'bloody' but expletives were not then commonplace in the American press—'so I decided this was not the proper climate for normal life.' This implies a significant change in the way Audrey viewed herself. Hitherto, her public statements had stressed her fear that staying up at night to cook her husband his meals might cause her to arrive at the studio in the morning not knowing her lines. She had seen marriage in terms of her husband's career. Now she indicated that she saw life very much in terms of her own career. 'I decided it would be unfair to Jimmy to marry him when I was tied to, and in love with, my work.' How humiliating it would be, 'making him stand by, holding my coat, while I signed autographs'. This was, perhaps, an improbable prospect considering that Hanson became the boss of one of the most powerful conglomerates in the world. But at the time Audrey's sense of what was right, for both of them, must be judged absolutely sound—and probably Hanson judged it so, too.

Audrey did not reckon with the effect of a broken engagement on her career. She became the object of much more concentrated and inquisitive media interest. For one thing, a broken-off love-affair paralleled the loneliness of the royal princess whom she had just finished playing, as well as the 'marriageable' Gigi she was once again playing onstage. Nothing fosters the growth of stardom so quickly as the gossip that fills the gap between the real person and the fictional character, making the one indistinguishable from the other. It mattered little to the media that Audrey's marriage had fallen through: if anything, the news was rather welcome to the then vitally important columnists like Hedda Hopper, Louella Parsons and Earl Wilson, from whose 'inside' information the mass public derived their vicarious, sometimes prurient gratification. Although James Hanson possessed everything a proud mother-in-law might wish for——wealth, good looks and the promise of greater things still——he was not natural name-dropping material. Hedda and company could now speculate freely on the much more glamorous liaisons in store for Audrey Hepburn.

Rumours of just this kind had already upset her while she was filming in Rome. Gregory Peck's marriage was breaking up, and he was soon to move out of the villa rented for him, his wife Greta and their family. Before filming was over he fell in love with a French journalist, Veronique Passani; and they were married a few years later. Gossip, unfounded but plausible, suggested Audrey as the cause of the marital break-up. She was hurt and puzzled for she claimed to have done nothing to set tongues wagging. Then it was explained to her by an interviewer from *Photoplay*, a woman wise to the ways in which rumours gathered credibility, that Audrey herself had unwittingly encouraged the story by the very enthusiasm she had shown for working with Peck: '[He] is down to earth, full of real simplicity, utterly kind to everybody.' Praise like that was not interpreted as a professional endorsement but as something warmer and more intimate. Audrey was startled by this revelation. Then she admitted thoughtfully, 'That may very well be.' It was a lesson in self-protection that she swiftly acted on: henceforth, interviews granted by Audrey Hepburn were notoriously cautious.

What was Audrey's status at this moment in her career before the release of *Roman Holiday*? Back in England, at the start of 1952, the imminent release of *The Secret People* had pushed her name and picture into the papers. The *Daily Mail*'s film critic, Cecil Wilson, under the headline 'Leap-to-Fame Year', noted that Ealing Studios had 'three attractive new faces all sparkling with star quality' ready for unveiling: Susan Stephen (co-star with Eric Portman in the comedy *His Excellency*); Audrey Hepburn, 'who has already found fame in the American theatre [as Gigi] and should go far, and that I fear means Hollywood'; and eighteen-year-old Joan Collins (the future dominatrix of *Dynasty* was appearing in *I Believe in You* as a delinquent girl placed on probation in the most unlikely care of Celia Johnson). After such a build-up, the reception accorded to *The Secret People* by the critics in February 1952 was a setback for Audrey. Reviews were lukewarm, even hurtful. Richard Winnington, a crypto-Communist critic and, therefore, far from sympathetic to the movie's muddled message about the perils of political do-goodism, wrote: 'Valentina Cortese's performance is occasionally moving, Reggiani's negligible, Audrey Hepburn's negative.' Fortunately *The Secret People* did not get released in America for several years and even then it was not widely shown. At least it did Audrey no harm there.

William Wyler was a slow—very slow—and meticulous craftsman. To Paramount's irritation, he would not have *Roman Holiday* ready for its premiere for almost a year. Audrey was a Broadway star before she began the film, but the gap of several months while she was filming in Rome, followed by the tour, removed her name from the important papers and magazines. When *Gigi* reached Los Angeles late in 1952, Paramount's publicists had a hard time persuading local newspaper columnists to interview Audrey and, in desperation, had to buy them tickets even to get them to see the show.

But this soon changed. Anticipation began building the minute Wyler had a rough cut of *Roman Holiday* to show to the Paramount executives and the opinion-formers. 'I knew that very soon the entire world would fall in love with her,' he said. The film revealed the very special combination of innocence, eagerness and youthfulness in Audrey's personality and performance. Paramount swiftly put its money where its convictions lay—by preparing a follow-up film for Audrey even before the first had been released. The new project was entitled *Sabrina,* an adaptation of Samuel Taylor's Broadway play, *Sabrina Fair.* Audrey had read it in typescript before embarking on the *Gigi* tour and—a significant clue that her instincts were leading to actions—she had asked Paramount to buy it for her even before Margaret Sullavan had played it onstage. What particularly appealed to Audrey was its story, a modern fairy-tale.

Sabrina is the Cinderella-like daughter of a chauffeur in the service of a rich Long Island family. Her father spends his wages on sending her to a finishing school in Paris, where she is turned into a 'princess'. In turn, she transforms the surly frog prince of the household, who was to be played by Humphrey Bogart. Billy Wilder was hired to direct: a shrewd choice since he immediately saw in the play something akin to the comedies of Ernst Lubitsch, which treated love as the pastime of people who were frivolous and rich, but not entirely worthless. *Sabrina* was one of the last films of the post-war American cinema to satirize the foibles of the very rich and take a tolerant view of their social uselessness. That it retains its innocence in this respect is in large part due to the casting of a girl so completely charming that one can only wish her to live happily ever after like a fairy-tale heroine.

Edith Head once again designed Audrey's wardrobe—with one important exception. The great designer took it as a personal rebuff but it led to one of the most influential and intimate encounters in Audrey's life. For *Sabrina*'s sequences in Paris, and for her return to the Long Island estate of her father's employers as an almost unrecognizable woman of the world, Audrey was to be dressed by the French couturier Hubert de Givenchy. When they met, in the couturier's salon at 8 rue Alfred de Vigny in Paris, the two became friends for life—and more. Givenchy helped to create Audrey Hepburn's image quite as much as any of her directors.

Audrey had first fallen in love with the Givenchy style when she went to France to make *We Go to Monte Carlo*. Givenchy was then preparing to leave the house of Schiaparelli to open his own salon. It was Audrey who suggested that he should design her costumes for *Sabrina*: early evidence both of her taste and of her quickly maturing determination to control the way she was presented to her public. It nearly did not happen. Gladys de Segonzac, wife of the Paris head of Paramount, favoured Balenciaga. But he was in the middle of the pre-collection period, and nobody dared disturb him. Audrey insisted on the newcomer, Hubert de Givenchy.

Only twenty-six years old, and standing 6′ 6″, Givenchy had the air of a man used to imposing his will on his art and his clients. No one should expect compromises to be made for the imperfections of their figures. Givenchy was a minimalist in conception and design. He pared away all inessentials, allowed for no mistakes, permitted no deviations from his designs. His clothes were as beautifully constructed in his atelier as they were on the page of his drawing book. Audrey brought him a figure that was made for his creations. In return he gave her an image as seemingly immutable as any Euclid proposition.

Since the appointment was made for 'Miss Hepburn' Givenchy recalled that he had been expecting Katharine Hepburn. Knowing the casual disarray habitually affected by the older actress, one wonders what thoughts crossed Givenchy's mind as he awaited his caller. His surprise must have been all the greater when in walked a girl wearing check trousers and a white T-shirt, who carried herself perfectly and had the clean lines of his own sketchbook.

That was not all. Givenchy's immediately recognizable style depended not only on a classical simplicity but on allowing the body to move without constriction. He introduced a feeling of comfort into her clothes that suited Audrey perfectly. He was fond of saying, 'Le vêtement habille la femme qui, en réponse, l'habite'——'A woman doesn't simply wear a dress; she lives in it.'

Givenchy was a Protestant schooled in the same work ethic as Audrey. It made for a closeness between them that went far beyond the usual relationship of couturier and client. It was a platonic love-affair. About that first encounter Givenchy later wrote: 'La douceur de son regard, ses manières exquises me séduisent sur le champ'——'The sweetness of her glance, her exquisite manners immediately seduced me.' And forty years later, in a prose-poem she wrote to celebrate Givenchy's contribution to French fashion, Audrey wrote of the shelter and protection his friendship had offered her:

'Les racines de son amitié
toujours profondes et puissantes.
Les branches solides de son affection
abritent ceux qu'il aime.'*

On that occasion Audrey had no trouble recalling the dresses Givenchy had designed for *Sabrina*. 'One was a very classic, almost severe evening dress, with a cheeky little bow high up on one shoulder which gave it the lightness and humour I love.' He also designed a superb gown in white organdie with jet-black embroidery which Sabrina wore in the scene in the winter garden where William Holden, playing Bogart's playboy brother, partners her in a slow, sensual dance. Givenchy named a special weave of cloth 'Sabrina' in honour of Audrey. Six years later he brought out a perfume, L'Interdit, which he dedicated to her. He even put a model called Jacky on his payroll because she resembled Audrey. In a very real sense Audrey Hepburn was the muse that inspired the house of Givenchy. In return he helped make her the trademark of everything young, elegant and rare.

Audrey's image retained the bloom of innocence; but it was at this time, and from this man, that she acquired the cosmopolitan touch that distinguished her from the other young stars of the day. When she came to Givenchy's salon, she was still in the bud, so to speak, her screen personality formed but not fully opened. The couturier held a mirror up to her in a more than literal sense: he showed her the woman she could become. Like him, she was to become surprisingly tough and cool-headed at taking

---

*The roots of his friendship forever profound and powerful. The firm branches of his affection shelter those he loves.

control of her own image once she had achieved the contractual power to do so. But to gain this power, she needed a different kind of man. It was not long before she found him.

It may have been while Audrey was in Paris to meet Givenchy in the summer of 1953, while pre-production work went ahead on *Sabrina,* that she saw a movie called *Lili*—and went back to see it again three more times. Its star was remarkably like herself: the same gamine face, the same lithe figure, the same natural air of waifishness. Leslie Caron was two years younger than Audrey and, like her, she had been a ballet dancer; was also the child of parents from different countries (America and France); had been singled out for fame by a well established personage, in Caron's case Grace Kelly; and had co-starred in a film that was already halfway to becoming a classic, *An American in Paris.* The resemblance between Caron's career and Audrey's, at this stage in their lives, is uncannily close.

Lili was an MGM love story with music about an orphaned girl who is wooed and won by a carnival puppeteer. Caron's *jolie laide* face had a beguiling sadness which Audrey recognized from her own mirror. Characteristically, she expressed only admiration for this potential rival. 'Wasn't she wonderful!' she later said to Hedda Hopper, who replied diplomatically (away from her typewriter), 'She's not a pretty girl, but on the screen beautiful.' 'It comes from the inside,' Audrey said, without a touch of resentment. 'No,' persisted Hopper, scarcely crediting that one star could express such golden opinions about another who might at any moment leap up and seize the bread from her lips, 'she's not beautiful like you.'

However, it was not Caron's beauty that attracted Audrey back to the film. She was drawn by Mel Ferrer, who was playing the puppeteer and whose skilful manipulation of the orphan's heartstrings wins him her love. The lean and handsome actor reminded Audrey of the princes in the fairy-tales that she had devoured as a child and still read to herself. Ferrer was indeed an energetic and graceful leading man though not quite a star. His charm was professionally adroit but a little too calculated, too much in his own good favours to allow an audience to feel it 'possessed' him. But Audrey clearly didn't see him this way. She met him in London that same summer, in 1953, at a party in her mother's apartment where Gregory Peck made the introduction. Peck and Ferrer were already friends through a common interest in the Actors' Playhouse in La Jolla, California. Ferrer was in London for the premiere of *Lili,* and to play King Arthur in *The Knights of the Round Table,* an American movie being produced in Britain. At thirty-five, he was twelve years Audrey's senior. She found him not only good-looking but well-read and multi-talented: an author of children's books; a stage, film and radio director; a man who seemed to know everyone in Hollywood and on Broadway. He had many irons in the fire, and was confident of setting the world alight with at least one of them.

People would ask, in years to come, 'What on earth did Audrey see in Mel?' The answer isn't hard to find. They had a great deal in common. Like Audrey, Mel Ferrer had begun his stage career as a dancer. His mentor had been Clifton Webb, one of Broadway's best dancers before he became a film star, who taught Mel enough tap-dancing in two hours to land him a job. Like Audrey, he had suffered a serious physical drawback; he contracted polio, spent three years in what he called 'a sort of non-alcoholic Lost Weekend' and was left with a semi-paralysed arm which he nursed back to flexibility by punishing exercises. Audrey always admired people with the strength of will to overcome their troubles; perhaps Mel reminded her of her benefactor Paul Rykens, who had likewise triumphed over polio. Like Audrey, Mel was multilingual. He had been brought up speaking French by his mother and Spanish by his father, a successful New York physician of Cuban descent. He was as much at home in Europe as America. Like Audrey, he sometimes looked almost undernourished. In fact, photographs of them together occasionally suggest a brother and sister, not a husband and wife. This was the man Audrey would marry.

In at least one respect they were radically *un*alike. No one ever found Mel relaxing company. He was a workaholic, always on the go. Where Audrey was assiduous, Mel was obsessive. But she could sympathize with his restlessness because, so far as she could remember, her father had been that way, too, forever devising new schemes, with the manipulative charm of the Irish. Like Hepburn-Ruston, Mel seemed to approach marriage with a certain impatience. He shuttled between New York, where he had married a sculptress and divorced her, and Hollywood, where he had married again, and then divorced his second wife and remarried his first. He had had two children by each marriage. When he met Audrey he was disentangling himself from marriage for the third time.

A profile of Mel which was published not many years later by a perceptive journalist, Charles Van Deusen, gives a graphic impression of his hyperactive personality. 'As a director, Mel would make his colleagues dizzy with his acrobatic gyrations; as an actor, upstage them into fury. His telephonitis was worse than a teenager's, and at nightclubs he was always waving to somebody across the room or getting up to table hop. "I often wonder," mused one of his early associates, "what Mel finds to keep him busy while he's asleep." ' Probably the answer was—dreams.

Meeting Audrey was, in all likelihood, like meeting his dream in the flesh. He told her, of course, how much he had enjoyed seeing her in *Gigi*. And she told him that she would be delighted to do a play with him, if filming permitted and if he could find something suitable. It was as simple and as sudden as that. It was also a brief encounter. Mel had to hurry off to play King Arthur at the court of the round table. Audrey had to fly to Hollywood to begin her role in *Sabrina*. The intrigues in that particular court, its jealousies, romances and occasional enchantment, soon put Mel Ferrer out of her mind—but only for the moment.

8

LOVES AND HATES

*I*N the middle of June 1953 people in Britain first became widely aware of the rumours that had been racing around the rest of the world. Princess Margaret, the Queen's sister, was openly associating with a divorced man, Group Captain Peter Townsend, a former equerry to the late King George VI, and wished to marry him. By the end of the month the princess had been whisked away from the media's reach on a nineteen-day tour of Rhodesia. Her lover had been advised not to be in Britain when she returned: he accepted a post as air attaché at the embassy in Brussels.

Thus the private life of a princess and her thwarted romance with a commoner became a trailer for *Roman Holiday,* which was to open at the end of August. No film studio could have bought such publicity. It was much less common then than it is today for a film to feed upon a news event; the scandal gave filmgoers the sense that they could be privy to what might be going on behind the scenes at Buckingham Palace. The news reports of the constitutional crisis, which a 'forbidden' affair precipitated in that more conventional era, and the columnists' speculation over Princess Margaret's supposed 'anguish', bled into the drama of the screen romance and sharpened anticipation of the film. The romances of the two princesses, real and fictional, had enough similarities to create the impression, well nourished by Paramount's publicity department, that one was a reflection of the other—even that the film was 'based on' Princess Margaret's star-crossed liaison. This was nonsense, of course, but manna to the publicists.

Audrey was still in London when the story started to break in the American press a few months before the more cautious English newspapers dared to reprint the Transatlantic gossip. She refused to return to Hollywood before starting work on *Sabrina* in June, pleading justifiably that she was worn out and needed a rest. This created a problem for Paramount. The vitally important American fan magazines were now desperate to interview Audrey, but most of them had three-month deadlines and all of them were several thousand miles away. In those days before jet travel and satellite links eliminated the difficulties of time and distance, Los Angeles reporters kicked themselves for ignoring her when *Gigi* had opened on the West Coast. So clamorous did the pressure for interviews become that Paramount helped at least one leading magazine, *Modern Screen,* to make a wire recording of questions for Audrey, and then flew the recording to London where she recorded her answers: 'the first interview for a fan magazine', *Modern Screen* boasted.

'One day,' said Audrey in reply to the predictable question at the top of the list, 'I'll just fall in love and get married, career or no career.'

Jane Wilker, *Modern Screen*'s interviewer, added her own perceptive commentary to Audrey's recorded answers: 'She seems to be a self-reliant, ambitious and courageous girl who has a deep capacity for love.' But, she said, 'The utter silence about her father suggests that the family rift disturbed her immensely: yet she has the taste [*sic*] to bypass the subject.'

Almost no columnist or interviewer in subsequent months mentioned the Fascist connections of Audrey's father. Hepburn-Ruston's absence from the family history, as Audrey related it, is put down to a simple 'disappearance' following his divorce from Ella. In one interview he is reported to have been 'shot by the Germans' (an inversion of what might have happened had he stayed in the Netherlands and collaborated with the Dutch Nazis, in which case he could have been shot by the Resistance). In an article by Anita Loos, the source of much that is mythical about Audrey, published in September 1954, the imaginative writer revealed that Hepburn-Ruston had 'disappeared into the far colonies of England. Nobody knows where he is today. [or] whether he has ever heard what happened to his magical child.' This was technically correct—he was now in Ireland—but reassuringly vague. Phyllis Battelle, a reporter for the International News Service, was virtually the only exception. In a syndicated series published in 1954 she refers to Hepburn-Ruston's membership of Mosley's Blackshirts. One can imagine the collective catch of breath this must have caused among the film executives to whom Audrey represented a sizeable corporate investment. Though logically Audrey was totally innocent of her father's transgressions, they would have been well aware that the public (or the press) does not react logically. Had the stigma of Fascism, with its unavoidable connotations of anti-Semitism, been attached to Audrey at this time when memories of concentration-camp atrocities were still fresh, her career would have been effectively ruined.

Fortunately, Battelle's passing reference provoked no response. Other writers, who might have been expected to have picked up Battelle's hint, were either unaware of Mosley's significance or else prudently kept quiet. Hollywood studios in those days possessed (and used) the power to ban writers who had incurred their displeasure from access to the stars. Few reporters would have wanted to incur the displeasure of Paramount.

No writer appears to have been aware that Audrey's father was imprisoned by the British throughout the war. As already remarked, it is highly unlikely that Audrey would not have discovered the truth for herself by now. An interview she gave Hedda Hopper is revealing precisely for what it does not divulge.

Hopper's papers in the Academy of Motion Picture Arts and Sciences Library contain the verbatim texts of interviews which she later shortened and edited for her newspaper column. The unpublished material is, not surprisingly, more intimate and often more telling than the image presented to the public. But even Hopper was probably ignorant of the fact that she was being thrown off the scent in her interview with Audrey, which took place on 11 September 1953. Decoying the media was a manoeuvre in which Audrey had already developed considerable skill.

Early in their conversation Hopper asked Audrey about 'your birth'. Audrey replied, and the awkward pause that ensued was recorded by Hopper's stenographer, 'I was born . . .' and then she diverted the columnist's dangerous curiosity by making a sudden and flattering comment on the *Time* magazine cover featuring Hopper displayed on the wall. Hopper took the bait, returned the compliment by saying that the picture of Audrey which had recently appeared on the cover of *Time* was not 'pretty enough', and then, no doubt to Audrey's relief, forgot to follow up her question.

Audrey's *Time* cover appeared on 7 September 1953 and caused a sensation. It was the first time many could recall this magazine awarding its supreme accolade to a star before her first big film had more than opened in America. The text was even more effusive than usual, suggesting a degree of prompting from the names highest on the magazine's masthead. 'Behind the sparkle of rhinestones, a diamond's glow,' said the cover caption. The illustration by Boris Chaliapin, then *Time*'s principal staff artist, showed Audrey in her royal attire with tiara, with the temptations of the commoners' world suggested by the surreal touch of a huge strawberry ice-cream cone against the background of the baroque architecture of Rome. The article inside made no secret that the writer was in love with Audrey.

'A stick-slim actress with huge, limpid eyes and a heart-shaped face . . . exquisitely blending queenly dignity and bubbling mischief.' Justifying the lapidary cover statement the text continued: 'Amid the rhinestone glitter of *Roman Holiday*'s make-believe, Paramount's new star glows with the fire of a finely cut diamond. Impertinence, hauteur, sudden repentance, happiness, rebellion and fatigue supplant each other with speed on her mobile, adolescent face.' (By now she was twenty-four—'not so young', as Audrey was to say herself.) A plug was given for her next film, *Sabrina,* whose director Billy Wilder was quoted as saying: 'Not since Garbo has there been anything like her, with the possible exception of Ingrid Bergman.' (With neither actress posing a threat to Audrey, since Garbo had become a recluse since her retirement and Bergman had disgraced herself in the eyes of America by her adultery with Rossellini, the way for their successor was plainly being prepared.) On a less lofty note, Wilder was later to praise Audrey for intelligence as well as beauty: 'She looks as if she could spell schizophrenia.'

Roman Holiday is as fresh today as it was forty years ago, despite the fact that we know so much more about the love-lives of princesses. The simplicity and purity of Princess Ann's responses have acquired an even rarer value now that royalty has been contaminated by mixing too much with the wide world. In 1953 the critics praised Audrey for her 'deftness and charm'. Her princess 'grows up in a day and a night' from the moment she awakens with the ravishing smile of a truant schoolgirl to the moment she lays her head on Peck's shoulder as they dance on the deck of the restaurant floating on the Tiber, dreams the last little bit of her dream and then appears to wake up and say 'Hello'.

The film opened in both New York and London at the end of August 1953. Audrey attended neither premiere but went to the screening at the Venice Film Festival as a compliment to the country where the film had been made. She arrived back in America to find herself truly famous yet feeling intimidated rather than elated by the even higher expectations she would now have to live up to. Paramount's chairman, Adolph Zukor had predicted: 'If Miss Hepburn gets the role to suit her, she would be the greatest actress the screen has ever seen.' Such a forecast should have made her jubilant. Instead, her reaction recalled the disillusionment she had expressed after that first-night triumph in *Gigi* on Broadway. Conscience robbed the moment of its sweetness, just as duty stripped the princess of her liberty. 'You can never feel tired any more, ever,' Audrey had said, almost before the cheers of New York playgoers had died away. It was a reflection that could have served Princess Ann equally well as she, too, like Audrey, prepared to fulfil the obligations laid on her.

The only place where *Roman Holiday* was a disappointment was, ironically, where it most needed to be a success: at the US box-office. The film had cost $750,000, a fair sum in the early fifties. In its first eight months it was to return a domestic profit of a little less than $300,000 instead of the projected $5 million, and its net return to Paramount was revised sharply downwards to $3 million. Audrey might be potentially the 'world's greatest actress' but it still had to be proved that she was major box-office. (The movie's Roman location may have been less of an attraction than William Wyler had supposed. For most Americans at that time, 'abroad' was still a rare experience. One year later *Three Coins in the Fountain* did much better business; by then American tourism had discovered the Eternal City and made it more popular than Paris. The theme song helped, too.)

Still, the success of *Roman Holiday* outside America was a formidable compensation. Whereas it remained the exception in Hollywood films for boy not to get girl—royal or otherwise—Europe had a long tradition of unhappy endings. The reviews in the European press matched the enthusiasm of the crowds outside cinemas. Ingrid Bergman saw the film in Rome and came out crying. 'Why are you weeping?' Rossellini asked his paramour, 'is it a tragedy?' 'No,' Bergman replied, 'I'm crying for Audrey Hepburn.' British critics, a less emotional lot, praised Audrey but found the film 'a shade too long' at just under two hours. The public, avidly following the doomed romance of Princess Margaret, had no such reservations. They flocked to *Roman Holiday* en masse. By 1953 Britain was in the grip of all things Italian: Vespa and Lambretta motor-scooters, pointy shoes, cuffless trousers for men, and the new espresso bars for teenagers. The street freedoms of a footloose princess in Rome fitted the bill perfectly. Associated British, which still 'owned' Audrey under her early contract, showed their customary acumen in dealing with fame and promise. They had nothing to offer her at the moment; but after *Sabrina* they would have a film ready for her: a life story of Gracie Fields, the Lancashire singer and comedienne.

Now that Paramount had Audrey back on American soil, they began her publicity build-up in earnest. She moved into a small apartment building on Wilshire Boulevard, near Westwood Village in Los Angeles. *Life* magazine ran a six-page photo-spread in its issue of 7 December 1953 which showed her image to be still in the making. 'What makes Audrey's charm?' asked the headline: and the answer *Life* supplied suggested a far from simple nature: '[She] defies definition. She is both waif and woman of the world. She is disarmingly friendly and strangely aloof.' The illustrations concentrated on her solitariness. She was pictured as a sleepy urchin waiting at the wooden gate of her little dwelling place at 6.30 a.m. to be picked up by the studio car: going over her lines en route like a child about to sit an exam; grabbing a quick breakfast with the technicians, one leg curled under her like a little girl, the other stretched out with the grace of a ballet dancer; having her eyeliner applied; and, in the only truly happy shot, riding her bicycle from make-up department to set. There was one concession to conventional glamour: in the first and last 'cheesecake' photo of her career Audrey was shown in a 'shortie' nightgown with the titillating edge of her panties just visible.

Significantly, the article did not raise the matter of romance. The qualities which *Life* singled out in Audrey were independence and self-reliance, 'I'd be quite happy if I spent from Saturday night until Monday morning in my apartment. That's how I feel,' she was quoted as saying. It's hard to imagine any other American star of the time admitting to a talent for entertaining herself. *Life*'s (unnamed) writer added: 'Hollywood is betting that the public will love Audrey for the very qualities that raise her above the popular stars.'

In one respect, Audrey was still well below the most popular stars. For *Sabrina* she received only $15,000 (£3000), little more than what she had been paid for *Roman Holiday*. 'You'd have gotten more money if you'd waited until after *Roman Holiday* before signing your contract,' said Hedda Hopper, in the role of financial adviser to the stars. Audrey answered, 'The important thing is not money—but being a good actress.' Hopper made no recorded reply. Heresy, like irony, is not well understood in Hollywood.

Ernest Lehman, who was to co-author the script of *Sabrina* with Billy Wilder, recalls the unorthodox greeting he received from Audrey when Wilder brought him to meet her in her two-room apartment. They took with them an Art Nouveau poster as a present. 'She was sitting on the floor with her legs curled up under her, like a child. She jumped up when I was introduced and kissed me on both cheeks—a very unusual greeting for a star to give a mere writer.'

Sabrina was not a happy experience for Audrey—or anyone else. Lehman explains that the film began in disarray and finished in sheer panic. 'It was the roughest introduction Audrey could have had.' Samuel Taylor had abruptly stopped working on the adaptation of his play half way through the rough draft, after Billy Wilder had begun deleting large chunks. Lehman, who was working at MGM one morning on what was to become the script of *Sweet Smell of Success,* found himself at Paramount in the afternoon after Wilder had sent an SOS asking to borrow him. The film was already in pre-production, and shooting would start in October. Audrey may well have had to study her lines in the car on the way to the studio because they had been ripped out of Lehman's typewriter as dawn broke that morning. '[Billy] directed by day,' Lehman has recorded on the copy of his script in the University of Southern California Archives, 'and wrote and rewrote by night. It was agonizing, desperate work and at times our health broke down from the effort.' Sometimes Wilder would arrive on the set with nothing to shoot, and would say, 'We'll do retakes.' Today Lehman calls it 'the scariest experience I've ever had in my life.'

If Audrey was spared this continuous creative panic, she was nonetheless in for a shock. She discovered what was meant by 'the Hollywood feud' when she became the blameless target of animosity and insult from none other than Humphrey Bogart. The star she had admired as the gallant, honourable and romantic adventurer Rick in *Casablanca,* one of her favourite films, she now discovered to be in reality an embittered bully. Bogart had a self-destructive streak in his nature that rebounded on anyone he disliked, felt inferior to or fancied was getting preferential treatment. This included the innocent Audrey. Part of the trouble was that Bogart had not wanted to be in the film at all, especially not playing the older and stuffier brother while William Holden got all the romantic opportunities. Cary Grant had turned down the part for much the same reason. 'You'll meet this enchanting girl,' Wilder promised Bogart by way of reassurance. Bogart started glowering the minute they were introduced. 'As soon as Billy started shooting tight close-ups of Audrey over Bogey's shoulder, he began snarling,' says Lehman. 'He knew who was being favoured. But whose face would *you* rather look at?'

When Audrey countered his needling with indifference Bogart's resentment turned to open hostility. He started mimicking her voice. Wilder intervened, so Bogart turned his anger on him, imitating the director's thick German tones, demanding 'translation into English'. Unlike Audrey, Wilder gave as good as he got—rather better, in fact. Turning on Bogart he barked, 'I look at you, Bogey, and beneath the surface of an apparent shit, I see the face of a real shit.'

The tensions increased as the day wore on. Audrey noted how Bogart ordered a glass of whisky to be brought to him on the set at five o'clock precisely. As he sipped it between takes, he became even more surly. Once or twice an upset Audrey would stumble over her lines. Then Bogart's delight was undisguised: this was a little English amateur with an overblown reputation. At the end of the day's shooting Wilder would invite Audrey, Holden and Lehman back to his office for drinks. Bogart was not included. Feeling ostracized, and having failed to goad Audrey into losing her temper, he turned his sarcasm on Holden—'Smiling Jim', as he called him— ridiculing his good looks, implying that he was more a matinee idol than a man. He even insinuated that Wilder was rewriting the script so that Holden and not he would end up with Audrey—and it has become part of the *Sabrina* myth that this revision was actually in the works. The truth is that the scene at the board meeting, where the younger brother renounces Sabrina and tells his sibling to go after her, was written under pressure of freeing Holden for his next film commitment, *The Bridges of Toko-Ri*. It was shot before Wilder and Lehman had any idea of how to script the scenes that would then settle the affair in Bogart's favour.

Meanwhile a romantic comedy was being attempted by the principals and, despite their soured relationships between takes, succeeding very well. But it was a brutal baptism for Audrey.

'The hardest scene for me to write,' Ernest Lehman recalls, 'was the one in the corporation penthouse where the stuffy elder brother and the radiant Sabrina, Bogart and Audrey, realize they're falling in love. Billy wanted to make it very intimate. He kept pushing me to suggest that the couple go to bed together. "Billy," I said, "that will ruin everything. No one sleeps with anyone in fairy-tales. The audience will hate us for it. We can't—no way." ' Thus Audrey was spared even the semblance of a sex scene, as she had been in *Roman Holiday*. An abiding innocence was becoming a vital part of Audrey Hepburn's image.

Off-screen the reality was very different. 'Audrey and Holden began an affair during the making of *Sabrina*,' Lehman remembers. 'A quiet one, very *sotto voce*, but very determined. It surprised us. Everyone thought they knew Audrey.' Lehman had occasion to enter the trailer of one or other of the stars—he doesn't recall which—'and there was no doubt of the warmth between them.' Holden was then married to Brenda Marshall and the fan-magazine photo-spreads of him with his family concealed the deep unhappiness of a promiscuous man. Monogamy could not begin to satisfy Holden. A heavy drinker, he struck up relationships with the casual air of a man striking a match. He had recently undergone a vasectomy to minimize the attendant risks and, as such men do, he put himself in increasingly risky situations in order to compensate for an even deeper-seated fear of sexual inadequacy. He took Audrey to his home for supper. Holden's wife was resigned to her husband's escapades, but Audrey felt guilty all through the meal. Yet she continued this romance, conducted in what might have been scenes from *Sabrina*.

Many years afterwards, in a self-excoriating account of his life, Holden recalled how 'sometimes at night, I'd get a portable record-player and drive out to the country to a little clearing we'd found. We'd put on ballet music . . . Audrey would dance for me in the moonlight. Some of our most magic moments were there.' Others were more down to earth. Audrey's interest in men, according to the few who got to know her intimately during her career, though strong, was intermittent and prudent. She had affairs when passing through emotionally tense times. She had a preference for men who made the first move, who were bold, even buccaneering, and—a few observers thought—who were far less romantic than she and didn't appreciate her rare nature. Such observers were surprised at Audrey's tolerance of her lovers' habits, their bluntness and sometimes downright crude language: so exactly the opposite of her own composed nature. Perhaps that was where their attractiveness lay. The robust and indeed combative Irish temperament of Audrey's father seems to be reflected in some of the lovers she picked, though not necessarily the men she was to marry.

After her broken engagement to James Hanson it is easy to understand why Audrey should have fallen for a co-star like William Holden, in the prime of his career and good looks. But whether she would have married Holden if he had divorced his wife is doubtful. A man who had deliberately denied himself the possibility of having children could not satisfy a woman whose thoughts would turn more and more towards starting a family.

Audrey's 'princess' role in *Sabrina* caused more problems than her royal role in *Roman Holiday*. Princess Ann had been virtually a child: Sabrina was a Cinderella girl transformed into a confident woman of the world by the attentions of the men she meets in Paris. The exact nature of those attentions is ignored; like a Lubitsch film, the comedy finds its best jokes in what it elides and leaves to our sophisticated intuition. In the Paris episodes, for example, Sabrina takes *cordon bleu* cooking lessons from a master chef played by Audrey's old friend and confidant from her pre-*Gigi* days, Marcel Dalio. But presumably the Givenchy wardrobe with which she returns to America has not been paid for out of her finishing-school fees. More likely it comes by courtesy of a fellow pupil, an elderly baron who is taking a refresher course in getting soufflés to rise. This is the earliest intimation of Audrey's other screen persona, not the innocent girl but the 'kept woman'. This dual nature, seen at its clearest in *Breakfast at Tiffany's*, was to tax screenwriters to the limit to ensure that her image remained pure even though her actions were questionable. Keeping the two in sync was to become an increasingly difficult task as Audrey grew older and the range of roles available to her was extended by the relaxation of screen censorship but restricted by the expectations of her millions of fans. In *Sabrina*, the star's own radiant nature preserves the heroine from moral contagion while she enjoys the benefits of newly acquired worldliness in cash and in kind.

Wilder and Lehman must be credited with a great deal of the taste needed for this moral balancing act. 'Billy showed Audrey exactly how he wanted a scene played,' says Lehman. 'She proved the perfect pupil.' It is their wit and ingenuity that Audrey relays with such sureness and lightness of touch. Wilder and her previous director, William Wyler, were transplanted European talents—like Audrey herself, in fact—and both were masters of timing, innuendo and those looks which, inserted in a close-up, transform the meaning of a scene. They brought to Hollywood the cynicism of their backgrounds—Wyler from Franco-German Alsace, Wilder from Vienna—but tempered it with wit to the benefit of their new star. Although Sabrina's status in the household of her father's rich employer is ambiguous, to say the least, the innocent way in which Audrey goes about winning the affections of the two heirs goes unquestioned—except by Bogart. His rasping rebuke to Holden, as his younger brother—'No gentleman makes love to a servant in his mother's house'—leads to a fistfight between them. The bad feeling between the two male stars made the fight real enough for a moment or two, before Bogart retreated to the relative security of the script. Such clever decoys on the part of the screenwriters—setting up the criticism in order to defuse it—help Audrey to make Sabrina the kind of girl who can ignore the financial motive while accepting its benefits. Only where love is concerned does she press her seductive advantage. 'David,' Sabrina asks Holden, 'would you like to kiss me?' Of course he would!

Here is a girl who disobeys her working-class father but reaches for the moon, not the money. In a role whose morality was much trickier to handle than that of *Roman Holiday,* Audrey's balancing act is faultless.

9

H USBAND AND W IFE

---

*T*HE telephone rang in Audrey's Beverly Hills apartment. It was the
last day of filming on *Sabrina* and she had returned, exhausted, from
the studio. Now Jean Simmons was calling. Audrey braced herself, remembering that Jean was the actress who would have played her role in
Roman Holiday if Howard Hughes, to whom she was under contract, had
been willing to share his 'property'. Now she heard Jean Simmons saying,
'I've just seen *Roman Holiday,* and although I wanted to hate you I have to
tell you I wouldn't have been half as good. You were just wonderful.'

A firm friendship was quickly established between Audrey and Jean
Simmons and her husband Stewart Granger. They were Audrey's first real
friends in Hollywood. She spent the now blessedly idle mornings at the
Grangers' home, lying beside the swimming pool—very seldom in the
water, for she hated swimming and rarely needed to take exercise of any
kind unless it were limbering up at the barre in the dance studio. Audrey
also smoked; moderately, it's true, and of course with little awareness of
the risks she ran from the cheap, exceptionally strong brand of cigarettes—
Wills' Gold Flake—which she had sent from England and smoked in a
long holder. She did not drive a car; she bicycled. Beverly Hills was a qui-
eter, safer place in 1954. The sight of a young star in pink pedal-pushers and
a man's shirt with the tails tied round her waist spinning along on her bike
caused few heads to turn in that small community of fellow celebrities. Occasionally Joan Crawford would sound off about the manners of the
younger set, quite forgetting what a wild thing she had been in her early
movies. 'Audrey Hepburn,' Crawford was reported as saying, 'now she
knows how to behave, I hear. I bet she dresses the way a young lady should.'
Hedda Hopper—not one to let Crawford be the arbiter of Hollywood
taste—responded, 'Have I got news for you, Joan . . . The "young lady"
showed up in this office wearing shocking pink matador pants, a tight-
fitting pale pink cotton shirt and shoes with just one strap.'

At this stage of her career, despite the intense anticipation which *Sab-*

rina was now arousing, Audrey lived 'out of a suitcase', so to speak. She had bought just one Givenchy dress for herself from among the gowns used in *Sabrina*. 'It's worn, of course, but to me it looks divine.' 'Divine' is a word that recurs frequently in interviews with Audrey: a useful, all-purpose word that sidesteps the risks of being more specific about a dress, a co-star or a relationship. She learned it quickly.

All those who got to know Audrey at this 'bachelor girl' time in her life agree on her genuine simplicity and absence of temperament. Emotionally she struck a few people as even a little immature for her years, but then she had a romantic outlook in a business and a town well known for disillusioned romantics. 'I've always wanted sloping shoulders,' she told Hopper, 'not ones that look padded.' The columnist supposed she meant a figure like a Southern belle in *Gone with the Wind*. 'That's right—crinoline and all.'

Audrey's love-life invited speculation but not scandal. Her romance with William Holden was not followed by any marital break-up; she had no wish to destroy anyone else's home life. She liked her independence. 'Mother and I are not alike,' she admitted when asked why the baroness had elected to stay in London rather than moving in with her, though she added quickly, 'but we get on awfully well.' There was a feeling that they got on even better at a distance. 'What about beaux?' was the inevitable next question. Wasn't there anyone else in her life since she 'turned down' her fiancé, James Hanson? The phrase stung Audrey with its slight imputation of cold-heartedness. 'I have no reason to turn down anyone,' she replied crisply, then, in what was now her customary defence when doing these publicity chores, she admitted her vulnerability, as if by doing so she would ward off a more penetrating inquisition: 'I've been so unhappy since the engagement was broken but I believe we did the right thing.' Around this time Paul Holt, a British critic visiting America, asked Audrey if she could put her finger on the quality that had brought her fame. She returned a surprising answer: 'Learning to do without things,' 'Such as?' Holt prompted. 'She gave me a bland, cool, half-amused look. "Marriage, for instance." '

Most stars see fame as a self-indulgent means of acquiring things, not as an austere obligation to do without them. Audrey's ambition burned as brightly as anyone's, but it did not illuminate the customary goals: there was a strong element of self-sacrifice in her attitude to stardom—and not only stardom. Marriage, too, was a dangerous state. It is as if she still felt too keenly the risks involved in the romantic ideal of marriage as an 'all or nothing' relationship, and was not prepared to accept them. Work was safer. Yet it was through work that she now found the pattern of her life radically changed by the man who reentered it, bringing with him exactly the kind of relationship she had learnt to 'do without'.

Audrey had told Mel Ferrer in London, just before starting *Sabrina,* that she would be interested in doing a play with him on Broadway if he could find one. Now, towards the end of 1953, he suddenly appeared in Los Angeles to tell her that he had done so. Maybe it was coincidence, but his remarriage to his first wife had recently been dissolved by a 'quickie' divorce in Juarez, Mexico. He was free to be Audrey's partner onstage and, over the months ahead, in an increasingly intimate relationship off it. Mel had a good eye for a play and he had chosen shrewdly. *Ondine* was another fairytale.

Written by the French playwright Jean Giraudoux, it was a fable based on the medieval legend of Ondine, a water-nymph who leaves her native element and trespasses on the alien territory of mortal man. There she falls in love with a chivalrous knight who is captivated by her magical beauty. But like all humans in the overworld, he is a fickle personage. Their union ends in Ondine's betrayal, her lover's death and the sprite's return to the sanctuary of her watery realm. The play exuded the melancholy fatalism that characterized much pre-war writing for the French cinema and theatre, but transposed its medievalism into a modern commentary on human love and its penalties. As played on the stage in Paris by Madeleine Ozeray and Louis Jouvet, *Ondine* had a lyricism that lightened its darkness. But by the 1950s it seemed an extremely artificial confection that had gone rather stale. Ferrer recognized that the play could still be a star vehicle if it had a magical presence to animate it and a distinguished name to direct it. Audrey herself needed no persuasion, and once her ready agreement had been secured to play the title role the distinguished actor Alfred Lunt was swiftly recruited to direct it. Ferrer would play the knight, of course. With names like these, financing was guaranteed, and the Playwrights Company in New York backed what would be a spectacular and expensive production.

The assembling of this package was an early demonstration of Mel Ferrer's strongest talent. Though he had made his name as an actor his creative needs remained unfulfilled. Playing the imaginative entrepreneur was more to his taste. At heart he was a producer-director, able to talk of art and quality in ways that made commercial sense. He had reached the highest point of his box-office popularity in *Lili;* now he was about to discover how much further his association with Audrey could take him.

Audrey exercised the clause in her Paramount contract which allowed leave for a stage appearance limited to a six-month run. It was sweetened for the studio by an option to produce a film of *Ondine* if the play were a success.

She moved to New York and rented a Greenwich Village apartment while the lengthy play went into rehearsal. Since much depended on Ondine's unearthly allure Audrey immersed herself totally in the minutest details of costume and make-up and, with Ferrer's encouragement, developed a control over every aspect of her role, and its place in the scheme of things, which was to guide her throughout the rest of her career. Valentina, the New York fashion designer, is generally credited with Ondine's sensational fishnet costume, which gave the impression that Audrey was naked except for a few strategically positioned wisps of seaweed. Only someone as beyond reproach as Audrey could have carried off an illusion that was then rare on the stage without courting accusations of tastelessness. In fact this minimalist costume—constructed on a flesh-coloured bodystocking—was devised by Audrey, inspired by childhood recollections of illustrations to the tales of Hans Christian Andersen. Lunt was delighted with the effect but he and Audrey fell out over the water-sprite's hairstyle. In pursuit of a flashing, quicksilver look Lunt asked her to dye her naturally chestnut hair a luminous blonde. She refused. 'But,' Lunt argued, 'salt water would bleach a sea-nymph's tresses.' Audrey retorted, 'Logic has nothing to do with it, Alfred. This is mythology.' Privately, she feared that blonde tinting was one immersion too much: it might wash out her own personality. Ferrer took her side.

The argument continued right up to the opening night in Boston, when Audrey, upset and unnerved by the dispute, suddenly gave in and made the change a few hours before the curtain rose. One look in the mirror and she instantly regretted it. With a restorative rinse she quickly reversed the disillusioning spectacle of a blonde Audrey Hepburn but accepted the champagne-coloured wig that Lunt had had the foresight to prepare for just such a sea-change. Even the wig eventually failed to pass her rigorous inspection. 'My hair looks dead. It feels stuffy and hot and horrible.' An hour or so away from appearing on stage, she found the solution. She sprinkled gold dust on her own dark hair. It caught the light like veins of precious ore as her balletic form flitted hither and thither. Occasionally, when Ondine pirouetted, the golden granules spun off behind her like a comet's tail. As she had hoped, the effect was magical though Mel Ferrer used to bring her down to earth after the curtain by serenading her back to her dressing room with an amended lyric from the raintub number in *South Pacific*: 'I'm gonna wash that gold right outa my hair.' Audrey also designed her own make-up: a blue-tinged powder to go with her aquamarine costume, a white shade to complement a pale cream dress. And she added two gilt 'points' to her ears to enhance the supernatural effect, thus anticipating Mr Spock by nearly twenty years. On opening night on Broadway, Mel would give her a tiny chaplet of real seaweed for good luck. Audrey was always charmed by people who could combine wit with inventiveness. They became closer companions than ever.

Just before *Ondine* had opened in Boston, Audrey had received a call from her Hollywood agent, Lew Wasserman, telling her that *Sabrina* had been previewed and was being hailed as another great success. She needed good tidings like this, for, as the New York opening drew near, she experienced not only bad attacks of anxiety but, to Mel's concern, began to show visible signs of the pressure of the last two years. A stubborn cold that refused to yield to treatment was one early-warning sign of how run-down she was, even though she refused to admit it. She stood in the wings waiting for her entrance, a bundle of nerves instead of enchantment, worrying that her skimpy costume might arouse comparison with the striptease shows at Minsky's. She worried, too, about the pace of the production, about Mel's wig, about half a dozen other matters outside her responsibility and anyhow beyond mending at that moment. But when the curtain rose, it was as if her anxieties had never existed.

As a production, *Ondine* was not received with total rapture when it opened on Broadway on 18 February 1954. Its pageantry, though spectacular, appeared laid on too thickly, as if to conceal a central lack of confidence in Giraudoux's philosophical embroidery. 'In [its] prettiness and lifelessness,' wrote the unnamed *Time* reviewer, 'it suggests not the court magician, but the court confectioner.' It was Audrey who gav' the play life and enlisted the audience's sympathies for Ondine. 'More than anyone else in the cast,' *Life* commented in a photo-review, 'she had the good sense to play the old fairy story as though she believed every poetic word of it.' The *time* reviewer uttered the verdict that most of the New York critics agreed with: 'however becalmed the lake, the sprite that darts out of it has a remote quicksilver witchery and wildness. Audrey Hepburn's is quite literally a mythical performance.'

The glowing personal notices failed to restore Audrey's sense of physical well-being and the strain of giving eight performances a week showed. Associates noticed that she was becoming more and more dependent on Mel Ferrer. Alfred Lunt sensed Mel's influence, however benignly intentioned, behind Audrey's occasional objections to his direction. At times he felt the show had two, or even three, directors. Moreover, the stage partnership of the two stars now reflected their personal closeness in a way that caused a murmur of professional disapproval. Traditionally, Audrey was entitled to take the final curtain-call—alone. After all, she was the nymph of the title, the linchpin of the spectacle. The sight of Mel Ferrer at her side night after night, sharing her applause, basking in a borrowed glory—and a suspicion also of a dominating influence—provoked a number of snide observations by the columnists. Mel was felt to be possessive and managerial. 'Chatter from New York,' Louella Parsons's column was headed in the *Los Angeles Examiner* of 3 March 1954, and it continued: 'All New York is talking about Audrey Hepburn and Mel Ferrer whose relationship is not only romantic, but on a business basis as well. Audrey [does] no interviews or photographs without Mel, and vice versa . . . Mel doesn't let her out of his sight for five minutes, and she seems completely fascinated by him. Audrey isn't the first one who has fallen for Ferrer's charms. He's free now, so anything can happen.' This last remark was a reference to Ferrer's recent divorce and a typical hint by the Hollywood columnists that a new 'mating season' in the menagerie of the famous had begun.

Perhaps it was coincidence but Audrey's mother, who had remained in England until *Ondine* opened, now reappeared at her side in New York. It was as if she too had heard the rumours of a love-match. Yet Audrey remained in the tiny downtown apartment she shared with her secretary and two curly-haired black poodles that had been presents from Mel. The mantle of self-protectiveness that Mel had encouraged was now wrapped even more securely around her. Her telephone number was kept a close secret, even from her press agent and the backstage managers at the theatre. When the need arose, she called them. On her rare social appearances she showed an uncharacteristic listlessness and soon left the gathering to go home and 'rest'. She had lost weight, which was visible through her skimpy Ondine costume. There were reports of anorexia nervosa. Worried friends blamed her condition on a career that had reached overdrive and a temperament that refused to let her luxuriate in success. A doctor was frequently on standby at the theatre. There was no doubt about it, the gossips said, Audrey Hepburn was having a nervous breakdown. And this time they were right.

Mel Ferrer, who possessed not only a demonstrative temperament but a talent for making cutting remarks at the expense of people whom he probably had good reason to suspect or dislike, was the most obvious 'villain'. He was not altogether believed when he protested that in keeping Audrey away from the intrusive media he was only protecting her precarious health. There was some truth in this, though not the whole truth. Audrey's anxieties stemmed as much from emotional tension as from a run-down constitution. She was now forced to make the sort of decision which last time she had postponed until love had expired like a statute of limitations. Like the water-sprite in *Ondine* she was captivated by the knight she had encountered, and now he wanted to make her his wife. But would marriage be the sort of 'world' she could adapt to?

Baroness van Heemstra clearly thought not, at least not to this enchanter. Audrey's mother, who had herself been vulnerable to just such charmers and married two of them, now distrusted the breed. For the moment, a tense and uneasy balance was kept between Ferrer, Audrey and her mother.

As Audrey fretted over the decision she must make, news reached her from Don Hartman, Paramount's production chief, that her performance in *Roman Holiday* had won her a 'Best Actress' nomination in the approaching Academy Awards. The New York film critics had already awarded her their prize at the end of December. But in her present emotional state this surfeit of good news numbed rather than elated her. Throughout her life, personal accolades acted as a depressant on Audrey not a stimulant. Praise carried an obligation, not a license to self-indulgence. It was part of her Calvinist heritage. 'All I feel is a responsibility to live up to success.' The level of achievement she set herself was high—higher than she felt able to reach or sustain.

On 25 March 1954 Audrey hurried offstage and, still partly clad in her Ondine costume and make-up, was whisked to the theatre which was receiving live coverage of the Oscar ceremony in Los Angeles. She had barely had time to substitute a white evening gown for her spangles before settling down beside her mother in the show-business audience, expectant yet disinclined to believe in luck. Then Fredric March, in Hollywood, called out her name. To a thunder of applause Audrey was virtually propelled by well-wishers towards the unfamiliar stage. She took a wrong turning and finished up in the wings, a *faux pas* from which she recovered with an exaggerated grimace of self-mockery that put a crest of affectionate laughter on the continuing waves of applause as Jean Hersholt, at her side in New York, passed her the gold-plated Oscar statuette—the supreme film award—from a supply that had been presciently flown to New York from the West Coast. To win it, Audrey had had to beat Ava Gardner (nominated for *Mogambo*), Deborah Kerr *(From Here to Eternity)*, Maggie McNamara *(The Moon is Blue)* and, perhaps the most poignant of all her rivals, Leslie

Caron, nominated for *Lili,* the film that had so fascinated Audrey the year before and which had co-starred the man who was now her lover.

She celebrated with warm champagne and didn't sleep a wink that night. In the morning, sitting at the head of the boardroom table in the big, padded oak chair twice as wide as herself that belonged to Paramount's chairman, she received the press and answered their questions. Inevitably, what they clamoured to know was not about art, but romance. 'Miss Hepburn grinned,' said one report, 'and said there wasn't any just now. She was, however, in love with the horses in Central Park.' Annoyed by her evasiveness, at least one journalist made the comparison with Mel Ferrer's long, lean and rather equine looks.

Audrey didn't miss a single performance of *Ondine* but this was a triumph against severe odds. Her weight loss continued and a doctor examined her after every show. She took the news that her Ondine had been rewarded with a Tony, Broadway's equivalent to the Oscar, with a wan smile. She had now made a clean sweep of every major American award (and several in Britain, too) yet she had never felt so ill. She (or Mel) turned down all social invitations and they spent the weekends together in a New Jersey health clinic. But her employers, Paramount, wished to strike while she was so 'hot'. Relentlessly, they announced a film musical with Danny Kaye, to be made immediately *Ondine* finished its run. But at the end of May 1954 Audrey collapsed. Resisting all management blandishments for her to return, her agents sent in her notice and *Ondine* closed. Even then, Audrey's press statement showed only concern for those she felt she had disappointed. 'I tried awfully hard to fulfil my obligations . . . I'm sorry if some people are mad at me.' The Danny Kaye musical was never made.

Robert Clark, the head of Associated British, understandably eager for Audrey's success to be turned to his company's profit and urged on by the impatience of the British press to see her return 'home' and make a film in England, chose this inopportune moment to arrive in New York. Pleasantly aware that, under the contract Audrey had signed several years earlier, he need offer her only £50 ($140) a week, Clark gave her a choice of two scripts: a comedy written by Graham Greene or a romantic drama, to be made before the end of the summer. 'By contract,' Clark said, 'the decision remains with us but,' he added, 'the important thing is for her to be happy.'

'Happy' Audrey wasn't. Her asthma had reappeared, a reaction to emotional pressures, perhaps exacerbated by her mother's objections to any plans she and Mel Ferrer had for marrying. It was one of the few occasions when Audrey and her mother parted in anger. She jumped at the doctors' recommendation to take a period of rest in the pure air of the Swiss mountains. This suited Mel Ferrer too. By arrangement or coincidence, he had accepted a role in an Italian film, *La Madre,* to be made in Sicily and Rome. Though they would be separated, it was not far from Italy to Gstaad, where Audrey planned to recuperate. Pale and thin, she set off for Europe alone, refusing her mother's plea to accompany her. 'I want to enjoy life and not become a wreck,' she had announced plaintively before leaving New York. But rumours of an impending marriage pursued her. She arrived in Gstaad to find herself an object of veneration and curiosity such as the reluctant princess had received in *Roman Holiday.* It seemed that there was no refuge from celebrity. Shop windows displayed framed pictures of her as they would of royalty. The local cinema was showing 'that film'. After a few days of involuntary confinement in her room, eating her meals alone and gazing out at unseasonably rainy weather, she felt she was a wreck already.

At the end of her resources, she called Mel Ferrer for help. He arranged for her to leave Gstaad and move into a better guarded hotel complex in an exclusive compound at Burgenstock overlooking Lake Lucerne, surrounded by mountains and small farms. Her privacy was guaranteed by the owner Fritz Frey.

It was an immediate improvement. Her châlet was furnished in a light, cheerful style, intruders were kept away by guards and Frey thoughtfully disconnected her outside telephone line and ordered all incoming calls to the hotel to be rigorously monitored. Only Mel and her mother were put through. The hotel doctor prescribed a nourishing diet, insisted she ate regularly and held her to it. She was in bed by 8 p.m. Soon she responded favourably to this regimen. Her blood pressure went down. Her asthma disappeared.

Audrey used the tranquillity of this enforced rest to take stock of the past and the exhausting acceleration of events that had brought her triumphs and a nervous breakdown with barely a pause to separate them. The future seemed incomplete without someone to share it. She had agreed to consider the marriage proposal that Mel made just before they left New York for Europe. 'Her decision came at the end of the summer,' says an intimate. 'Mel's thirty-seventh birthday was coming up. He was still filming in Italy. Audrey sent him a platinum wristwatch inscribed "Mad about the boy"—from the Noël Coward song. That was the signal that she accepted him.'

'My greatest ambition is to have a career without becoming a career woman,' Audrey said soon afterwards. Her separation from Mel Ferrer had confirmed how much she missed him; her illness had given an urgency to her need for someone to advise her and help take care of her talents. She had now enough evidence that those who were making plans for her did not value her at her real worth. Marriage, Audrey felt, would enable her to be a woman and at the same time enjoy a career. Besides, she loved Mel. Exactly one month after Ferrer's birthday would be their wedding date.

The first person Audrey told the news to, besides her mother, was her grandmother in Vienna. She didn't want her to learn of it from the papers first, she said, stressing that the great day would be ruined for her if the press became aware of it—how touchingly hopeful, the thought that they would not! She emphasized (her instructions heavily underscored) that the old lady was not to breathe a word to *anyone*. Though someone exposed to the public eye's fierce gaze may feel an understandable concern, one senses that a disturbing degree of obsessiveness about protecting her private life was now present in Audrey's outlook, as evidenced by the minute and admonitory instructions she impressed on her dearest granny. The consequence of this perhaps exaggerated need to control her life was not long in occurring. And it was to be one of the few occasions that didn't reflect too well on Audrey.

Mel Ferrer took a Geneva-bound flight from Rome the weekend before the wedding, after the company for which he was filming, aware that its production would benefit from the publicity of the star's marriage to the most newsworthy girl in movies, had accommodatingly altered his schedule. He sealed the engagement with a kiss, not a ring. Meticulous plans had been made to ensure that the ceremony was as private as possible. Audrey now knew enough about the drawbacks of being famous to resolve that she wasn't going to order her life according to other people's agendas. She remembered Valentina Cortese's advice: she was going to make the rules. An uncharacteristic flash of anger was directed at a local photographer who turned up uninvited in the back room of the Mairie at the lakeshore town of Buochs, where the civil ceremony was being held a day before the church wedding. Once they were husband and wife, she and Mel fled through the kitchen and into a car waiting in the back yard.

The next day, 25 September 1954, a reassuring posse of Swiss police was on hand and the door of the small thirteenth-century Protestant church at Burgenstock was locked once the bride and groom and their two-dozen guests were inside. It was pouring with rain and Audrey, looking pale, held the skirt of her white organdie dress above the wet ground in one hand, carrying a white leather prayer-book in the other. Encircling her dark hair was a chaplet of white rosebuds. She was given away by Sir Neville Bland, a former British ambassador to The Hague. Mel's sister and his two children, Pepa and Mark, from his marriage to Frances Pilchard, were present. Audrey's two half-brothers, Jan and Alexander van Ufford, were absentees: both were working in the former Dutch colonies. Baroness van Heemstra wept copiously as the ceremony was conducted in French.

The presence of Richard Mealand, Paramount's man in London, was a reminder of the studio's benign but watchful brief as the two film stars made their vows. Hollywood corporations were not usually overjoyed when their prize assets entered into another kind of contract. To the usual problems of handling one career, and keeping the star successful and sweet-tempered, were added the potentially more troublesome ones of reconciling two careers so that the stars could lead a married life and at the same time earn their living. Among the wedding guests was a man who would also give Paramount its share of headaches on that score: Kurt Frings, Audrey's new agent, who had come to her on Mel's invitation. Frings looked what he was: a formidable character. Born in Germany, he had been a boxer and bore the scars of that life as well as several tattoos on his muscular biceps. In the United States, Frings had first established himself among the émigré talents—including Wyler and Wilder—and then attracted other stars who saw how well his pugnacity in the ring could be applied in contractual wrangles, for a bigger sum of prize-money. Soon he had a large client list. Kurt Frings, more than anyone else, was to make Audrey the highest-paid star of her time. Mel Ferrer hardly needed to give her a wedding present: when he introduced Audrey to Frings, he gave her riches in a very real sense.

After a short reception at a private golf club the newlyweds scurried into their car and left for Italy—or so it was meant to appear. In fact, they returned by a side road and spent the weekend in front of a roaring log fire in Audrey's châlet, luxuriating in their happiness and blissfully unaware of what some columnists—those, at least, who had not received wedding invitations—were predicting for their future together. The journalists behaved as if Audrey had not only stolen a march on them but had been stolen away by a man who was of a mind to keep her to himself. Resentment lingered over the 'custodial' care which Mel had exercised over Audrey in New York. It was felt he hadn't 'earned' her: a reference, even at this early stage, to their unequal celebrity, and it was forecast that Audrey would soon be chafing against what was seen to be Mel's manipulative nature. Hadn't his two previous marriages quickly ended in divorce? And what about the age difference—twelve years—between them? *Ondine,* it was muttered darkly, contained a message for people like Mel who married out of their sphere. If the marriage didn't prove quite as mortal as his stage romance with a water-sprite, it would nevertheless bear the curse of their mismatched natures.

However, the two figures at Lucerne's railway station behaved as if it were all a light-hearted game of hide-and-seek. When Audrey's secretary signalled that the ground was clear of lurking lensmen by pulling out her hanky and blowing her nose, they emerged from a waiting room well muffled against the cold (and easy recognition). They stood giggling as more than a dozen pieces of light-grey luggage (hers) and six valises and several attaché cases were passed through the windows of their private compartment in the express waiting to ferry them to Rome. The smiles were wiped off their faces when, on arrival, they encountered the indefatigable animals that Fellini's film, *La Dolce Vita,* would soon baptize *paparazzi.* Dozens of them were waiting, ready to spring. Like bank robbers making their getaway, Audrey and Mel jumped into a studio car which roared off with carloads of pressmen in hot pursuit, not at all fooled by an evasive detour in through the front gates and, after a deceptive pause, out through the back gates of Cinecittà studios. The speed limit was roundly broken as they raced along the Via Appia Antica and through the gates of a twenty-room farmhouse-villa high in the Alban hills near Anzio. The paparazzi broke through the cordon of servants before the gates could be shut. They rapped on the door and rattled the windows with the resentful desperation of people unwilling to believe that a few minutes' exposure to cameras could make the victims feel as if their bones were being picked bare. The Ferrers eventually gave in to the ferocity of the siege and posed for a few moments.

Two hours later, all was silent again. In the darkness of their rural stronghold Audrey stepped outside for a breath of clear cold Campagna air before retiring. Suddenly, dozens of flashbulbs went off simultaneously around her, like one of the electric storms common at that season. Before she fled indoors she had the impression of silhouetted figures hanging from the trees and emerging from the bushes. Publicity had been part of her day's work when she was a single girl at Paramount Studios. Now she was discovering that marriage redoubled the world's curiosity about her. She had entered a new stage of her career, and she would need the strongest of defences.

Audrey's resolution on this score was soon tested by an event that must have caused her much private distress. It involved administering a stern rebuke to her own grandmother, who had been so kind to her since childhood and was, after all, mother of the man she missed most in the world.

Shortly after the marriage in Switzerland, the German-language weekly *Wochenschau* published a front-page article about Audrey illustrated with several photographs of her and her grandmother. Audrey recognized one of them as a wedding photograph which she had organized for private distribution to a very few members of her family and her closest friends—a souvenir of the event which they could treasure in the knowledge that it was not something that every single person in the world could view freely. Now here it was, publicly displayed. Audrey bitterly reproached her grandmother, recalling that the old lady had once supplied a photograph of her as a child to the papers. (Perhaps this accounts for the barely veiled warning she had issued in the first place.) The letter to Frau Foregger is written in dignified but unmistakably blunt terms, and is unsweetened by any affectionate signature, simply a curt 'Yours . . .' Frau Foregger was living on a very reduced income at this time; no doubt what money she had been paid for the use of Audrey's private photograph was welcome and possibly it didn't seem very wrong to her to sell a picture that only showed Mel and Audrey coming out of church as husband and wife on the happiest day of their lives. But Audrey regarded it as a breach of trust, and this worried her more than any pin-money granny might have picked up. Her reaction was to be characteristic of the way she would protect her privacy throughout her life: she always expected the highest degree of confidentiality from those whom she called friends. In this case, one cannot help feeling the reaction was excessive. All the same, she was deeply wounded by feeling that millions of eyes had been enabled to view one of the most personal moments in her life due to her grandmother's thoughtlessness.

Audrey reminded her that she, Audrey, had always tried to be open in her meetings with the press, but that she treasured certain things in life and wanted to keep them private. Not because she wanted to hide them; simply that they were too close and dear to her. She ended by hoping that the old woman had been taught a lesson. In future, she should try to keep her grandchild for herself, rather than share her out to a world that would soon leave nothing to be treasured for itself. The chastened old lady complied; and the affectionate relationship was soon resumed with a Christmas cheque arriving every year until her death, and an accompanying letter of love from her grandchild. But the fact that Audrey resolved to issue such a hurtful rebuke, rather than take the easier way and overlook a transient trespass, was itself a measure of her growing determination to control her life.

10

SUMMIT CONFERENCES

AUDREY recovered her health and strength under Mel's diligent su-pervision. He could be quite a disciplinarian. 'No, darling, milk,' he would respond to her request for a bedtime whisky. There was one good thing: they could have withstood a long siege in their villa without starv-ing. Nearby farms delivered meat and fresh eggs; vegetables came from the landlord's garden next door; their own acreage had ripe grapes hanging on the vines. Audrey taught her Italian cook-house-keeper to prepare ham-and-eggs and hash browns American-style and she, in return, showed Au-drey how to cook Italian peasant dishes. A taste for pasta that Audrey acquired then remained with her all her life. 'Puts meat on your bones,' she would tell everyone for whom she cooked it. Fish, too, fetched from the Roman markets and cooked with rice, saffron and asparagus, formed the regimen that kept her figure in enviable shape. Her periodic spasms of anorexia became things of the past as her worries receded. She took to making her own bread after a few lessons from the village baker. And, to her joy, she became pregnant.

Home, childhood, family: these represented the things lost or endan-gered by the war years. Now they were what Audrey desired above all else. Throughout her life, some of her attitudes, and even her manner of talking, appeared to close friends to be a little childlike—she approached much of life like a wise child playing a game. But she had a childhood robbed by divorce and war to make up for. From it she retained her trust in people, along with a lingering apprehension that the day might not turn out as sunny as it had promised to be. This air of expectation tempered by caution, her way of seeing the best in others and tying them more securely to her by little knots of affection, endeared her to her friends and was felt even by fleeting acquaintances.

The newlyweds had a problem common to their condition: how to support themselves. Audrey and Mel had lived up to, and beyond, their in-comes. She had been paid very little in proportion to the magnitude of the stardom she had attained so quickly. *Ondine* had brought in $30,000 (approximately £10,700), twice what she was paid for *Sabrina;* but agents, lawyers, professional expenses, the cuts taken by Paramount and Associated British, to say nothing of US taxes, had stripped it to the bone. Mel was working—at the moment—and they planned to live on his film fees while Audrey waited for her child. But a family would require much more money, and quickly, too.

They were in this happy domestic setting, but aware of their financial plight, when Michael Powell and his partner Emeric Pressburger arrived at the villa. Powell and Pressburger had made the ballet film *The Red Shoes,* one of Audrey's favourites, and other movies distinguished by a special combination of design, imagination, highly original stories and a mood more European than English in its interplay of incidents and ideas. Powell viewed his hosts with an approving but not uncritical eye. He noted Audrey's 'flair and intelligence and continental elegance allied with simplicity and a natural feeling for form' but added drily, when he came to write his memoirs, 'She was the right shape for that year.' He had seen her in *Ondine* where '[Mel's] lean height carried him through, just as Audrey's charm and flair made up for her small voice in that vast 46th Street theater.' Audrey, wrote Powell, 'is the kind of woman who gives all or nothing. I don't know how [Mel] lit this torch, but, by heaven, it flamed!' He looked around at their demonstrably happy rural existence and judged that they 'were escaping from other obligations and entanglements . . . out of America and into Europe'. He proposed something that might assist them on that escape route: a film of *Ondine.*

However, it soon became obvious that they were both still wedded to their stage roles as water-nymph and knight. Ferrer hadn't impressed Powell as an actor. 'He had no warmth, nothing to give. Clever, yes—kind, no.' More to the point, Powell already sensed the possibility of a rival impulse in Mel—he might want to turn producer, too.

Even so, Powell and Pressburger were soon outlining their plans for a film of *Ondine,* to be made in England, modernized and transmogrified into a magical dance operetta in the style of *The Red Shoes.* It would begin, Powell told Audrey and Mel, with the Technicolor camera navigating its way through the crowded marina of Monte Carlo, dipping under the surfaces of the Mediterranean into Ondine's world. 'A modern aqualung film,' he said, 'much better than a medieval romance.' Audrey would be discovered as Ondine, darting through submarine caverns in a bodysuit sewn with glittering fish scales while Mel, no longer in knightly armour, would be clad in a scuba-diver's suit and carrying a torch and a harpoon. But even while

Emeric Pressburger was giving 'a magician's performance' in front of the log fire explaining his new vision of the old myth, Powell sensed that his listeners were putting on an act of welcome for a highly inventive concept that they—Mel in particular—judged might divert attention away from the stars.

Talks continued over several days. Finally, Mel and Audrey provisionally accepted the idea, and left it to Powell to negotiate the film rights with Giraudoux's widow. If made, the film of *Ondine* would follow the one that Powell and Pressburger had already set up in England, a fancifully revised version of Strauss's operetta *Die Fledermaus,* relocated in a post-war Vienna still under four-power occupation and retitled *Oh . . . Rosalinda!!* Mel had already signed to appear in this as a singing and dancing American officer. He did so reluctantly, but Audrey and he needed the money urgently. Paramount had eventually agreed to contribute £250,000 of the £375,000 budget, though everyone concerned had to agree that half their fee would be paid only after the film went into profit—if it did at all. It made good economic sense to begin the film of *Ondine* hard on the heels of *Oh . . . Rosalinda!!*

Privately Audrey and Mel remained unconvinced. Besides Audrey's uneasiness in the water, they would have preferred to film their own stage version of *Ondine,* with which they felt safe. 'Their' *Ondine* was what had brought them together and shaped their love-affair. Powell imagined Mel and Audrey, after their visitors had left, engaging in 'pillow talk' far into the night, with Mel devising ways to ensure that *Ondine* was filmed the way they wanted. It was not, he felt, a good basis for a collaboration.

Meanwhile, offers for Audrey kept arriving from other independent producers. She turned down all of them because of her pregnancy—and sometimes was very glad later that she had done so. Otto Preminger wanted her to play Shaw's St Joan, calculating that her flat-chested, androgynous figure would be perfect for the Maid in man's armour. (Jean Seberg was eventually cast, and it blighted her career for a long time.) Another proposal was for the dual role of Viola and her brother Sebastian in Joseph L. Mankiewicz's production of *Twelfth Night*—scheduled for February 1956—two years away, at least. Producers were now placing orders for Audrey's services as far ahead as that—or at least placing stories in the newspapers saying they had. Mel had persuaded Audrey to set up their own production company—an early sign of his hard-headed approach to what he considered to have been exploitation of his wife by her employers—and that provided another good reason for not rushing into new commitments. They planned to film *Hedda Gabler* in Norway, with Mel directing Audrey.

Sabrina had opened very strongly in America, by coincidence (or more likely by Paramount's design) on Audrey's wedding day. Just how impatient the public was to see her was apparent from the lines outside the cinemas from the day of release. 'The most delightful comedy-romance in years,' wrote the *New York Times*'s Bosley Crowther, whose review read like a love-letter: 'a young lady of extraordinary range of sensitive and moving expressions within such a frail and delicate frame.' By now the 'Hepburn image' had a firm outline although a note of caution was sounded by the columnist Dorothy Manners: 'After seeing the limpid-eyed Audrey for the second time, I am beginning to believe she is not the easiest actress in the world to cast. In a lovely, enchanted, breathless way she is almost as stylised as the other Miss Hepburn . . . Her material will have to be selected very carefully.'

There was a great deal of truth in this. The fact was, Audrey was hard to fit into a wide range of roles. As Hollywood was coming to realize, she was a rarity in the storehouse of staple attractions then on display. She didn't personify sex or glamour which was the hallmark of the top stars of the post-war years and the early 1950s: Betty Grable, Rita Hayworth, Elizabeth Taylor, Lana Turner and, soon, Marilyn Monroe. Nor was she cast in the American mould of bubbly, mischievous teenage knowingness as represented by Debbie Reynolds, Natalie Wood, Pier Angeli or Janet Leigh. She was not a 'mammary woman' or a 'bobbysoxer'. In posture, looks and accent, she exemplified grace without prissiness, virtue without stuffiness, quality without snobbishness. She could pass for an innocent, yet it was soon evident that she was by no means a helpless child in the world of older men. She went her own way, but with curiosity rather than desire sparkling in her wide-eyed look. She offered reassurance to conservative America that virtue could still lead to a happy ending and remain intact. She appeared delicate, yet possessed a tomboy's agility and strength of mind. It was this that distinguished her from Leslie Caron's tougher sort of waifs. Caron always looked as if she could take care of herself; so could Audrey, of course, but her defence was her very vulnerability. She seemed to assume that life itself would take care of her by extending its special protectiveness over her like a shield.

Thanks to her ballet training Audrey carried herself with a dignity beyond her apparent years. (At twenty-five she was hardly a child but could pass for one if she wished.) She was 'mother's girl' in all the things she had been brought up to do: 'stand straight, sit erect, use discipline with wine and sweets' was how she remembered it. But she was also 'daddy's girl' in the asexual delight she took in the company of older men. 'Oh, you beast,' she cries in *Roman Holiday,* half giggling, half genuinely alarmed—a flattering sound to a man's ears—when Gregory Peck pretends his hand has been bitten off by the carved stone head known as the Mouth of Truth. One feels sure this is what Audrey herself might have said, as if Wyler, for a second time, had left the camera running after Audrey thought the scene was over.

But innocence has a price to pay. Sexual knowledge cannot be intimated, only love—or the loss of love. Sabrina, planning to kill herself in a rather comic manner out of unrequited love for the Holden character, adds a wistful postscript to the suicide note addressed to her father: 'Please don't have David at the funeral. He probably won't cry.' This is the comedy of immaturity: it doesn't require acting, simply 'being'. That is the rarest of gifts, and Audrey possessed it. As Marjorie Rosen, the American critic and feminist, wrote: 'She simply out-dazzled by the sheer force of her *joie de vivre* and the apposite way she was put together . . . a narrow, bony body which she carried like a queen and an elfin face whose doe eyes were contradicted by the strength of intelligence in the look, the irregular nose and wide mouth whose smile was at once sensuous, mischievous and absolutely sincere.'

Audrey's individual features were so well defined that they did not blend into an image of classical beauty. This, too, proved an asset. Stardom invests the star with a patent on his or her appearance, instantly recognizable and unique, which is theirs for life. Audrey patented her 'look' early and enduringly. Cecil Beaton ran a professional eye over her and noted down the photographer's view: 'her huge mouth, flat Mongolian features, heavily painted eyes, a coconut coiffure, long nails without varnish, a wonderful lithe figure, a long neck, but perhaps too scraggy . . . Everything very simple about and around her.' But her vast and growing public did not see the construction the way Beaton did: they saw the animation, what Richard Schickel called 'an eager coltish innocence', coupled with 'the utter seriousness with which she seems to take herself'.

The tone of Audrey's voice was as distinctive as any physical feature. 'With its sing-song cadence that develops into a flat drawl ending in a childlike query, it has the quality of heartbreak,' wrote Cecil Beaton, whose ear was as sharp as his eye. And one of her future directors, Stanley Donen, commented that it wasn't only film that loved her. 'It was also the sound track. You didn't have to see her: her voice was enough to soothe your jan-

A little amateur modelling. Audrey in Amsterdam, 1946, shows off a dress designed by a friend of her mother's. She had recently recovered from a near-fatal illness.

Show-business beginnings: Audrey (standing) shares a publicity pose – but wisely not the block of ice – with two of her fellow artistes from the revue *Sauce Tartare* cheating the heat on the rooftop of the Cambridge Theatre, London, in 1949. The ice was borrowed from the theatre's cooling system.

Auditioning (with blonde Babs Johnston) for the chorus of the musical *High Button Shoes* in London, 1948. 'I don't know how I had the nerve to try for it,' she said. Certainly, she had the legs.

Enter the 'Swinging Sixties' girl: Audrey in the 'new look' – spoof skidlid and bubble sunglasses – dreamed up for *How to Steal a Million* in 1965.

That 'liberated' look: Audrey's marriage was shaky while she was filming the Stanley Donen–Frederic Raphael marital comedy *Two for the Road* in 1967. The two of them reportedly had an affair. 'You sometimes get to the edge where make-believe and reality are blurred,' Finney admitted.

The photo of herself that Audrey signed for those who worked with her on her films. This one is dedicated to Margaret Gardner.

AUDREY HEPBURN

As Eliza Doolittle, the Covent Garden flower-seller in *My Fair Lady*: a game attempt at streetwise vulgarity. But Audrey herself preferred being 'loverly'.

THE CALL OF FASCISM

**By Baroness
Ella de Heemstra**

It is comparatively easy for those versed in politics to understand the ideas Fascism brings to the people of England: our loyalty to King and Empire, the Corporate State, and the revolt against alien domination of banking and trade.

It is quite another thing to point out to them that if we want our hands and feet to work freely and our brains to be delivered from the impressions of current falsehoods, and if we want to reorganise things material, we have to aim, first and foremost, at a reorganisation of our thought.

NOT ONLY MATERIAL

It is not our sole desire to get Empire bread and butter, homegrown vegetables and homespun clothes. We do not merely aim at bettering conditions for the body and easing the condition of humanity. Such amelioration cannot and will not be based on materialism or intellect, but on ideals and the spirit.

Too long has the world attempted to improve itself by self-destruction, to purify by a decimation of numbers. Too long have we thought that matter paid for matter, and that earthly things could improve the earth.

It is not so.

We who have heard the call of Fascism, and have followed the light on the upward road to victory, have been taught to understand what dimly we knew, and now fully

BARONESS ELLA DE HEEMSTRA

realise that only the spirit can cleanse the body, and only the soul of Britain can be the salvation of Britain.

THE ROAD TO SALVATION

Too long have we been fettered by the fetish of materialism. At last we are breaking the bondage and are on the road to salvation.

It is not by changing laws, not by breaking fresh political ground, not by laying down new rules, that we shall save this country.

It is not by forswearing all that Britain has stood by during this last decade, not by only material rebirth, not by just the facts contained in our programme, that we can reorganise the State. By the spirit that inspired them they shall bear fruit, by the spiritual meaning of the reforms we propose, by the light behind the veil which we shall draw aside, by the rebirth of the soul of our country.

And this rebirth is possible through Fascism. In this creed we find expressed all our hopes, all our desires, all our faith.

It is the spirit and not the letter, the creed and not its outward manifestations, that count. If to-morrow all words were washed away and all sentences became meaningless, if our language ceased to exist and the Ten Points became obsolete, their essence, the spirit that inspired them, would hold out.

THE FOUNDATIONS OF SPIRIT

The activities of a Corporate State are not in themselves our Faith. The Ten Points of our programme are an enunciation of our beliefs, not a dogma unto themselves. The growth of prosperity and the material ease of our people will be the result of our creed, not of material expectations. Only on the unshakable foundations of spirit can a new world be rebuilt.

And we who follow Sir Oswald Mosley know that in him we have found a Leader whose eyes are not riveted on earthly things, whose inspiration is of a higher plane, and whose idealism will carry Britain along to the bright light of the new dawn of spiritual rebirth.

"Britain dares to be great," said our Leader. Britain dares to have a soul!

One of the articles contributed by Audrey's mother to the Mosleyite publication *Blackshirt* in 1935.

Audrey's mother, Baroness van Heemstra (second from the left) on the steps of the Nazi Party headquarters, Munich, 1935. Also pictured are Michael Burn (in lederhosen) and (on the extreme left) Pamela Mitford, sister of Hitler's fervent English admirer Unity Mitford.

Audrey's father snapped in a London street, 1938, when he was the director of a press agency that put a pro-Nazi spin on its information. It led to his arrest and internment.

In her mother's arms. 'She had great love,' said Audrey, 'but was not always able to show it.'

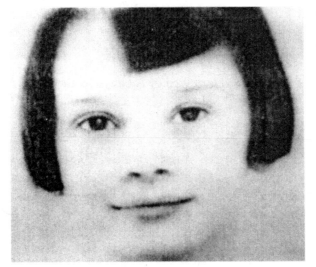

The 'Dutch Girl' look, aged three.

Aged about four, with her father. A few years later, he walked out. 'I was always searching for someone to cuddle me,' she later admitted.

Above A modelling engagement, circa 1952: the gamine fringe identified by Cecil Beaton as 'rat-nibbled' and her 'Oriental look' are already in place.

Above right and right Publicity chores, 1952. Put under contract by a British studio, Audrey submits to their view of her as an outdoor girl defying wind and waves. Otherwise, ideas failed her employers.

In *We Go to Monte Carlo*
(with Cara Williams),
in 1952, playing a movie
star. Soon she *was* one.

A triumphant debut. In
Gigi, on Broadway, she
was given voice
exercises and tutored
off stage by Cathleen
Nesbit (right), but it
was her 'fresh and
frisky' personality, 'like
a puppy out of a tub,'
that bowled over the
critics.

Bit-part film actress: a day's work, a twenty-second scene. Audrey passes through *Laughter in Paradise*, in 1951, with Guy Middleton.

Playing a ballet dancer, her first substantial role, in the political thriller *The Secret People*, 1952, with Valentina Cortese in the background.

Two studies in Angus McBean's surrealist style in 1951. The first offered her three views of herself; the second, advertising Lacto-Calamine skin lotion, offered something more solid: a fee.

gled nerves. What a celestial sound flowed from her throat. It had a soft-
ness that supported her distinct, but never pedantic diction, it embraced
her words and surrounded them with the consistency of honey. She captivated even in the dark.'

Not only was Audrey immediately identifiable, she was also temptingly
easy to copy—at least a few of those disparate features were. The Hepburn
eyes, for instance; and, especially, the gamine haircut of those years. Leslie
Caron may have had that ragamuffin look first but from the moment in
Roman Holiday when Audrey the truant princess ducked into the hairdresser's and emerged tossing her head in the shingled cut of freedom, that
style became hers. It was projected repeatedly through the pictures taken
of her by the half-dozen master photographers of the day—Avedon,
Beaton, Penn, Anthony Beauchamp, Dorothy Wilding, Bob Willoughby—
and the magazines and movie screens repeated the 'Hepburn look' until it
attained an iconic vividness. Any shopgirl could do as much with her hair,
and many did. Not since Garbo's pageboy bob of the 1930s had a hairstyle
conquered the world of youth so quickly and so feverishly.

By the middle of 1954 the *Los Angeles Times* was reporting that 'Audrey
Hepburn's hairstyle is causing something of an uproar in Japanese bath-
house circles. It costs Japanese women ten yen, about three cents, to wash
their heavy tresses at public baths. But women sprouting the straight, short
Hepburn-type coiffure contend they should get a reduced rate.' Western
women did not dare threaten their stylists with similar demands for cut-
price hairdos but the sweepings on the salon floors were thicker after Audrey's image had established itself on the screen. Cecil Beaton observed in
Vogue that 'Nobody ever looked like her before World War Two . . . now
thousands of imitations have appeared. The woods are full of emaciated
young ladies with rat-nibbled hair and moon-pale faces.' The gamine cut associated with her lasted long after Audrey had abandoned it—even after she
was no longer there to revive it. In the 1990s supermodels on the cat-
walks and in the photo spreads of glossy magazines—Linda Evangelista,
Lucie de la Falaise, the skeletal Kate Moss—appear as Hepburn reborn.

Soon the fashion alliance that Audrey and Givenchy were forging would
add a new identity-tag to her persona—the elegance of minimalism—as
well as a price-tag that few women would be able to meet. That did not
matter much. In the 1950s stars did not dress like the mob; they were
held to be special beings, and the public expected them to be gowned accordingly. Elegance gave them authority as well as confirming their rarity.
Audrey's wardrobe signified a simplicity that never courted the vulgarity
of costly extravagance. One could guess at the price, for it was by Givenchy.

But his 'line', so closely identified with her 'form', was the visible signature of Audrey's personality.

While Audrey's two films, supplemented by Paramount's publicity machine and the willing collusion of journalists and picture editors the world over, built up interest in her and increased the impatience with which her next film was awaited, the subject of this attention remained apparently at peace with herself and the world in the farmhouse-villa at Vigna San Antonio. She and Mel soon collected a menagerie of household pets: two dogs, half a dozen cats, a donkey and a couple of fantailed doves seemingly every bit as much in love as the newlyweds. Still keeping her pregnancy secret from the outside world, Audrey was not disposed to commit herself even to long-term plans. Inter-office memoranda indicate that all the impatience was on Paramount's side. Her agent, Kurt Frings, was in no hurry to make a deal, either, reckoning that a studio's sense of urgency could only inflate the price it was prepared to pay for gratifying it.

Not that business matters went undiscussed. Near neighbours and frequent visitors were Carlo Ponti and Dino de Laurentiis with their wives Sophia Loren and Silvana Mangano. 'Two Italian producers,' Michael Powell described them, 'of awesome magnitude and unimaginable wickedness, with wives of sultry splendour.' De Laurentiis was even then planning an epic film of Tolstoy's *War and Peace*. He had already told Mel that he would be most suitable for the role of Prince Andrei. Of course the great role is that of the heroine, Natasha; but the cunning Italian producer indicated that he was keeping his options open . . . he hadn't yet assigned it . . . there was time . . . and it must be perfectly cast. Who on earth could play it? he would wonder aloud over supper with Mel and Audrey. Clearly de Laurentiis knew that it was sometimes easier to get whatever one wanted by giving things a gentle sideways push. If de Laurentiis saw Audrey as Natasha, he implanted that thought in her mind by nudging Mel.

Apart from carefully planned visits to a private clinic in Rome to monitor the progress of her baby, Audrey rarely interrupted the country idyll she was enjoying while Mel finished *La Madre*. She went to a reception given by the American ambassador Clare Booth Luce, then travelled on to Amsterdam at the beginning of November 1954. This was a duty trip: part of a five-day fundraising tour on behalf of Dutch charities for disabled war veterans. It taught Audrey a lesson that was unpleasant yet formative. She was besieged by thousands of young—and many not so young—people every time she appeared in public, precipitating a near-riot in a department store, which brought home to her the dangerous dimension of her stardom.

It made a well-sheltered refuge even more essential if she and Mel were to protect their private life.

On the last day of 1954 she and Mel arrived in London where he was to start filming *Oh . . . Rosalinda!!* They brought with them their Christmas presents—a yellow cashmere sweater for him, a dress in white eyelet embroidery for her—and rented an apartment not far from Audrey's mother in South Audley Street. Again, as he had done in New York, Mel made sure that a distance was kept between Audrey and the media. She went along with this gladly. For Audrey, childbirth was always going to be fraught with problems: the physique that so enhanced her charm was not best suited to having babies easily and painlessly. She was in considerable distress at times during these weeks, and Mel no doubt wished to spare her any unnecessary strain, although his curt manner with the photographers and journalists who were lucky enough to catch Audrey visiting the set of *Oh . . . Rosalinda!!* was attributed to possessiveness, even jealousy. This writer remembers Mel, playing the amorous American army officer with well-drilled ease and considerable charm, rushing over to Audrey immediately Michael Powell called 'Cut' and hustling her off to his dressing room. After that, he demanded that no photographer, not even the stills man employed on the film, was to be allowed on the set while Audrey was there.

'I know my part already,' Mel had told Michael Powell when rehearsals began that January. Powell conceded in his memoirs that 'Alfred was a part he could play on his head' and then, he added, 'spend half the night intriguing against us over *Ondine*'. The many questions over the film of *Ondine* had not been resolved and the British producers suspected, rightly or wrongly, that delays were being deliberately engineered while a counter-plan was worked out to allow Mel and Audrey to film it themselves—in a manner much closer to their stage production of the previous year. Powell continued to resist. 'Mel was certainly no Louis Jouvet,' he recalled. 'When Jouvet paused [in the original Paris production], we all paused. When Mel paused, the whole play stopped.' In any case, Powell and Pressburger had decided to forsake the text of the Giraudoux play—for which the author's widow was asking what they considered an exaggerated sum of money—and revert to the original legend as told by the French fabulist La Motte Fouquet. It was a thoroughly uncomfortable situation. The showdown came at a meeting to which, according to Powell, Mel Ferrer brought along his own designers. 'Audrey never said a word, but Mel spoke for two . . . It was quite clear that the meeting was about who was going to be boss.' Any hope of Paramount assuming the financing of such an 'iffy' project was swiftly extinguished. The studio did not see Audrey as a nymph in an underwater ballet. It was the end of the *Ondine* project. A few blunt words were spoken, for Paramount was now without any Audrey Hepburn film in the works and felt it had been patient long enough. Suddenly, Audrey and her husband found themselves again in the unromantic position of worrying about money, for they had been stretching their credit to the limit.

There was also a more heart-rending reason for getting back to work as soon as possible: Audrey suffered a miscarriage. It was a particularly cruel blow for a woman so set on starting a family and bringing up a child in the love and security that her own interrupted childhood had never known. Her faith came to the rescue of her need. Instead of looking back on what might have been, she fixed her mind on what she could now be— one of the great heroines of literature, Tolstoy's Natasha.

By mid-March 1955 Audrey and Mel were back in Switzerland. They went to St Moritz, and it was there that Dino de Laurentiis called Mel some time towards the end of the month. 'King Vidor,' he said, mentioning the veteran American film-maker already signed to direct *War and Peace,* 'has his heart set on Audrey playing Natasha, and you know I've wanted you for a long time for the part of Prince Andrei.' Mel must have recognized the technique, but he was equal to it. Though he and Audrey badly needed an infusion of fresh funds, he showed no undue eagerness to take advantage of de Laurentiis's 'suggestion'. Just the reverse. The Italian producer was told that much as Mel and Audrey wanted to work together, and would like nothing better than for it to be in a de Laurentiis production, they would have to think it over very carefully. It was a huge project. It would impose a great strain on Audrey, particularly after her miscarriage, and it was not a thing to rush into. De Laurentiis made understanding noises. He knew the coded message. Soon, he suspected—maybe as soon as Mel put down the telephone—a call would be placed to Kurt Frings in Hollywood and the order would be issued: 'Deal time!'

'Mel had a great amount of influence over Audrey, particularly in those early years,' says the actor Robert Flemyng who had known both of them in New York, 'and there's no doubt Audrey did what he told her.' Her obedience to what she was told now laid the secure foundation of her wealth and—with it—her power.

Kurt Frings hurried over to Europe. All the parties assembled at a hotel on Lake Como at the beginning of April 1955: de Laurentiis, Frings, King

Vidor, Mel and Audrey. Vidor explained to his potential stars how he saw the film and, equally important to them, their roles in it—particularly that of Natasha. Then Audrey, Mel and Kurt Frings climbed into a chauffeured limousine and began a leisurely drive along the shore of the lake while they discussed Vidor's vision of things. Meanwhile Vidor and de Laurentiis followed in another limousine, preserving a discreet if impatient distance. After several miles of this 'shadowing', both cars halted at a signal from the one in which Frings was riding. He joined de Laurentiis, presumably to relay his clients' agreement in principle and to hear the producer's financial proposals in greater detail. Vidor joined Audrey and Mel, the conversation in their car being somewhat less tense and more general. The deal was sealed by a triumphant honking of the de Laurentiis vehicle's horn. Kurt Frings must have felt entitled to blow an even louder blast on his trumpet.

The deal that he had just concluded made Audrey one of the highest-paid stars in the cinema. For twelve weeks' work she was to be paid $350,000 (about £125,000); expenses ('per diems') of $500 (£180) a week and $27,500 (almost £10,000) for each week she might have to work beyond her agreed shooting schedule. She was to have a car and chauffeurs on twenty-four-hour call for the duration of her work on the film. She was also granted approval of the script, cast, lighting photographer and make-up artists.

The deal was not quite so rich for Mel, but still generous: $200,000 (about £71,000) plus $250 (£90) a week 'per diems'. Paramount guaranteed Audrey's fee in dollars—still necessary because of foreign-exchange controls and the shaky status of the Italian lira—and, in return, received US distribution rights in the film. Her 'home' studio, Associated British, was offered the chance to invest in the production, but, true to its nature, preferred the sure thing over the risky gamble and agreed to let Audrey do the film in return for British distribution rights.

The deal made headlines. It also provoked the first serious signs of chauvinist resentment in the British press, which had already turned sour over Mel Ferrer's 'proprietorial' attitude towards his wife during the filming of *Oh . . . Rosalinda!!* at Elstree Studios earlier in the year. Wasn't it time that Audrey made a film in her 'home' country? The strong identification of the princess's escapade in *Roman Holiday* with the plight of Princess Margaret contributed to the common and enduring view of Audrey as a 'British' star—despite the fact that she was half-Dutch and now residing outside the country. Other British stars who had migrated to the United

States—Jean Simmons, James Mason, Deborah Kerr, Stewart Granger were the best known—had felt the same backlash a few years earlier. Now Audrey caught the tail end of it. 'Instead of earning dollars for Britain,' said a *Daily Mail* feature writer, 'Audrey Hepburn will continue to help Hollywood earn money from British stars.' Mel was blamed for this drain in the currency reserves. Aware that financial analysis did not have the same readership pull as romantic speculation, the press hinted that he was able to take advantage of her because she was so madly in love with him. Mel obviously could not win. A shrewder option came from a man who had good reason to think he knew Audrey more intimately than most. 'I think Audrey allows Mel to think he influences her,' said William Holden, her former lover and co-star in *Sabrina*.

To some extent, and eventually to a fatal extent, love did dictate the working relationship of Audrey Hepburn and her husband. They had resolved that, as far as humanly possible, they would not let film-making separate them. They would appear in films together or, if that could not be arranged, find films to do simultaneously within reasonable distance of each other. 'We dread the thought of separation,' Mel declared. 'Look what it's done to so many Hollywood marriages.'

For all his protestations to the contrary, the rumours that Mel dominated Audrey took firm root. In defence Audrey was forced to give *Photoplay* magazine an interview which it headed 'My Husband Doesn't Run Me'. She said she would put marriage before her career if work threatened to keep them apart for any serious length of time. As always Audrey appeared the conscientious pragmatist. 'I don't think any job we went off to do under these circumstances could be very well done,' she said. 'I think we would each have a very heavy conscience.'

However, as filming of *War and Peace* got under way even her current director was to concede that 'Audrey let Mel do the shouting for her'. In an interview with Thomas Wiseman, King Vidor confessed: 'I had the feeling that Audrey needed someone to make the decisions for her. She's an innocent who doesn't know the business the way Mel does. He did all the talking for her. He knows what is right for her. He knows how much money she should be getting and he's a director himself, so he understands whether she's getting a fair deal . . . I believe he collects her salary personally.' This benign interpretation provoked an outburst from Audrey, showing how sensitive she had become to the accusations that she had contracted marriage to a Svengali. ' "Protection!" ' she echoed, on reading Vidor's remarks, 'protection from what? As a husband [Mel] naturally advises his wife. But that's all. I assure you I don't need "protection".' And indeed, considering that within six months of his marriage to Audrey Hepburn, Mel had been instrumental in increasing her fee 233,000 per cent, why should he not advise her? If this was 'protection' money, it put a new and welcome spin on the term—it was money coming in, not being paid out.

11

PRETTY FACE

---

*A*UDREY was one of the most benevolent monarchs to rule over a film. She hardly ever abused her powers. She expected to be able to advise, to warn and to be consulted: which the *War and Peace* contract stipulated in clause after clause. 'I never realized so many things could go wrong,' she said after a first reading of the contract. Nor did she realize, until she started to exercise the powers she had been granted, how hard it was to achieve what she thought was in the best interests of herself and, she hoped, the film. The first test came early, with the choice of star to play opposite her in the role of Pierre Bezukhov.

The illegitimate son of a Russian nobleman, Pierre is Tolstoy's voice of reason, intellect—and pacifism. Amiable, ungainly, good-natured, short-sighted and chronically vague: few Hollywood stars could embody such human but decidedly unheroic qualities. But Audrey knew who would be perfect for the part: Peter Ustinov. She pushed very strongly for him, despite the premonitory wince that Dino de Laurentiis gave at the mention of the British actor's name. Not that de Laurentiis deemed it a bad choice: on the contrary, Ustinov was literate, cultivated and, on the strength of his Nero in *Quo Vadis,* an actor who brought to his characters valuable undertones of his own invention. 'But Audrey,' said de Laurentiis, 'he is not a star as big as you.' Tolstoy could afford to let his matchless heroine Natasha be fascinated by an intellectual; Hollywood could not take such risks. It was bad enough having a hero like Pierre who wore spectacles that distinguished him from the men of action and battle. De Laurentiis, insisting that intellect and weak eyesight be counterbalanced by visible sex appeal, pushed hard for Gregory Peck.

This put Audrey in a delicate dilemma: as de Laurentiis probably intended. How could she not welcome a rematch with the man who had so generously conceded her equal billing in *Roman Holiday?* But would Mel be happy with a star around whom rumours had circulated while he was filming in Rome with the woman who was now Mrs Mel Ferrer? When de Laurentiis set off for Hollywood to pick 'his' Pierre, it was to Henry Fonda that he paid court. Fonda met with Audrey's approval—and no doubt with Mel's too.

Audrey used her contractual powers to protect how she looked—the way she was photographed, made up and costumed—with more immediate success. When her first choice of cinematographer Franz Planer, the Austrian who had been co-photographer on *Roman Holiday,* proved unavailable, she asked for Jack Cardiff, one of the best colour photographers around, who was particularly close to her and Mel. (He had been their secret nominee to film the aborted *Ondine.*) She sought out a husband-and-wife team of make-up and hairdressing experts, Alberto and Grazia di Rossi, and they served her well not only on this film but on several subsequent ones. The 'court circle' was forming around her, the insulation that every major star depends upon for a sense of familiar security. She asked Givenchy to do Natasha's costumes but he begged off on the grounds that to do 'period' costumes might undermine his newly acquired status as the leader of starkly modern contemporary fashion. However, he flew to Rome several times to approve the fabrics and colours selected and their suitability for Audrey.

Her characteristic hairstyle had to be sacrificed in the interests of period authenticity. This drew laments from some columnists that Audrey had 'grown up' too fast since making *Sabrina;* they would have preferred to see her enjoying a prolonged screen adolescence, ignoring the fact that even as she was preparing *War and Peace* she was celebrating her twenty-fifth birthday. As it was, she photographed much younger than her age. Fortunately so, since Tolstoy's Natasha is a bare fifteen at the start of the story (the script discreetly added a year or two). Age aside, looks and personality of the character in the great Russian novel were an eerie presentiment of Audrey Hepburn: 'A black-eyed, wide-mouthed girl, not pretty but full of life, with childish bare shoulders which, after her run, heaved and shook her bodice, with black curls tossed backward . . . at that charming age when a girl is no longer a child, though the child is not yet a young woman.'

'A darling . . . a sport . . . to know her is to have a new joy,' E. M. Forster once said of Natasha; he might have been echoing those who knew Audrey. King Vidor, who had moved to Rome in the late spring of 1955 to prepare a screenplay, declared: 'Audrey is Natasha. She is fresh out of the book.' If physical resemblance were the only thing that counted, the combination was foolproof. Unfortunately it was not.

Audrey began costume and camera tests, during an exceptionally steamy Roman summer, at Cinecittà studios known popularly as 'Dinocittà' in tribute to the energetic entrepreneur and his $6 million production. She needed all her dedication to survive the heat and humidity at a time when air conditioning was still a relative rarity. It took nearly an hour to drive to the studios from the villa that had once again been rented for her and Mel in the Alban Hills. The peace and privacy they enjoyed after work was like a second honeymoon and only very privileged—or powerful—members of the press were invited there. One was Louella Parsons, already sweetened up by small bouquets of summer flowers, wild as well as cultivated, that Audrey picked and despatched to the Los Angeles columnist's suite at the Excelsior Hotel. In return, Louella reported that Audrey was so happy 'she unconsciously reaches over to pat Mel's hand as they talk'. Even though it wasn't her intention, Louella conveys something of the strain that stardom was imposing on the work routines of her hosts, if not yet on their married life.

Having so often stressed their determination not to let work separate them, they were now obliged to try and line up projects many months in advance. Obligations piled up while current commitments were still being discharged. Even before Audrey had shot her first scene in *War and Peace* she was being approached to make a comedy entitled *Ariane* (or, as it was more pleasingly retitled, *Love in the Afternoon*), with Gary Cooper and Maurice Chevalier as her co-stars, to be directed by Billy Wilder in Paris more than a year later. Not wanting to be apart from Mel, Audrey delayed agreeing to it until his needs were catered for. Fortunately, he was able to find a part in a Jean Renoir comedy, *Eléna et les hommes,* which was to be shot in Paris at the same time. For the moment, the equation 'togetherness is happiness' went unchallenged.

William Wyler was impatient to take his place in the queue, or, rather, to jump it. He had bought the European rights to Rostand's play *L'Aiglon*—the property was in the public domain in the United States—and had sold Audrey on playing the young son of Napoleon and the Empress Marie-Louise, who had died of consumption before he could reach man's estate or inherit his father's empire. Born in Alsace, Wyler had a strong Franco-German affection for European dynasties. He proposed shooting the film at the Schönbrunn palace in Vienna, where the boy had been raised after Napoleon was sent into exile. But Wyler's grandiose plan foundered on the absolute refusal of Paramount's bosses to allow their expensive new star to appear as a boy. That kind of cross-dressing had gone out with Garbo!

With the intensive day-to-day concentration needed for *War and Peace* it was perhaps no surprise that Audrey said no to George Stevens when he proposed a film of *The Diary of Anne Frank*. There was more to her refusal than an overcrowded schedule. There was too much in the story of the resilient Jewish girl, whose spirit remained unbroken through years of being immured in a secret hiding place within feet of passing German soldiers and Gestapo officials, that reminded Audrey of her own wartime risks and privations. Besides, she had misgivings about 'playing a saint'. This objection only made Stevens more eager and importunate. Jennifer Jones had shown in *The Song of Bernadette* that saints enjoyed a dependable box-office and won Oscars for their earthly impersonators. But Audrey was not to be persuaded. She told Stevens that she had read the Anne Frank diaries as early as 1946, in Dutch, when a proof copy was given to her 'by a friend'. The 'friend' was her mother's benefactor, Paul Rykens. 'I read it,' she told Lesley Garner in an interview many years later, 'and it destroyed me . . . I was not reading it as a book, as printed pages. This was my life . . . I've never been the same again, it affected me so deeply.'

Eventually the moment would come when Audrey could open the Anne Frank diary again and this time find there a determination to survive, an inspirational quality that would serve a humanitarian cause infinitely more forcefully than any role she could have played on film. But in Rome in the mid-1950s, playing a heroine in an earlier era who also sees her country, her home and her family devastated by war, that time was still a long way off. Audrey confided to friends that if she had succumbed to George Stevens's blandishments, 'it would have brought on a breakdown'.

Audrey's role in *War and Peace* stretched well past the twelve weeks stipulated in her contract, earning her a fortune in 'overage' but it was at a price to her health and stamina. She was an indefatigable pupil, learning all the skills required for Natasha's role. Though always nervous of horses, she steeled herself to acquire the seat of an aristocratic girl on a genuine Russian-bred pony. In the great halls of the Russian nobility, recreated in astounding detail on Cinecittà's sound stages, she took lessons in the convoluted dances performed at court balls in early nineteenth-century Moscow. She stood for hours on end amid a host of costumiers, being gowned in creations skillfully adapted from styles her own great-grandmother might have worn at royal occasions in the Netherlands.

As so frequently happens in film epics, the production design was fuller and more rounded than the roles. The chief quality with which Audrey endowed Natasha was the one she embodied herself without any effort at all—a limpid radiance. The part gave her little to rely on beyond her looks. King Vidor was a pedantic adapter of Tolstoy, not an inspired one. 'Of course, the temptation is to put the whole damn book in,' he wrote ominously to the novelist Irwin Shaw, who was ultimately conscripted (though uncredited) along with five other writers to compress Tolstoy's multitudinous plots and sub-plots into a clear, if oversimplified, narrative. The University of Southern California archives hold Vidor's own two-volume copy of *War and Peace;* at the foot of each page he has noted the principal event in the clear if mistaken hope that it could be found a niche in the screenplay. What he left out, however, did the film more harm than what he included, and Audrey was the chief sufferer. The film does not reflect the crucial transformation of the book, as war, death, pestilence, privation and destruction take their toll on Natasha, toughening her resolve to survive, annealing her spirit and turning her into a woman who has known every sort of weather and sky, happiness and folly, ruin and recovery, before achieving the final bounty of contentment.

Was such a transformation too much to ask of Audrey at this stage of her career? Perhaps so: but Vidor does not give her the chance to see if her reach can exceed her grasp. She looks at her loveliest in the film; but she is denied what any actress, however great, needs to develop a character—namely, a director's skill at showing the insights that come with experience. Lacking both, Audrey falls back on simple innocence. To judge by his notes on the project, and his letters to Irwin Shaw, Vidor seems to have been so much in love with Audrey's own charm that he was reluctant to allow Natasha to 'grow up'. He wrote to Shaw that he recognized, intellectually, that the mainspring of the story was 'the maturing . . . of Natasha. She represents to me the anima or soul of the story and she hovers over it like immortality itself.' Yes: but immortality usually excludes the more interesting features of humanity.

In less exalted moments Vidor appears to have drawn on *Gone with the Wind* for his inspiration. Naturally this brought no objection from de Laurentiis, but it did nothing for Audrey. She was not an actress in the mould of the obsessive Vivien Leigh. Vivien was a performer whose own lack of concern for the consequences of her actions exactly tallied with the character of Scarlett O'Hara. Audrey needed subtle steering through waters of emotional experience which she had not travelled in before. She did not get it from Vidor.

Her Natasha is irresistibly charming. The description of her provided by Prince Andrei—Mel handsomely made up and giving a competent yet curiously mechanical performance—fits Audrey perfectly. To embrace this creature would indeed be 'like holding spring-time in your arms'. Unfortunately for her role and for the film, her autumn and winter never arrive.

Audrey did not fare badly in the reviews of the film, most of which were respectful. The harshest censure came from the British critic Paul Dehn who pronounced that 'her pretty face with its large Muscovite eyes equiv-ocally recalling fawn and faun scarcely changes'. Dilys Powell acknowl-edged that Natasha does not 'mature' but added sympathetically that this deficiency, though just, made it seem 'as if the poor girl were some kind of port or cheese'. And C. A. Lejeune, mixing asperity with appreciation, de-clared that 'although anachronistic', she was 'a charming little goose'. Crit-ics who had been complaining that Audrey was sacrificing the best years of her youth by abandoning waifish roles now complained that she wasn't adult enough.

Who knows what Audrey would have achieved in *War and Peace* had Vidor been a bolder adapter and a more imaginative director. By 1955 he was sixty-one and well past the brilliance of his silent spectacles of the 1920s such as *The Big Parade*, or even the flamboyant commercial confi-dence of the recent *Duel in the Sun*. He lacked the social sophistication or historical grasp to produce more than token Tolstoy. To be fair to him, the screen grammar of a 'directors' cinema' had not yet evolved the psycho-logical resources it would have acquired ten years later. He was falling back on tested Hollywood forms when his material needed new concepts of story-telling. Audrey fitted the former very trimly indeed, but her short-comings become painfully obvious in her character's most dramatic se-quence and the film's biggest failure: Natasha's seduction by the dashing reprobate officer played (with unbelievably coarse dubbing) by Vittorio Gassman. Her momentary infidelity costs Natasha her reputation and the love of Prince Andrei. Because Audrey has established Tolstoy's heroine on no firmer ground than girlish innocence, the note of fickle heartlessness she must strike as she prepares herself for elopement sounds false, and em-barrassingly so.

Vidor's correspondence reveals that he was aware of this and half ac-cepted the blame. He wrote to Irwin Shaw: 'I asked my wife'—the writer Elizabeth Hill, by his third marriage—'to read the sequence as it now stands, and she spent most of this morning telling me how I had harmed Natasha's character.' The fault, it has to be admitted, was compounded by Audrey's inexperience. Though her relationship with Vidor was in no sense unprofessional, it is likely that they were too close for their individual good. Audrey was more Vidor's muse than his star. He never quite fell out of love with her even though *War and Peace* was a box-office disappointment that had a long haul to reach profitability. In Vidor's words, she was still 'a director's delight'. In his memoirs, bluntly titled *On Film Making* and a work that revealed him to be a gifted illustrator rather than a conceptual artist, Vidor breaks into rhapsody over Audrey: 'Whenever I am asked that most embarrassing of all questions—'Who is your favourite actress of all those you have directed?"—one always comes immediately to mind.' There was really no need to name her: the love-affair between them shows in every shot of *War and Peace*.

Vidor at least enjoyed the satisfaction of seeing his critics proved, if not exactly wrong where Audrey was concerned, then less than reliable. Although he never deviated from his conviction that she was 'ideal from my viewpoint', he had feared 'she would probably not fulfil a Russian's concept of the part'. Yet when the Russians made their own version of *War and Peace* in 1966 (directed by Sergei Bondarchuk), 'they cast an actress [Ludmilla Savelyeva]', Vidor noted with a smug sense of vindication, 'who was exactly Audrey's type.'

12

F U N N Y F A C E

A UDREY had discovered that no sooner has a star achieved personal success than she needs something else—corporate protection. She now had her pick—or at least approval—of the top directors, screenwriters, lighting photographers and make-up artists. Her talents were taken care of; and Kurt Frings took care of her escalating fees. All this had to be safeguarded by good public relations. This necessarily more discreet requirement of stardom was entrusted to a handsome, urbane and Europeanized American called Henry Rogers. For most of the next decade, every interview Audrey gave, every public appearance she made, every announcement about her plans or her personal life (of which there were very few) was given Rogers's close but sympathetic scrutiny before Audrey approved it. His recollections of their relationship throw interesting light on the person Audrey had become in her year or so of marriage and the film-making treadmill.

'Audrey had a gift for striking up an immediate relationship,' Rogers recalls. 'As soon as we met, she closed the business gap with her friendship.' Rogers and his wife, Roz, had arrived at Rome airport tired enough to let the chauffeur of the waiting limousine sweep them off without inquiring where they were going. To their surprise, they were deposited on the doorstep of the de Laurentiis mansion, which was crammed with a huge dinner party of voluble Italians whose language neither of the Rogerses spoke with any fluency. The telephone rang. To their great relief it was Mel Ferrer, who had discovered the involuntary detour they had made. 'You don't understand one word,' he hissed, 'get out of there.'

'Audrey met us as we entered the driveway of their farmhouse,' says Rogers, 'almost as if she'd been waiting for us for an hour lest we missed the turning—and probably she had. I'll never forget the impression she made. Black slacks, a black turtleneck sweater, the biggest grin you ever saw on a face and her arms stretched wide open like someone at an aerobics class. She didn't give me the usual business handshake. She embraced me. "I'm so happy you've come to stay with us." Not, you notice "to work for me".' Like Ernest Lehman, Rogers wasn't used to such sudden and apparently genuine affection from a Hollywood star. 'But then Audrey wasn't ever really "Hollywood," ' he later reflected.

Roz Rogers noticed what a close eye Mel kept on his wife, anticipating her needs and sometimes insisting gently but firmly on things to do with her diet or some matter of domestic routine. 'It was second nature for him to manage things. Where her career was concerned, Audrey let him—for a time, anyhow. I don't really think acting meant all that much to Audrey. Not as much, in any case, as being a wife or becoming a mother.' For both roles Mel was needed and valued.

After-dinner talk turned to future projects—what else? At this time, Audrey had finished her main scenes in *War and Peace* and was being buffeted afresh by producers with ready-to-go pictures—'ready-to-go', that is, if she (and Paramount) were ready to agree. Most would never be made. One that was not, however, is revealing of what Audrey did not often disclose about herself. In this instance, she definitely disapproved of the project, but found a way to escape the embarrassment of a blunt no.

Tennessee Williams and the producer Hal Wallis had recently visited her in Rome with the offer of the star role in the film of Williams's play *Summer and Smoke*. It would have been a considerable step forward for Audrey, into new if taxing dramatic territory. She had several lengthy talks with the two men and their hopes were high. But those hopes were abruptly shattered when Audrey insisted that Givenchy would have to do her dresses for the film. Since her character was a dowdy, repressed spinster living in small-town America during the First World War, this demand was particularly incongruous. Negotiations foundered and eventually collapsed. (Geraldine Page played the role five years later.)

What made Audrey so obdurate and apparently insensitive to a heroine whom Tennessee Williams described in his memoirs as 'the best female portrait I have ever drawn in a play'? *Summer and Smoke* is an actress's 'dream' vehicle, but it contains a scene that suggests, physically as well as metaphorically, the attempted rape of innocence. Audrey was not ready to face this. She instinctively recoiled from anything that would strip her of her greatest asset. Many dreadful things happen to the heroines of fairy tales but rape as such doesn't figure among them. Audrey had got by very well with her screen virginity intact and she did not want to face the world on its own more realistic and violent terms, even if Tennessee Williams had turned them into poetry. Characteristically, she did not break off the discussions with him and Wallis. She avoided unpleasantness. 'When something black happens to me—like my miscarriage—I make a decision and carry on, and then later I'll be numb.' The talks 'carried on' until Givenchy was to be made part of the deal. Then, as she had anticipated, they broke down.

She had told Kurt Frings and Henry Rogers that she wanted something light-hearted and modern as a contrast to the historical surcharge of *War and Peace*—'which felt like endlessly dressing up for the opera'. Now she told Henry and Roz Rogers her philosophy: 'Not to live for the day—that would be materialistic—but to treasure the day. I realize that most of us live on the skin—on the surface—without appreciating just how wonderful it is simply to be alive at all.' The Rogerses returned to Hollywood in thoughtful mood: in their job, this combination of worldliness and idealism seemed a contradiction. Could Audrey have both?

It seemed that she could. A series of fateful accidents—not too uncommon in the film business—soon brought her a project that would allow her to reap great material rewards while preserving, in the warmest and most attractive fashion, the unworldliness of her screen personality.

Funny Face began life as an unproduced stage play by Leonard Gershe called *Wedding Day*. It was the story of a Greenwich Village bookshop clerk who is discovered by a fashion photographer doing a shoot for a glossy magazine. She is turned into a model and whisked off to Paris for a romantically styled picture-spread. Like Eliza Doolittle after she has been 'improved' almost out of recognition, the girl feels unappreciated by her Pygmalion mentor; and he, in turn, fails to recognize the unprofessional feeling she inspires in him for what it really is—love. Gershe intended his play as a musical with an original score, something completely modern in tone and treatment. Accordingly, he wrote a libretto, with a score by Vernon Duke, which was enthusiastically received by Roger Edens, the most talented arranger and producer of musicals in Arthur Freed's production unit at MGM. Edens's enthusiasm brought in director Stanley Donen, with whom he had made *On the Town,* that groundbreaking musical of 1949 which utilized real Manhattan locations as 'sets' for song and dance, and allowed stylized numbers to flow effortlessly into and out of the reality of the passing scene.

'Leonard was reading the screenplay to me,' says Donen, 'and had reached the scene in the darkroom where the photographer is developing the shot he's taken of the Greenwich Village waif. He hangs the print up, wet and dripping, for her to see. And she says, "Oh, no! You could never make a model of that. I think my face is perfectly funny." '

'Stanley and I exchanged a quick look,' Gershe recalls, 'and at the same time he shouted, "What a great song cue!" I shouted "Gershwin!" We immediately stopped everything and dug out the songs from the George and Ira Gershwin score for the Broadway musical of 1927, *Funny Face*.'

'We found that the songs might have been written for the new situations we had created,' Donen continues. 'The song "How long has this been going on?" became the melody that the bookshop girl sings to herself in the lonely let-down following the explosion of activity when her store is invaded by the sophisticated folk from uptown and she finds herself yearning for their glamorous world.'

Gershe adds: ' "Let's kiss and make up" fitted perfectly into a quarrel scene. And probably the most delightful surprise was to discover that the lyrics of "S'Wonderful", when sung by the lovers, could provide a charmingly sentimental summary of the entire story.'

In short, the lyrics relieved the script of much of the burden of explanatory dialogue, while placing the characters in that melodic limbo where anything can happen. The project was transformed and, in the hands of Edens and Donen, one of the most innovative Hollywood musicals of the post-war era began to take shape. But then came the casting. The producers struggled while, unknown to them, the playful gods held Audrey in reserve.

Cyd Charisse was one early choice for the girl, strongly favoured by MGM's production chief, Dore Schary, but just as strongly resisted by Roger Edens: not for lack of talent in dancing and singing but on grounds of credibility. 'I don't think an audience would ever believe that Cyd had just graduated from Barnard [College],' Edens wrote to Schary, 'and she wouldn't somehow [have] got round to knowing what was going on in the outside world.' In other words, she lacked the essential innocence of Audrey Hepburn, despite the fact that the girl in *Funny Face* was around eighteen, nearly ten years younger than Audrey. At this stage of her career, age was never a problem for Audrey: she played younger with total confidence. A *Christian Science Monitor* interviewer, Volney Hurd, shrewdly analysed the way in which Audrey unconsciously neutralized the signs of age. 'You become almost completely oblivious of [her] as a physical personality,' the journalist remarked to Roger Edens, 'and see, rather, an illuminated presentation of the thought she is giving out . . . It is as though she were a transparency.'

Edens and Donen pushed for Audrey to be borrowed from Paramount. 'If she needed a change after *War and Peace*,' Donen recalls them saying, 'here it was—a happy musical. She must have felt that way, too. We sent her the script and three days later she said yes.' The deal took much, much longer. First Paramount said no to a loan-out to a rival studio, so Donen tried to make *Funny Face* one of the three films Audrey still legally owed to Associated British. That didn't work, either. Then he and Edens hit on the solution: if the star couldn't come to them, why shouldn't they go to the star? Thus an 'MGM musical' came to be made as a Paramount picture.

One major difficulty remained, this time raised by Audrey's agent. Her agreement hinged on *Funny Face* being shot in Paris. For tax reasons? Not at all: simply to allow her to be in the same city as Mel while he was shooting the Renoir comedy *Eléna et les hommes*. The Billy Wilder film, *Love in the Afternoon*, that Audrey should have been shooting while Mel acted for Renoir wasn't yet ready to go. It tells one a lot about the strength of their marriage, Paramount's desire to accommodate Audrey, and the studio's muscle power, that the Renoir film which was scheduled to begin in the early weeks of 1956 was put back until *Funny Face* was ready to shoot in its Paris locations, allowing Mel and Audrey to stay together. Not until Elizabeth Taylor and Richard Burton held a whole production to ransom during the making of *Cleopatra* in 1962 was a husband-and-wife team able to dictate its terms so bluntly and triumphantly.

Without exception, every American film Audrey had so far made had cast her opposite a well-established star: Peck, Holden, Bogart, Fonda. Yet there had never been any sense of their stardom reflecting onto her: she had shone with equal, sometimes superior brightness from the moment she stepped before the cameras—as if a stage magician had conjured her out of nowhere. In *Funny Face* she had to match herself against someone who was more than merely great. Fred Astaire was legendary. 'I am realizing the dream of my life in making a musical with Fred Astaire,' she told Louella Parsons over the telephone from Paris, where she had been getting herself in trim at a dance studio before reporting to Hollywood for rehearsals and song recordings in mid-February 1956.

'What she didn't admit,' says Donen, 'is that she was also terrified.'

After elation at the prospect of dancing with Fred had worn off, alarm set in. 'Understandably so. Astaire was acknowledged to be the finest dancer of the twentieth century by Balanchine and Jerome Robbins—and, much later on, Baryshnikov would say so, too. It would have frightened anyone with a grain of understanding about dance.' What Audrey didn't know—though Donen did—is that Astaire was just as jittery at the prospect of appearing with Audrey. 'He had been dazzled by her earlier couple of movies. But he was now fifty-seven—thirty years older than she, and, he thought, perhaps too old.' As the film proved, their misgivings were groundless. The partnership that made a young girl into the protégée of an ageing mentor was romantic, not sexual: their mutual attraction appeared to be based irreproachably on tutelage, not seductiveness. Astaire's character, Richard Avery, whose name paid tribute to the photographer Richard Avedon (a buddy of Leonard Gershe's in the US Marine Corps), was a manipulator of his art. In the darkroom he operated with a sleight-of-hand skill that was echoed in the sleight-of-foot precision which guided Audrey through the choreography. In matters of the heart, Audrey's character led the older man a dance of a different, but no less charming, kind.

Twenty-five years later, Astaire, then eighty-two, was honoured with a Life Achievement Award by the American Film Institute. Audrey presented it to him, describing the moment when they had first met on the Paramount rehearsal stage. Astaire cut his usual debonair figure, his lighter-than-air look co-ordinated in the upbeat mood that his graceful feet would set: yellow shirt, grey slacks, red scarf instead of a belt, pink socks and well-waxed black moccasins twinkling impatiently to 'go'.

'I could feel myself turn into solid lead,' Audrey recalled, 'while my heart sank into my own two left feet. Then, suddenly, I felt a hand around my waist and, with his inimitable grace and lightness, Fred literally swept me off my feet. I experienced the thrill that all women at some point in their lives have dreamed of—to dance just once with Fred Astaire.'

They had only five weeks in which to rehearse and record the fourteen separate musical sequences ahead of shooting. This was because Audrey's availability for *Funny Face* was limited by her commitment to begin *Love in the Afternoon* almost immediately she finished her stint on location with *Funny Face* in Paris.

Each morning Audrey reported to Roger Edens's office for song rehearsal at the piano. Then she would go on to the set where Stanley Donen would stage the number and plot it for the camera. After that she went across to the rehearsal hall to work on the dance steps. Recording the songs took a week: an amazingly short time considering their complex arrangements and a testimony to the blueprint precision of Donen, Edens and their team. The first number was one of the trickiest: the 'Bonjour Paris' sequence in which Audrey, Astaire and Kay Thompson, playing the astringent editor of a *Vogue*-type glossy, arrive at the airport, then set out singly to explore the delights of the French capital. Each of them is photographed against a 'typical' Paris landmark, sometimes separately, sometimes on a screen split in three, until they converge unexpectedly on the viewing platform of the Eiffel Tower—the place they had sworn they would never visit because it was so 'touristy'. The number was to last precisely five minutes, incorporate 518 lines of music and jump-cut through thirty-eight Paris locations.

All of this had to be rehearsed and recorded in Hollywood in front of a full orchestra of over fifty musicians, then mimed to playback once the unit went to Paris. Roger Edens was extremely nervous. 'Even for seasoned musical artists, it's a nerve-racking business doing all the takes and retakes necessary. I was afraid Audrey wasn't up to it.' Donen had misgivings now, too, for a slightly different reason: 'Fred was a great dancer. But some people, including George Gershwin, Irving Berlin and Cole Porter, had good reason to believe his singing of their songs was even better. I said to myself, "Oh, God! Can Audrey match him?" She was jittery, and Fred felt it too. She kept missing a note on the first three or four takes and we had to stop and start and stop and start—the very thing that causes even a professional singer to crack. Fred could see she was getting more flustered with each take. On the next one, she blew it again. Fred didn't stop, but immediately hit a wrong note himself, deliberately so, and then said, "Hold it, hold it . . . I muffed that one. So sorry, Audrey." It was a corny little ruse, and no doubt she spotted it, but it did the trick, relaxed the tension, showed we were all fallible and from then on it was plain sailing, or nearly so.'

Donen realized the trust that Audrey was putting in him when, before shooting began on the interior scenes at Paramount, she confessed to him something that she swore she had never told anyone before. Her director, in recalling it, quoted George Burns's old quip that 'Acting is nothing but telling the truth. Now if you can fake that, you've got it made.' Audrey refused to fake it. 'She knew she had to experience the emotion before she was able to show it to the camera; and this took so much out of her that she could do it once, and once only, to her own satisfaction. Summoning up the feeling over and over again was impossible, or so she told me. Repeated takes only made it worse.' Directors customarily first shoot an overall view of the scene called a 'master', then take whatever medium shots or close-ups are needed. 'Audrey asked me if we couldn't do it the other way round, so that she was fresher when it came to do the close-ups. This was more difficult. It meant that we had to work out the action in detail and light the scene for the master shot, then undo it all and start with a close-up of Audrey. But if it meant she was better, I agreed.' Donen admired her all the more for owning up to her anxiety. Most stars, in his experience, would have covered up such a deficiency, if such it was, for a lifetime.

Another cause for concern emerged: Audrey suffered from vertigo in a mild form. Her first sequence with Astaire was in the bookshop, which he and a noisy horde of glamorous models invade with a view to doing the shoot there and then. Impatiently, without looking, Astaire trundles a tall ladder on wheels out of his way along the full length of the bookshelves. Perched on the ladder is Audrey, trembling with real nerves. Though slotted into runners, the ladder had to be additionally secured by invisible moorings before Audrey felt safe enough to do the scene. Even so, her expression of alarm as Astaire shoves at the ladder as though launching a boat is more real than simulated.

Richard Avedon acted as the film's colour consultant. One of his happiest touches, adopted with delight by Donen, gave Audrey's first scene in *Funny Face* its fairy-tale aura. This was the long floating veil on a straw hat left behind in the bookshop by Astaire's minions after the photo-shoot. Picking it up when all have gone Audrey dances with it, alone and totally entranced, as if it were a partner in her arms. Its chiffon weightlessness gives shape to her own suspended disbelief that all this is happening to her. It is one of the film's simplest and loveliest images.

Donen remembers having only one major difference of opinion with her, 'a rare moment of friction' which showed that Audrey's eye for detail was as sharp as her director's. Anything that looked, somehow, 'wrong' to Audrey created a disproportionate amount of heart-searching: 'In one of the dance numbers, she had to wear an all-black outfit—sweater, slacks, shoes. Black, you see, was the shade of choice of the trendy Parisian sect of poseurs we called the 'Empatheticalists" in the movie, a spoof on the then fashionable "Existentialists". With this all-black outfit I wanted Audrey to wear white socks, so as to draw the eye to her dance steps. She would not hear of such a thing. She was really shocked. She said it would ruin the line of her costume, be a distraction from the scene, damage the integrity of the dance number, my God, maybe ruin the film . . . all for a touch of white!'

They did a test shoot of Audrey performing the number with white socks, and without. Still they couldn't agree. 'When you get to that impasse,' says Donen, 'there's only one way to handle it. Just before we shot the scene for real, I went to Audrey's dressing room. She was very tense, expecting what was coming maybe. And I ordered—commanded—her to wear white socks. Period. She very nearly burst into tears. She looked miserable when she wasn't performing in front of the camera. For about four days—the time it took to shoot the solo number with her—she took direction impeccably, but was like a kitten who'd been spanked. But never once did she refuse to do what she was told, or create an "unhelpful" mood. And no trace of what thoughts I'm sure were seething in her mind appears in the sequence. She waited until she'd seen a rough assembly of it, then simply sent a note round to me. "You were right about the socks." That was all. Audrey was honourable. She was ready to defend her position to the death, because she knew what sweat it had cost her to reach it: but she was never paranoid about it.

'When she realized you appreciated her gifts and were doing all in your power to make her look as good as possible—and with Audrey that was very, very good—she entrusted herself to you completely. I admit, though, it was something she made you earn.'

During the filming of the *Funny Face* interiors Audrey lived with Mel in a house rented from the director Anatole Litvak. Litvak, though born in Russia, had made his reputation in Germany before emigrating to Hollywood, and would become another of those émigré European directors— Fred Zinnemann would also soon join the group—who formed a special working relationship with Audrey Hepburn which was part of Hollywood and yet, by reason of their common culture, distinct from it. Though Hollywood had always been a cosmopolitan town, it was becoming increasingly American in the post-war years. It is difficult to pin down the qualities that these collaborations brought to Audrey's work for, of course, the films she made for these directors had to conform to the demands of the big studios which financed them and fall within the experience and sympathies of the American public. The declining box-office appeal of Dietrich, until she recast herself in the American mould as the queen of the Last Chance Saloon in *Destry Rides Again,* showed the dangers now facing European imports—of which Audrey was one. Garbo had responded to the problem by retiring from the screen altogether. When one looks back at *Roman Holiday,* or *Sabrina,* and even at *Funny Face,* one senses the degree of sophistication that their makers brought to them. Stanley Donen, though a son of South Carolina and as native an American boy as ever appeared in the chorus line, had wide cultural interests and a strong bias towards Europe; he was to settle in Britain and make films there in the 1960s.

Audrey's gifts were not of the kind that Hollywood traditionally nourished; they were more common on the continent of Europe. She responded to her early European (or Europeanized) directors with freshness and trust, and they, in turn, recognized the quality of the material in their hands, found it responsive to their own cultural backgrounds and made the most of it while they could. They were aware that Hollywood was changing. The new generation of teenagers required its own icons—Brando, the short-lived James Dean, Monroe, Elizabeth Taylor, Sinatra. The new breed of independent producers, spurred on by television's abduction of habitual cinemagoers, would soon be making movies that reflected American social reality in ways that the old 'escapist' film factory had rarely seen the

133

need to do. Audrey was probably unaware that the scene was changing. She had come in at the tail end of a glorious harvest, and was profiting from the talents of ageing directors who gratefully seized on her to show that they still knew how to handle a commodity that was not quite Hollywood, nor yet entirely American—and was getting rarer all the time.

The *Funny Face* unit moved to Paris in April 1956 for the main location film. Audrey and Mel checked into the Hotel Raphael which was to be their home for the next few months. Mel would start work on the Jean Renoir film in a few days.

Margaret Gardner, a former freelance writer now working for the firm of Henry Rogers and his partner Warren Cowan, had been assigned by Rogers to take care of Audrey's public relations in Europe. She recalls the surprise awaiting her when she called at the Ferrers' hotel suite. Almost every piece of hotel furniture had been removed and replaced by furnishings belonging to Mel and Audrey. The entire style and atmosphere of the suite had been transformed. Pictures, rugs, sofa and chair coverings, table lamps, bedlinen, vases, cushions, silverware, crystal, tablecloths, decanters and drinks trays: all had been in store in Switzerland, awaiting the day when Audrey and her husband would have a home of their own (apart from the hotel chålet at Burgenstock which they still rented from Fritz Frey). As if she felt a growing need for roots, Audrey had decided to assemble a familiar world around her wherever her work allowed a lengthy stopover. From now on, this would be the pattern of Audrey's peripatetic life: grand hotels, elegant if anonymous suites, but the protective cordon of familiar bits and pieces around her to fill the void until her dearest wish, a child, arrived on the scene to give it a real sense of permanency.

In lieu of a family, Audrey took her 'home' with her: one she could unpack and reassemble. True to her meticulous nature, she kept itemized and numbered lists of everything she owned so that wherever she was, she had only to cable details of her requirements, thus 'coded', and the furniture would be in place when she arrived.

In interviews at this time Audrey admitted to 'underlying feelings of insecurity . . . Sometimes I think the more successful you become, the less secure you feel. This is kind of frightening, really.'

Yet Margaret Gardner felt that as Audrey was a very practical woman, able to mend fuses, fit taps with new washers and repair recalcitrant bits of machinery—including on one occasion, her tape recorder 'when it most embarrassingly broke down in mid-interview'—the rites of refurbishing her hotel suites were both a pleasure and a consolation. As well as recalling Audrey's artful manipulation of journalists during interviews, Gardner testifies to just how closely her client monitored press releases. 'She was a stickler for factual accuracy. Occasionally, if necessary, she would correct the spelling in even a rough draft.' Thus the phrase 'poured over the script' was quickly amended in Audrey's large, round schoolgirl handwriting to 'pored over the script' (a correction many a native-born English speaker might fail to notice). 'She had veto power over all photographs of herself and every production still in which she featured,' says Gardner, 'and she used it.' She did not give interviews while filming on set or location but this had more to do with keeping her concentration unbroken than with any airs and graces she gave herself. 'I never heard her utter a rude word or deliver a public reprimand,' says Margaret Gardner.

Paris was unseasonably cold and exceptionally rainy in the spring of 1956. With a suitably wintry smile Stanley Donen recalls ordering the firefighters to turn on their hoses and simulate rain in the Tuileries Gardens so that the footage of the previous day could be matched up with what he was now about to shoot—'on the rare dry day we got. It rained for twelve out of the fourteen days we shot outside.'

Audrey made good use of the time lost through bad weather. When rain stopped filming she rushed over to the studios of the Paris Opéra ballet for a 'refresher' session in the film's choreography. The unit itself was scarcely in one place for more than the few hours it took to set up its cameras and get the shot. Even with film extras pretending to be real 'flics' so as to keep sightseers out of the shot, it did not pay to stay too long in the same spot. The tourist season was getting under way and it cost a dizzying amount to close a French landmark to the public even for a few hours. 'It was the most start-stop-start schedule I've ever mounted,' Donen declares. Just like *Roman Holiday*.

Without split-second timing from Audrey, it could probably not have been accomplished so well. As she danced along one of the quais with the Grand Palais in the background, she had to keep to the choreography of her steps, lip-sync her prerecorded song, and still hit her mark so precisely that when the film extras on the upper bank leant over and shouted 'Bonjour', she, they and the Grand Palais would all be in the shot.

The most arresting sequence in *Funny Face* is a series of set ups, each of which ends in a freeze-frame, of Audrey modelling a collection of Givenchy clothes in a variety of Paris locations—a railway station, the flower market, the Louvre and so on—while Astaire imitates the fashion photographer's techniques that Richard Avedon had taught him. The freeze-frames of Audrey are enchantment caught on the wing. She became so proficient at 'modelling' that in the last shot of the sequence, when she comes out from behind the statue of *Winged Victory* at the top of the Louvre's grand staircase and runs down the steps with a red veil fluttering around her like her own pair of mythical wings, it is she who calls the shots, telling Astaire when to click the shutter. 'I was scared stiff I'd break my neck,' she said later, 'high heels, all those steps, Givenchy's full-length gown . . . Thank God, Fred got me in one . . . or do I mean Avedon? . . . or Stanley Donen? Oh, I forget who!' Paris reality and film fantasy had become one for her, which is how it appears in the movie.

Astaire had already had the challenge of playing opposite a much younger actress. The year before, he had made *Daddy Long Legs,* the story of a little orphan girl who discovers that her patron and surrogate lover is old enough to be her grandfather. By coincidence, his co-star on that occasion was Leslie Caron, at one time Audrey's virtual alter ego. But a comparison of the two films shows how much more he gave to Audrey. Towards Caron he adopts a tone of amused benevolence, charming in its slightly patronizing way. Between him and Audrey the tone is warmer, more impish, mutually magnetic. Physical love was out of bounds, of course, but the romance sometimes comes close to it. When the two of them discuss the 'Empatheticalist' philosophy, whose disciples project their feelings on to one another—Audrey being very grave and Astaire treating it with amused scepticism—he suddenly gives her a quick peck on the cheek. 'I put myself in your place,' he mischievously explains, 'and I felt you wanted to be kissed.' That's all there is to it, but it is a fleeting union that intimates what still could be.

Audrey's declaration of love for Astaire is likewise conveyed through the protective filter of stylization. As they twirl in each other's arms she is heard singing a snatch from 'S' Wonderful': 'You've made my life so glamorous / You can't blame me for feeling amorous.' Words do duty for deeds; atmosphere annihilates the age-gap. The photograph of Audrey used on the poster for the film is one that Avedon took of her, replicated by his alter ego Avery/Astaire in the dark-room scene: the infrared lighting is broken only when he turns on the lights to show Audrey on the printing paper, present only in the romanticized hints of her eyes, nose and lips. The film is, in a very real sense, an amorous photo-session of the utmost elegance and artfulness.

The hard sweat it all required rarely shows, and the most explicitly romantic number in fact proved to be the most exasperating one to shoot. All kinds of hitches arose before Fred and Audrey could dance off together. The location had been selected months before: a small hunting lodge in a meadow near Chantilly, which had been skilfully dressed to look like a rural chapel. An acre of grass grown specially in hothouses throughout the early spring had been laid in this fairy-tale setting, with its stream, wild flowers and mute swans looking as if they had glided up specially to see what was going on.

When the unit set up its lights and cameras they started to sink. Recent rains had waterlogged the turf. Audrey and Astaire found themselves frequently waltzing on bare earth, camouflaged by green paint and the slightly hazy filter on the camera lens but visible if one looks closely enough. 'It's like dancing uphill,' said Astaire. After slipping and skidding in what was intended to be an effortless dream sequence, Audrey suddenly cracked up with laughter: 'Here I've been waiting twenty years to dance with Fred Astaire, and what do I get? Mud in my eye!' Another snag was caused by— of all things—Audrey's underwear. As she and Fred waltzed on the 'lawn' the short white bridal gown from Givenchy kept floating up gracefully, just enough to show that her panties were pink. To avoid a colour clash at the climax of so meticulously coordinated a picture, Donen called a halt. An assistant drove furiously the eight miles into Chantilly, pulled up at a chain-store, dashed in and bought a single pair of white briefs—in a child's size— for the star. Thus, beneath the thousands of dollars of Givenchy couture that Audrey wore for the fade-out was 98 cents' worth of panties.

Baroness van Heemstra was now living in Paris, but true to the friendly but independent relationship between mother and daughter, she rarely came to watch Audrey filming with one of the legendary Hollywood stars. On one occasion when the baroness was present, for a scene in Montmartre, she was more concerned with her daughter's health than with her celebrity. Audrey, seeing a continuity girl shivering in the cool of the afternoon, impulsively stripped off the sheepskin jacket she herself was wearing over one of Givenchy's lightest creations and hung it round the girl's shoulders. The baroness said something reproving in Dutch. Audrey just laughed.

The baroness's visit, however, was notable for something other than motherly concern. This was one of the very rare occasions on which the tight-lipped woman whose injudicious political sympathies were now buried in the past, was persuaded to give an interview. Possibly the fact that the reporter was from the *Christian Science Monitor,* the lay organ of the baroness's own spiritual faith, elicited a more candid admission of her attitude to the recent war than she ever gave again. It flatly contradicts the hints that she was a Resistance heroine which had been scattered by publicists and were later perpetuated by some of her daughter's biographers.

Volney Hurd, of the *Monitor,* describes the baroness as 'a charming, dignified woman with vigorous-looking grey hair and clear blue eyes which contrast so strikingly with Audrey Hepburn's dark eyes . . . she is the essence of the gentlewoman.' Hurd continues: 'We talked about the war years. "We really came through it remarkably well," said the mother. "You see, instead of getting burdened down with the terrible picture of war occupation, I always took the attitude in all the day's work that there never had been nor was a war. You'd be surprised how much this positive attitude broke the spell, so that all kinds of things came to us at the right time from the most unexpected places." '

Hurd commented: 'Mrs Hepburn's [sic] eyes gave me a penetrating but smiling look. By this, I understood Mrs Hepburn to be expressing the conviction that life is spiritual and that mankind has the ability to prevent untamed occurrences, however drastic, from destroying the harmony of that life.'

This may be a revisionist view of the baroness's wartime memories, almost as thorough as her obliteration of the Fascist sentiments she had put her name to before the war. It certainly gives some idea of the strength of will that also sustained Audrey.

13

STRAINS AND STRESSES

W ORK on *Funny Face* ended in the first week of July 1956; but Audrey had no rest to look forward to. The Billy Wilder film, *Love in the Afternoon,* was ready to go almost immediately. She had a short break—really no more than a long weekend—at Burgenstock before flying to London to see friends, and then it was time to report back to Paris.

It was at this time that rumour insisted she was about to seek Swiss citizenship in order to avoid paying British taxes. They were steeper than anywhere else in Europe, and would soon be claiming 98 per cent from top earners like Audrey. She laughed that off, saying, 'I'm quite happy with my British passport.' This was being slightly frugal with the truth. Though she never did surrender her British nationality she now concluded arrangements that recognized Switzerland as her legal place of domicile. Noël Coward was the influence here. At the start of 1956 Coward had reluctantly decided to quit England and settle in Bermuda rather than pay the astronomical taxes levied on his earnings. 'You'd be a silly little ninny not to do the same,' he had told Audrey. Being in love with a cold climate, she preferred the Swiss Alps to the Caribbean; eventually, of course, Coward came to be her near neighbour. This arrangement meant Audrey could spend no more than three months in England in any tax year, but this was no hardship, as she had not spent even that time there since *Gigi.* The savings were enormous.

Mel was due to start work on an MGM film called *The Vintage,* a manhunt drama co-starring Pier Angeli, which was to be filmed on location in Provence and at the Victorine Studios near Nice. For once, Audrey, filming at the Studios de Boulogne in Paris, would not be by his side. She comforted herself with the thought that he wasn't far away. They would talk on the phone daily and join each other for weekends at the Hotel du Cap, Eden Roc, or further down the coast at St Tropez.

On the eve of the first day's shooting of *Love in the Afternoon,* a telegram was delivered to Audrey at the Raphael. 'How proud I would be, and full

of love I would be, if I really had a daughter like you—Maurice.' Maurice
Chevalier, then sixty-eight, was playing Audrey's father, a private detective
hired to keep tabs on an American playboy millionaire and unaware that the
mysterious woman whom the fellow is romancing is his own teenage
daughter. 'Actually,' Audrey said later, 'it would have made more sense for
Gary Cooper to have played my father and Chevalier my lover.' This wasn't
ungallant of her. Even Wilder was a bit worried by the lubricious twinkle
in the Frenchman's eye when what the plot called for was no more than a
paternal sparkle.

Gary Cooper, on the other hand, aged fifty-six, looked and seemed
older than his years. Though Cooper was notoriously laconic, he was a fervent womanizer and his lined, indeed haggard face suggested that his pursuit of the opposite sex in his declining years was taking a physical toll. He
kept this propensity for philandering well concealed behind the mask of the
strong, silent man of conscience that he had developed in Westerns and in
the populist comedies of the 1930s like *Mr Deeds Goes to Town*. There was a
sexy Gary Cooper, of course, which Lubitsch had put to good use, but Billy
Wilder was aware that the age gap between him and Audrey would need
the most careful attention if it were not to acquire undertones of the recently published novel *Lolita*.

Fortunately, Wilder realized, Cooper's talent for straight-faced, if not
strait-laced, comedy could be enlisted if the script were remodelled by him
and his collaborator, I. A. L. Diamond, along the lines of the one they had
written for Lubitsch in 1936, in which Cooper had played a seven-times
married American millionaire pursuing Claudette Colbert. As in the earlier film, so in *Love in the Afternoon:* Audrey frustrates her Casanova until he
becomes—almost—a reformed man. Only now, instead of having a combative flirt like Colbert as the opposition, Wilder had a heroine who behaved herself with the serene composure of a self-confident schoolgirl. It
would work, he was sure.

Truant and pert, Audrey bubbles along, sticking her oval chin out as if
to invite love, then putting up her guard just in time. Cooper of course sees
through the adolescent affectations that are part of her arsenal of seduction.
He spots the child beneath. But what this man of the world doesn't see are
the wiles that she unscrupulously uses to disarm him. She flatters Cooper
by arousing his masculinity and at the same time protects herself by bringing out his better nature, producing the effect that one critic described as
'feeling like Red Riding Hood gobbling up the wolf'. Just as Gregory Peck
in *Roman Holiday* was put in touch with his decent self—by not exposing
the princess's follies—so Cooper, too, is turned inside out and likes him-

self the better for it. The rake's progress is towards a recuperative affection. Or so we can believe, if we wish.

The film was to draw fire from critics whose imagination led them beyond the end credits aboard the train into which the roué has snatched this captivating child at the fade-out, albeit with her father's blessing. What might they be getting up to together? American audiences (and moral censors) had to be reassured by a conciliatory end title which stated firmly that Audrey and Cooper got married. European audiences, assumed to be more sophisticated (or decadent), were left free to speculate. Either way, salaciousness was sidestepped by being postponed until all the parties to it were safely off-screen.

As he had done in *Sabrina,* Billy Wilder gave Audrey the reading he wanted and she returned the lines with the exact degree of wide-eyed aplomb needed for a girl who covers her own astonishment at the world with an expression that suggests nothing would surprise her. A difficult double: but Audrey's peculiar gifts create some of the finest light comedy since Lubitsch.

Making the movie was no picnic. Even the picnic in the film, on an island in the river Chevreuse, serenaded by the troupe of violinists whom the millionaire hires as a movable orchestra for his seductions, proved a trial rather than a treat. The day's shooting was first delayed by ground fog—in August!—and then by mosquitoes which had everyone, including the players, cocking an ear for their telltale whine. Finally, the drone of Orly-bound aircraft necessitated innumerable retakes. 'Never was a seducer's work so hard,' Cooper cracked, as he was required to uncork the champagne for the fourth or fifth time, while Audrey gnawed on yet another chicken leg and wished the location chef had heeded her pleas to hold back on the garlic.

She found Cooper attractive, though hardly in the way he might have hoped. Playing opposite a man old enough to be her father restored a little of her lost childhood. Chevalier did not have the same appeal. Indeed he held very little attraction for her or for anyone working on the film.

Chevalier was lucky to be in the movie for it helped him regain some of the popularity he had lost following his wartime 'accommodation' with the Germans: he was not a collaborator but it was felt that he had made himself a little too much at home on the uncomfortable ground occupied by those who entertained the enemy. His English was good, but almost too smooth for the part. Wilder was forever begging him to 'put back some French' into his accent. The crew regarded him, with some justice, as a tightwad. Audrey had the *déjà-vu* experience of seeing Chevalier being left out of the cocktail gathering that Wilder presided over at the end of the day, just as the rebarbative Humphrey Bogart had been during *Sabrina*.

When the musical version of *Gigi* came to be made by Vincente Minnelli in 1957, there was general surprise that Audrey was not reprising the role that had made her famous. She usually replied that it clashed with other commitments but that was not the only reason she allowed the part to go to Leslie Caron. She did not want to work again with Chevalier who was cast as Uncle Honoré. Professionally, she admired him. How could she not? Personally, his brand of flirtatiousness seemed too close to the real thing for comfort. She also found the attitude he so carefully cultivated, which seemed to say there was more to him than appeared on the screen, far too regal. Perhaps, too, Audrey's inherited reluctance to look back in life had its part in her refusal to replay the past and appear again as Gigi, even if it now came with words and music.

Audrey was not in the best of moods during *Love in the Afternoon*. Mel's absence, filming with Pier Angeli in the South of France, brought home to her how much she depended on him. Even with her possessions around her the suite at the Hôtel Raphael seemed empty without his continuous activity: calling the West Coast for long phone conversations with Frings about movies to star in or possibly direct; sounding out publishers on the rights of books he had read and impresarios about plays for Audrey and himself; or simply gossiping his multilingual way through an address book almost as thick as a volume of the Paris telephone directory. Just before he left Paris he had bought a Yorkshire terrier, in the hope that this tiny companion would ease their enforced separation. It was a fractious little dog that had its master's restlessness, and few took to it save Audrey who adored it. She christened it 'Famous' and kept it on a couple of yards of bright red ribbon whenever she took it out. Some people were disconcerted to see a grown woman, and one as intelligent and apparently self-assured as Audrey, lavishing such extreme affection on this minute creature. It is easy to imagine that it was receiving the mother-love Audrey had not as yet been able to give to the children she yearned for. She was paying visits to a gynaecologist over these months, hopeful of another and more successful pregnancy.

Overwork was catching up with her. She spent a little longer than usual at the cocktail parties thrown by Billy Wilder and drank rather more than was customary—Mel wasn't there to switch her whisky-and-soda for a glass of milk. Perhaps it was seeing the result of this on her bathroom scales, compounded by guilt and worry over Mel's absence, that brought on a mild attack of anorexia. She lost seven pounds within a week or so. At

The marriage that never was: With James (later Lord) Hanson, the British industrialist to whom Audrey was engaged in the early 1950s. After they called it off, she said: 'I was also in love with my work.' Work proved the more seductive suitor.

Princess and commoner. Audrey in her Oscar-winning role as the royal personage who plays truant on a visit to Rome; tastes the joys of eating ice-cream on the Spanish Steps; and the more erratic excitement of taking Gregory Peck's newsman for a motor-scooter ride. 'She was as funny as she was beautiful,' Peck said. She was also an instant star.

Mentors and pupil. From these two directors, skilled in Hollywood's star-making ways and Europe's sophisticated taste, Audrey learned her craft. Billy Wilder (left) directed her in *Sabrina* and *Love in the Afternoon*; William Wyler (right) in *Roman Holiday, The Loudest Whisper* and *How to Steal a Million.*

In *Sabrina,* with co-star William Holden. Off-screen the romance continued more seriously. But Audrey broke off the relationship on learning that Holden could not have children.

Sabrina time: a studio portrait.

Leading man in her life: Audrey and Mel Ferrer, the thrice-wed, 37-year-old star of *Lili*, twelve years her senior but in every way – it seemed to Audrey – the perfect partner. Others thought differently, and labelled him 'a prickly Svengali'.

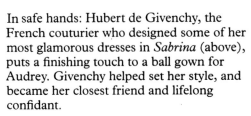

In safe hands: Hubert de Givenchy, the French couturier who designed some of her most glamorous dresses in *Sabrina* (above), puts a finishing touch to a ball gown for Audrey. Givenchy helped set her style, and became her closest friend and lifelong confidant.

Bachelor girl: a small flat in Beverly Hills was Audrey's modest habitat while preparing for *Sabrina*. She soon exchanged the California life-style for wider horizons.

Receiving the Oscar, still in her *Ondine* makeup.

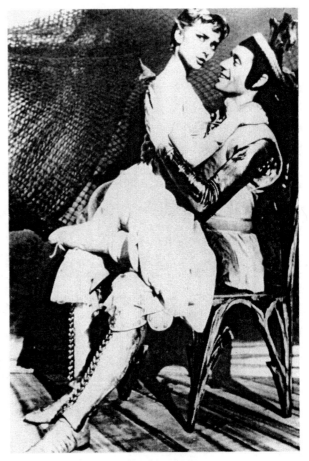

Nymph and knight: in *Ondine* on Broadway, in 1954, with Mel Ferrer. But by now she had discovered that 'success is like reaching an important birthday and finding out you're exactly the same.' What mattered to her more was ... Mel.

'If I get married, I want to be *very* married.' The 'if' became a 'when' on 25 September 1954. Mel and Audrey walk across a Swiss pasture in their wedding clothes.

this time, too, she fell out with the Hôtel Raphael, allegedly because she could not get her favourite cocktail, a martini, mixed exactly to her liking, and moved into a service apartment—entailing the packing and unpacking of her personal furnishings—and then into another hotel where the barman mixed the drinks to the proportions she decreed. It was uncharacteristic behavior for Audrey.

It was obvious to friends that a void had opened up in her life with alarming suddenness. She became withdrawn, and even more insistent that all publicity work be minutely prepared in advance. 'She was never bad-tempered,' says Henry Rogers: and Margaret Gardner adds, 'She never made difficulties, but you knew she meant business. She was always polite to interviewers, but the conversation was kept to the point—the picture she was finishing, never her personal life.' Not so long ago, with touching meekness, she had called journalists 'sir', deferring to their professionalism and flattered by their interest. Now an interview with Audrey was not unlike an audience with royalty—more relaxed, of course, but demanding a deference from the journalist appropriate to the discreetness of the star.

Political events may have accounted for some of her reclusiveness. In the early autumn of 1956 street violence erupted in Paris in protest at the Russian invasion of Hungary. The Soviet Embassy was stoned and fire-bombed. It became difficult to move around the centre of the city. One of the crew on *Love in the Afternoon* was hit by a missile and died later in hospital. Concern for Audrey's safety meant she had to travel with an armed bodyguard and make a wide detour of likely trouble-spots to reach the film studios. Wilder speeded up work, hoping to get them all out of Paris earlier than scheduled. Mel Ferrer was now in Hollywood finishing *The Vintage,* whose distinctly unpromising prospects were made shakier by several panicky changes of title—from the original one to *Purple Harvest,* then to *Harvest Thunder,* and then, despairingly, back again to *The Vintage.* Mel was on the telephone at every convenient moment, calling Audrey or imploring MGM to rush him through his remaining scenes so that he could rejoin his wife.

Things worsened with the invasion of Egypt by British and French forces in retaliation for Nasser's nationalization of the Suez Canal. There were more street demonstrations in Paris and fuel shortages occurred overnight. As Israel joined the anti-Nasser forces, real fear developed of the war spreading to Europe. United Artists made block bookings on airlines almost daily so that the stars of the Wilder film could be evacuated to the safety of America. Baroness van Heemstra telephoned her daughter from London to report that she had seen the first casualties of the war arriving at ports in England. All of this reminded Audrey only too vividly of the last months of the Second World War.

The various crises mercifully subsided about the time *Love in the Afternoon* wound up. Mel returned to Paris from Los Angeles on a Scandinavian airline, one of the nations that had declared neutrality in the Egyptian conflict. The world events had given him and Audrey a shock, making Switzerland seem more of a haven than ever. They were committed to attending the London premiere of *War and Peace* on 16 November, but agreed to keep the date only provided that a collection was made for the Hungarian Red Cross. 'The film has an interval,' said Audrey, 'let's put it to some good use.'

Audrey's arrival in London disclosed a change in her appearance: one considered so radical by the press that it almost stole the headlines from the epic film she had come to promote. The urchin hairdo to which she had reverted for *Funny Face* was gone, and in its place was the soft, sweeping pageboy with a centre parting which Grazia di Rossi had designed for the well-brought-up music student of *Love in the Afternoon*. 'I thought people might have got tired seeing me in the old style,' she explained. 'Now I have decided to keep this new look, even off the set.' Age had something to do with it, too. The new cut was more in keeping with a woman of twenty-seven.

The mixed reception of *War and Peace* was the first jarring note in Audrey's seemingly effortless ascent. She awaited the opening of *Funny Face* with some concern. Mel Ferrer, too, had his career worries and these were rather more real than Audrey's. His last few films had been either in a foreign language or, if American-financed, made in Europe: either way they were outside the Hollywood mainstream where stardom is gained and sustained. Mel had come within sight of real success in *Lili*, but that was several years ago, and even then he was regarded as a good leading man rather than star material. Asked about Mel's chances of stardom, the director Herbert Wilcox rated them low: 'They [the public] do not go for lean types with thin hair.' (Unless, of course, they could dance like Astaire.)

There was always the possibility of Mel's co-starring with Audrey, yet this kind of pairing was contrary to Hollywood custom. The reason that producers usually gave for rejecting such a pairing was that stars who were married to each other had a diminished curiosity value when they appeared in movies cast as lovers. They held no real surprises for the fans—certainly not as many as a couple who were not husband and wife but who became lovers in the course of shooting and continued their affair during the publicity build-up before the film's release.

For all these reasons, Mel had not done his career the favour that his detractors alleged by marrying Audrey. As things turned out, professionally he was going to be the loser by the decision he and Audrey had made not to allow work to separate them. For Audrey this agreement was still an essential part of life with her husband. She said at the time of the *War and Peace* premiere, 'Whether we work together or not, we shall avoid long partings at all costs. We haven't done so badly so far—only two months' separation all told in two years of marriage.'

But whether they recognized it or not—and the likelihood is they did not, with Audrey still receiving so many film offers which required Mel's trusted advice and assistance—a not uncommon Hollywood phenomenon was about to drive a wedge between them. As in the plot of *A Star Is Born,* while one partner's stellar career continued to rise, the other's began to dip. An event now occurred that made their professional relationship even more problematical.

They spent Christmas 1956 at La Quinta, California, relaxing at Anatole Litvak's home before joining the director in New York early in the New Year for a television film in which they would both star: a lavish ninety-minute production for NBC entitled *Mayerling.* It was to be shot in New York over eighteen days in February 1957. Audrey's fee was $157,000 (about £30,000), then a record for television drama. Her considerable hesitation about appearing on television had been finally overcome by the reassurance that all the elements of the package seemed to generate. *Mayerling* was an almost exact copy of the French film of the same title that Litvak had directed in 1936 with Charles Boyer and Danielle Darrieux playing the Crown Prince Rudolf von Habsburg, heir to the Austro-Hungarian Empire, and his mistress, Marie Vetseva, who ended their lives in a suicide pact in 1888. It had been an international success, doing particularly well with American audiences. The new version with Audrey and Mel would co-star Raymond Massey and Diana Wynyard, have a cast of over a hundred, and incorporate special material that Litvak had shot in Vienna after Audrey and Mel had committed to the project. What could go wrong?

What went wrong was the all-important chemistry between the star-crossed lovers. Mel and Audrey, it seemed, did not have what it took—or what was expected of them—to be convincing as lovers in one of the great *affaires* of history. Audrey got by on the strength of her beauty and aristocratic grace; critics didn't question her courtesan credentials too closely. But the reviews of Mel's performance were embarrassing. Although at thirty-nine he was only two years older than Charles Boyer had been, and certainly he bore a closer physical resemblance to the dashing Crown Prince, he signally failed to generate the romantic obsession that was the driving force of this tragic *folie à deux*. He and Audrey behaved like a husband and wife rather than a couple locked into a suicide pact. 'The lovers seemed more fated to bore each other to death,' said one review. That was the general opinion. Even Litvak put up a very weak defence. 'It is very difficult to get Mel to treat her roughly,' he said apologetically, 'I had to work with him to get him to do it.' That may have been to the credit of the Ferrers' marriage but it hardly inspired the confidence needed for them to be cast together in a major movie. Audrey had been trying to persuade Paramount to co-star her with Mel in a film of Thomas Wolfe's novel, *Look Homeward, Angel.* After *Mayerling,* the studio turned that down, saying tactfully that perhaps the part of Laura was too small for a star of Audrey's magnitude.

She herself showed her good sense in turning down several pictures at this point in her career, among them a version of Françoise Sagan's *A Certain Smile* (Jean Negulesco was obliged to import a French starlet, Christine Carrère, with small success) and the role of Maria the nun who became governess to seven Von Trapp children, in the non-singing, non-dancing version of the story that would become *The Sound of Music.* And once again she turned down *The Diary of Anne Frank* even though the importunate George Stevens brought along Anne's father, who broke Audrey's heart with his account of his child's captivity. Stevens went on to make the film with the ingénue talents of Millie Perkins: it was a disaster.

Most stars turn down more films than they ever make and Audrey was no exception. In the case of *Zuleika Dobson,* it was Audrey who proposed, and was turned down. *Zuleika* was not a film project: it was a stage version of Max Beerbohm's satirical novella set in the Edwardian era, about a captivating beauty who bewitches the undergraduates of Oxford to the extent that they commit mass suicide for her in the River Isis. Diane Cilento, star of the musical version in London, had been unable to obtain a green card to work in the United States and Audrey was strongly attracted by the idea of returning to Broadway in the role. She still hankered after a stage career that could run parallel with her film work, believing that Mel's talents as a director would find an outlet there more easily than in Hollywood films. But she made one condition: she wanted Laurence Harvey as her co-star.

Harvey, then twenty-nine, Lithuanian-born but British by upbringing, style and temperament, had a growing reputation as a leading man, and Audrey had seen and liked him in both the Anglo-Italian version of *Romeo and Juliet* and, especially, as the Christopher Isherwood figure in *I Am a Camera.* Two years later, *Room at the Top* was to make him an international star. Harvey appealed to Audrey because, in some ways, he resembled Mel Ferrer:

he had great self-confidence, an opinionated manner that was often witty and sometimes scathing, limited but real talent as an actor though without the mysterious chemistry that would make him a star, and the capacity to make himself attractive to women of intelligence. He was also uninhibited in what he said and how he said it and although Audrey's own expletives rarely went beyond 'Shoot!' or 'Damn!' she was not at all put off by a man who sprinkled his table-talk with four-letter words. Her own father had had an Irishman's command of barroom vocabulary. She liked Harvey's malicious sharpness, forgave him his narcissism and probably did not know of his bisexuality or care, if she did. Audrey had the broad-mindedness of those who refuse to judge others.

It would have been interesting to see what she and Harvey would have made of *Zuleika,* but it was not to be. James Woolf, the film producer who was Harvey's mentor and in large measure responsible for his career, vetoed the project on the irrefutable grounds that, as the title suggested, the female role would dominate the play. If this seems a trivial objection, it is worth remembering that an even bigger star than Harvey had come near to turning down a musical version of *Pygmalion* because it was then entitled *Lady Liza.* When it was given a possessive emphasis by being changed to *My Fair Lady,* Rex Harrison changed his mind.

Meanwhile, Mel's plans to turn independent film-maker were not bearing fruit. He agreed to direct a drama very much like *The Vintage* in plot and atmosphere, entitled *The Black Virgin of Gold Mountain*—even Louella Parsons said, 'Some title!'—and recommended signing an eighteen-year-old Franco-Italian actress, Jacqueline Sassard, whom he had met and taken to while working in Nice. But the project was put into turnaround and sold, mysteriously, to Carol Reed who, perhaps fortunately, did not make it either. Then it was announced that Mel would direct Brigitte Bardot in *Venus and the Cat.* That fell through. So did an admittedly uncertain invitation to direct Cecil Beaton's play *The Gainsborough Girls* on Broadway. Even after constant rewrites by Beaton over a period of six years, this vanity production failed to cross the Atlantic after its ignominious first-night flop in England in 1951: another lucky escape for Mel.

Instead he accepted the last-minute offer of a role in *The Sun Also Rises,* which was to be shot in Madrid followed by Mexico City and the colonial town of Morelia. This decided Audrey's plans. They were simple: she was going to do nothing for a year. Her announcement, plus the news that she would be accompanying Mel to Mexico had a predictable effect on the press—she must be going to have a baby! 'No, no,' the surprised Audrey protested firmly, if vainly, 'one wouldn't go to a way-off place like Mexico [to have a baby].' Almost as an afterthought she made an observation that showed the strain she had been under. 'Up until now, Mel and I have been working hard and living our lives in hotels . . . We have been married two years and haven't even set up house. A home is necessary to a happy marriage.' And a home, she implied, had to come before a family.

The truth was, Audrey was caught in an ever-tightening web of career commitments. Try as she might, she could not break out of them to set herself up in a life that was not ruled by production plans and shooting schedules. She was by nature a determinedly private person; yet she had next to no private life, no place she could call home, no children she could call a family. Time was passing. Although she was not yet thirty, she knew that each passing year she devoted to film-making—by its nature a protracted occupation that couldn't be interrupted for child-bearing—shortened the joyous span of motherhood. There were medical problems, the nature of which she never divulged: if the cure for them might be no more complicated than simply to slow down and relax and rest, this nevertheless was not going to resolve her problems quickly.

So it was without any regret at not having a movie to make that Audrey accompanied Mel to Mexico City and then to Morelia, deep in the hinterland, with sophisticated facilities for foreigners who loved its clear air and high altitude. It was from Apartment 152 of the Villa San Jose hotel compound in Morelia that she sent a letter—undated, but probably in mid-April 1957—to Roger Edens. 'How happy I am and what a relief,' it began. 'I say "relief" because of the nasty scare *Time* gave me.' She was no doubt referring to the review of *Funny Face* which had appeared in the magazine's April issue. It had begun ambivalently, comparing the film by which Audrey set such hopes and in which she had invested so much of her singing and dancing talents to 'one of those big Technicolor musicals that staggers towards the culminating nuptials like a determined but over-equipped bride'. It continued in a hardly less ominous vein: 'The thesis [is] that Audrey Hepburn is really just a dud who can wear duds. It is a hard one to credit—"Clothes for the Woman Who Is Not Interested in Clothes." ' But then *Time* had to modulate its scepticism into grudging but genuine admiration, calming the flutter of alarm it had prompted in Audrey's heart. '[She] not only looks her limpid best from first to last; she also does some pretty snazzy dancing (though not with Astaire) and even manages to sing quite effectively in a sort of absinthetic *Sprechtstimme* with a touch of wood alcohol in the low notes.' This notice, almost a parody of *Time* style, was slightly cooler than had been hoped for; but it was reassuring, and the rest of the reviews were lavish in their praise.

Audrey had put herself firmly back at the centre of the critics' admiration and, as time proved, the public's affection. The final cut of *Love in the Afternoon* was being screened and advance reports assured her she had nothing to worry about there, either. Audrey's letter to Roger Edens reflects the ease of mind, calmness and contentment she had regained: '[This place] is a settlement of cottages scattered around a sloping garden of bougainvillea, geranium roses and trees—you can eat the salads and drink the water! Hot sun by day, cold nights and of course the altitude makes you feel like a million dollars. What I really like is *no telephone*. The perfect place for a real rest. PS. Famous loves it here. Can scamper in the garden all day.'

14

A GOLDEN VEIL

---

*A*UDREY'S sense of well-being in Mexico was fostered by more than good reviews for *Funny Face*. While in New York in January 1957 she had signed a letter of intent to make a movie that Kurt Frings had been urging on her for some time. It was called *The Nun's Story* and was to be directed by Fred Zinnemann.

The terms were anything but austere. Though the fee of $200,000 (£75,000) was far less than Audrey had received on her last two films, this was only a beginning: she was to get ten per cent of the gross box-office receipts—that is to say, from the first dollar earned—after her fee had been recouped. The film would eventually cost $3.5 million—a large budget at that time for a non-epic—but it was to earn this many, many times over in profit. Audrey took full advantage of her star status. She demanded that her 'parent' company, Associated British, should guarantee the fee in the event of *The Nun's Story* failing at the box-office—and she had their guarantee notarized before she signed the contract.

In addition to all her now customary rights of approval she recommended to Fred Zinnemann a number of artists and technicians with whom she had worked 'comfortably' on *War and Peace*. Zinnemann, a native of Vienna, just turning fifty and with proven artistic and box-office success after such films as *From Here to Eternity* and *High Noon,* was no stranger to Audrey. He also had hoped to direct her in a film of *War and Peace* using the Todd-AO-Scope ultra-wide-screen process developed by Mike Todd, who was to be the producer. That project folded abruptly the moment Zinnemann read that de Laurentiis had cast Mel Ferrer as Prince Andrei in his version. Zinnemann guessed, correctly, that 'this meant that Audrey was automatically set to play Natasha'. Now the curious eddies of international film production had carried his star back to him.

The Nun's Story, which Warner Bros. were producing, was based on a novel by a former lawyer, Kathryn Hulme. Though cast as fiction, it closely followed the experiences of a real nun in a small Belgian nursing order who had renounced her vows after seventeen years' work as a missionary among the lepers of the Belgian Congo. She had left her order early in the Second World War to play an active role in the Belgian Resistance. The theme of both book and film was the conflict between conscience and obedience, the sacredness of the spiritual vows being tested against the pressures of the secular world and found wanting. Sister Luke, as she is called, chooses to live for herself, not for Christ or the Church. Understandably the novel was frowned on by the Roman Catholic hierarchy. It was, at the very least, a bad recruiting poster.

The book had reached Zinnemann by an unlikely route. Gary Cooper had sent it to him by way of a favour in return for the new lease of life *High Noon* had given its star (and its genre) on the cinema screen. Its attraction for Cooper is unknown, but it struck an immediate chord of sympathy with Zinnemann, a film-maker whose own conscience had felt the pressures of Hollywood several times already in his life. Though recognizing its commercial potential, Warner Bros. were initially wary of the project—the Catholic Church was still able to bring its weight of disapproval to bear at the box-office of films that seriously offended against morality or the orthodox faith—until Audrey said she would do it. Could such a movie be irreverent, much less blasphemous, with Audrey Hepburn warranting its sincerity? Of course not! Could it be profitable? Of course!

It is often assumed that Audrey agreed to do the film because she was attracted by the parallel between her own childhood in war-torn Belgium and Sister Luke's role in the underground battle against the German occupation. There is no truth in this. As with *The Diary of Anne Frank,* Audrey saw herself as unworthy to step into the shoes of a real-life heroine, refused to 'borrow' someone else's suffering in order to enhance her own status. Her willingness to do the film arose from a more interesting coincidence. The author, Kathryn Hulme, had been commandant of a camp for displaced persons which the United Nations Rehabilitation and Relief Administration set up in post-war Germany. To this camp had come the real-life Sister Luke, now a civilian nurse whose name was Marie-Louise Habets, and the novel had grown out of the close friendship formed by the two women. For Audrey, filming such a story was a way of paying tribute to UNRRA's work in saving lives, including possibly her own, in the months immediately following the end of the war. Any lingering hesitation was dispelled when she was told that the Second World War scenes were to be dropped. The reasons were not only running time but also the desire to stress the nun's moral struggle, not the wartime one. 'That pleases me,' said Audrey, as unwilling as ever to speak about those years.

As a Christian Scientist she was not unduly troubled by playing a Roman Catholic nun who broke her vows. Conscience, not dogma, always came first with Audrey. In any case, she was assured that the film could not easily be made without the agreement and, it was hoped, the practical assistance from some broad-minded members of the Church. It became the task of both Zinnemann and his producer, Henry Blanke, to locate suitable 'vocational consultants' and arrange for Audrey's introduction to the spiritual rites and obligations of the nun she would be playing. Reassuring, too, was the absence of sex in the book and film script. Though there is a very powerful sexual undertow generated by an Italian surgeon, Dr Fortunati, at the Belgian mission hospital, the tension derives from Sister Luke's resistance to a physical relationship with him. Thus Audrey, in her first venture into something other than a Cinderella fantasy or a literary classic, would not have to test her as yet untarnished innocence and chastity against the demands of physical love—and a forbidden love at that. Gérard Philipe was considered for the role of Dr Fortunati but withdrew because he was dissatisfied with its size. Yves Montand demanded an even higher fee than Audrey was getting. Jack Hawkins, Audrey's preference, was unavailable. The final choice was Peter Finch who, just turned forty and able to project sensitivity combined with sensuality, had proven himself a serviceable leading man in *A Town Like Alice* and several other outdoor adventures. He had romantic looks of a kind alternatively described as weatherbeaten or hungover; either way, he gave the impression of a man who knew what was available in life and didn't scruple to help himself.

There is no record that Mel Ferrer was considered for the Fortunati role. Though he was equipped to carry it off professionally, Warner Bros. might have feared that satisfactory sexual and spiritual frictions would not be generated if the star playing the nun were known to be married to the player cast as her potential seducer. Moreover, Ferrer had another and, to him, more important mission on hand: one in which Audrey was intimately involved.

The history of *The Nun's Story* is unusually well documented in hundreds of letters, memoranda and cables that passed between Warner Bros. in Hollywood and Zinnemann and others preparing production in Europe and Central Africa. In the late autumn of 1957—the film was to be Warner Bros.' major production in 1958—cables to and from Zinnemann make reference to Audrey's increasing anxiety, not over the film's start—which had been set for January—but over its likely finish date. This eventually caused real alarm that she might withdraw, using the failure to let her know this crucial date as a reason for breaking her contract. Eventually Zinnemann sent a cable from Rome—the production had its offices at Cinecittà—to Steve Trilling at Warner Bros. Dated 6 November 1957, this communication stated the problem in blunt terms: 'Believe we are courting disaster if Audrey left unaware finishing date much longer. Will decline all responsibility for picture unless Audrey fully aware of true situation. Find myself increasingly unable to cope with endless uncertainty.' The reason for Audrey's uncharacteristic fractiousness must have been very serious for a man as iron-nerved as Zinnemann to infuse a message with such anxiety.

It was. On the finish date for *The Nun's Story* hinged the date for the film Audrey was gambling would put her husband's career back into play, namely *Green Mansions*. She owed MGM a film after that studio had agreed to let Roger Edens and Stanley Donen take *Funny Face* over to Paramount. Now Audrey had personally gone to see Sol Siegel, head of production at MGM, and told him she would star in *Green Mansions* provided Mel Ferrer was hired to direct. It was her generous return for Mel's support in those early years when his command of Hollywood manoeuvring had helped turn Audrey from a compliant pawn into an independent power. Now she had placed her own stardom on the line to back a film that, frankly, MGM didn't give a damn about. The project had been mentioned briefly in an interview which Audrey and Mel gave Hedda Hopper in August 1957.

Mel Ferrer had asked Hopper, 'Do you think Audrey could play Rima in *Green Mansions?*' In her printed reply the columnist said, 'I told him I hadn't thought of it, but now that he'd brought it up I thought she was the only one who could play her.' That was flattering, but Hopper added, 'But she'd have to make the picture before having a baby. Rima can't have any maternal look about her.' Mel pondered this in silence. Later in the interview Hopper asked Audrey, 'When are you going to start a family of your own?' The star replied, 'Any time,' which might have meant anything. The truth was, she wanted a baby as desperately as ever; and she was caused some pain when Hopper's frankness found its way into print for everyone to read. Having committed herself to *The Nun's Story* she had an additional reason why she could not try to start a family. All the same, Hopper's observation stayed with Audrey and worked its way into her thoughts every time she fretted over the lack of a finish date for *The Nun's Story*—and a start date for *Green Mansions*. On both dates depended, in a very real sense, the possibility of her becoming a mother for the first time.

Green Mansions was based on the once celebrated work by W. H. Hudson, a pantheistic evocation of the still undefiled wilderness of nineteenth-century South America as seen through the hallucinatory eyes of a naturalist who encounters a strange and lovely native girl, Rima, the spirit of the place and the guardian of its flora and fauna. Rima the wood-sprite is cousin to Ondine the water-nymph. In both cases contact with a personage from the alien world leads to death, though this time it is the girl who perishes, sacrificed in the despoliation of her forest and her innocence. The novel had come near to being filmed several times since RKO had bought the rights for Dolores Del Rio back in the 1930s. Most recently, in 1953, it had been considered as a vehicle for Pier Angeli, with Alan J. Lerner writing the script and Vincente Minnelli directing. Each time, budgetary considerations and box-office uncertainties had caused the project to founder. The heroine had to be of almost transparent virtue and spirituality: which ruled out all the current sex goddesses. Gradually the story of Rima had dropped out of fashion, then out of sight—until Audrey's offer to star in it gave it the green light. Having secured MGM's agreement to produce the film, Audrey and Mel were naturally anxious not to let the front office's interest wane. Hence the fretfulness conveyed in the cable from Rome to Hollywood.

Green Mansions meant a very great deal to Mel professionally. His part in *The Sun Also Rises,* which had taken them to Mexico for several months, had not given his reputation the boost he had hoped. In Peter Viertel's adaptation of Hemingway's novel, the character of Robert Cohn, the Jewish drifter around the bullrings of 1930s Spain, had been stripped of the Semitic traits that lent it colour, leaving Mel little to play with except, as Viertel said, 'a diffident aloofness'. Mel made a stronger contribution to the production by suggesting a French singer for the role of a prostitute in the film: and thus Darryl F. Zanuck met Juliette Greco. Once *The Sun Also Rises* was finished, Mel and Audrey had headed back to Europe where Mel was to film a predictable disaster entitled *Fraülein,* directed by Henry Koster, set in East Germany and financed by 'frozen' German marks, and co-starring Dana Wynter as a Greek professor's daughter who is reluctantly rescued from life in a brothel by a post-war knight errant in a US officer's cap—none other than Mel. His performance on this occasion was described as 'restrained to the point of apathy'.

Though it was her sabbatical year, Audrey was far from idle. She used every hour away from Mel to prepare for her role in *The Nun's Story,* which was due to start production on 1 January 1958.

It was Fred Zinnemann's idea that Audrey and her co-stars, Peggy Ashcroft (as a Mother Superior) and Edith Evans (as the Mother-General of the order), should spend several days in a convent, witnessing and wherever permissible participating in the nuns' ritual observances, from prayers at 5.30 a.m. until vespers and retirement for the night. The search for a religious order that would allow this showed the stubbornness or flexibility of the various Roman Catholic orders they approached. In Paris, they were 'liberal, intelligent, relaxed', according to Zinnemann: in Belgium, 'suspicious and almost hostile': in Italy, 'the opposition . . . was as concrete as a stone wall.'

Audrey backed Zinnemann's search for authenticity to the full. She was well aware that *The Nun's Story* would mark a vital transition in her career from gamine girlhood to mature womanhood. She approached the role with the concentration and humility of a genuine postulant, learning Latin prayers to get the feel of the liturgy. She acquainted herself with every detail of a nun's habit—the fact that the veil left only a small triangle of her face on which she had to show a range of complex emotions was a major worry. She practised the rituals of the services, saying the rosary and genuflecting, and put on a nun's habit to discover what it felt like to walk about in public as a representative of a holy order. She even visited a hospital to watch nuns assisting the doctors in the operating theatre. She also flew to Los Angeles to meet Marie-Louise Habets, the nun on whom the character of Sister Luke was based, and spent several hours with her at Kathryn Hulme's home. This friendship was soon to be repaid.

As to costumes, there was little Givenchy could do for a nun's habit. But he gave his blessing to the sketches that Audrey showed him. By December 1957 it had still not been decided whether to shoot the film in black and white or colour. Zinnemann wanted to use both: monotone for the early sequences set in Europe, then deeply saturated colour to dramatize the exotic and sensuous nature of Central Africa. Jack L. Warner vetoed this: too arty. It must all be in colour, he decreed. Although Audrey had requested Jack Cardiff's services, she gladly accepted Zinnemann's choice of his countryman, Franz Planer, a cameraman with whom she had already worked and who had proved his talent for lighting women's faces both in colour and in the subdued, desaturated tones that Zinnemann now intended for the convent sequences. The natural predominance there of black and white was something that even Jack L. Warner couldn't banish from the screen.

Audrey was well tutored by the time Zinnemann announced his success in gaining the cooperation of a Belgian order, the Sisters of Oblates d'Assumption, based at Froyennes, near Tournai, who wanted to demonstrate their independence from the monastic authorities. In return, Warner Bros. placed a suitable donation on their collection plate.

Zinnemann has recalled in his autobiography how, on 2 January 1958, he 'stashed away' his 'nuns'—Audrey Hepburn, Peggy Ashcroft and Edith

Evans—for a four-day 'quarantine' at three different convents in Paris, with other actresses with speaking roles in convents elsewhere. 'Making the daily rounds at 10.00 a.m. to see how they were doing, I'd arrive in the warmth of a taxi . . . The winter was immensely cold and the convents were hardly heated . . . All of them would come out of the cloisters absolutely purple with cold but fascinated by what they were involved in and very excited by the way they were getting prepared for their characters.'

The production files of *The Nun's Story* make clear that spiritual matters were not alone in the forefront of Audrey's mind at this time. She wanted assurances that the best doctor the studio could find would accompany her to Africa: that the latest sulphonamide drugs would be available in case of viral infection; that canine quarantine laws in the Belgian Congo would be waived for Famous so that the tiny terrier could accompany her; and, most important of all, that a bidet would be installed and waiting for her at the Sabena Guest House, Stanleyville, where the key members of the unit were to be quartered. It was probably the only bathroom fixture of its kind in Central Africa at that time.

Audrey's last chore before flying off on location was to do costume tests for the colour cameras. 'Wonderful!' said the one-word cable from Jack L. Warner, not wasting a cent in his enthusiasm when he saw the result.

The location severely tested Audrey's own enthusiasm as well as her delicate but well-protected constitution. Fog and cold at night made her fear chest congestion while the blanket of humid heat that enveloped them by day was even worse, and not helped by the fact that the air conditioner which had been sent at double speed from Hollywood turned out to be a humidifier. Thunderstorms with sheeting rain interrupted work. The religious garments felt like a slimming cabinet at a health spa. 'I'll bet all nuns are skinny underneath,' she said, managing a laugh. For four days she worked in a leper colony, refusing to wear the protective gloves available to cast and crew out of sympathy with the afflicted. At the end of the day's shooting she would lie back and listen enraptured to the rhythmic beating of native drums summoning the canoes—'just like taxis'—to take her and the others back to Stanleyville, along rivers where hippotami wallowed, sank out of sight and occasionally surfaced dangerously near the long thin boats. Then Audrey would hold on to the sides and giggle like any child on a Big Dipper. She still smoked her favourite Gold Flake cigarettes and sometimes the native bearers expressed amazement at seeing a nun with a cigarette-holder between her lips. Zinnemann told them she was 'an American nun'—and they nodded understandingly.

Everyone was eager to see how Audrey and Peter Finch would get along. Finch's reputation as a hell-raiser and womanizer gave him a lot in common with Dr Fortunati, of whom another character says to Sister Luke: 'Don't think for a minute your habit will protect you. He is a devil.' Like Fortunati, however, Finch was a professional. Perhaps he judged that Audrey's concentration on her role—she even asked that a jazz record which a crew member had been playing between set-ups be turned off, as it was inappropriate music for a nun to hear—was so sincere that it ruled her out as a potential bedmate.

The role of Fortunati is crucial to the film's success. It is his brutal but candid remark to Sister Luke, 'I've seen nuns come and go and I tell you this—you are not like them. You have not got the vocation', that tilts the emotional balance of the story in favour of the nun's self-discovery and ensures her survival as a free-thinking individual. Finch plays this short but vital scene with all the force of personality that it requires. He uses his magnificent voice like a scalpel, cutting out what he sees as a sickness in a woman dedicated to poverty, chastity and—most difficult of all to achieve—obedience. It was the most dramatic scene that Audrey had yet played. One wishes—perhaps ungratefully—that she had been put through such stern tests earlier in her career, with co-stars who had more dramatic weight, in stories with more emotional volume, for her self-searching reaction to Finch's coldly measured dissection of her weakening grip on the Catholic faith admirably conveys the feelings of a woman shocked into self-awareness.

To the disappointment of the publicists, no affair sprang up between Finch and Audrey. She was faithful to Mel; and despite Finch's reputation, he was in reality very dependent on the women he made love to or lived with, looking to them to shore up the self-doubt that he otherwise drowned in bouts of heavy drinking. 'For Audrey, I had only respect,' he later admitted and then, unconsciously contradicting her role in the film, he added: 'She had no time for affairs. She had a vocation.'

Audrey managed to avoid the main health hazards of the Congo. The only call for a doctor came when an overzealous monkey gave her a small bite. Ironically, illness caught up with her savagely once she returned to Rome for the interior scenes, when she collapsed with a kidney infection brought on by dehydration in equatorial Africa. Cables to and from Warner Bros. convey the pain she went through—in them she was always referred to as 'Sister Luke' lest news of her illness reach the press, causing her harassment and prejudicing her recovery. One night she awoke in agony in her suite at the Hotel Hassler, bathed in sweat. A cystoscopy revealed kidney stones. Strict rest was enforced, under sedation, in the hope of avoiding the need for an operation. As always, it was her conscience rather than the physical pain that troubled Audrey. She couldn't forget the fortune she was costing Warner Bros. as she lay in bed, Famous at her side. Her concern was scarcely reciprocated. Cables from Hollywood grew less sympathetic and more intemperate as irritation at the delay turned into alarm at the prospect of having to close the picture down while she recovered. Audrey knew that this would delay the finish date, and hence prejudice *Green Mansions*. Mel flew to her side, having just returned from a couple of months spent reconnoitring Venezuela, British Guiana and Colombia.

Audrey's fever worsened. Her mother arrived from London and her half-brother, Jan van Ufford, from the Hague, where he worked for a company manufacturing toiletries. Zinnemann took one look at the burly young Dutchman, such an improbable relative for his star, and assigned him a role as an extra in the film. Fortunately the kidney stones, and the crisis, passed. Audrey returned, looking appropriately pale, to the magnificent convent set that Alexander Trauner had designed. There, extras recruited from the Rome ballet were putting their professional grace to good use in following the convent rituals, and members of the city's oldest and noblest families were lending the character and wisdom inherent in their looks for the close-ups of the elderly nuns in return for a pittance.

Viewing *The Nun's Story* again when he came to write his memoirs, Fred Zinnemann was struck by Audrey's success in suggesting, physically as well as vocally, the latent strain of independence in Sister Luke which eventually makes her opt for the secular life. He admits, however, that he slipped up—and therefore perhaps deprived Audrey of an even more interesting dimension to her acting—by failing to suggest adequately the passage of some seventeen years in the nun's life. '[There was] hardly a strand of grey hair when she shakes it free from the confining wimple [at the end of the film].'

Principal photography finished on 25 June 1958 on location in Belgium. Just in time; for Audrey had caught the flu. But at last she was free to go out in the sun again with a *nihil obstat* from her director about acquiring a tan. She flew to California at the end of the month, with four weeks' rest ahead of her before starting *Green Mansions*.

Audrey found the mood at Warner Bros. strangely subdued. The front office had screened a final assemblage of *The Nun's Story* and was not wholly pleased with what it saw. The film seemed too long, too downbeat, too undramatic, and included too much documentary detail about a nun's life. It was crushingly disappointing for her and Zinnemann to find their faith—

quite apart from the agonies they had suffered to make the film—being brushed aside by people who sat in office and conference rooms second-guessing the public. But revenge was at hand.

Zinnemann recalls the day that the film opened in New York. Warners had chosen Radio City Music Hall, a vast multi-decker auditorium more like the tomb of a Caesar than a picture palace. Director and stars gathered upstairs for cocktails before the first screening in an atmosphere not unlike a wake. Then someone glanced down into the street and cried 'Look!' Even before the doors had opened, an ever-lengthening queue was forming on the sidewalk until it curled round the corner of the block. Unlike the nun who gradually lost her faith, those who had backed the movie suddenly and miraculously regained theirs. *The Nun's Story* went on to become one of the greatest money-earners of all time, rewarding Audrey handsomely until the end of her days. It was the most profitable film she was ever to make.

In retrospect she had reason to be grateful to Warner Bros. for being so indecisive about its prospects that they had held its release back until June 1959. The delay was a blessing in disguise for Audrey. The triumphant reception of *The Nun's Story* was to limit the damage done by the film she made after it—*Green Mansions*—which opened three months earlier. It was to be the first serious setback to Audrey Hepburn's career—and to her marriage.

15

RIDING FOR A FALL

THE interviews that Mel and Audrey gave prior to starting work on *Green Mansions* on 21 July 1958 give the impression of two people talking up their courage while privately doubting the wisdom of their enterprise.

The film was costing $3 million, not far short of that for *The Nun's Story* and a huge sum then for such a rarefied movie: nuns were traditionally more popular than wood-nymphs. The studio, having opened its purse to Audrey, was holding its breath for Mel. He had certainly been an assiduous explorer in South America. While Audrey had been filming in Africa he had travelled 25,000 miles into W. H. Hudson country, pushing his way up the Orinoco river with one of the newfangled stereo recorders to capture such exotic sounds as the lion-like roars of uruguato monkeys. He and his scouts had chopped their way through the jungles on foot, in dugout canoes or aboard light aircraft. No location filming would be possible, because there simply wasn't enough light in the dense forests where W. H. Hudson had set his fantasy. Air cargo was arriving daily at MGM, rare South American birds, animals and plants to be used for dressing the sets, making the studio look like a zoo. The feeding bill for the wild animals and birds resembled a supporting star's salary. There were coral flamingoes (which ate only shrimp), herons (wheatgerm), a rare blue hyacinth macaw (papaya), a jaguar (200 lbs of horse meat daily), a montjac (warmed-up baby food) and a miniature deer called Little Ip. Christened on the set, Little Ip would be Rima's constant companion and the emblem of the girl's free spirit and gentle nature. Since it was impossible to train the nervous and delicate animal, Little Ip spent the first three weeks of his fame living in the Malibu house rented by Audrey and Mel, fortunately forging a friendly alliance with Famous. On one occasion he escaped, giving MGM a bad moment or two as they contemplated the prospect of their four-footed star being savaged by the fiercer terriers of the neighbourhood. Audrey didn't miss the irony that she who was still yearning for a baby had to interrupt her sleep at night in order to bottle-feed a deer.

Anthony Perkins was signed to play the part of Abel, the young explorer who falls instantly in love with Rima—if love is possible for such an insubstantial and quickly vanishing vision—and, at the end, sees her consumed in the fires of ritual sacrifice. Mel and Audrey had made a special trip to see him playing in *Look Homeward, Angel* on Broadway to confirm that he had the requisite romantic looks. Perkins passed this test, though he was to be bitterly embarrassed by the specially composed theme song, 'The Ballad of Green Mansions', which he crooned to a small guitar and which became a byword for camp for many years afterwards.

Mel did not stint on quality. He was determined that *Green Mansions* would show Hollywood what artists he and Audrey were. He engaged the Katharine Dunham dance troupe to choreograph the native dances; Heitor Villa-Lobos to compose the 'primitive' music; and Rufino Tamayo to paint the poster for the film—naturally featuring Audrey as Rima. Givenchy had had no hand in the wardrobe, but then Audrey's costumes were not so much clothes as camouflage. The script, written by Mel on his off-days while filming *The Sun Also Rises,* was highly poetic. Rima was to be first glimpsed 'reclining against the massive roots of a huge tree. So perfect is her camouflage against the ferns and herbage, the greenish-grey of her brief chemise blending with the moss and the roots, the dark mass of her hair so like the rich brown of the tree trunks that she is invisible to Abel and becomes visible to us gradually as the camera moves slowly closer.' That was all very well, said one MGM executive memorandum, but couldn't the star be a little clearer in the picture? 'We aren't paying for the Invisible Girl.'

Audrey had anxieties about letting herself be photographed in Scope. She had always thought her chin too square, and she knew that the tendency of the new wide-screen format was to 'fatten' faces. But tests of the recently developed Panavision lenses put her fears to rest, when it was shown that any distortion was removed. Unfortunately, even a spirit like Rima had to part her lips occasionally and utter dialogue. Instantly the nymph of the primal forests became risibly banal as Audrey struggled with sentiments that had clearly defeated the screenwriter. 'Out here, I believe in everything. Every leaf, every flower. Birds. The air. It's just a feeling I have, I can't explain.' It would have been wiser not to try.

Mel had worked himself so hard that he was very nearly exhausted before shooting began. Not only had he travelled to the ends of the earth but he had managed to squeeze in an MGM movie entitled *The World, the Flesh and the Devil* about three people (himself, Harry Belafonte and Inger Stevens) who are the sole survivors of a superbomb that has discharged its gas across the surface of the globe. After all three had been saved from catastrophe on-screen they perished in the reviews. Mel knew, therefore, that his career might depend on the success he made of *Green Mansions*. The truth was even more brutal. It was Audrey who would bear on her slender shoulders the responsibility for a picture that, without her as its star, would never have been made.

Possibly for this reason, much play was made of the love scenes she would share with Perkins. The publicity carefully distinguished between her being 'in love', which she had certainly been in a number of earlier films, and the physical coupling which she would now attempt on-screen for the first time. This was promoted into a major selling point. 'Audrey Hepburn's Husband Orders Another Guy To Make Love To Her' was how the MGM press material put it, perhaps a shade gaudily for such a tasteful enterprise. Poor Audrey. Her embarrassment must have been complete when she read the quotes attributed to her in the publicity. 'For the first time in my career,' she is alleged to have said, 'I lost my shyness . . . Love scenes have always been difficult for me. But with my husband directing and leading Tony and me through the emotional passages, things fell into place'—not the happiest of phrases. Reviewers (not led by Mel) found these scenes so stilted that they drew sniggers at the press shows. In a silent movie the notion of a child of nature awakened to love by the tender caresses of a handsome young man might have had some naïve impact. By the late 1950s such scenes were patently old-fashioned and so remote from contemporary taste that even Audrey's doe-eyed presence failed to earn them a grudging approval.

Newsweek's review was particularly harsh: 'Bird Girl, Go Home', it was headed, and the opening sentence was a shrewd judgment of the only reason why one of the world's most celebrated stars should have undertaken this sort of antiquated whimsy: 'Audrey plays her part like a loyal wife—cradling fawns, warbling bird calls and running barefoot in a thick cotton nightdress, hair astream, through the imported studio forest. Tony loping disjointedly along after the wispy girl, bleating out his uncertainty about her reality status, looks pretty silly.' *Time* was even more dismissive: 'Ferrer works hard to recreate the misty mood of the book but unfortunately he goes about it like a man trying to spray the whole South American rain forest with an atomiser full of dime-store perfume.' Audrey was 'sprightly enough': but this was tame praise for someone who had featured on the magazine's cover before her first American film had even opened. The *Los Angeles Times* critic, Philip K. Scheuer, found her 'for the first time less than sparkling . . . colorless . . . and sexless, too'. *Variety* responded adversely to an interview in which Mel had talked about 'the religion of nature' by predicting that *'Green Mansions . . .* probably will get its heaviest response if billed as a high-grade jungle film . . . a pseudo-poetic Tarzan-Jane epic'.

Green Mansions dipped out of sight at the box-office as swiftly as *The Nun's Story* climbed into the blockbuster class. The damage was not so much to Audrey's career as to the trust she had placed in her husband. She had done the film for love. She had acted not only against her better judgement but against her instincts. She blamed herself for trying to be 'sexy' when, as she later observed, 'the truth is, I know I have more sex appeal on the tip of my nose than many women have in their entire bodies. It doesn't stand out a mile, but it is there.' It did not show on screen.

The *schadenfreude* that greeted the embarrassment of Audrey and Mel spilled out of the review columns on to the gossip pages. Little Ip's 'performance' had been hailed more warmly than Audrey's by some critics and now the columnists were suggesting that the deer would be seen around town wearing dark glasses and negotiating a new contract. Audrey managed a wan smile though she burst into genuine laughter on the occasion when she and Mel called in at Jungle Land on their way back from visiting two of Mel's children and asked to see Little Ip. 'The deer's away doing stills,' they were told.

· The couple's premonitory pessimism is almost tangible in their inevitable interview with Hedda Hopper soon after *Green Mansions* had finished shooting. What were Audrey's plans? 'I have none for the moment,' she said softly. Hopper referred to *The Roots of Heaven,* a film in which Mel might have hoped to star and which instead featured Trevor Howard, Errol Flynn and Eddie Albert, and offered consolation. 'Who wants to see three drunks and a herd of elephants?' A film was going to be made of *The World of Suzie Wong,* observed Mel (or Audrey) in the desultory chat recorded by Hopper's stenographer. Well, Hedda didn't encourage Audrey to try for a role in that! 'Who wants to sit in a house of prostitution for three hours?'

Audrey confessed that, more than anything, she would like to do a play. But the old vow she and Mel had made about staying together and working together was now more of a stumbling block than an incentive. 'It's difficult and impractical,' she had to admit to Hopper, 'unless we could both do one together. If I were working in a play, what would Mel be doing? We would probably be meeting at the door. That's not a life for a married couple.' In fact, it seemed that only one thing could constitute a suitable occupation for a married couple—starting a family. If that thought occurred to Hopper she was merciful enough not to mention it this time. Her guests' spirits were low enough already.

Audrey's depression did not—and could not—last long. Kurt Frings had been busy on their behalf. All too aware that *Green Mansions* would not be a money-maker, he had thought it prudent to close several new deals before its negative impact was felt. So, even though her thoughts were turning more and more anxiously towards trying again to have a child, Audrey was forced to assent to two particularly attractive film projects to be directed, respectively, by John Huston and Alfred Hitchcock. *The Unforgiven* was a Western that was going to be shot entirely on location in Mexico. Huston had jumped at the chance of directing it—it was paying him $400,000 and would give an outdoor man like him time to ride and shoot game. Audrey's role was by no means ideal, or even at first sight natural casting for her. She was to play Rachel Zachary, a Kiowa Indian maiden rescued in childhood from a tribal massacre in the 1860s and reared by a white family whose sons (Burt Lancaster and Audie Murphy) behave like brothers towards her. A 'Method' actress, Molly McCarthy, a protégée of Elia Kazan, had been pushed for the role and Huston was interested in her. But once Audrey expressed interest the part was hers—for a fee of $200,000. Huston greeted her acceptance with a typically laconic remark: 'She's as good as the other Hepburn'—Katharine, whom he had directed in *The African Queen*.

Having committed herself, Audrey immediately had misgivings. As the film was to be shot around Durango and on an Indian reservation in a parched and burning strip of the Sierra Madre—sentimental territory for Huston, where he had shot *Treasure of the Sierra Madre,* one of his earliest successes and his only Academy Award-winner—Audrey knew she could only expect heat and dirt: discomforts comparable to those she had suffered while filming *The Nun's Story.* Moreover, Mel could not be with her: he was busy with post-production work on *Green Mansions.*

Just before work on the film was due to begin, she received the news for which she had been hoping for years: she was pregnant. This made her even more reluctant to do a film involving hard outdoor activity, including horse-riding. But she allowed Huston to convince her that her scenes would be over and done with well before the baby was expected.

The only delay would be to the second of the two projects: the Hitchcock thriller called *No Bail for the Judge.* Hitchcock reluctantly agreed to postpone his start date until June 1959 by which time Audrey's child would be safely delivered.

Hitchcock told friends that the pregnancy was a bit of a nuisance. Privately, this closet misogynist had no great love for actors and thought women stars especially needed more attention than they were worth. But recruiting Audrey Hepburn allowed him to indulge his fascination for the sort of woman who was, in looks and manners, undoubtedly a lady—a woman of breeding or, as Hollywood put it, 'class'. Who knew what sensual core reposed within Audrey's well-bred exterior, which might be gratifyingly exposed by his direction, as he had touched the carnality that lay beneath the cool surfaces of Ingrid Bergman and Grace Kelly? Audrey, he concluded, would be worth the wait.

This agreed, Audrey started preparing for her more gruelling role as a grown-up papoose in *The Unforgiven,* 'a little red whelp' as Huston called her character. She paid little attention to the still evolving screenplay for *No Bail for the Judge.* This was to prove a great mistake.

All Hitchcock had told her of the role was that she would play a courtroom lawyer, the daughter of the eponymous judge, who defends her father when he is accused of murder and hires a professional criminal to bring in the real killer. That sounded fine to Audrey, particularly as Laurence Harvey would be the crook turned knight errant and John Williams, who had played her father in *Sabrina,* would once again be her on-screen parent. Hitchcock had assured her, in the tone he used when wheedling actresses into doing what he wanted, that she would make 'a very pretty Portia' wearing one of those chic horsehair wigs that English barristers wore in court. What he neglected to tell her was that the plot would require her to be sexually assaulted. The pleasures that come from assaulting well-bred ladies in motion pictures were not then as well recognized a Hitchcock trademark as they became when the auteur theorists got to work.

When Audrey reported for work on *The Unforgiven* in January 1959, buoyed up by her pregnancy, a supply of drugs and heat-resistant creams and the support of her favourite cameraman, Franz Planer, she could not have guessed that what lay in store for her with Hitchcock would be even worse than getting dust in her hair at Durango. Almost immediately her misgivings about the Western reasserted themselves.

For one sequence she was to ride bareback on a stallion, a grey named Diablo that had been a favourite mount of the ex-Cuban dictator Batista. Ever since a pony had thrown her as a child, dislocating her collarbone, Audrey had been uncomfortable with horses. But such was her concern for integrity that she refused a stand-in and took her place in the saddle. At the last minute, it was decided to shoot the scene another way; a horseman was despatched with the news. Audrey's stallion saw the other horse approaching, threw up its head, reared—and the next thing Audrey knew she was flat on her back on the hard desert soil. Instinctively she lay still. She was in great pain. A Mexican physician had her carried to a truck on a stretcher which was placed on the vehicle's bare boards under a hastily rigged canvas sunshade. She was driven, very slowly, but not slowly enough to spare her the torture of the bumpy dirt road, to the nearest hospital. She fainted several times en route but insisted on breaking the news to Mel herself.

As soon as he heard her weak and anguished voice, Mel chartered an aircraft and flew to Mexico with a Beverly Hills orthopaedic physician, Dr Mendelssohn. Audrey was brought home in an air ambulance a few days later, on 3 February 1959. The flight took six hours; she was fitted with a back brace but was unable to eat, sleep or rest, so great was her pain. She put on a brave face, and her blue cashmere sweater and the gay magenta hair ribbon round the ponytail she had worn for her Indian role belied the extent of her injuries. Her Mexican maid, Juanita, carried Famous, as Audrey insisted, 'I'm perfectly all right.'

Such was far from the case. The X-rays revealed that her condition was even worse than she feared: four ribs had been fractured, two vertebrae had been broken and her ankle was badly sprained. But her first and overwhelming concern was for the welfare of the foetus within her. The prognosis was maddeningly inconclusive. The growing child might have suffered damage, or it might not: it was too early to say. This was the dreadful anxiety that Audrey now had to bear as she underwent daily physiotherapy. Huston had 'shot around' his absent star as much as possible until Hecht-Hill-Lancaster, the independent production company, had to close the film down and make the insurance claim that would tide them over until she was certified fit to return. No amount of insurance money could have compensated Audrey Hepburn for the loss of the prospect of motherhood. Physical pain she bore easily, but her mental pain was cruel. She said later that she could not have got through those days in hospital without the presence—the unexpected presence—of a woman who was close to her in spirit: Marie-Louise Habets, the original of Sister Luke in *The Nun's Story*, who now showed up at her bedside to read to her and comfort her. In an inspired moment that brought a giggle to Audrey's lips, Marie-Louise even offered to put on her nun's nursing uniform and tell any unwelcome visitors that they could not be admitted.

By 20 February 1959 she was up and walking—albeit cautiously—around the house that she and Mel had rented in Beverly Hills. Her doctors permitted her to return to the film a week earlier than expected. 'I've no pain unless I make a violent movement,' she said, walking to the aircraft on Mel's arm at Santa Monica airport. 'I'm sure John Huston will rearrange the script and have a double for the remainder of her riding scenes,' said Mel, who would have preferred her to wait that extra week. His hopes were misplaced. Possibly with Audrey's compliance, Huston had her ferried to the location daily, stretched out on mattresses in a station wagon, Mel beside her holding her holding her hand. Because the footage already shot had to match that which she still had to do, she had to complete the scene that had been interrupted by her accident on the same horse, Diablo. No accidents occurred this time although no risks were taken, either. The scene was the very last one shot in the film.

Sadly, considering the suffering it caused her, *The Unforgiven* did not enhance Audrey's reputation—nor Huston's. He acknowledged that he was at fault. He had cherished the hope that he could lift a cowboys-and-Indians action adventure out of its class by turning a period tale of racial prejudice into an allegory of contemporary tensions in urban America. He felt that if Audrey's Indian girl could be represented as a sort of 'Red Niggah', then the tribal wars would reflect on America's current colour problems. But in the course of filming the concept went sour on him—and this was not helped by having to halt production because of Audrey's injuries. The reviews reflected Huston's failure to live up to his ambitions. 'A massive and masterful attempt . . .' *Time* magazine began, which sounded promising, '. . . to gild the oat.' Instead of making a cow-country epic, a kind of heroic tableau, Huston ended up with a pretentious piece of ersatz folklore. Despite the possibility that Audrey's high cheekbones and large clear eyes could be evidence of Indian ancestry, she continued to look like a sophisticated model girl, and what *Time* called 'her elocution-school accent' was much too cultivated for the rough-tongued folks of this territory.

Characteristically, Audrey didn't hold anything against Huston—neither so-so reviews nor her disabling accident. A year or so later, she added a postscript to a letter she wrote him: 'Have you read any good stories lately with a small part in it for a girl who's good at falling off horses?'

Though it was a relief to be finished with the film, Audrey still had to live with the anxiety about her pregnancy. Her real wretchedness began when she and Mel returned to Switzerland. She was rushed into hospital in Lucerne at the end of May 1959 and suffered a miscarriage. The blow was all the more cruel since medical opinion had been reassuring: her accident, it was thought, would not prevent her becoming a mother. The farm in the Alban Hills which she and Mel loved had been rented in anticipation of the birth and furnished with all the nursery necessities, and Audrey had already begun knitting baby clothes—both blue and pink, in the same pattern, 'in case of either one'.

Now she was brought home from hospital to Burgenstock in a state of severe despondency, saying plaintively, 'I can't understand why I don't have children.' Her doctors ordered two months of complete rest.

In Hollywood the news was received with compassion tempered by more commercial considerations. 'This means that Alfred Hitchcock will be able to go ahead with [*No Bail for the Judge*] which was postponed when he learned she was to become a mother,' wrote Hedda Hopper. In fact, it meant just the opposite.

While convalescing in her Burgenstock châlet, Audrey took her first comprehensive look at the completed script of the Hitchcock film. In her present state, having just lost a child, she reacted with disbelieving horror. Her character was going to be raped in a London park; even in her usual good health, she would have found the scene repugnant. The idea of suffering violence in a film of her own, or even witnessing it in other films, made Audrey flinch and cover her eyes; she had once nearly fainted at the premiere of a film containing a sexual assault and had to leave the cinema. She could not—and resolved that she would not—play this part. But she had signed a contract with Hitchcock, who was reluctant to lose his star and any thrill he would have got by putting her through the wringer. His determination to hold Audrey to her contract was strengthened when *The Nun's Story* opened in New York in June 1959 and put Audrey securely back in the front rank of bankable stars. Hitchcock's exasperation was all the sharper because the success of *The Nun's Story* delayed the opening of his own new film, *North by Northwest* at the same cinema.

There was only one way out of the dilemma—and it did not require the threat of litigation from Hitchcock to make Audrey embrace it. She became pregnant again. Even Hitchcock would not compel a mother-to-be to proceed with a film in which she would have to simulate traumatic suffering and accept a certain degree of rough handling. He was furious. The term of her pregnancy, plus an indefinite period of maternity leave, would make it impossible for him to wait until Audrey was certified fit to make his film. With bad grace he tore up the agreement—and forever held it against her, considering it a deliberately engineered breach of contract.

While Mel went off to Italy and France to appear in two stylish and grisly horror films, *Blood and Roses* and *The Hands of Orlac,* Audrey remained home in the Swiss châlet, looking after herself. This time she did not dare to knit lest she invite the gods' retribution for her presumptuousness. But she admitted, 'There is not a second of the day when I am not thinking of the little one. I am like a cloistered woman, counting the hours.' The hour struck prematurely. On 17 January 1960, around mid-morning, she gave birth to a boy in the maternity ward of Lucerne's municipal clinic, where Henry Rogers had advised her to move in order to avoid the risks of paparazzi and reporters laying siege to her in Burgenstock. The child was christened Sean, which means 'gift of God'.

'Let me see him, let me see him at once,' she demanded. While Mel stood by her bed in a white medical coat, she turned the baby this way and that, examining him from all angles, fearful that he might not possess the perfection she had always striven for. 'Is he all right? Is he all right?' He was, and a wan smile of contentment eventually settled on her face.

Two months later, in the same private chapel on the Burgenstock estate where she and Mel had been married, Sean was officially baptized. By then he had been unofficially baptized by his mother as 'Pooh', after the bear in the A. A. Milne stories. (He was to bear the nickname with commendable stoicism as he grew up.) He became a Swiss-American citizen though the US Ambassador, present as a godfather, pretended to tip the balance by pressing a miniature Stars and Stripes into the baby's fist and handing the radiant mother an American passport for her first-born.

16

THE GIRL WHO CAME TO
BREAKFAST

---

*P*ARAMOUNT had grown impatient with the number of films Audrey was turning down as the joys of being a mother filled her days in Switzerland. She still owed the studio three pictures. Not at all misty-eyed at her good news, it notified her that she was not to think of working for anyone else until she had settled this obligation. She was in no hurry.

Early in 1960 Audrey accompanied Mel to Rome where he was to star in the vampire film *Blood and Roses:* it was her first trip abroad since Sean had been born. There she posed for a Cecil Beaton photosession that reflected her maternal contentment. 'She has lost her elfin looks,' Beaton said, 'now she has a new womanly beauty.'

The 'new woman' soon received a new proposition: a version of Truman Capote's novella *Breakfast at Tiffany's,* which George Axelrod, author of *The Seven Year Itch,* had adapted for the screen with Blake Edwards as director. It was a Paramount picture, too: useful for discharging her obligations. There was one major snag. Holly Golightly, the heroine, was (not to put it too bluntly) a 'kept woman'. Even though her wardrobe contained only a single 'working outfit'—a little black dress—and another for day wear, this frugality only reflected the dubious basis of her existence: most of the work she engaged in was done on the night shift. If Audrey accepted, she would have to cope with a radical change of image: the role called for the cheerful amorality of a high-class call girl. Or, as Kurt Frings described the character when he tactfully presented the role to Audrey—'a kook'. 'That sounds better,' she said. 'They'll pay you $750,000,' her agent said, adding, 'Doesn't that sound even better?'

'Kook' was the vogue word in the early years of the new decade. Up to a point it was an apt description of Holly Golightly. A 'kook' was the kind of dauntless waif who unrolled her sleeping bag in any part of town, preferably where the action was thickest, and lived without conventional moral principles, seemingly protected from the retaliation of landlords and ex-lovers by her own ingénue innocence of the world. In *Breakfast at Tiffany's,* Holly's principal benefactor is a gangster doing a stretch in Sing Sing prison. She also gets by on what were euphemistically called 'cloakroom tips' of $50, supplied by a series of gentlemen whom she strings along without per-forming the services they have paid for—and which have nothing to do with the powder room. She abandons her obligations as heedlessly as she once, in her deliberately dim if not so distant past, abandoned her husband, her stepchildren and her small-town origins for the promiscuous excite-ment of New York. Holly Golightly, in short, is a predator posing as a pussycat; a tramp pretending to be a free spirit; a truant from life who views each day as a holiday from responsibility; a playgirl whose sense of fun almost, but not quite, conceals a badly damaged woman. Audrey was not at all sure she liked the sound of her.

In retrospect, it is hard to understand why the character of Holly Go-lightly, as Audrey eventually played her, should have caused her a moment's hesitation. But fan worship, a fickle thing, is a force that even as well bal-anced a film star as Audrey Hepburn was reluctant to jeopardize. She knew she needed a film that would speed her transition to roles with a newer take on morality in tune with the accelerating permissiveness of the 1960s. She tried to rationalize Holly Golightly's sweetly mendacious mores by recall-ing her own hand-to-mouth days in London fifteen years earlier, when she was starting out in nightclubs and cabaret revue. 'She was caught off base. Lost. But she was pretending just as conscientiously as I did. And she had her identity,' she reminded her interviewer, Henry Gris, sounding as if she were talking herself into doing something basically disagreeable. Then, recollecting that Holly's schizoid attitude to life depended on her hiding her true identity as a small-town girl and runaway wife, Audrey added, 'which was a total lack of identity.' She was tying herself in knots and she knew it. But there was some truth in her assertion that she had been 'luckier' than Holly: 'I had a purpose.' Capote's heroine clearly wasn't a Christian Scien-tist, as Audrey still was in a general way, but, as Audrey said, 'If you pass the man with the canapés more often than usual, you may get yourself a kind of meal.' Such sanitizing remarks helped reconcile her to the risks inher-ent in playing an adorable hooker. One man, at least, was not taken in— Truman Capote.

Audrey was a friend of the novelist's and, as Capote put it, one of his 'favourite people', but she was not his choice for a role which he clearly had written with Marilyn Monroe in mind. Marilyn was an authentic kook, a daughter of all those blondes whom gentlemen preferred. She was also an actress whose self-absorption, as complete as Holly's, acquitted her of moral responsibility for the results of her actions as completely as if she had not been present at the time. 'Marilyn would have been absolutely mar-vellous', Capote stubbornly maintained; Audrey, though he liked her, 'was just wrong for the part'.

But Monroe was under contract to Twentieth Century-Fox and would be expensive to borrow. Paramount pressed Audrey to make up her mind. What sealed the decision was the reassurance of her director, Blake Ed-wards, that the character of Holly would be effectively purified by the style in which he would shoot the picture. After the opening scene, Ed-wards promised, there would be no doubt that Holly's predatory nature was only a charming aberration. And so it turned out.

Even before the title began to roll, *Breakfast at Tiffany's* established its heroine in a world-famous sequence which showed that she had an eye for the main chance but without suggesting that it was in any way the product of rapacious calculation. The opening shots had the surreal novelty—rarer in 1961 than it became later when cinema exploded into sheer fantasy—of a television commercial for a very exclusive brand of consumer goods. Dressed in one of Givenchy's starkly simple black numbers, with a rope necklace of outsize pearls and long gloves of black satin, and sporting a hairdo like a black pineapple which she carries with the graceful deport-ment of a native woman bearing her worldly goods on her head, Audrey emerges from a yellow cab on an apparently empty Fifth Avenue in the dawn hours and, with a purposeful stalk, she advances on the windows of Tiffany's jewellery store. The glittering pieces behind the glass—implau-sibly, but helpfully, left on display overnight—form an ironic contrast with the styrofoam cup of coffee from which this vision of whimsical cupidity occasionally sips, and the proletarian breakfast pastry in her other hand from which, now and then, she takes a delicate nibble. It was a television-like staging that turned concupiscence into a childish daydream, much as the old newspaper advertisements had sold Maidenform bras by picturing ladies dreaming that they went walking in them in broad daylight. After this introduction, no one could possibly think anything bad about Holly Go-lightly.

Audrey was nervous when filming that opening sequence. What the cameraman—the faithful Franz Planer—didn't pick up, but Audrey could when she looked to her right, were several thousand curious New Yorkers who had risen from their beds early enough to line the police barricade closing off that stretch of Fifth Avenue for the few hours granted to the film-makers to shoot the scene. An additional, if minor, worry was the Danish pastry. Audrey hated that buttery, flaky item and asked if she might substitute an ice-cream cone. 'No way,' Blake Edwards said. He had enough to control without worrying about a freezer full of ice-cream scoops for the ten retakes that the scene might require. Filming had to be completed by 7.30 a.m. because the Russian premier, Nikita Khrushchev, was in New York and crowds made police and Secret Service bodyguards distinctly fretful.

Audrey concealed her nervousness at the ambiguous demands the rest of the film would make on her. Walking alone to Tiffany's, like a model on the catwalk, was one thing: the set-up and the evening gown at that hour of the morning provided the comic dissonance with reality. But playing opposite her co-star George Peppard, as the writer whose pad Holly uses to crash out in when it is necessary to elude her male 'admirers', had no guidelines. Audrey played her film roles 'on instinct', or followed the cues of directors like Billy Wilder who gave her line readings. Peppard, a rising hopeful of the 'Method' acting school, was a technician who analysed his part thoroughly in advance. He and Audrey were not out of sync with each other when the shooting began, only slightly out of sympathy. It did not show, however, because of the way their respective characters had been conceived. Though it is difficult to believe, this was the first time—barring the wretched *Green Mansions*—that Audrey was playing opposite an actor of almost her own age. Hitherto she had been either an ethereal sprite or an adorable child whom older men pursued but never got to grips with— in any sense. *Breakfast at Tiffany's,* though a fantasy, took place in a recognisable urban setting where a sexual relationship between boy and girl was plausible and to be expected. None occurs: the attachment remains platonic. Peppard as the writer is a personable male but not really an available one, since he is also a 'kept man', what a later generation would call a 'toy boy', attached by the purse strings to an older (and richer) woman played by Patricia Neal. Peppard's character would today be thought a closet gay, a 'midnight cowboy' able to make himself agreeable to men, women and the 'tutti-frutti' in between. Holly becomes a den sister to him, rather than a lover. Though this relieved Audrey of one worry, it left her with a sense of the incompleteness of her own character. Holly shows more feelings for the cat in the film, called 'Cat', than she does for Peppard.

What endows Holly's character with the sort of purity with which Audrey felt comfortable is nothing contained in the script. It is Henry Mancini's composition 'Moon River', probably his most famous theme song. Its invocation to 'my huckleberry friend' hardly suits Holly's urban sophisticate, but it hints convincingly at her rural origins as the runaway wife of a country vet. As Audrey croons it to the accompaniment of her guitar, seated outside on the fire escape, it sums up the party girl's wistful yearning for innocence and simplicity. 'Moon River' is the keynote to which her ambiguous nature is pitched, and Mancini credited its gentle melancholy and wishful lyrics directly to Audrey Hepburn. 'I knew how to write it the first time I met Audrey. I knew the exact quality the song would take on when she sang it in that slightly husky voice of hers.' Such moments in movies, when a theme song attaches itself to a character and then follows her off screen, are rare. This was one of them. 'Moon River' became Audrey's 'aura', so to speak, throughout the years to come. When she died, Tiffany's paid tribute to her with, among other things, an advertisement dedicated—with touching simplicity considering the usual extravagances associated with the store—to 'Our Huckleberry Friend'.

When people think of *Breakfast at Tiffany's,* they chiefly remember Audrey in the opening apparition, the haunting theme song and an overcrowded party sequence where someone's hat catches fire. It is a tribute to the star that her presence induces collective amnesia, for very few fans recall the film's parasitical concern with greed and exploitation as well as mental dysfunction. There is not a single principal character who is not living off someone else. Holly gets by, just. She belongs to the golden-hearted tradition of the Little Girl Lost, and one seldom really asks what she would be lost without. The answer is, rich men friends. Audrey's untarnished image is the alibi for the film's cupidity. 'Mail me a list of the fifty richest men in Brazil,' she demands, through her sniffles, when her Rio millionaire jilts her and she resolves nonetheless to fly south and exploit the gold mines there. One laughs at her pertinacity. But one would have laughed more had it been a charming airhead like Marilyn Monroe pulled along helplessly in the perpetual motion of her life. When Peppard's character says, 'I can't help her, and she can't help herself,' it is not really believable.

When Holly goes shoplifting in a five and dime, it is amusing because of her scatterbrain assessment of what can be stolen without detection, including a goldfish bowl which she hides under her fur cloche. But when she suffers actual pain—news of her brother's unexpected death—the play world she lives in suddenly and uncomfortably reverts to the one of damaged infancy so painful that Audrey is excused from playing it. Instead, she busts up her apartment and passes out in a snowstorm of floating cushion feathers. Contrast this failure to write the scene that's required with the extremely well-written and cruel scene where Peppard tries to end his dependence on Patricia Neal and she simply writes him a cheque to buy a Caribbean holiday for himself and Holly. She puts her cynicism where her signature is. Holly, by contrast, remains a moral illiterate and only the fact that it is Audrey Hepburn in the role prevents one's discomfort from surfacing more than momentarily.

The casting of Audrey and the sanitizing of Holly's promiscuity meant that, as the critic Marjorie Rosen acutely observed, *Breakfast at Tiffany's* was successfully geared to the family audience. It is important to put it in the context of the time it was made. Elizabeth Taylor in *Butterfield 8,* a film made in the same year as *Breakfast at Tiffany's* and also centred on a high-class call girl though more realistic in tone, had to pay the redeeming price of death for the sins of the flesh. Morality still ruled the American screen, whether in light comedy or melodrama. It would be left to Billy Wilder's bitter comedy *The Apartment,* starring Shirley MacLaine, to show that a woman could put herself about with a series of men and still retain the audience's sympathy. MacLaine made promiscuity pardonable, but Audrey kept it intangible. The torch of ladylike propriety with a hint (but not too strong a hint) of fun underneath would soon pass to Julie Andrews. She took over where Audrey left off, as Marjorie Rosen said, 'on a love-affair with conservative America', as if to assure moviegoers that virtue and happy endings still existed. But for the family audiences at whom *Breakfast at Tiffany's* was pitched, Audrey was still unrivalled when it came to portraying—in the love-struck words of one of Holly's men friends—'a phoney, but a real phoney'.

Yet motherhood had subtly changed Audrey; it had brought about a questioning of values. Holly Golightly's search for happiness coincided with Audrey's re-evaluation of what life held for her. Holly is vulnerable. She hasn't found what she wants. Fun fills her life, just as film-making filled Audrey's, until she has to consider what such a life really means. Then what she calls 'the mean reds' descend and Holly curls up, foetally and without sexual intent, in the bed of the writer, luckily an unpredatory man, like a child fearful of the dark, lamenting: 'You're afraid and you sweat like hell, but you don't know what you're afraid of, except something bad is going to happen. Only you don't know what it is.' Audrey spoke of her own concerns more tranquilly, but one can feel the tension that her work has set up with reality. 'I suppose it's true that no woman finds complete fulfilment until she has a child. I feel that to be a really good actress, equipped to play the widest variety of roles open to me at my age, it is essential to have experienced childbirth. I didn't realize it before. Now I know.' One satisfaction achieved still left others unattained. Motherhood also made Audrey take even more serious stock of her career, balancing her own need to work against the needs of her baby. Now that she had a child, it was no longer convenient to lead a life on the endless treadmill of the movie factory. She was less and less reconciled to the peripatetic existence that she and Mel had led in hotel suites and rented villas. While Mel's nature demanded constant activity, settling down in a home of their own became Audrey's goal. Gradually their paths and satisfactions began to diverge, though with the commitments they had already accepted filling the calendar in advance it is unlikely that they realized then what had begun to happen.

They spent Christmas 1960 in Hollywood while Audrey wrapped up *Breakfast at Tiffany's.* Baby Sean was flown over from Switzerland with his Italian nanny. Audrey spoke of this holiday 'with my two men' as the happiest she could remember. But in the New Year it was Mel's turn to fix their itinerary—and hers to follow with the baby. They went first to Paris where he was appearing in a French film, *Le Diable et les Dix Commandements,* and then back to Burgenstock. At least life there was peaceful, secure, routine—all the things Audrey loved. She awoke early, usually at 6.30 a.m., to feed the baby and cook for Mel if he was there—she generally did all the cooking, even for guests, if they were at Burgenstock for only a short time, otherwise a woman from the village came in to cook. Mel played tennis to work off his surplus energy; they did a lot of reading; and two or three times a week they drove down to the markets in Lucerne.

By now Sophia Loren and Carlo Ponti had moved to Switzerland and were near neighbours of Mel and Audrey in a villa they rented from the same hotel corporation that owned the Burgenstock compound. Audrey and Sophia had more in common than a career in films. Like Audrey, Sophia was finding it difficult to bear a child and was still in that unhappy limbo where she yearned for motherhood without being able to fulfil her yearning. She often arrived on Audrey's doorstep to have supper with her while Ponti was away on business in Milan or Rome, and Mel was away filming. Becoming a mother had released Audrey from the vow that, where possible, she and Mel would never be separated. Now Sean was the heart of her family. Audrey would cook pasta for Sophia and herself and, after Sean had been put to bed, the two women—among the world's most famous and beautiful stars—would eat alone in the kitchen like neighbourhood housewives. What motherhood did for Audrey was to confirm her lifestyle in the European mode. Part of the joy of rearing a child came from the relative simplicity of life in a country whose rhythm was peaceful, if dull sometimes; where the change of seasons mattered; and where she could breathe pure air on the top of a mountain and raise her eyes to the snows she loved instead of hiding away in some Hollywood canyon with a canopy to exclude the sun.

But film-making was a slipstream that it was hard to pull out of. It was back to Hollywood she had to go just as the spring of 1961 was arriving in Burgenstock.

Broadening her range and varying her roles became Audrey's concern as she approached early middle age. She had considered retirement. After all, with Sean's birth she felt herself 'married, really married', as she had once said she needed to feel. She had no need to work again. She was beginning the search for a permanent home, which had to be a safe retreat since Sophia had convinced her that film stardom had become not only an onerous occupation—when was it not?—but a risky one. During the 1960s the rich and famous would find themselves singled out by radicals on the extreme wings of politics, not to mention conventional criminals from the Mafia-linked gangs of international extortionists. Not just their wealth and possessions, but the safety of themselves and their families, were to be in constant danger. Once unimaginable hazards soon became the daily preoccupation of Audrey and others in her supposedly enviable class.

Militating against early retirement were her contractual obligations. She still owed Paramount two films, though her British 'parent' studio, Associated British, had accepted that it was unlikely they would ever have anything remotely suitable for her. There was the question of Mel's career, which was now of concern to them both. Mel, now in his mid-forties, without a recent box-office success as an actor and with one embarrassing failure as the director of *Green Mansions* (the only Audrey Hepburn film to have lost money), was no longer a contender for leading roles in Hollywood. Male stars like Brando, Newman, Lancaster, Douglas, Clift, Lemmon, Curtis and Heston, boys who stayed in California to wheel and deal on their employers' doorsteps, had supplanted Mel and his peers who seemed to come from another age. Although he was in demand for Franco-Italian-German-Spanish co-productions where his multilingual talents and the prestige of a Hollywood name were useful at the European box-office, a generation had grown up in America which might not readily recognize that name. (Some younger journalists of the time, reporting on Audrey, confused Mel with Jose Ferrer.) More than ever Audrey's was the name that deals were made on; so long as she stayed in films, her husband could feel he carried weight in the industry, receive its courtesies and enjoy consultative status.

Even before finishing *Breakfast at Tiffany's* Audrey had agreed to do a film that sounded as if it would fulfil her need for a part that took account of her maturity. *The Children's Hour* would surely open up new territory for her: its subject was lesbianism. It was part of the new trend in Hollywood, as the film industry waged war against television's seduction of its audiences by producing films that had themes, characters and stories considered too daring for the networks to imitate. Lesbianism—and indeed every so-called 'perversion'—was still officially banned in the offices of the Motion Picture Association's production code administrator. But this individual, once considered powerful enough to halt a film when it was only a gleam in the eye of a studio head, had lost much of his taboo in the current struggle for survival. Soon he was shortly to lose what remained of his power as the American screen began to ape the frank sexuality of the new imports from 'permissive' Britain, like *Saturday Night and Sunday Morning* and *Tom Jones,* to say nothing of home-made landmarks of violence like *Bonnie and Clyde.*

The Children's Hour was based on Lillian Hellman's play about two women teachers whose lives are ruined by allegations that they are lovers. It had already been filmed in an extremely adulterated form by William Wyler in 1936, under the title *These Three,* and it was Wyler who now contemplated a remake, retitled *The Loudest Whisper,* which would strike an artistically liberated pose on a commercially safe base. Lesbianism would not be mentioned by name in the film, not even in a whisper: but the publicity would dare to speak it loud enough for all to hear. Wyler was to assure a press conference: 'We haven't attempted to make a dirty film . . . We plan to do everything possible to keep children away.' Audrey was part of this strategy. Her presence in the film would intrigue the public (Could Audrey Hepburn be a lesbian?) while at the same time appeasing the censors (Audrey Hepburn could never be a lesbian). Shirley MacLaine, who was cast as the school principal, brought to the film a more ambiguous screen persona.

Audrey had little to worry about where her image was concerned since active lesbianism never arose in word or deed. But, she also had less material to work with. In MacLaine she was paired with a professional of practised naturalism, known for her laconic, ribald and relaxing sense of humour, who was riding high in the box-office charts and in the critics' opinions. Assurances were sought that Wyler would protect Audrey's interests. The presence of the cameraman Franz Planer, now an almost imperative part of every contract Audrey signed, was one safeguard. As things turned out, she also needed protection from James Garner, four years in the saddle in the *Maverick* television series and miscast as Audrey's gallant fiancé. His performance was that of a man helplessly aware that the women were getting all the attention.

Not quite all . . . Some of it went to Sean, quartered in a playpen in Au-

drey's trailer. Now it was her child, not her husband, from whom she refused to be separated. It was lucky that Famous, to whom Audrey still
showed an almost maternal devotion, had 'bonded' so well with the baby
and didn't compete for her attention.

It was not Audrey's fault that *Loudest Whisper* failed to establish her as a
'serious' actress. The material was second-rate; the antiquated plot showed
its age, and Wyler's direction showed his age, too. He was scoffed at for the
naïveté of his approach to lesbianism—the very reticence of the film was
a disadvantage in an era becoming increasingly candid about sex and its so-
called aberrations. Worst of all, the drama was inert. Pauline Kael wrote:
'There has been some commiseration with Wyler about the studio hack-
ing out the centre of his film'—a reference to a last-minute attack of
cutting-room nerves—'[but] that's a bit like complaining that a corpse has
had a vital organ removed.' MacLaine emerged from this critical and commercial disaster with her reputation for integrity intact. Audrey won points
for winsomeness: she clearly failed the stiffer exam that the new realism
was setting established stars. *Time* magazine declared that she had given 'her
standard frail, indomitable characterization, which is to say that her eyes
water constantly (frailty) and her chin is cantilevered forward (in-
domitability)'.

As if another symptom of intrusive and painful reality, Audrey lost Famous during her stay in Hollywood. The little dog was crushed by an au-
tomobile on Wilshire Boulevard. Mel did the best thing to distract her
from her grief. Once back in Paris he bought her an almost identical Yorkshire terrier, a pedigree speck of tawny hair with the grandiose name Assam
of Assam. She speedily rechristened him, simply, Famous; and with the
strength of mind that enabled her to close her eyes to reality and wish the
best view of life into existence, she behaved towards the second Famous as
if he were both the once and future Yorkie, and his predecessor had never
met his end on the boulevards of Beverly Hills. She treated *The Loudest
Whisper* likewise; it simply ceased to exist in Audrey's remembrance of
things past.

More than ever, Audrey valued the safety of being able to retreat to
Switzerland. Getting her to commit herself to a new film now involved a
pilgrimage to Burgenstock and a stay of several days to 'audition' for the
project and win her confidence in it. She knew how lucky she had been in
catching the mood of the times with her Holly Golightly, a beguiling kook
whose propensity for play coincided with a generational change in values
and the start of an infectious hedonism that would culminate at the Wood-
stock festival of 'love, music and pot'. Meeting Audrey again around that

time, this writer ventured to suggest that Holly Golightly probably finished up among the flower children at that event. 'Yes,' she said, 'look what I started.'

She was still weighing up the pros and cons of going on with films when Richard Quine came knocking on the door. At this time, 1962, Quine had made such lively and offbeat comedies as *Bell, Book and Candle* and *The Notorious Landlady* (both with Kim Novak) as well as the romantic musical, *The World of Suzie Wong,* whose success belied Hedda Hopper's prediction that no one would want to sit for three hours in a house of prostitution. Light comedy done with flippancy and style was Quine's specialty, and he brought with him to Burgenstock a George Axelrod screenplay. It had a role tailor-made for Audrey: the sprightly young assistant of a Hollywood screenwriter who helps him over his writer's block by acting out his fantasies of possible plots. In the soon-to-be-voguish word of the era, it had a 'swinging' beat to it—as Quine related it, anyhow, on Audrey's walks with him over the Swiss hillsides. (Mel was in Rome, acting in yet another Italian potboiler.) *Paris When It Sizzles* was the name of the project. The Gershwin associations seemed to Audrey a good omen.

She hesitated, though, when she was told that William Holden would play the scriptwriter. Even though she was now a married woman and a mother, it revived memories of the affair they had had while making *Sabrina*. She finally came round to the idea by a curiously ironic route. Quine had brought a print of a film he had recently directed and showed it to Audrey in order to increase her confidence in him. It was a romantic drama called *Strangers When We Meet*. Audrey admired Charles Lang's photography and was absorbed by Quine's handling of the love-affair between Kirk Douglas's architect and Kim Novak's married woman: two people caught in a romantic bind, unable to cope with it and deciding it is better to go their separate ways. Afterwards she made an odd comment: 'Perhaps it's what I need at the moment.' Quine took the remark as a gratifying vote of confidence in his talent. But to a friend, Audrey admitted that *Strangers When We Meet* brought back the feelings she and Holden had had for each other before deciding to kiss and part ten years earlier. She was tempted to say yes—and yielded to a hankering for the old romance.

The film was to be made in Paris which meant she would be close to Hubert de Givenchy, always an inviting prospect. He would of course design her wardrobe, but he offered her something less tangible: advice. Almost the same age (there was less than two years between them), Audrey and the reserved and remarkably perceptive couturier were as close as brother and sister. He seemed able to read her thoughts before she had disclosed them. No one knew Audrey Hepburn better than this discreet and loyal man. Like her, he embraced the rigours of the Protestant work ethic and, where Audrey was trying, he was succeeding in imposing a serene and disciplined order on his personal life despite the frenzy of the industry which had made him internationally famous. To Givenchy she confided that all was not well with her marriage. The disparity between her career and Mel's was generating strains and fracturing that sense of togetherness they had attempted to build, just when she needed the security of a permanent dwelling-place in which to bring up and educate Sean.

Alas, *Paris When It Sizzles* was a soufflé which refused to rise. Holden was well past his prime and deep into a phase of heavy drinking. There was a pathetic irony about the fact that the scriptwriter who consumed one Bloody Mary after another in his hunt for inspiration was played by an actor who tippled covertly throughout the day and had to be carried to his car when paralytic inebriation had set in. It was plain to Audrey that Holden was still in love with her. But his alcoholism, plus the self-inflicted impotence of his early vasectomy—undergone for convenience in his philandering but now bitterly regretted as a deterrent to any fresh marriage—had made him erratically unprofessional during filming and sour and unpredictable off the set. Audrey had to endure endless retakes because of his forgetfulness or mistiming. For Audrey, retakes meant a deadening of her performance.

She had other worries. Claude Renoir, though a lighting photographer of brilliance on traditional movies, adapted badly to the needs of this film. The humour of *Paris When It Sizzles* depended to a large extent on parodying the styles of half a dozen genres, as Audrey and Holden imagined how the film-within-the film, entitled *The Girl Who Stole the Eiffel Tower,* would look if made as a comedy, a spy thriller, a musical, a romance and even as a Western. Panic-stricken at how she was being photographed, Audrey demanded that Renoir be replaced by Charles Lang who had photographed *Strangers When We Meet.* Half-way through shooting, Holden's drinking got heavier and his behaviour worse. He was discovered shinning up the wall outside Audrey's dressing room on the second floor of the Studios de Boulogne like some knight errant striving to reach his lady's chamber, and had to be put into a clinic to be dried out. In July he attempted to drive to Burgenstock where Audrey was having a weekend off, and had a car accident which set the film's shooting schedule back even further. By now Audrey was wishing she had never got involved in it.

The film's appearance was delayed for a year, and it showed the effects of all this dislocation. It failed utterly to live up to the pleasurable promise of its title, director and stars, who included Noël Coward in a guest role and passing-through appearances as 'themselves' by Marlene Dietrich and Mel Ferrer. The only good notices were earned by Givenchy's dresses.

Around this time, as if to add to her unhappiness, the first open hints were being dropped in the gossip columns that all was not well with Audrey's marriage. She was certainly unhappy: unhappy at being separated from Mel, and unhappy when Mel returned from his own film to see the mess that was being made of *Paris When It Sizzles*. He told her bluntly what she already knew, that she had made a bad error of judgment. Mel's brief appearance had been as a party guest dressed as Dr Jekyll and Mr Hyde, with one mask on his face and another on the back of his head. It was a suitable symbol of the state of his marriage. Once success had brought out its best features; now a sense of frustration was putting a different complexion on it. For the moment both of them postponed facing up to the dilemma. In work, as always, lay the seduction that might alleviate the strain, if not cure it.

Before she left Paris Audrey received formidable compensation for what she had had to put up with on the Quine film. An old friend and skilled film-maker came to her rescue with a proposal that she instinctively knew would be as stylish, elegant and flattering as any outfit run up by her favourite couturier. Stanley Donen offered her *Charade*: in every detail of its art and styling, it was a 'designer movie' for the 1960s. Even better, the package was to include almost the last of those great stars whose appeal seems timeless: Cary Grant.

'I knew Cary well,' Donen recalls. They had already made *The Grass Is Greener* and *Indiscreet* together. Donen was now living and working in England, and surprised Grant by turning up on the doorstep of the Bristol nursing home where the English-born actor's elderly mother was now living and presenting him with the script of *Charade*. Grant thought it great fun. 'If only Audrey would play the girl,' he said.

A romantic adventure set in Paris, *Charade* applied the semi-fantasy of the James Bond movies which were currently all the rage to the sort of film usually labelled 'Hitchcock suspense'. It was a post-modernist joke in which absolutely nothing was to be taken at face value. Fun and fright met head on. A funeral mourner in an early sequence suddenly sticks a pin into the deceased to make sure he is really dead; half-slumbering delegates at a Unesco conference are jerked awake when a romantic *tête-à-tête* in the translation booth goes out over the system; an ugly-looking pistol pointing at the heroine discharges no more than a jet of water from its menacing muzzle; and so on. Like many people who value the security of a conventional lifestyle—like Hitchcock himself, in fact—Audrey had a penchant for innocuous practical jokes. *Charade* was an extended and inventive jape: she loved the script. 'If only Cary would play the man,' she said. The film, Stanley Donen said, came together as easily as that.

Grant was then fifty-eight, nearly twenty-five years older than Audrey. The odd thing was that despite their eminence they had never met. Donen decided to be the one to introduce the old legend to the new. 'Before we began the film, I reserved a table at an Italian restaurant in Paris—no longer there, alas!—and collected Audrey. We were already sitting at the table when we saw Cary wending his way towards us, looking immaculate in a tan suit. We stood up, both of us—the sort of courtesy that came instinctively to Audrey even though she was as big a star as he—and I said, "I needn't tell each of you who the other is." Audrey said she could scarcely believe she was going to have dinner with Cary, never mind work with him. "But I'm so tense," she went on, "I'm sure I'll never get through dinner, much less the picture."

'Even then, Cary had been taking relaxation courses. He had a remedy on the tip of his tongue. "Sit down," he said to Audrey, "put your hands on the table . . . Good . . . Rest your forehead on your hands . . . Good . . . Now take a deep breath . . . Relax." At which point Audrey's elbow upset the bottle of red wine, all down the front of Cary's immaculate tan jacket. She was horrified, like a child who'd disgraced herself at a party.' But it tested the famous 'cool' that Cary Grant maintained on all public occasions. Just as nonchalantly as in the film, where he lightens up a love scene by taking a shower in his wash'n'wear suit, he quickly stripped off his wine-soaked jacket, which was despatched to a dry cleaner's that the restaurant knew was miraculously still open, and sat down calmly in his shirt-sleeves to begin his dinner with Audrey. Thus was established a relationship that was reflected in every scene they played together.

Like all the other 'mature' stars with whom she had acted, Grant was concerned by Audrey's relative youth. He was aware of the risk of appearing too physically attracted to her, lest his age tell against the acceptability of their relationship. His easy fooling around in *Charade* was a conscious—and successful—effort to achieve a romantic attachment closer to the screwball comedies of the 1930s in which two mismatched people 'meet cute', fall out of love, then fall back in again after they have spent the film teasingly sniping at each other. But Audrey was not going to be done out of her love scene with Cary Grant. The solution worked out with Donen allowed her to give him a kiss: not a long lingering one but a little light flurry of kisses like the pattering of raindrops over Grant's celebrated chin.

'I love the moment,' says Stanley Donen, 'when Audrey says to Cary, "You know what's wrong with you?" "What?" he says. And she replies, "Nothing." That was her attitude to him all through the film.'

Winter came early in 1962, one of the coldest on record, and because much of *Charade* had to be filmed outdoors, and during the freezing hours of the night, Audrey moved into the Hôtel Raphael for greater convenience and security. Mel, however, stayed on at the Château Crespierre at Fontainebleau where the lease, taken during the summer while Audrey was making *Paris When It Sizzles,* had not yet expired. This looked to the press like a falling-out, and rumours of a separation surfaced again. Audrey reacted by tightening the cordon that kept reporters away from her while filming. When a *Cinémonde* photographer managed to penetrate her dressing room, her first reaction was to snatch up the photo of Sean and hide it. Kidnapping the children of the rich was a burgeoning crime in Italy. Audrey's Burgenstock villa had recently been broken into and she had lost her *Roman Holiday* Oscar, though not for long. The Swiss police found it discarded in a nearby field, presumably because it wasn't easily marketable. But even though the burglar turned out to be only a twenty-two-year-old student with a crush on Audrey, she could have done without this reminder of her vulnerability.

Between takes she was frequently on the telephone to Mel. Her concern to bridge the growing gap between them—or to kill the rumours—extended to slipping away from the location in the gardens of the Palais Royal at two o'clock in the morning and calling him from an all-night bistro. It was clear that she was under strain.

There is a line of dialogue in *Charade* that pulls the attentive listener up with a jerk. It probably passed unnoticed at the time it was spoken but now it seems strangly prophetic. It occurs as Audrey is being escorted to an unknown destination by Cary Grant, when she is not yet sure that the seductive but mysterious man is entirely to be trusted. As they emerge from an elevator and Audrey asks where she is, Grant's character replies, 'On the street where you live.' The line, of course, is identical with a lyric in *My Fair Lady.*

The Lerner and Loewe musical had opened on Broadway in 1956. Audrey had it very much in mind as she continued shooting *Charade* that cold winter in Paris, for the film of it was being prepared. It was several years since she had first expressed her desire to be in that film: 'I ought to campaign for it, I suppose,' she had said in 1960. 'There's no other role I'm dying to do. *I* must be Eliza.' But she was well aware that there was another outstanding contender for the role of the cockney flower girl who is turned into a lady by Henry Higgins, the professor of phonetics, and goes to the ball. The English actress and singer Julie Andrews had created the role of Eliza Doolittle on Broadway and it had made her a star as decisively as *Roman Holiday* had immortalized Audrey. She had repeated her success in London in 1958. To millions who had seen her, or listened to her recordings of the songs, Julie Andrews appeared to have a patent on the part: *My Fair Lady* was surely unthinkable without her.

Audrey had never before had to fight for a role, and it was an unwelcome sensation to know that if she won the coveted part she would be doing Julie Andrews out of what even Audrey considered to be her due. It would also be the first time Audrey had stepped into a role so famous and so inextricably associated with someone else. Cruel comparisons would be inevitable and would rob her victory of some of its sweetness. The Cinderella roles that Audrey had played in the past came to mind as she continued to shoot *Charade* in Paris and wait for news of Eliza. Would the glass slipper that had been made for someone else fit her own foot as well?

17

M ILLION - D OLLAR   L ADY

I N truth, it was no contest. To recoup the fortune that Jack L. Warner had paid for the film rights to *My Fair Lady* he needed a proven star of the movies, not just of Broadway.

Kurt Frings opened the bargaining for Audrey's services in September 1962. By October the muscular agent had worked out a deal which left no one in doubt that Audrey would be the one carrying the money on the screen. Warner Bros. had bought the film rights from CBS Television, which owned 'the property' called *My Fair Lady*, for the then record sum of $5.5 million. By an agreement signed on 20 October 1962 Audrey was to be paid a million dollars in seven annual instalments of $142,957.75 between 1 July 1963 and 1 July 1969. The instalment system would reduce even more the relatively small tax bite that the Swiss would take out of her income, which was already well protected by offshore, tax-free accounts in the Bahamas and Liechtenstein. (Later she would move considerable sums of money to Spain where pre-war tax laws, established by General Franco to facilitate the movement of both Jewish and Nazi Party funds, were now being used to protect the financial confidentiality of the world's very rich.)

Audrey was also to be paid a contingency sum of $41,444.67, or pro rata thereof, for every week or part of a week that the production ran over schedule. Her per diem payments ran at nearly $1000 a week and she had the usual star privileges of chauffeurs and first-class travel, but not her customary approval of cast and crew. There were some things, apparently, that money couldn't buy.

Audrey received five times as much as Rex Harrison, who was paid a mere $200,000. Rex had restored his reputation after a fallow period by playing the abrasive Professor Higgins on the New York and London stages; but as a film star he no longer rated as bankable. Peter O'Toole, twenty-four years younger and fresh from his triumph as Lawrence of Arabia, was Warner's preferred choice and would probably have landed the part if his demands had not been pitched so steeply—$400,000 against a large percentage of the box-office. Even Audrey drew no percentage. But Rex Harrison was already earning royalties from the recordings of the songs he 'sang' in his own eccentric but effective version of talking on pitch, or *Sprechtgesang*—a technique that had been used from the earliest days of the English music-hall by comedians who wanted to end their act with a song in a patriotic or sentimental vein but who couldn't sing in the conventional way. He would also draw royalties from his recording of the songs on the film soundtrack. Frings's deal included one vital clause governing Audrey's future remuneration. If her singing were good enough to be used in the film she too would participate in recording royalties. This meant that hundreds of thousands of extra dollars might be coming her way—and helps to explain the anxiety she showed over the quality of her singing while the film was in production.

Julie Andrews took Warner Bros.' decision gamely though her natural disappointment showed in a mild warning she gave Audrey. Although Audrey was likely to be 'enormously successful' she should beware of the pitfalls awaiting her. 'Two of the songs [in particular], "Just You Wait, 'Enery 'Iggins" and "I Could Have Danced All Night", are not easy. [The former] requires a lot of power, [the latter] has a great range [of notes]." Left unspoken was the thought: Is Audrey up to it?

Audrey arrived in Los Angeles on 15 May 1963 wondering the same thing. She was accompanied by Mel—who had a part in *Sex and the Single Girl* which was going into production at the same time—and Sean with his Italian nurse. After resting overnight at the Beverly Hills Hotel they all moved into the large house in Coldwater Canyon that Warner Bros. had rented for Audrey. From the start she established a living pattern like that of an English lady. Early callers were Cecil Beaton and George Cukor. Over cups of Earl Grey tea, tiny plates of thinly buttered sandwiches and jammy rounds of the Swiss roll that Audrey permitted herself despite her diet, Beaton scrutinized the star he was to dress for the film. It worried him to see how 'terribly thin' she looked. It is unlikely that he knew Audrey was still subject to spells of anorexia, otherwise he would have noted the fact in his voluminous diaries. Her vitality, however, animated what flesh there was on her bones and would cancel out any impression of wanness the cameras might otherwise have caught: 'a phenomenon', Beaton called it. 'Her mouth, her smile, her teeth are enchanting, the expression of her eyes adorable and her whole quality overcomes any deviation from the norm of beauty.'

Cukor was more down-to-earth in his connoisseurship of the million-dollar lady. In her early scenes as the uninhibited flower girl he wanted her to 'look slightly comic, but not chic'. Reconciling these contradictions, Beaton wrote with a sigh in his diary, was 'a great problem'. In fact relations between the two highly-strung men were soon to freeze over and, despite a temporary truce declared on Jack L. Warner's orders, would never quite recover. Their attitude to Audrey was the problem, for each claimed a kind of proprietary precedence: Beaton as her early admirer, confidant, photo-chronicler and costumier; Cukor as her director, jealous of anyone snatching her image away from him. Audrey expended precious energy during the film trying to make peace between her two mentors.

Almost as soon as they met Audrey asked Cukor, 'Are you going to use my voice in the film?' If she could sing the songs satisfactorily, he answered, then yes. No definite promises were made. This worried Audrey. It wasn't just the financial loss she would incur; it was the feeling of incompleteness that the role of Eliza would always possess for her if someone else was called in to dub her rendering of the tricky libretto. Such a surrender would rub salt in the wound opened by allegations that she had stolen a part which properly belonged to Julie Andrews. She attacked the songs early on with the aid of a voice coach skilled at expanding a singer's range. What made her task all the harder was Rex Harrison's refusal to record his songs in advance of shooting. Although Rex was never unduly concerned about the difficulties his demands frequently made for other people, his reasoning wasn't entirely selfish. He pointed out that he 'acted' the songs, not just voiced them, and if he recorded them in advance he would not be able to match his camera performance to the playback. Thus Audrey would have to perform some of the most difficult numbers she shared with Rex 'live' on the set, with only the fallback protection of revoicing them later on if her vocal proficiency wasn't up to standard.

Audrey had of course sung on the stage and in earlier films, but now she had a purist standing by. Alan Jay Lerner would be the judge of her success: a biased judge, she feared. Lerner had campaigned hard for Julie Andrews to be assigned the role. Though he understood the economic reasoning behind Warner Bros.' decision, Lerner felt that the artistry of his and Fritz Loewe's musical was compromised by entrusting the role of Eliza to someone who, great star though she was, was essentially not a singer. All these pressures weighed heavily on Audrey as she faced André Previn conducting a fifty-piece orchestra. Even though she had widened her range by five notes and, according to Previn, 'sounded happy and confident', this was far from being the case. She was later dismayed to be told that, as a precaution, all her songs had also been recorded by Marni Nixon, a professional opera and concert singer who had been the singing voice of Deborah Kerr in *The King and I*. Whether Nixon's version would be used, or Audrey's, or a mix of the two incorporating Nixon's voice as the notes still beyond Audrey's range, was a decision left until the film's rough cut. No one wanted to give an answer at this point: no good would come of upsetting Audrey too early. Yet she *was* upset: she felt in less than total control of her performance.

Mel was used to ironing out tensions between her and the studio's top brass. He got nowhere. Jack L. Warner had been generous but, of all the Hollywood moguls, he was the one who most stubbornly resisted any *démarche* by an out-of-temper star. Mel's attempts to calm Audrey's nerves or to assure her that, because of the adroit dubbing now possible, no one would notice any shortcomings in her performance, were met with a rare show of temper. Henry Rogers, her public relations counsellor, interpreted these upsets between Audrey and Mel as indications of some deeper dysfunction in their marriage. Rogers himself was soon to discover the penalty paid by anyone who took sides.

Audrey was also concerned lest she look unattractive as the Covent Garden urchin and tried to trim back the realistic 'dirtying-up' that was to be done on her. She allowed smudges on her cheeks, to indicate a lack of acquaintance with the soap and water that was later to be liberally bestowed on her; but she wanted only a token disfigurement. Once again the front office prevailed. An unpleasant week or so ensued. Wearing stained and dingy skirts and bunched-up petticoats with tatty bloomers, Audrey crawled on her knees—capped with rubber gardening pads—over studio cobblestones gritty with street dust to collect the few coins that Professor Higgins disdainfully threw at the flower girl. She also had to blacken her nails and have grimy-looking greasepaint smeared on the backs of her hands. It was a relief when she became part of the Higgins household.

One of the crew observed Audrey tossing pills into her mouth. 'Ill?' he asked in surprise, knowing how stubbornly she refused to admit to any indisposition. 'It's to make my tongue red,' she said, sucking furiously. 'It must be madly crimson when I stick it out for Professor Higgins.' A few minutes later, confronting the bullying professor of phonetics, Eliza bawled, 'I won't do my vowels agine. I knew 'em before I come here anyway.' And the impudent girl shot out a bright red tongue.

Beaton said afterwards that Audrey had been miscast. The flowergirl's big test came when she was introduced into a ballroom, but Audrey as the Cockney waif looked more out of place on her Covent Garden pitch than when she climbed into the magnificent white sheath Beaton had designed for her and displayed her elegant new personality under the chandeliers. The early scenes of Eliza Doolittle contain some of the stiffest acting of Audrey's career. She felt out of place and therefore out of character. This was a role that went against the grain of Audrey's own personality. Her acting technique was stretched valiantly, but to no avail. She was chagrined at the lost opportunities to run riot with Beaton's gowns since Eliza had a strictly limited wardrobe until the grub burst out of its chrysalis. In Beaton's workrooms she looked enviously at the range of designs for the 'upperclass extras' in the 'Ascot Gavotte' sequence. *My Fair Lady* was one of the last films to enlist the talents of an army of Hollywood craftworkers and here they all were, dozens of women putting the finishing touches to an abundance of period costumes—attaching aigrettes to turbans, stitching on false pearls, threading bunches of artificial Parma violets into corsages, ruching yards of intricately-worked lace and ribbon, even embroidering the parasols of the elegant *beau monde*. The sight set Audrey's taste buds watering with desire. She told Beaton, 'I don't want to play Eliza. She doesn't have enough pretty clothes. I want to parade in all these.'

Impulsively she started trying on the exotic hats and wrapping the silk shawls around her until, emboldened, she slipped into a dressing room and emerged in an elegant society lady's outfit. As she sashayed up and down between the trestle tables, the seamstresses cheered and applauded her like guests at a Paris fashion show. Jack L. Warner finally overcame his resistance to any additional expense and let Audrey do a photo-session with Beaton in the *My Fair Lady* wardrobe. It is one of the great series of Audrey Hepburn images. Anyone seeing it would immediately acknowledge her as the most beautiful woman of her time. Audrey's own looking-glass had always reflected an imperfect face. She used to denigrate herself, unconvinced by what anyone else said. Her eyes were 'too small' and needed a lot of cosmetic attention to achieve that entrancing oval look; and as for her chin—well, you could see what that did to her jawline. She once appeared on the doorstep of a near neighbour in Switzerland, Doris Brynner (the ex-wife of Yul Brynner and one of her intimates), and tilted up the famous Hepburn face, completely without make-up, for the inspection of her friend. 'See how square it is,' she said. Ever afterwards Doris Brynner called Audrey by the nickname 'Square'. Now, as she looked at herself in Cecil Beaton's glass of fashion, Audrey's doubts vanished. 'Ever since I can remember, I have always wanted to be beautiful,' she said in a thank-you note. 'Looking at those photographs last night, I saw that, for a short time at least, I am—all because of you.'

Her relationship with Rex Harrison was friendly but not especially warm. Harrison regarded *My Fair Lady* as his show: probably rightly, where the film version was concerned. He did not give away a point to Audrey in the acting game and of course won hands down when it came to the singing. He was under strain himself, for he was trying to cope with the heavy drinking of his new wife, Rachel Roberts, whom he had married after the death of his third wife, Audrey's old chorus-line partner Kay Kendall. Rex was also keeping a wary eye on George Cukor, aware of his reputation as a 'women's director' who had made some of his best films with Garbo, Norma Shearer and Katharine Hepburn. Cukor had a tedious time assuring Rex that he would not favour Audrey unduly. This didn't reinforce Audrey's confidence.

Too many born perfectionists were trying to work together. Rex Harrison in particular took endless pains—and gave endless trouble—over his scenes. To make sure they were just right—for him—necessitated frequent retakes. This was not right for Audrey, and may explain why, particularly in the early sequences, she performs with a clockwork punctiliousness instead of her customary spontaneity. Beaton had been told by Baroness van Heemstra that her daughter 'lived on her nerves'. Although she never let it show, her stomach was often in a knot. One terrible incident released her pent-up feelings in a manner she could never have anticipated.

She had just finished performing to the playback of 'Wouldn't It Be Loverly?' on a closed set from which all visitors were banned save Mel Ferrer. Cukor called her into her dressing room to break the news he had just heard from a studio security man: President Kennedy had been wounded in Dallas and was feared dying. Audrey fell onto her bed and buried her face in her hands, remembering perhaps that, like Marilyn Monroe, she too had sung 'Happy Birthday' to the US president only a few months before. Then she got up. 'We must tell the crew . . . We must say something.'

As Cukor recalls the morning, she walked with great purposefulness to an assistant director who was carrying a loudhailer, 'took it out of his hand and, still in her lumpy flower-girl skirt and shawl, stood on a chair'. The crew stood frozen in curiosity, wondering what all this was about. In a small, tight, clear voice, Audrey broke the news she had just heard and called for two minutes' silence. 'Please pray, or do whatever you feel appropriate.' Getting down off the chair, she knelt on the fake Covent Garden paving stones and leaned her head in prayer against the chair back, like the illustration of Christopher Robin saying his prayers in the A. A. Milne books that she now read nightly to Sean. 'May he rest in peace,' Audrey announced, after a minute or two. 'God have mercy on our souls and his.' Then, as if in a trance, she walked back to her dressing room. Looking in a few minutes later, Cukor found her crying her eyes out. What motivated such an uncommon show of feeling by someone who made it a rule not to let her emotions run away with her in public? The shock of the news, certainly. But also, as Audrey said in a calmer moment, 'the tradition in the theatre in England—and America—for the leading lady or the leading man to make any special announcements of tragic significance to the company. I just did what had to be done.' No doubt: but it was a relief to Audrey to have a licensed outlet for emotions she had to suppress in the exceptionally nerve-ridden circumstances of this production.

The minutiae were exhausting. Cecil Beaton was forever fussing over her. 'Strands of hair to be placed in this direction or that,' he wrote about his own labours on Eliza, 'suggesting more or less eyelash, selecting a brooch or a trinket.' Cukor, being ridden hard by Jack L. Warner, did not take any chances: everything had to be checked twice over, and reserve takes shot 'just in case'. Eventually Audrey demanded that black screens be placed at strategic points so that she wouldn't be distracted by any off-the-set movement. Crew members were ordered not to cross her line of sight while shooting, or even rehearsal, was in progress. A notice saying 'No Admittance Without Permission' was now posted on Audrey's bungalow dressing room. A small fence was built around it, ostensibly to keep her Yorkshire terrier in but very much an indication of the pressure she was under and her desire to have all worries kept out.

Then Rex Harrison turned moody on her, reprimanding her in the manner of Higgins—which indeed was very much his own, as Lerner and Loewe had written the part with him in mind—and declining to feed her lines from behind the camera for her close-ups. That chore was left to an assistant director, which may account for a minute but detectable overemphasis in some of Audrey's dialogue.

Mel visited the set during the eighteen-week shooting schedule, but it was the impression of some of the crew that the last thing Audrey wanted to discuss with her husband were his plans for future projects together. Mel had been busy while filming *Sex and the Single Girl*. For some years he had been developing a film version of J. M. Barrie's *Peter Pan*, with Audrey as Peter in the English stage tradition of casting androgynous females in the role, and Peter Sellers as Captain Hook. (Sellers had recently become an international star after appearing with Sophia Loren in *The Millionairess*.) However, Walt Disney, who had made the animated *Peter Pan* ten years earlier, claimed remake rights in the property and the project came to nothing. Audrey would never have to learn to fly. Well then, wouldn't she look good on a throne? Mel, who had developed business interests in Spain while taking a minor role in Sam Bronston's epic *The Fall of the Roman Empire*—Audrey was making the ill-fated *Paris When It Sizzles* at the time—now announced that he would direct a $5-million spectacular about Columbus's patroness, Queen Isabella. This project, too, faded into history. There was a feeling of frustration between them. Audrey's temper gave way once or twice owing to lack of sleep and loss of weight and she snapped at a stills photographer though she was as quick with her apology as her uncharacteristic outburst. 'There are people who blow their tops, and people who don't,' she said. 'I am told it is bad to bottle it all up inside you, but then if you blow you have to go around apologizing . . . I suppose I should just let it come out of my ears.'

Her tenseness diminished as the film neared the sequences where Eliza moved out of her guttersnipe background and began to acquire ladylike graces: the shift into high society improved Audrey's looks as well as her temper. Gone was the hairstyle which Cecil Beaton insisted was worn by working girls of the day, but which Audrey thought made her face even squarer. Not quite gone was Eliza's gawkiness. Beaton demanded she let her walk reflect traces of it and tied padded weights to her calves to remind her to drag her feet as if treading on cobblestones, not the drawing-room Axminster. With the successful acquisition of an upper-class persona and accent Audrey thankfully reverted to her own poise and dignity. When she was helped into Eliza's ballgown she looked more than a lady: she looked a princess.

In her alabaster-white Empire-line dress, her hair rising in a false cockade of intricately plaited tresses secured by a diamond pin, her long neck clasped by a high diamond collar, and her arms (whose thinness had made her self-conscious whenever they were left bare) now looking like delicate tapers in white satin gloves that came above her elbow, Audrey made her entry onto the set escorted by Rex Harrison and Wilfrid Hyde White, who was playing Colonel Pickering. The action suddenly stopped. Every extra in the ballroom, arrayed in his or her own finery, was standing in line looking expectantly towards the entrance. As Audrey came through it, their applause stopped her in her tracks. The film crew cheered. There was a strange feeling, Beaton recorded, that 'the little princess of *Roman Holiday* had grown into a queen's estate'.

But even her new-found resilience couldn't stand the pace. After Sean had fallen ill with a temperature of 103°, Audrey collapsed with a virus infection. Work halted for a long weekend while she rested and, for once, allowed her physician to prescribe sleeping tablets. Her mother, who was now living in San Francisco for part of the year, flew down to be at her side. Her weight loss continued even when she returned to work, and her smoking got the upper hand over willpower, which at first had resisted cigarettes until the day's shooting ended. She took short, sharp puffs on a Woodbine handed to her by a member of the crew. One reason she had tried to curb her smoking was its possible effect on her singing voice.

She need not have bothered. The day came when she had to be told that her rendering of the lyrics was not quite good enough. Marni Nixon would sing all Eliza's songs. In utter dejection Audrey declared that this would leave her giving only half a performance. She asked to go home early that day, later admitting that she felt like a child who had failed her exams. That evening she implored Jack L. Warner to let her rerecord the songs, 'and this time I'll get it right'. Warner told her curtly that there was no provision for re-recording in the budget. She protested that there must be. No, she was told, it had already been spent when Marni Nixon recorded the songs. So the decision had been taken from the very beginning! That was the cruellest blow. In order to avoid upsets, Audrey had been allowed to go along in the false hope that she still had a good chance of voicing her own lyrics. 'Audrey,' said Jack L. Warner, 'for a million dollars, you've enough to sing about. Nothing personal.' No, indeed: just Hollywood's way of doing business.

Audrey finished *My Fair Lady* a few days before Christmas 1963. But instead of sinking back thankfully into the peace and comfort of Burgenstock, she took only a few weeks' break before following her husband from France to Italy and Spain as Mel directed or produced a series of movies, three in quick succession, over the next year or so. The pact he and Audrey had made to stay together was still being honoured but now it was at the expense of Audrey's comfort and peace of mind. At all costs, she was determined their marriage would remain intact, so she 'bottled it up inside' and decided 'not to blow'.

During those months she acted as a script girl, production factotum, sometimes even den mother to young members of the unit: chores she performed with convincing goodwill, her concern being to keep close to Mel since 'he is so demanding of himself . . . I thought if at least I went along I could somehow help.' The effort was hardly worth it. *El Greco,* a life of the artist of which Mel was star, producer and music composer, had trouble getting shown in some countries. Visitors who witnessed Audrey doing the menial errands on Mel's films described her as looking as if she were on automatic pilot. Mel's attachment to Spain and all things Spanish had grown stronger over the years—his father's Cuban ancestry probably played its part—and when he and Audrey spoke of settling down, it was Spain that Mel suggested. This did not please her. Being a Northern European, she had little natural affection for the hot, dry plains of Extremadura and the other Spanish provinces where Mel's film-making caravan halted.

The date of *My Fair Lady*'s world premiere in New York, 23 October 1964, drew nearer. The fact that Audrey was only miming to Marni Nixon's singing was common knowledge in Hollywood, where the trade papers had got wind of it. Warner Bros., concerned about the negative effect on expectations of the film, put out a statement that—by error or intent—gave the impression that Audrey's voice would be heard on at least half of Eliza's numbers. This was a great exaggeration and it wrung an indignant denial from Marni Nixon's husband who claimed that his wife would be heard singing 'virtually 99 per cent of the notes'. This undignified wrangle fanned the indignation that many members of the Motion Picture Academy, which awarded the Oscars, were already feeling over Julie Andrews's being denied the 'right' to film the role she had made famous. While Audrey was making *My Fair Lady*, Julie Andrews had been filming *Mary Poppins* for Disney. Now it looked as if Audrey and Julie would once again be brought into contention, with the sympathy swinging towards Julie.

The premiere of *My Fair Lady* drew a celebrity audience from all parts of the world, anxious to judge how the film version stood up to the stage show (and Audrey Hepburn to Julie Andrews). Riding on their verdict was Warner Bros.' investment which, at $15–16 million, made *My Fair Lady* the most expensive musical then made.

Audrey's early scenes as Eliza, 'the squashed cabbage leaf', as Higgins calls her, in which she cooed her cockney vowels 'like a bilious pigeon', were so much at odds with the Hepburn image that the audience watched in an uncomfortable hush. Audrey's customary romantic air was swamped by her untidy look, dirty face, vulgar grimaces and unwonted feistiness. This girl was pitiable but not vulnerable. Audrey's East End accent was broad and, frankly, unconvincing. Compared to the Greenwich Village bookworm who so effortlessly elicited love and sympathy with her first plaintive air in *Funny Face*, Audrey's Eliza gave an uneasy impression of puppet strings being pulled. It is when Eliza loses her common accent that the film is transformed as if a wand has been waved over it, and Eliza too. The lyrics of 'The Rain in Spain', purged of their gutter vowels and glottal diphthongs and resonant with a girl's joy at speaking like a lady, show Audrey having burst the hobbling chains of language and celebrating her freedom with a vocal buoyancy familiar to all Hepburn lovers. This writer recalls an almost palpable thrill going through the cinema and applause crashing out—almost with relief—as Eliza darts about the Higgins household like a newly hatched dragonfly sunning herself in her mentor's approbation. It must be admitted, though, that it is Marni Nixon's singing voice which makes the transformation work at a deeper level than the visible joy which Audrey radiates with such physical élan. If the transfiguration didn't resonate with such confident clarity, it would be a false annunciation. From this point on, Audrey and the film get better and better.

Lerner and Loewe neglected to provide scenes defining the steps by which the rough edges of Eliza's newly-cast persona are smoothed away. But Audrey's own persona insinuates itself into the dramatic gap and fills it to perfection. We accept the vision of elegance—'By George, she's got it!'—and, unlike the social arbiters at the ball, don't question its pedigree. It is here that having Audrey Hepburn as the star is worth every cent of a million dollars. Eliza's emotional deflation after her night of triumph, when she fails to win the love and esteem of the bullying professor who only thinks of the wager he has won and not of the woman who made it possible, is a faultless account of pride, dignity and heartbreak by Audrey, one of the best scenes she ever played. As the premiere audience left for its round of receptions and parties hosted by Warner Bros., it was confidently expected that the film would garner an armful of Oscar nominations, including one for Audrey.

It won twelve nominations in all. But not one for Audrey. She had been snubbed by the actors and actresses in the Academy, in a show of professional displeasure directed less at her than at Jack L. Warner and the studio that had rebuffed the rightful pretender to the role.

Audrey heard the news on a February afternoon in 1965. Inwardly deeply disappointed, she put up a good show in public, congratulated Julie Andrews who had been nominated for *Mary Poppins* and wished her success in the final Oscar contest. Jack L. Warner was less chivalrous. Speaking at a trade luncheon a few days later he had occasion to refer to his film. As well known for his social gaffes as Sam Goldwyn was for his malapropisms, the boss of Warner Bros couldn't remember the name of his *My Fair Lady* star. 'That girl, what's her name?' he hissed to an aide. A million dollars without an Oscar nomination to show for it presumably left a certain numbness.

Audrey's namesake, Katharine Hepburn who had already been nominated eight times (and won once), sent her a consoling cable: 'Don't worry. Some day you'll get another one for a part that doesn't rate.'

Behind the scenes at Burgenstock, a smaller and more painful drama had been unfolding, not unrelated to Audrey's failure to appear among the Oscar contenders. Her relationship with Henry Rogers, her publicist, came to an end a few months after she had finished *My Fair Lady* and returned to Switzerland. The row involved her oldest friend, Hubert de Givenchy.

'Audrey always looked on Givenchy as God,' Henry Rogers recalls. 'He'd created her fashion image. She went to all his shows. She was photographed wearing things from his collections. He'd created the fragrance L'Interdit for her, and a special concentration of it for her exclusive use. But Audrey never received any money for the way she promoted Givenchy. She even bought the perfume, and paid for it at the retail price, too! Mel Ferrer shared my view that this arrangement was a bit one-sided, and he said to me, "I think you should talk to Givenchy—but see his brother Claude, who's his business manager." I said I'd see what could be done.' Rogers called at the Givenchy fashion house and, according to him, Claude de Givenchy saw the force of his argument that Audrey should derive some financial return for the close liaison that had developed over the years with the couturier and his creations and products. 'It was all settled very cordially,' says Rogers.

At the same time the Cannes Film Festival was trying to prevail on Audrey to attend in May 1965. Henry Rogers put an idea to the festival's president, Robert Favre LeBret. Would it not be a coup for the festival to have Audrey present with the status of a *patronne*—a patroness? Indeed, the festival might adopt this idea permanently, and celebrate world cinema under the aegis of a different celebrity each year. Rogers left Favre LeBret feeling well pleased with his work.

'The next I knew, I got a message from Audrey asking me to come and see her most urgently. I took a plane to Geneva and was soon with her in Burgenstock. There was just the two of us: which was somewhat odd. Mel was usually present. We had a drink and then started dinner. Audrey looked upset. She started to cry at the table. I was very concerned and puzzled. I said, "Audrey, what on earth's the matter?" She looked up at me and said, "How could you come between me and my best friend!" Givenchy had told her of my visit to his salon and the financial arrangement that had been proposed. I pointed out to Audrey that it had been done with Mel's full agreement. If she knew that, it apparently didn't make any difference. A close relationship—perhaps the most intimate she'd formed with any man besides her husband—had been turned into a commercial transaction.

She wasn't having any of it. And she didn't like the approach that had been made to Cannes, either. Favre LeBret had presented it to her in terms that made her think we were putting pressure on the festival.'

In these circumstances, believing he could not continue working for a client who had been so deeply, if unintentionally, wounded, Henry Rogers courteously agreed to dissolve their relationship. 'We still stayed good friends and later on I went back to giving Audrey advice.' Rogers took the full force of Audrey's displeasure but before long events occurred that would leave him with the thought that she had fired him on that occasion because she was not ready to face the prospect of 'firing' her husband.

As a result, Rogers was not around when Audrey needed him most: to combat the groundswell of Academy opinion in favour of Julie Andrews.

Audrey attended the Oscar ceremony at Santa Monica on 5 April 1965 knowing she would win nothing but that her absence would be interpreted in a way far more hurtful to her. A good loser was better than a jealous absentee. She would still have a role in the ceremony, though as she arrived at the presentation she was unaware of how ironic that role would be. Patricia Neal, who had won the 'Best Actress' Oscar the year before for her role as the housekeeper in *Hud*, was to have presented this year's statuette to the winner in the 'Best Actor' category but had recently suffered a stroke, semi-paralysing her and depriving her of her faculty of speech. Audrey agreed to deputize for her: a severe test of stamina, considering her own omission from the list of contenders. She found herself handing over the 'Best Actor' award to her co-star in *My Fair Lady*, Rex Harrison.

Rex showed an untypical touch of gentlemanly generosity by suggesting that the award be split between them. Then, turning towards Julie Andrews who sat holding the 'Best Actress' Oscar for *Mary Poppins*, Rex united the stage and film Elizas by thanking '. . . er, both of you'. A potential embarrassment seemed to have been avoided until Audrey, tense and wracked by conflicting emotions, entirely forgot to mention Patricia Neal. 'Pat's husband, Roald Dahl, wouldn't believe that Audrey hadn't deliberately slighted the poor woman,' says Henry Rogers, 'though anything less in keeping with Audrey Hepburn's nature would be hard to find.'

Roald Dahl told the newspapers later, 'Pat made gurgly noises of fury . . . Audrey telephoned me from Kennedy Airport on her way back to Paris. I told her to bugger off.'

Later, to Audrey's great relief, Patricia Neal regained her power of speech sufficiently to be able to tell her that she bore no resentment and understood what a jangle Audrey's nerves must have been in. But the incident and its unpleasant publicity haunted Audrey's thoughts for months afterwards and, Henry Rogers believes, strengthened her determination to build an even more secure wall around her life. In a literal sense, that is exactly what she did. For the first time since her marriage nearly twelve years earlier—and indeed for the first time in her life—Audrey found herself the owner of a home of her own.

18

O f F a s h i o n a n d A f f a i r s

A T LONG last she had put down roots. They sank into Swiss soil in a pretty-looking village called by the jaw-breaking name of Tolochenazsur-Morges, which lay just off the main motorway from Geneva about fifteen minutes' drive from Lausanne. It was chosen for Sean, rather than her or Mel, because French was the language of that canton and Audrey was anxious for her child to start speaking it as soon as possible. He would be able to go to the village school a hundred yards from the gate. 'It is everything I long for,' she said, surveying her new property; and she immediately called it 'La Paisible'——the place of peace.

It was not quite as peaceful as all that. The main road ran past it, several yards from the front gate, as if it had been cut through the vine fields which the house overlooked. But the garden wall was a strong bulwark. And though a notice begged callers to 'Enter and Ring', not everyone was equally welcome: another message on a ceramic tile warned, 'Attention au Chien'. The house itself, for which Audrey paid a sum equivalent to £18,500 in 1965, was a long, low, eighteenth-century *ferme:* but actually more of a manor house than a farm dwelling. Its plastered walls were peach-coloured and the shutters on the windows a duck-egg blue. The roof was steeply angled, which left plenty of space for bedrooms and attic. Two fancy metal finials decorated the gables like miniature ships' masts. A glassed-in front door was reached by four or five steps, which allowed for cellars and kitchen premises underneath the main reception rooms. The house faced north. Virginia creeper would redden the front walls; two tall cypresses stood guard at the western end and a large tree, probably a sycamore, buttressed the eastern end. Audrey had been guided to La Paisible by her great friend, Doris Brynner, who, after her divorce from Yul Brynner, had built a house for herself in Lully, the neighbouring village.

The garden was Audrey's delight. It stretched out behind the house, running south on a gentle slope to the main village street and ending in a high stone wall and white picket fence. It was studded with mature apple trees that, each spring, turned every view from the garden side of the house into an ocean of blossom. The first thing Audrey did was plant an English garden and fill it with flowers for cutting—but only white flowers. Coloured blooms were not to Audrey's liking, and red was particularly detested. A child's swing and slide were set up close to the house, where she could keep an eye on Sean and his playmates. The precious bits and pieces of furniture which she and Mel had amassed over the years were taken out of storage for the last time and set in place. Immediately the house took on an atmosphere of unassuming but elegant comfort: not a 'film star's house', but one that would soon be home to a child growing up and provide a welcome both for friends from abroad and film folk on business trips suggesting six-figure deals in an atmosphere of such unaccustomed relaxation that it was all the easier for the mistress of La Paisible to turn them down. This was to be Audrey's home for the rest of her life. This was the place where she would die.

In her contentment, she probably did not see that this settled existence was not the sort to infuse her marriage with tranquillity. La Paisible was a place to rest; but rest was something Mel Ferrer adapted to poorly. Mel was an obsessive globetrotter, never happier than when moving from place to place, film to film, enjoying the cosmopolitan ease of slipping from one country's culture into another just as he slipped from one foreign-language film into the next. Tolochenaz wasn't exactly off the beaten track, but in the days before the fax machine and all the facilities of instantaneous international communication, it was a poor headquarters from which to do business. Though Audrey was indisputably 'the star' in the relationship, she had been living at Mel's pace for a decade and a half. He still fretted over expanding his range and opening new career opportunities, if possible for both of them. Audrey followed loyally, but now the attachment to home was a prize—as she said—'worth more than a second Oscar'.

She had accompanied Mel to Spain after the last Oscar ceremony and the contretemps over Patricia Neal. The attraction Spain held for Mel was plain. It was not simply its warm Mediterranean ambience that he found congenial. He also took to the talents of a sixteen-year-old Spanish girl called Marisol, a high-tempered and precociously voluptuous beauty, whom he and Audrey saw dancing a flamenco at a party given by the Duchess of Alba. Smitten by her looks and high spirits, Mel decided she had the makings of a film star; and there and then he and Audrey devised a scenario about a girl rag-picker, a *trapera,* who exchanges her rags for the costume of a *caballera,* a mounted bullfighter, and wins the day against Spain's fiercest bull riding her beloved pony Cabriola. It was the sort of Cinderella story—literal rags into populist riches—that had been devised several times for Audrey. Now it was Marisol who would get the star role and the attention of Mel as he directed, co-authored and executive-produced the movie. Unfortunately for Mel, *Cabriola* or *Every Day Is a Holiday* appeared just as the steam went out of the Spanish film production scene with the collapse (and later bankruptcy) of Samuel Bronston's empire. It was evident that Mel's future didn't lie in Madrid.

But Mel felt the pull of the Iberian peninsula too strongly to give up any idea of working or living in a latitude he found so congenial. The strain of the unsettled life he and Audrey led seemed to be taking its toll on him. While Audrey had been making *My Fair Lady,* he had paid a trip to Portugal to investigate the prospects for a historical film on the life of the pioneering seafarer Vasco da Gama. He had fallen ill suddenly with a fever and turned to an old friend of his and Audrey's, the Duchess of Palmella, who had him transferred to her own home and nursed him through the ailment. 'Alligator', she called him, a teasing allusion to Mel's splendid set of teeth which his wide mouth revealed to advantage, at least to those who didn't consider them slightly menacing. Shortly after Mel had recovered and returned to America and Audrey, the duchess took delivery of a small light-blue Tiffany box: a present from Audrey, for the kindness shown her stricken husband while work prevented her from being at his bedside. It was a gold brooch in the shape of an alligator, with emerald eyes. The Hepburn touch—an apposite thoughtfulness combined with perfect taste— hadn't lost its power to charm.

Mel and Audrey bought a property in Marbella—a town that Sean Connery would soon pioneer as a rich man's enclave and the travel agencies of the world would turn into a tourists' nightmare. Their house was on a green hillside overlooking sandy beaches that Audrey felt would make the ideal summer resort for her son. Whether Mel intended it to be a more permanent location for the family is unknown: anyhow, the purchase of La Paisible decided the matter to Audrey's taste.

For her, the future held an opportunity—and a problem. It was time to reinvent Audrey Hepburn by fitting her image more closely to the look and taste of the youthful generation that had shaken off the old restraints in every field of the arts and entertainment. At thirty-six, this would require skill, boldness and stamina. She used all three at the first opportunity Kurt Frings presented her with: a movie on the lines of the then popular 'caper' plots that took crime lightly and laughed all the way out of the bank.

The Audrey Hepburn who began work on *How to Steal a Million* at the Studios de Boulogne in Paris, was a newly-styled woman. The old elegance was still there, but Givenchy had given her what the fashion writers quickly called 'the Mod-ish look', after the groups of sharply tailored young people who distinguished themselves from the more raggle-taggle 'Rockers'. Gone was her customary conservatism; in its place, a boyish sense of last-minute dash. She wore the diamond-patterned tights then in fashion on the King's Road, which had become the Via Veneto of London. Her smooth-layered hair had been given a spiky cut. Her skirt had been hiked up a couple of inches and her shoe heels lowered to balance it. She wore the latest in herringbone suits and cord blazers with flat brass buttons like a sailor's reefer jacket. There was a distinctly 'fun' element in her new look: one of her hats resembled a streamlined white motorcycle helmet. Big 'bubble' sunglasses made their appearance on her nose, vaguely suggesting that Audrey Hepburn was some kind of extraterrestrial, but were quickly copied by hundreds of thousands of women who wouldn't have been seen dead in them but for her. (Later, when she came to wear glasses, she chose the same outsize style, whose exaggeration displayed her lack of concern at wearing them. Her friend Sophia Loren swiftly followed suit.) In all this there was an unmistakable nod of homage to the sparky, mop-topped Beatles then (and for many years to come) feeding the mania of the worshipful young.

The second Beatles film, *Help!*, had come out the previous year. It was directed by an inventively iconoclastic young American, Richard Lester, who would one day direct Audrey. Movies that put the emphasis of interest on the newly liberated teenager—like *The Knack, Girl With Green Eyes, Georgy Girl*—delivered the message of change to those older stars, among whom Audrey had now to be classed, who could still claim a convincing connection with the new generation and its icons. *How to Steal a Million* showed that Audrey could do so: her chic urban waif was reborn as a sixties' pussycat.

She was paired with one of the most idiosyncratic and beguiling of the new generation of British actors: Peter O'Toole. He played the cat burglar whom Audrey engages to save the honour of her father, an art forger (Hugh Griffith), by stealing one of his sculptures from an art gallery and so preventing his deceit being discovered.

O'Toole accepted the chance of working with Audrey Hepburn in this William Wyler-directed comedy like a man who has been made the gift of a Fabergé bauble. 'I was in danger of becoming known as a dramatic actor, always self-tortured and in doubt, always looking off painfully into one of the world's most distant horizons,' said the star of *Lawrence of Arabia* and *Lord Jim*. He had deliberately set out to surprise people by making *What's New,*

Pussycat? with a harem of co-stars who included Romy Schneider, Capucine, Ursula Andress and Paula Prentiss. Now he wanted to continue his sex-attraction therapy with Audrey Hepburn. A less hectic piece of fun, maybe: but it would give him the chance for 'a touch of the Cary Grants'.

He was a wilder, younger, more extrovert edition of Grant, perhaps; rather more hit and miss, too, without the glint of hardness that gave Grant's persona its amorous cutting edge. Any reservations Audrey had were dissolved by her awareness that she was once more in touch with the times and working at a modern tempo. *How to Steal a Million,* a light romantic comedy with a fantasy feel to its frivolity, was the film that *Paris When It Sizzles* should have been. Having Charles Lang to photograph her again was an added security. She and William Wyler had an unspoken bond, developed on their previous two films, so she knew exactly how he wanted the scene played before he gave her his precise, even pernickety, directions. The film had the good sense not to try to be more than the sum of its comic situations, which played like a parody of the very similar 'caper' comedy *Topkapi.* The lightness, one might almost say the giddiness of the plot, carries the performances up to the same cruising altitude: no sweat.

O'Toole also helped bring Audrey up to pitch. As Stanley Donen had done, he soon discerned that she was always holding a little of herself in reserve. To a man with an Irish temperament, this was a niggling challenge. Early on, though, it was clear to him that any romance between them was going to be confined to what was in the script. So he sought another way past her guard—through a sense of fun. During the big robbery Audrey and he had a sequence in which they shared a broom cupboard and were thus in close physical proximity. Since each was fairly skinny, this caused little distress, but it offered O'Toole an opportunity to joke with Audrey in the impromptu way that had always appealed to the giggly child in her. In the pause between rehearsal and Wyler's cry of 'Action', he murmured into Audrey's ear, 'This must be what death feels like when you're in your coffin.' To his delight, Audrey whispered back, 'Are you afraid of dying?' He replied that the thought of it petrified him. 'Why, Peter?' she asked. Came the reply in a deadpan Irish whisper, 'Sure there's no future in it.' At which, Audrey gave vent to the biggest belly-laugh anyone had ever heard explode in that slender body of hers. Wyler called both of them out of the cupboard and demanded to know what was going on. Doubled up with mirth, Audrey tottered off helplessly to her dressing room to lie down and steady herself. O'Toole, well pleased with his success, licked his lips lecherously as if a more intimate encounter had taken place.

The film proved popular. It also proved to Audrey that she could adapt herself to the faster, more throwaway tempo of sixties' movie-making. There was another change in the air, however: a slight but inescapable one. There was a three-year age difference between herself and O'Toole. Audrey was growing older than her leading men.

At the beginning of December 1965 Audrey was delighted to find herself pregnant again. She had wanted to have a second baby for several reasons. One was that she had no desire for Sean to remain an only child. Though she herself had half-brothers, she had always felt—and indeed been treated by her father—as if she were the only one in the family. With her parents' marriage break-up, she was left on her own: no sister or brother to help bear the shock of separation. She also hoped a new baby would steady her marriage. Mel had not accompanied her to Paris while she made *How to Steal a Million;* and though he had been active from June onwards, discussing projects for her with Warner Bros., their relationship appeared to be more and more a professional one. But early in January 1966 she was rushed to a Lausanne clinic where she suffered yet another miscarriage. She returned home in a mood of depression. She had lost her baby and had fears that she might lose her husband.

Yet the setback had an unexpected compensation. It meant that the new film she had been offered could now go ahead much earlier than expected. Work was a kind of refuge in her current mood, even if it was work on a movie that, coincidentally, was built around the strains and stresses of modern marriage once the euphoria had gone. *Two for the Road* was a comedy with bitter undertones. It was about a couple whose life and circumstances should have kept them comfortable and happy but whose contrary natures propelled them into continual domestic discord.

The screenwriter, Frederic Raphael, fresh from his success with *Darling,* which had won Oscars for Julie Christie and himself in 1965, had the idea for *Two for the Road* 'while I was driving down to the South of France. How strange it would be, I thought, if we could overtake ourselves—pass our old selves on the road and look back and see how the people we were then had become the people we are now. No sooner had that thought entered my head than I said, "Hey, that's a film script!" ' Yes, but for whom? Raphael took the idea to Stanley Donen: the upshot was that both of them went to see Audrey. 'She was then still living in Burgenstock, in what must have been her last months there,' Raphael recalls. 'She said, "This is a great idea, but it will never work." Stanley said, "We'll do a script." Audrey said, "It's very clever, but I've been burned that way before." She was thinking of *Paris When It Sizzles,* with all its jump cuts into and out of fantasy.'

Raphael's impression of Audrey—'very smart, relaxed, but like an elegant cat that dozed with all its senses open'—corresponded to Donen's. He found her ravishing, but as if she were withholding some inner, vital part of herself. 'There was a very slight, but detectable formality in the air. Mel was around: she called him "Melchior." ' (Mel had been christened 'Melchior Gaston Ferrer'.) 'We spent more time talking about his film, the one he'd just made, *El Greco,*' Raphael recalls with an audible wince.

Raphael had to put in a lot of work on the script, for its 'time slip' structure was novel then and rather daring for an English-language film. Time jumps back and forth during four trips the couple in the film make to the Continent over a period of twelve years, spanning their lives from courtship to marriage, infidelity, near-divorce and finally, it is suggested, a sort of armed truce. They declare war on each other when tempers snap, then make peace and love almost in the same breath that they bawl at each other. There was an advertising slogan of the late 1960s which characterized the materialistic young of the period as 'Getaway People'. The couple in Raphael's script were this sort, but brought closer to daily reality than their doubles in the TV commercials. The husband comes across as an abrasive, truculent and sometimes bullying boy-in-a-hurry, but with great reserves of sex appeal. The wife is well able to hold her own in verbal abuse. She frequently keeps her mate at tongue's length with a rebuke that congratulates him on the way he's changed with the years—from 'a bad-tempered, disorganized and conceited failure' to a 'bad-tempered, disorganized and conceited success'.

Though they love each other, they are held together by mutual tensions the way a drop of water is kept whole by the tensile strength of its surface. They constantly use the underground bunker of their affections as a stronghold from which to sally forth and conduct verbal skirmishes in a war of nerves. 'Bitch,' says Mark to Joanna. 'Bastard,' says Joanna to Mark. These are the last two words in the script Raphael wrote, but two other words are comfortably implied in the modern mood of the banter: they are 'happy ending'.

The script was radically different from anything the well-protected Audrey Hepburn had ever been presented with before. She hesitated. She said she could not quite see 'the story'. Understandable: for there was none in the traditional sense. What Raphael had done was use the narrative freedom won by the French 'New Wave' film-makers like Truffaut and Godard to deconstruct and then reinvent the classic American screwball comedies. The dialogue had a brazenness that was unfamiliar to Audrey. There appeared to be semi-nude scenes, an adultery, a bedroom scene of the sort that called for a closed set. Raphael recalls: 'Audrey wasn't prim,

Learning the intricate steps of a nineteenth-century dance for *War and Peace* in 1955 ... and doing the real thing on the set at Cinecittà Studios. As Tolstoy's heroine Natasha, she won critics' approval: the film fared less well.

A bookshop waif lives a mannequin's daydream just by trying on a hat: Audrey singing her first number in Stanley Donen's *Funny Face*.

Could this be the image of love? Fred Astaire's famous fashion photographer produces magic in a darkroom.

Audrey's white socks, as she dances for a *Funny Face* number set in Paris, produced friction. She wanted to be all in black; Stanley Donen said no. He proved right: cats with white paws cut classier steps.

'In *Funny Face*, I experienced what all women dream of sometime in their lives: to dance with Fred Astaire.'

Curiosity gets the better of the cellist: Audrey in Billy Wilder's *Love in the Afternoon*, in which co-star Gary Cooper tries seducing her ...

... and, of course, has the picnic tables turned on him by this not-so-innocent child.

reflective mood, Audrey looks over Paris
the height of her stardom ... and comes
wn to earth dancing 'the Twist' with Mel
the evening.

Unhappy interlude, 1959: Miscast as a half-breed Indian in John Huston's *The Unforgiven*, she finds her horse is definitely not a fan. When it threw her, her injuries contributed to a miscarriage. Later, she jokingly asked her director if he had 'any parts for a girl who's good at falling off horses'.

W. H. Hudson's unforgettable
story of South America...
of Rima, mysterious as
she was beautiful...
of the Strange Secret that
lay hidden in a forgotten
land unknown to man.

M·G·M presents

AUDREY . ANTHONY
HEPBURN PERKINS

GREEN MANSIONS

...the forbidden forests beyond the Amazon

co-starring

LEE J. COBB

SESSUE HAYAKAWA · HENRY SILVA · Screen Play by DOROTHY KINGSLEY

in METROCOLOR and CinemaScope · Directed by MEL FERRER · Produced by EDMUND GRAINGER

As Rima in *Green Mansions*, directed by Mel Ferrer. A would-be eco-romance intended to restore her husband's career, it turned into a box-office flop. Critics complained they could hardly see Audrey's wood nymph for the trees.

Her biggest success: as Sister Luke, in Fred Zinnemann's *The Nun's Story*. The conscience-troubled woman who gives up the veil brought her an Oscar nomination – and a lifetime percentage of the profits.

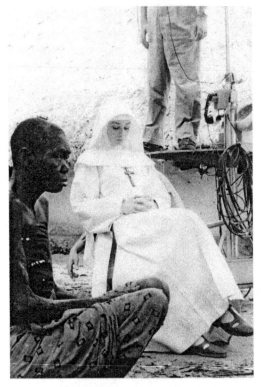

Sister Luke meditates before the cameras roll: Audrey in the Congo.

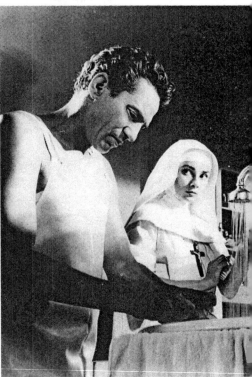

'He is the devil incarnate ... Don't think for a moment your habit will protect you, Sister.' But the higher powers of stardom preserve Audrey from Peter Finch's non-believer in *The Nun's Story*.

but she was what the French call "pudique". "Modest", I suppose, is the nearest word. It was a limitation, I always thought: she worried about what her public would think of her.' However, what she didn't lack was courage. She finally gave Donen and Raphael the green light.

Stanley Donen had sent the script to Paul Newman, hoping he would play the husband. Newman replied that it was a 'director's picture', not one for a star. At that halfway point Audrey had become pregnant and the film-makers had thought their project would have to be postponed for a year at least, maybe longer, if not indefinitely—which effectively spelled the end of it as far as Audrey was concerned. The pain of her subsequent miscarriage was at least mitigated by the prospect of the picture going ahead again. She had her customary approval of co-star. The script was now sent to Albert Finney.

As with Cary Grant, Audrey had never met Finney. Film stars sometimes lead extremely self-contained lives. Either they are working flat out, or else they are between pictures and looking ahead to their next one. Anyone else's movie has to be fitted in as, and when, there is free time; and there may be a strong if irrational reason for not rushing to see a possible rival in a movie one regrets not having done oneself. Audrey had few of these inhibitions but she had found little to attract her in the contemporary cinema, and quite a lot to repel her 'pudeur'. Albert Finney, at this stage of his screen career, had made his domestic mark with *Saturday Night and Sunday Morning* and then become an international star with *Tom Jones*. Audrey had seen neither film. She inquired how old Finney was and, after a reference book had been consulted, was told he would be thirty in May. Seven years difference: her co-stars were certainly getting younger. However, the fact that there were only a few days between the date on which each of them was born—Audrey on 4 May and Finney on 9 May—seemed a good omen. Audrey nodded agreement. For this film she received her now customary $750,000 (£312,500); Finney got $300,000 (£125,000). A dinner was arranged to introduce them to each other.

Albert Finney, at that time, had the look of a mischievous lad, tousle-headed and cocky, with the natural vitality of a Midlands upbringing where a wary eye was needed to thrive and not too much care shown for other people's feelings. He had none of the English theatrical vice of well-mannered but low-voltage characterization. He had come up—and quickly, too—playing working-class boys and his attitude to life, though increasingly comforted by its good things, was cavalier rather than polite. He was boss, and made it plain. Completely relaxed about his own celebrity, and no respecter of other people's, he was a type that Audrey had not worked with before. He sometimes deliberately went out of his way to disconcert people in order to see how they reacted. Marlon Brando and Jack Nicholson, the two Hollywood stars most like him in this respect, cultivated a joky, though sometimes brutal attitude towards newcomers with whom they were going to work—producers, directors, actors—to see how far they could test their tempers, ruffle their vanity or play upon their obsequiousness. Finney did the same thing more artfully.

The year before, 1965, he had been cast against type in Peter Shaffer's ingenious stage play *Black Comedy,* in which the characters, enduring a power cut, continue to move on a fully lit stage as if they were in the dark. The reversal of expectations, where Finney was concerned, was reflected in this very masculine actor playing an extremely effeminate antique dealer, hand on hip, limp-wristed, campy-voiced—the sort of character that gays today would find highly offensive. Stanley Donen recalls, 'Albert called me up before dinner with Audrey and said, whatever happened, I was not to laugh when he turned up.' He arrived at the restaurant accompanied by a male friend. 'To my amusement,' says Donen, 'he minced his way across to our table, extended an over-courtly hand to Audrey and said in a lisping drawl, "We're ever so happy to be working with you." ' His friend played up. Donen kept quiet. At first Audrey wondered if she was jumping to the wrong conclusion. Surely this couldn't be the Finney who had played a factory worker forever leaping into bed with his mates' wives or Henry Fielding's eighteenth-century roustabout who could turn supper with a wench into a visual feast of carnal innuendos?

Finney went on and on, always referring to himself as 'we'—'We did enjoy your last film, Miss Hepburn . . . We think you're absolutely sweet, Miss Hepburn.' 'He was totally convincing,' Donen says. 'Audrey caught my eye and made a face, as if to ask how she could possibly play a love scene with this man. I shrugged my shoulders, as if to say, "What can I do?" To her credit, Audrey looked resolved to make the best of a bad, or at least an ambiguous situation.' But after half an hour of delicate lisping, effete gesturing and florid compliments, Finney could sustain it no longer. 'He cracked up,' Donen remembers, 'and the belly-laughs exploded. Audrey's eyebrows shot up, her eyes opened to their full enormity and, realizing the deception practised on her, she joined in the mirth as Albert spluttered over his assurances that all was aboveboard and completely hetero.'

The trick not only broke the ice; it also set the tone of engaging banter, and sometimes physical combat, between the young married couple in the movie.

In worldliness, of course, Albert Finney was much older than Audrey.

He hadn't led the sheltered life that stars of her generation did, protected by protocol if, happily, not yet by the armed bodyguards that a later generation would require. The young actresses of the 1960s, headed by Julie Christie (born 1941), Sarah Miles (1941), Faye Dunaway (1941) and Vanessa Redgrave (1937) had become the challengers, and even the winners, of the prizes that Audrey had carried off fifteen years earlier. Audrey seemed to enjoy eternal youth. But if there was as yet no great difference between her outward appearance and most of these new, younger actresses, the distinction lay in the types of roles and kinds of films. The young, uninhibited generation was in thrall to stars who were naturally tuned in to their own iconoclasm and contempt for their parents' taboos. This was the gap Audrey now prepared to span in *Two for the Road*.

'It's no surprise that she was nervous,' Donen says. 'She was very concerned who the cameraman would be.' It wasn't Franz Planer or Charles Lang this time, but Christopher Challis, who gave some of the decade's American-financed and British-made films their distinctive 'swinging' look. After she saw the first day's rushes, Audrey exclaimed, 'But this man is wonderful!' Her make-up was done precisely according to her instructions. It was with the choice of wardrobe that the crisis came. Even Donen had not reckoned with the resistance Audrey put up when he broke the news that Givenchy would not be doing her costumes for this film. 'He was her other great protector, and I was depriving her of him.' It was the Henry Rogers row all over again: a third party was coming between her and her closest confidant. Donen remained adamant.

He pointed out that the young couple in *Two for the Road*, while comfortably off, were not the sort to pay the prices of a top Paris couturier. And however much Givenchy tried to 'dress Audrey down', without completely losing his own 'look', Donen flinched at the thought of having to argue over each and every one of Audrey's dresses and accessories. He wanted her to feel a changed person—without the security of a wardrobe containing only clothes of her own style. He wanted her to feel like the girls who shopped off the racks in the boutiques of youthful designers like Mary Quant, Michelle Rosier and Paco Rabanne. 'We shopped together from the collections of designers like these, as well as Ken Scott, Foale and Tiffin, all prêt-à-porter stuff,' says Donen.

Even so, it was an uphill task. Audrey quibbled over every detail. Ken Scott, the fashion designer who had been hired as consultant, resigned rather than suffer Audrey's endless quest for the thing that was 'just right'. Lady Rendlesham, a fashion adviser, was made of sterner stuff, and scoured the boutiques and wholesale showrooms for over a hundred outfits, of which twenty-three were used in the film. In place of the Givenchy trade-marks—Euclidean-angled lines, boat necklines and rouleau belts—were clinging jersey mini-shifts in violent red and yellow stripes or shocking emerald greens. In place of the Empire-line gown that had taken Eliza to the ball there was a dazzling silvery shift made out of aluminum discs from Paco Rabanne. There was a blouse of cotton cretonne in turquoise and lime that could have been bought at a King's Road boutique for five pounds. A yellow plastic visor cap came from the same shop; a slithery PVC trouser suit, as black and slim as a liquorice stick; trendy wraparound sunglasses. 'Audrey Hepburn in *Two for the Road*,' wrote one fashion magazine, 'is a lesson for any girl who thinks that 30-plus is time to put up her hair and let down her hemlines. She proves it isn't.' It was exactly what was hoped for.

As well as her new-look wardrobe, other elements in the film were a test for Audrey's ingrained reserve. For any woman approaching forty to expose her body in close-up to the camera was a test of faith: for Audrey, it was like a delayed initiation. 'She was very strung up as we began filming,' Donen remembers. 'It was Albert who helped put her at ease.' Some observers felt that Finney was very blasé and didn't really appreciate his luck at being in a film with Audrey Hepburn. The truth was that his own unimpressed attitude to stardom, coupled with a total lack of inhibitions, made it easier for Audrey to slip into an unself-conscious mood for the semi-nude love scenes. The production took over the Hôtel du Golf at Beauvallon, near St Tropez. Instead of keeping a polite distance between each other until called to do the scene, as is customary on location, the two stars romped around together like the couple they played in the film. Donen was delighted, and encouraged them. Soon it was obvious they needed no such encouragement. Audrey formed a warmer relationship with her leading man than she had done on any film since *Sabrina* and her affair with William Holden.

In none of her earlier films—not even in the romantic comedy she had just done with Peter O'Toole—had Audrey felt her leading man's sex appeal taking charge of their relationship on the screen. Now she became the willing partner of a man whose natural inclinations enhanced a woman's sense of her own desirability. He took pride in showing how he commanded her attention. To those like Raphael, who had noted Audrey's 'modesty' when she was with her husband, this was a surprise. Audrey's sexuality had never been the sort to burst its banks. But her relationship with Finney revealed the reservoir of feelings that had been dammed up in other movies.

Not infrequently stars assume screen roles and then play them in a way that becomes a kind of unconscious autobiography. Their roles awaken sentiments that are usually dormant, not always with beneficial results. The manic-depressive state that kept Vivien Leigh so close to the edge of tragedy proved balefully receptive to the extremes of sexual desperation that she portrayed so effectively in *A Streetcar Named Desire* and *The Roman Spring of Mrs Stone*. She didn't find it easy to shake them off: they 'tipped me over into madness', she said in the violent aftermath of one of these parts when she had required electroshock therapy. Other actresses were luckier or sturdier. Elizabeth Taylor re-enacted the crises through which her life was passing in some of the roles she played. With an almost eerie exactness they paralleled the events that were making headlines off-screen. Her love-affair with Richard Burton at the time of *Cleopatra* was virtually scripted by her writer-director, Joseph Mankiewicz, in the pages of the screenplay he delivered to the stars each day. Similarly, the feelings fostered by Audrey's encounter with Finney, on-screen and off, came at just the right moment in her life. They showed her what was missing from it. 'If he and Audrey did make love,' says one of the moviemakers, 'then they were discreet about it.' There was none of the flamboyant, defiant association between the stars that filming in exotic locations frequently leads to. 'But no one doubted the warmth between them.'

Audrey was very nervous about doing a swimming scene in the nude and suggested a flesh-coloured bathing costume. This was rejected. It was Finney who gave her the confidence to expose more of herself than her concern with 'my dreadful thinness' had ever allowed her to do. This was not just permissible in the context of the scene, he told her; he added, 'You're really an eyeful, Audrey.' His manner was cool and casual, sometimes blunt and vulgar: it loosened her up at such moments of self-disclosure. He had a disrespectful way with conventions that she felt put him in charge of things. To be with someone who was her opposite in so many ways proved peculiarly attractive.

Finney and Audrey were like children in some ways, too, inventing their own world, bonded by their roles in the film, developing the intimacy of a surrogate marriage in the jokes they shared, the nicknames they traded, the mental and physical closeness that the film—and they were in almost every scene together—promoted long after the cameras had stopped turning for the day. 'I'd never seen Audrey like this before,' says Donen. Irwin Shaw, a visitor to the location, added, 'They behaved like a brother and sister in their teens. When Mel dropped in to watch, Audrey and Albie got rather formal and a little awkward, as if they now had to behave like grown-ups.' The love scene was performed with a truth that those privileged to watch it on the closed set of a hotel bedroom, with the windows curtained against the blinding Mediterranean light outside, felt they had not witnessed in any other Audrey Hepburn film. Audrey's character has had her adulterous fling, come to regret it and now returns to the bed of her husband. It is a complex scene requiring not only depth of feeling but a shift of mood as guilt turns to gratification on receiving his forgiveness. All of this had to be performed by Audrey naked except for a pair of briefs and a sheet partially covering her own and Finney's bare torsos. Chris Challis behind the camera talked her through it, assuring her that it was 'sexy but proper'.

'I discovered Audrey's curious dread,' says Donen. 'She hated being in water, whether the sea or a swimming pool. When we came to do the scene where Albert picks her up and dunks her in the hotel pool, she said to me, "Can't you use a double?" I said, "Audrey, this is a scene I can't possibly shoot with a double. People have to be able to recognize it's you being thrown in." "Well," she said, "if Albie throws me in, I may well have a heart attack." ' It took three days' coaxing to get her into the pool. But she went through with it, though with mounting trepidation as Donen poured water over her head so that she would not have to duck it beneath the surface. Two assistant directors, stationed just out of the shot and wearing swimming trunks, mistimed their dive into the water to rescue a struggling and spluttering Audrey Hepburn and the scene had to be done again.

'You see,' Audrey later explained, 'when I was nine years old, in Holland, I was caught up in the weeds in a pond. I couldn't swim very well. The weeds were holding me down and I was losing my strength. I swallowed a lot of water as I tried to disentangle myself and before help arrived and they pulled me out I was sure I would drown. Even today I can't swim more than a few strokes without the panic coming back. When I can be persuaded by Mel to go into the sea, I keep my head well above water. All my nightmares, when I have them, are about water swamping me and suffocating me. It's hideous and frightening.' When mentioning her phobia, Audrey said it might also have something to do with the time she had had to hide herself from the Germans in the darkened cellar in wartime Arnhem.

Frederic Raphael had no complaints about the way Audrey played the part he had created for her. A fastidious writer, he found she treated his dialogue with an intense curiosity about the character's inner life that went beyond respect for the dialogue. 'She suggested that one of the important scenes needed clarifying. I rewrote it, and thought it an improvement. Audrey didn't: on second thoughts, she preferred the slight ambiguity of the first version. "Would you read it with me?" she asked. We did, and went back to version number one. She could change her mind, admit her mistake, go back to the start and make it all an improvement. With a star, that's rare.

'I remember hearing her give Stanley eight different readings of the words "Hello, darling." Number six, she thought, was the right one. Always needed to be perfect, that was Audrey. It was the Hollywood in which she had been brought up, where the big studios would shoot and reshoot until it was absolutely right. She had a lightness in her playing, but she held on to her status as a movie goddess. It was at times very odd. There was a tension between the star she was and the woman she wanted to be. She didn't let "the woman" be seen as clearly as she did when making our film—for which, I think, she should have received at least an Oscar nomination. As an actress, she didn't feel obliged to emote. She just let her feelings show: intuition stood in for technique. Looking back, I think she reminded me of Princess Diana. You know, the feelings were there to be drawn on, but there had to be a correctness of occasion.'

Two for the Road drew mixed reviews when it was released; but it has prompted more critics to revise their view of it over the years than any other film Audrey made. Nowadays it is admired for the way it mixed genres and juggled with time, and turned a shrewd eye on the gruelling journey through married life, disillusionment and endurance without losing its trust in romance. It was thus a very Anglo-American creation, wedding the British sense of irony with the Hollywood feel for fairy tale. Finney's performance, surprisingly sour-tempered at times, contributed to the former ingredient; Audrey guaranteed the latter. Nearly twenty years later a critic in New York's *Village Voice* wrote: 'The disparity in shapes and temperament between the thin, ethereal Hepburn and the chunky, earthy Finney makes the romance more moving and the relationship more challenging. Their slice-of-life vignettes are as biting as those devised by Raphael for *Darling*, but their acting presence is rendered in the emotionally rewarding American tradition of star appeal.' It was exactly the sort of picture that American producers were rushing over to England to make. England had been dubbed by *Time* magazine, in another catch phrase of the times, 'the place where it's all happening'. Audrey was brought back into fashion by more than the fashions on her back.

19

THE END OF THE ROAD

'We ought to get a divorce.' The words were Albert Finney's, spoken in *Two for the Road;* but spoken lovingly, as if the married couple he and Audrey play are so secure in their mutual affection that they can indulge themselves by pretending it's all going wrong.

Between Audrey and her husband, though, it *was* going wrong, gradually but surely. At first she shut her ears to the gossip in the newspapers about Mel and other women. A foundering marriage frightened her. Sean was now six, the same age as she had been when her mother and father broke up. She didn't want her son to suffer the same devastating sense of loss that she had felt. She was willing to put up with much in order to prevent, or delay, the possibility. She was even willing to appear in another film produced by her husband.

Mel had been active in setting up a new project, *Wait Until Dark,* while Audrey was away making *Two for the Road.* Audrey had initially approached it with reservations. For one thing, the heroine was a blind woman. The mere thought of blindness—never mind having to counterfeit it—unsettled Audrey. She could not imagine what life was like without sight: it held terrors for her. But Warner Bros. had been so keen on the story that the studio had bought the play even before it opened on Broadway. Written by Frederick Knott, best known for another thriller called *Dial 'M' for Murder,* it was a one-set melodrama about a blind woman in jeopardy from a gang of drug dealers whose Machiavellian leader tries to trick her into surrendering a package of heroin hidden in her apartment. The files of Warner Bros. show that negotiations for Audrey were started by Kurt Frings as early as June 1965, just before she began making *How to Steal a Million.* The long gap before production of the film began in 1967 is explained by the need to allow the play to come out on Broadway and enjoy what was correctly anticipated would be a successful run.

Audrey's reservations are apparent in the memoranda exchanged between Frings, Mel, Warners's executive Walter McEwan and others at the studio. On 24 June 1965 McEwan wrote to Jack L. Warner to say that 'if we plan to make a deal with Audrey Hepburn to do *Wait Until Dark,* she would like it announced as soon as possible—in order to avoid the possibility of another "Fair Lady" situation. If the actress who does the play on Broadway (I believe it's going to be Lee Remick) makes a big personal success in the show, Audrey does not want to be again accused of taking over a role which someone else might say belongs to the Broadway actress.'

Other problems arose, of a no less personal nature. Warner Bros. wanted the film to be shot in Hollywood. This would have presented Audrey with a tax problem. There was talk of setting up a personal corporation under whose fiscal umbrella she would make this one film. Frings thought that might be possible and pushed the matter of Warner Bros.' indebtedness to Audrey a little further forward. She had recently won awards for *My Fair Lady* in Italy and France. 'Frings would like you to consider taking local trade ads—to offset the fact that she did not get even [an Oscar] nomination here,' McEwan recorded. It is never too late to have balm rubbed into wounded vanity. Audrey's health also gave Warner Bros. cause for some concern. Her anorexia had staged a comeback. Who knew how she might look by 1967? 'Be sure we have a good protective clause in the event her health might possibly affect her appearance, etc. etc.,' Jack L. Warner wrote, as always putting work before sentiment.

By 12 July 1965 the deal was done. It was a quick negotiation: Audrey would pick up $750,000 (£312,500) against ten per cent of the gross; she would draw a per diem of $1000 (£416) a week. She would have director approval. Mel's remuneration for producing was set at a maximum of $50,000 (£20,883.) The picture would be made at Warner Bros.' Burbank studios and elsewhere—which turned out to mean Toronto, the Canadian location presumably chosen to accommodate Audrey's tax position—and then New York for location exteriors.

Alfred Hitchcock was considered by Warner Bros. as a possible director. News speedily came back: 'No chance of getting A.H. to direct.' Hitchcock's memory of how Audrey had 'double-crossed' him over *No Bail for the Judge* still rankled. Terence Young was proposed by Audrey, and agreed to by Warner Bros.—for a fee of $250,000 and $25,000 expenses. Young, an ex-officer in the Brigade of Guards and a film-maker with suspenseful action films like the James Bond adventures to his credit, had a well-mannered civility on and off the set which reassured Audrey. In other works, he was an ex-officer and a gentleman. While Audrey prepared for *Two for the Road,* Mel continued to set up *Wait Until Dark* which, it had been agreed, would begin shooting 'around the end of December, 1966'.

No sooner had the agreement with Audrey been signed than she began to have doubts about making the film in Hollywood—a place she now disliked very much after the cold-shoulder shown to her over *My Fair Lady*. England was proposed by Mel and Terence Young, then Paris. The bait for Warner Bros. was that, if shot in Europe, the film would cost $2.5 million (£1.04 million) instead of the projected budget of $4 million (£1.66 million) if it were shot in Hollywood. With some of the money saved Audrey could receive fifteen per cent of the gross instead of ten per cent and $900,000 (£375,000) instead of $750,000 (£312,500). '[Mel and Terence Young] looked at me innocently,' noted Walter McEwan, who was serving as executive producer. 'Have you any comment?' he asked the studio's head of contracts. Indeed he had. The figures were wrong and the proposal to make the film overseas, 'for the convenience of Miss H', was totally unacceptable. Warner Bros. now got tough. An ultimatum followed, warning of legal action for damages should 'Miss H' or Mel or Terence Young not comply with their contractual obligations. 'We wish to remind you that *Wait Until Dark* is a very costly and important theatrical property. If we are deprived of the services of a star of the magnitude of Miss Hepburn and forced to make the picture with a lesser artist, damages could amount to a very large sum . . . This is a public corporation and we cannot do business for the personal convenience of stars and others to whom we pay such tremendous sums.' Within the week, Audrey had reluctantly given way. 'Audrey will be a good girl and do picture here as always planned', McEwan cabled Jack Warner in New York. Warner now had the upper hand and let it fall where he knew it would hurt most. No, he ordered, Givenchy would not be doing Miss Hepburn's costumes for the film. Those days were over, he implied. 'We are spending enough money on her.'

Audrey spent the time between finishing *Two for the Road* and beginning *Wait Until Dark* in supervising the completion and furnishing of the villa she and Mel had bought in Marbella. Privately, though, she was pining for the crisp air of the glorious autumn days at the place she considered her one and only home, La Paisible. She was back in Switzerland for Christmas 1966 and present at a Nativity play done by the village schoolchildren in which Sean appeared as one of the sheep watched over by shepherds—in a costume made by his mother with paper tissues screwed up to resemble a curly fleece and black crêpe-paper ears. He also recited a short poem in French. 'He did us proud,' Audrey commented, 'and spoke good and loud as I'd asked him to. [Mel and I] were absolute wrecks . . . We were afraid he would forget or lose his confidence. But he didn't . . . It was a big thrill.'

She herself was being tutored at the time, in feigning blindness for the approaching film. She went to a clinic for the blind in Lausanne to consult a professor about the compensations available to the sightless. She left for Hollywood in January 1967, stopping over in New York to continue her researches at the Lighthouse Clinic. She wore one of the 'blinders', specially made to give people who are losing their sight some experience of what confronted them; learnt how to move tentatively, tapping with a white cane; listened to the various sounds made by footsteps which could determine the position of the walker; practised using a telephone 'blind' (there would be a lot of this in the film); made tea and felt the cup fill up by the rising heat of the liquid; and determined where a light bulb hung by the heat of it on her face. This would be very important in *Wait Until Dark*, since the beleaguered heroine frenziedly smashes all the bulbs in her apartment in order to reduce her tormentor to something like equality with herself in the battle of nerves, brains and brute force. It made Audrey recall the rigorous drill she had put herself through when preparing for *The Nun's Story*, except that this time the discipline was physical, not spiritual.

When she began the film in New York, her pride in the sightless look she thought she had assumed was rudely dispelled after the first rushes had been seen. Her eyes—an Audrey Hepburn trademark, after all—still sparkled too much. Contact lenses were ordered. These were not the flexible water-thin discs common today but hard glass objects that made her feel she had grit in her eyes and, along with the wind of an exceptionally cold winter, left her eyelids red-rimmed. Charles Lang—at least she had a favourite cameraman—listened to her unhappiness. She was a very different Audrey, he felt, from the woman he had worked with so happily in the past. In virtually every scene she was the only woman, and it wasn't only the rough treatment she had to endure as the gang used increasingly brutal methods to undermine her confidence that made her feel she was being manipulated. Oh, where was the glamour of Holly Golightly? Warner Bros. maintained its reputation for stinginess until the unit moved to Hollywood, where Audrey and Mel took over a bungalow in the grounds of the Beverly Hills Hotel, making use of every 'perquisite' that Kurt Frings had had written into their contracts, including a tea-break at 4 p.m. which was taken on a small replica of an English tea-garden run up next to the apartment set in the studio. It was a reminder of more decorous days on *My Fair Lady*.

Audrey had been tempted to take Sean with her, but feared disrupting the friendships he was forming with Swiss schoolmates. They talked for a good half-hour at weekends over the line to Tolochenaz, and he arrived to spend Easter with her, which included a day at Disneyland.

The tension between Mel and herself was remarked on by those on the set. There were plenty of informants to reroute rumour into the gossip columns. One of Audrey's closest friends, who had recently parted from her own husband, suggested she seek psychiatric counselling. She recalls the star's reaction. 'Her chin shot up as if her head had been yanked high by horse reins and she almost spat out the word, "Never!" She would get through this on her own.' She never called on her mother, perhaps because she was unwilling to admit that her marriage was going the same way as the baroness's own two had done. Audrey realized at this period of her life how very few close friends she possessed. Work, and following Mel around Europe, had not left time. There was Connie Wald, the widow of producer Jerry Wald, who lived in Hollywood; and Doris Brynner, Yul's ex-wife, in the next village in Switzerland; but that was almost it. She needed all her Christian Science resilience as she blindly suffered the tortures that filming put her through daily.

Despite the talent involved—which included Alan Arkin as the gang leader (contenders had been George C. Scott and, incredibly, Robert Redford)—*Wait Until Dark* remained a stage-bound potboiler. It did not even preserve the logic of its own far-fetched premise. The vicious Arkin puts on a variety of physical disguises with matching voices to make Audrey believe that a series of different people, some benign, others threatening, are coming and going in the apartment block in which she seems to be the sole resident. Why a blind woman needs to be fooled by make-up jobs is never explained; and nor is Audrey's failure ever to lock the front door of her apartment. If she had, there would have been no play (and no film). Despite being roughed up by the gang, she remains implausibly unruffled, with a tiny smudge of blood on her dress as a token nod to reality.

It all brought home to her how Hollywood—her Hollywood—had changed. It was in other, tougher hands. The pace of change was accelerating monthly, as screen taboos collapsed like dominoes. Even when it appeared, halfway through 1968, *Wait Until Dark* looked *passé* compared to films like *Rosemary's Baby* starring the waif-like and victimized Mia Farrow ('Mia will get my roles now,' Audrey commented drily); *The Detective*, a serial murderer mystery using medical frankness as bait for sensation-hungry filmgoers; *The Graduate,* a social satire combining a romance between an older woman and a virginal boy in which Audrey had been offered the part of Mrs Robinson; and *No Way to Treat a Lady,* with Rod Steiger as a multiple murderer who, like Alan Arkin, adopted different disguises, but with an infinitely more bizarre effect. Still, with all its formulaic banality, *Wait*

Until Dark did extremely well at the box-office and was even to bring Audrey an Oscar nomination.

She returned to Switzerland in late April 1967, feeling she was out of joint with the times as well as with her husband. The latter problem she tried to mend. In July 1967 the doctors confirmed she was pregnant again. Mel was not by her side: he was in Marbella. Within a few weeks, the same sad story occurred: she lost her baby. Her despondency was now total. Her weight dropped to below 112 pounds. In this mood, she did what events were forcing on her: she asked for a separation, for time to reconsider where life was taking her. She did so without dramatics or rancour, in the most level-headed way she knew. Uppermost in her thoughts was her desire to protect Sean.

Despite the rumours that preceded it, the announcement of the separation took everyone by surprise. It was made in the name of both parties by Kurt Frings's Hollywood office. Audrey and Mel had agreed to pursue separate lives and careers 'for the time being'. No reasons were given; divorce was not mentioned. The announcement coincided with the release of *Two for the Road,* the story of a troubled marriage, and there were suggestions that it was a publicity stunt. This might have been more widely believed had any other actress than Audrey Hepburn been involved. No, this was real marital discord. The Ferrers had been seen only a fortnight earlier maintaining a brave face in public at the Gala des Courses, the main social event of the Deauville racing season, where they were guests of honour of Baron and Baroness Guy de Rothschild. Mel was working on his next production in Paris, a third version of the Mayerling story to be directed by Terence Young as the second film in the company the two men had recently set up. Audrey would not be in it: Catherine Deneuve was to play the Crown Prince's mistress this time round. 'I'm so glad,' was Audrey's only comment to a friend when asked if she was sorry not to be in Mel's film. The doomed union of history was echoed in the ruptured union of stardom.

With the announcement of the separation, Mel flew to Geneva and went on to Tolochenaz, tight-lipped and unusually uncommunicative except to say that he was 'going home'. Audrey was not 'at home', however; she was behind heavy security at their old villa in Burgenstock. She returned to La Paisible three days later and husband and wife were seen walking pensively between the yellowing apple trees on the lawn, his arm around her slim shoulders and their heads close together in conversation. Whatever they talked about, it was low-key in every sense. Some years were to go by before Audrey could bring herself to comment publicly on that moment. But when she did, it was in terms which showed how tenaciously she had clung to the fairy tale. 'When my marriage broke up, it was terrible,' she said to Henry Gris, one of the very few journalists to retain her confidence. 'More than that, it was a keen disappointment. I thought a marriage between two good, loving people had to last until one of them died. I can't tell you how disillusioned I was. I'd tried and tried. I knew how difficult it had to be to be married to a world celebrity, recognized everywhere, second-billed on the screen and in real life. How Mel suffered. But believe me, I put my career second.' Into that simple confession may be read Mel's own bitterness at the tailing off of his film career and Audrey's unsuccessful attempts to come to his aid by agreeing to 'rescue' projects, which only prolonged her disillusionment with film-making or else left her with no sense of personal fulfilment.

She did not at this stage contemplate a divorce because she still shrank from Sean's being involved in a possible custody battle. A lot had to be worked out by the lawyers. Fortunately, there was no public acrimony. Mel was granted access to the boy. What Audrey found hard to bear was the residual feeling that responsibility for the breakdown might in part be hers. She knew what she owed her husband: he had guided her career, helped her earn huge fees by his astuteness and toughness, constructed their life together, given her a son. All these things were on her conscience as the new isolation of the Tolochenaz house closed around her. Mel immersed himself in work and planned to return to the theatre, where a large part of his heart lay, and which had suffered as he dedicated himself to film-making and to Audrey. 'Reconciliation would still have been possible, and that's what she was hoping for,' says a friend of Audrey, 'but as the months passed, Mel found work more satisfying than going back home.' He did not join her when she took Sean to Marbella for the winter holidays in 1967. Her few friends rallied round, and as a result of the social consolations arranged for her over Christmas, Audrey found new acquaintances which caused speculation. One was Don Alfonso de Bourbon-Dampierre, a pretender to the throne of Spain. They saw the new year in together in a Madrid nightclub. 'Actually, that was when Audrey stopped blaming herself,' Henry Gris says. 'She had sustained the shock of separation and now she began to enjoy some of its liberties.' Her son remained at the centre of her concern: 'her salvation', Gris believes. Mel waited at Kennedy Airport, New York, early in 1968 for the boy to arrive off a Swissair flight to spend a few weeks with him in Manhattan and then at the house in California that he had rented for them. The boy did not turn up on the flight, but a message from Audrey did: she couldn't bear to part with him. Very little communication between the parents followed; the lawyers did most of the talking. The inevitable division of property and other settlements was painfully worked out. Audrey had reached the point where divorce was a preferable alternative to this half-wedlock.

But there was another reason for her desire to make the break a clean one. That summer of 1968 she joined a cruise round the Greek islands in a yacht chartered by Paul Weiller, the French industrialist, and his Italian wife, Princess Olympia Torlonia. Another member of the party was a smooth-cheeked, youngish Italian of good family who enjoyed socializing but, in Audrey's eyes, had a serious side to him as well. Andrea Dotti, at thirty, was assistant director of the Rome University psychiatric clinic. There could have been no profession or concern more likely to commend him to the lonely woman with a child of her own and no father on hand to care for him.

Yet it was not quite love at first sight. Where Dr Dotti was concerned, whether or not he recognized it, it was partly fan worship, too. He had first set eyes on Audrey Hepburn when, as a fourteen-year-old schoolboy, he had seen *Roman Holiday*—and returned to see it again several times, captivated by this girl who enjoyed the freedom of the city streets he knew so well. He had not missed a single one of her films since then. He had been on the fringe of the circle around Audrey when she and Mel attended a large society party in Rome in the 1950s. Now events had closed the distance between them: she was asking his advice and confessing her troubles. To the good doctor, it was like a movie.

Dotti's charm had been well practised on the Roman party circuit before he acquired, through hard work and intelligent career-building, a professional ease and considerable success with patients. He was very knowledgeable about the use of many of the new drugs, like lithium, which were then establishing themselves as stabilizers in the treatment of manic-depression. He was also an energetic conversationalist on the more faddish opiates like LSD. Friends in Rome who knew him well and who were themselves Italian, tended to be a little less impressed than foreigners with his charm and loquaciousness: things that were not so uncommon in their society. Even hard-headed foreigners, meeting Dotti at dinners or parties, generally surrendered to the efforts he made to entertain them with wit mixed with professional talk. Clare Booth Luce, who had been US ambassador to Italy, was seated next to Dotti at one dinner, and her hostess was slightly disconcerted to see how the doctor monopolized the conversation with this powerful woman who didn't suffer fools or bores gladly. At the end of the evening Mrs Luce effusively thanked her hostess, saying what a 'fascinating' man the doctor was: he knew all about the medical use of drugs.

The mood Audrey was in when she and Dotti met aboard the Weiller yacht may have been familiar to him through his psychiatric practice. She still had a residual guilt over the break-up of her marriage and was deeply worried about the possible effect of the split on her child. In the confined surroundings of the vessel, Audrey soon made a confidant of her new acquaintance. Very soon they were on terms of intimacy. Had she stopped to reflect, she might have been struck with the similarity between this encounter and her first meeting with Mel Ferrer thirteen years earlier. Then she had been desperately grateful to Mel for taking her in hand when too much was happening all at once and, feeling lonelier than she could ever have imagined, she was heading for a nervous breakdown. Often no one is more in need of friends than the star, whom everyone thinks of as not having a minute to spare for herself. Dotti's professional counsel, supplemented by his personal attentions, offered Audrey the support she needed at exactly the right moment in her estrangement from Mel Ferrer.

Audrey was always professionally cautious about allowing anyone to get too close to her, particularly self-declared film fans. But she was grateful for the insights that Dotti offered into her emotional distress and the likely effect of divorce on Sean. 'And he's such an enthusiastic, cheerful person,' she said of him some time later, when she had a chance to analyse what was happening. 'Obviously, as I got to know him, I found him a thinking, very deep-feeling person also.' The fact that Dotti was a man of established status, with a good income, from a well-off family, encouraged her to drop her guard with more confidence than usual. Although the divorce settlement with Mel would be costly, she would still be rich. But Dotti was certainly no fortune-hunter. He was a confident charmer, an effective comforter. His fondness for Rome's social life was obvious; but that, too, was part of the 'cure' to keep Audrey's depression at bay. Her intuition, that instinct which role-playing frequently sharpens, acquitted Andrea Dotti of insincerity or self-aggrandizement. He 'passed'.

As she got to know him better, she was struck by a similarity to her own background. Though his family were prominent Roman Catholics, Dotti's parents had separated—like hers—and their marriage had been annulled. His mother had been a countess, just as Audrey's had been a baroness. His stepfather was a prominent newspaperman; his brother, a respectable banker. There was nothing that would cause Audrey to resist the growing closeness of the relationship. Sean got on well with Dotti: that was the most reassuring thing of all. And Dotti expressed to her his wish to have 'many children' of his own. After the vain attempts she had made to add to her own family of one, Audrey could not object to this aspiration. To someone with her painful gynaecological history, an early remarriage was advisable as well as desirable.

She obtained her divorce from Mel, quietly and secretly as Swiss law guaranteed, on 20 November 1968. That Christmas, in Rome, Andrea Dotti formally proposed to her and, when she accepted, slipped a ruby engagement ring on her finger. Even so, there is the evidence of friends that Audrey was still hesitant about marrying him. She did not want any future husband to be turned into a surrogate celebrity, best known for being married to Audrey Hepburn the film star. She knew how invasive such a reputation could be to a man's self-esteem, never mind his professional standing, particularly in a field where discretion was essential. 'I said to him that people—women, I mean—might be attracted to him because he was married to me, and that this couldn't be helpful or might indeed hold risks for his professional reputation,' she confided to a friend.

Dotti pooh-poohed her apprehension. He wasn't a public figure, he said. True; but what he neglected to mention, either through prudence or because it was so much a part of his nature that he did not recognize it, was the strong fascination that celebrity possessed for him. Despite the genuine pleasure he got from Audrey's company and her flattering dependence on his advice, the Audrey Hepburn he had loved on the screen still shimmered in Andrea Dotti's imagination. The glamour sparkled more brightly than an engagement ring. Mel Ferrer had at least had a professional understanding of how such uniqueness could be created and what humdrum reality often lay behind it. It was to be part of Dr Dotti's education to discover this for himself: that the woman he married was not exactly the one he had fallen in love with when he was a fourteen-year-old schoolboy.

His mother, his brother and his extended family were all delighted with the engagement. Andrea was going to settle down, get married—to a film star, too—and start a family. To have a son unmarried at the age of thirty would be a source of concern to the average Roman matron. Though the fiancée was almost ten years older than her husband-to-be, she behaved in every way as if she were already part of the family. It is not uncommon that when the son of a prominent Italian family marries 'outside' his circle or even his nationality, the woman can expect to undergo a rigorous examination, even an initiation that cruelly, if discreetly, tests her suitability. This was never to happen to Audrey. Her fame, as well as her nature, somewhat overawed her future relatives. 'She will be an ideal daughter-in-law,' Paola

Roberta Bandini, the former Comtessa Dotti, was quoted as saying. 'For years and years, [Andrea] has spoken of getting married and having a handful of children, but he just never was able to make up his mind.' From Audrey's mother, Baroness van Heemstra, there was no published statement of any kind.

The wedding took place not in Rome, but on Swiss soil. The choice was no doubt dictated by Audrey's recent divorce which rendered remarriage in a Catholic church an impossibility at this time (it wasn't until after 1974 that Italy liberalized its divorce laws). The banns between 'Andrea Paolo Mario Dotti, 30, medical psychiatrist, and Audrey Kathleen Hepburn, 39, British citizen', were posted on the wall of the tiny post office at Tolochenaz-sur-Morges on 6 January 1969. Ten days' notice was required. The parties did not drag their feet. On 18 January Madame Battaz, registrar in the town of Morges, joined the doctor and the actress as husband and wife. Witnesses for the bride were Doris Brynner and the French film star Capucine. Dotti's witnesses were Paul Weiller and the painter Renato Guttuso. Just over three dozen guests attended. The bride was dressed in a pink jersey outfit, the gift of one of her oldest admirers, Givenchy.

20

THE DOCTOR'S WIFE

*A*UDREY and her new husband spent part of their honeymoon house-hunting in Rome—to be precise, looking for an apartment. A top-floor one was eventually chosen, a spacious, high-ceilinged place in a converted palazzo that had belonged to a church dignitary several centuries before. It had broad views over the Tiber, and Audrey was delighted with it. In her favourite word, it was 'divine'. She was also prudent. To anyone inquiring about her 'palazzo' she replied crisply, 'We have no palazzo in Rome, only an apartment.' The attitude that ostentation was not only vulgar, but unsafe, was even then permeating life in the city. The free and easy spendthrift days of the *Dolce Vita* era were being forced rudely out of fashion by the urban terrorists of the Red Brigade and the kidnap threats to the rich and politically prominent.

The overflow of a life that until recently she had kept in storage, except for what the house at Tolochenaz could accommodate, preoccupied Audrey's days. She fitted her possessions, old and new, into the apartment, working alongside the carpenters and masons who were remodelling it, her hair powdered with the fine dust that falls from old plaster. Her slender form suggested a tent pole under the sort of shroud that fashion models wear when being made up, which Audrey used to protect herself from the dust and dirt.

She entered into the tempo of her husband's life, both on and off duty. Dotti loved hitting the nightclub circuit two or three times a week after work. Audrey's old acquaintances in the movie world, who had known her as an early-to-bed person when married to Mel, were astonished to see her doing the Twist and other trendy dances on the crowded floors of late-night restaurants and clubs. Dotti was an excellent dancer. He was understandably proud of showing off his wife. To her relief, she had no worries about the effect of her new marriage on Sean. She told friends that her child's proficiency in Italian, which he had learnt from his nurse Gina, was one of the reasons why he had developed such a quick affinity for Dr Dotti. Since she had lived away from her half-brothers for most of her life, almost as an only child, she now found it a novel and exhilarating experience to be a newcomer in the extended Italian family of a matriarchal household. At first she fitted easily into Signora Bandini's routine, religiously attending Sunday lunch and, though not a Catholic herself, accompanying her in-laws to their church on special occasions.

She was becoming Italian in looks as well as protocol. Givenchy and she remained on the closest of terms, but the celebrity spotters at the Paris collections missed Audrey's face in her usual front-row seat. 'Obviously,' she told Henry Gris, 'it's impossible for me to take off for Paris, just like that, to look at Givenchy's latest models.' This was said with regret. She still preferred his designs to anyone else's; but now, as if to compliment her adopted country, she shopped in Rome's smart boutiques and found the clothes 'quite beautiful'. Asked if it wasn't a sacrifice, she said bluntly, 'Nonsense, I can do without.' What she didn't discuss were her efforts to live within her husband's salary and not indulge herself—and maybe humiliate him—by splashing out on the Paris couture fashions she could well afford.

Film scripts still flowed in, but were more often than not put aside unread and sometimes unopened. People had assumed that Audrey Hepburn would resume her film career, perhaps making movies in Rome instead of Paris. She showed no inclination at all to return to the screen. When she said 'I'm functioning as a woman should function', she left it unspoken, but implied, that too many years had been spent functioning as a film star. Domesticity was the dreamed-of state; the hard labour of film fantasy had been the obligatory occupation. Now that she was free to take up the former, she felt she was 'not robbing anyone of anything'—least of all herself.

This was understandable following her recovery from the divorce. But danger signs were already there, had Audrey cared to look for them. Andrea Dotti had married a movie star. For him to watch her become a Roman housewife took the lustre off the treasure he had brought home. A close friend of them both says, 'It took him some time to find out that Audrey wasn't the girl in *Roman Holiday,* but when he did it was like being awakened from a wonderful dream. Reality did not compensate for it.' For Audrey, it was attractive to be leading 'a normal, healthy existence [such as] I never experienced before'. For Dotti, a routine life was not enough. It needed glamour. Her husband's personality was warm and naturally affectionate; but he liked to relax after work in that easy, drifting Roman way that makes time fly and surprises one at how little has been done with it. Audrey was someone who liked to see results. The ground for a clash of temperament was being laid even in these honeymoon months.

Then an event occurred about four months after their marriage which could not fail to absorb any spare time she felt hanging on her hands. She was found to be expecting a child. In any Italian family, the arrival of a grandchild is the real test of a good union. When the son of the house was Dotti's age, it was double cause for rejoicing. Audrey suddenly gained a maternal importance far above her wifely status. She would be nearly forty-one by the time the baby came along; and her history of miscarriages probably meant that this would be her last opportunity. She took great care of herself that spring and summer. She spent the middle months of 1969 in virtual seclusion on a Mediterranean islet where the Dotti family and other members of the rich Roman bourgeoisie had holiday homes. The wives and children were escorted there by their husbands and made comfortable, then the menfolk returned to the mainland for the weekday work and, in many cases, the night-time pleasures of girlfriends and mistresses.

Come September, Audrey retreated further still. Rather than return to Rome, she made La Paisible her *place d'accouchement*. She received weekend visits from Dotti; otherwise, she rested, walked Sean the hundred yards or so to school, did the shopping at the village store and some light gardening, and felt the sudden drop in temperature that told her of approaching snows. Distance doesn't necessarily make the heart grow less fond of a loved one. But it can sometimes help to create misunderstandings. Audrey's friends believe that this is what now began to happen—and sometimes the problems were not just misunderstandings.

To most of the Italian paparazzi, Andrea Dotti was no longer simply a well-connected and hard-working psychiatrist. He was also the husband of a world-famous film star. In a word, he was 'newsworthy'. Reports of what he did, where he went, whom he was seen with, were of interest even if his wife were not in the photo; indeed, they became even more interesting if Audrey were absent but the actresses and fashion models whom Dotti met in his after-work hours were present. He remained the ever-attentive husband and father-to-be. But the old Hollywood syndrome held true: fans who had been elated by a star's marriage waited expectantly for news of the divorce. Rome was a bad place to try and quell such rumours. And Audrey was shrewd enough to know that denial only kindled the suspicions. She kept quiet—and waited for her child.

He came by Caesarian section, 8 February 1970, at the Cantonal Hospital in Lausanne, where Dr Dotti was holding a temporary lectureship in order to be near his wife and still keep in touch with his profession. The child weighed 7 pounds 8 ounces. The father's joy was all one might have expected; so was his pride in claiming how great it was 'to have another man in the house'. 'Luca,' it was stated, 'strongly resembles his father.' Audrey was jubilant at her success in becoming a mother again. Her fans were perhaps the only ones to suffer a twinge of disappointment. Perhaps they would never see her on the screen again.

As if to clarify her intentions, she gave interviews to a few carefully selected journalists. Could she be 'just a wife? Surely not forever?' She countered with, 'Why not for ever?' and then added, 'Let me put it simply. I have absolutely no desire to work. And it's not worth going to a psychiatrist to find out why.' (This was obviously meant as a house joke.) Her interviewer persisted. 'But with all that God-given talent?' This was the wrong approach. 'I never believed in my "God-given talent". I adored my work and I did my best. But that was all.' She declared that she felt relaxed for the first time in her life and insisted that she would hate to become 'unrelaxed' again: that is to say, go back to work 'and let "them" lock me up in a studio all day, far from husband and children, tense and worried about the next scene'. Her life was now hers to command.

Usually she rose early, about 5.30 a.m., fed the baby and made breakfast for the rest of the family, frequently dismissing the housekeeper's efforts to help. Her own diet had hardly varied over the years: a single square of grilled ham, a lightly poached egg, wholemeal bread showing just the faintest browning from the toaster, herbal tea and a large glass of mineral water. Dotti left every morning at 8.30 a.m. to report to his clinic at the university. He spent the mornings teaching or seeing a patient or two, then frequently came home for lunch, which Audrey had arranged for the cook to prepare for them, and returned to the clinic to devote the afternoon to his patients. Unless they had a dinner party invitation, he didn't usually come home again until 9.00 p.m. and when he was on hospital duty in the evenings, Audrey would not see him until lunchtime the following day. Occasionally she went down to the clinic in the evening, carrying a pasta meal she had cooked at home, and ate with him in his office with baby Luca beside them.

Inevitably, such closeness to her husband and his work drew her interest to the sad condition of some of the patients he treated. Occasionally her practical help was invoked. 'They know me as Dr Dotti's wife,' she emphasized. Children with emotional problems earned her special attention.

When she thought about films at all, it was in terms of going to see them. Her reaction when she did was not the kind to encourage a swift return to the screen. The escalation of violence horrified her. She thought *A Clockwork Orange* 'one of the most brutal, heartless things I've ever had to sit through'. The James Bond comedy adventures amused her. She adored Sean Connery, but she disliked Bond's frivolous attitude to death. 'Like so many paper hankies', was how she referred to Bond's penchant for despatching his enemies with a light quip on his lips. Of the new generation of women stars, she liked Jane Fonda best, especially in *Klute*. But she asked herself where the romantic comedies were, like *Breakfast at Tiffany's* and *Charade,* and had to admit that they seemed to have gone the way the world had: it was now a 'darker, less secure place . . . no longer very funny'. Sure, she agreed, 'some films are lovely. Obviously there is a place for them in a present-day society, but somehow I don't see myself in them right now. I keep my eyes and ears open to what goes on out there. I cannot help but be painfully aware of the unhappiness and discontent and anguish around us. Nobody is escaping it. Every so often, it hits home.' Rome was no longer Hollywood-on-Tiber. And London was no longer a trendy centre for American-made films: Hollywood, suffering a severe box-office decline due to the collapse of expensive pictures and an overstocked inventory of unreleased ones, had called back the money. The charms of home were sweeter than ever, even if, as she observed, 'Rome is a bit of a jungle.' With money, status and circumspection, one could live there comfortably and fulfillingly—or so it seemed to Audrey then.

Luca's arrival had created no sibling jealousy. His nurse took him and his twelve-year-old half-brother for afternoon outings to the Villa Borghese park, where Sean watched over the toddler. One day a photographer spotted Luca atop a low marble plinth, looking up at the statue above him, and waving his little arms as if he was hearing a symphony orchestra in his head—or imitating what he had seen on Italian television. Audrey, when told of this, recalled how, as a child not much older than Luca, she had been found 'dancing' to the music of the bandsmen in a park at Folkestone.

What were the most important things in life, she was asked. She must have sighed at the profundities she was expected to put into her answer. Yet she made an unexpected reply. 'Love', she nominated—of course—but she also mentioned 'fear'. 'Because whatever you love most, you fear you might lose.' She confided to some women friends at this time, 'If I ever lost Andrea through infidelity, I would throw myself out of the window.' She spoke so emphatically that the friends fell silent, conjecturing the likelihood of such an event. Then one of them said, 'And I would open the window for you'—and the general burst of laughter, in which Audrey joined, dispelled the uneasy ruminations.

The truth was that beneath Audrey's protestations of contentment, there was growing a muted vigilance. Like her mother, Audrey deliberately refrained from dwelling on the things that could go wrong with one's happiness lest she invite them to happen. It was not a fool's paradise that Audrey created around her during these years; it was an optimist's one.

Outwardly, the Dottis lived modestly. They drove a production-line Fiat. When they went sailing on Lake Como, it wasn't in a vessel borrowed from their rich friends: they simply hired a small sailing boat. They did not lease the sort of summer beach-house that wealthy metropolitans rented in places like Fregene or Rocco di Mare, but stayed in a good family hotel and rented a beach cabaña for the children. Only indoors were there evident signs of wealth, and the thick palazzo walls protected them. At Tolochenaz, the villagers themselves were a natural security cordon. No media people were ever admitted to these domestic retreats. The baroness stayed in the Swiss manor house when Audrey and the family were away.

Audrey was now in direct touch again with her ex-husband. As Sean grew older—at fifteen he was taller than Audrey and could pass for a young man—she had no scruples about letting him rejoin his father: 'Pooh' would always come back to her. Sean had been present when his father remarried in London, in February 1971. Mel's new wife was Elizabeth Soukhotine, an editor of children's books. (Mel had written a book for children before he met Audrey.) He would spend the 1970s producing and acting in films made in Germany, Italy, Sweden and Mexico.

Children momentarily lured Audrey back in front of a camera in 1971 when she joined Barbra Streisand, Richard Burton, Harry Belafonte and other stars in a television documentary, *A World of Love,* to which they donated their services since it was made to raise funds for the United Nations children's charity, Unicef. It was Audrey's first commitment to the great cause that would occupy her final years.

If she wavered at all in her determination not to resume her movie career while her family were growing up, it was when Sam Spiegel came to Rome to ask her to play the Russian tsarina in his production of *Nicholas and Alexandra.* Spiegel was prepared to pay her a million dollars to say yes. She read the script and said no. Her instinct was good. The film turned out to be a ponderous museum piece. Janet Suzman played Alexandra, a lifeless part which not even Audrey could have made much of, except perhaps the woman's love for her massacred children.

She did one surprising thing in the early seventies: surprising for Audrey, anyhow. She made her first and only television commercial—for wigs, of all things! It was intended for screening in Japan. She had always been fascinated by that country, whose aesthetic concern with the essence of things reflected her own pared-down style. Givenchy was a much honoured designer in Japan, and the Japanese were the greatest fans of an actress whose own high and delicate cheekbones and large eyes suggested an Asian connection. If there was sentiment in Audrey's making the commercial there was also a very large profit: $100,000 for a day and a half's work in a studio in Rome. Then she went back to bringing up her baby.

She maintained the state she refused to call 'retirement', but referred to simply as 'not working', for several years. But her pleasure in watching her children grow up became tempered by concern for their personal safety. In common with big cities in the other democracies of Western Europe, Rome was now suffering an escalation in random violence and organized terrorism. Sophia Loren and Carlo Ponti had already removed their two young children to Paris. After receiving several threatening telephone calls, seemingly designed to frighten her into ready agreement to a future ransom demand, Audrey followed the Pontis' example. One day soon after dawn towards the end of June 1975, a car drew up at the Dottis' residence. A few minutes later, accompanied by an armed policeman, Audrey and the children were driven to Leonardo da Vinci Airport; a few hours later, they were all in Tolochenaz. The Roman 'holiday' had come to a premature end.

The move was to have considerable consequence for her marriage and her resolution not to resume film work. Dotti had not resigned from his post at the clinic in Rome, and the new location of his wife and family meant that he (or Audrey) would become a commuter to the other's place of residence. Thus a marriage already suffering strain from the media's depiction of Dotti as a nightclubbing playboy when his wife was out of town began to experience more serious dislocation from the geographical distance between husband and wife. 'Not an ideal situation,' Audrey acknowledged. 'My husband goes up and down, and so do I. We seem to be forever in airports or airplanes.'

Pulling up her roots in Rome also loosened her resolve not to go back to work, reviving a hankering that had been dormant while the new life had fed her contentment. But opportunity had to be present as well as impulse. The former arrived in the shape of a screenplay by James Goldman, author of the play and screenplay of *A Lion in Winter*, which had won Katharine Hepburn her third Oscar. Though called *The Return of Robin*

Hood when Kurt Frings had sent the script to Audrey, the project was quickly retitled *Robin and Marian* when Audrey said she would do it. In the production were two other talents then at the height of their respective reputations. One was Richard Lester, its director, who had made the first two Beatles films as well as a string of contemporary and historical comedy-satires employing surrealistic sight-gags and anachronistic humour. The other was Sean Connery, who had by then handed in his James Bond licence to kill and was itching to step into roles that allowed him to show his age and develop his capacity for humour and warmth of character. He had just finished *The Man Who Would Be King,* with Michael Caine, directed by an old friend from Audrey's past, John Huston. Connery was to be paid a million dollars (£555,555) as Robin Hood; Audrey $760,000 (£422,222) as Maid Marian—or, rather, as Reverend Mother Marian, since the film was based on the romantic but realistic encounter between an ageing Robin Hood, weary from the Crusades and stiff in the joints, and a Marian who had opted for the convent life and risen to be abbess. The plot not only fitted the talents of its stars; it fitted their ages.

Richard Lester went to Tolochenaz to clinch Audrey's interest in a screen comeback. 'Once we had promised to shoot the film during her children's school holidays in the summer, so that she could take them with her to location in Spain, and also assured her we could finish shooting in time for them to get back to their classes, she needed no arm-twisting. Reassuring her about how she would look on the screen . . . Now that took some doing. After all, she had been away from the screen for eight years. Film-making had changed a lot in that time.'

'It's always been frightening for me to start a picture,' Audrey admitted to the *International Herald Tribune*'s Mary Blume. 'I think I'm basically an introvert. It's always been hard for me to do things in front of people. And it's not like riding a bicycle, it just doesn't come back [on its own]. Even with a lovely script, fine actors and director, you're always alone.'

Lester saw this 'aloneness' at its most touchingly pathetic when Audrey flew to London for costume fittings. 'Yvonne Blake did her costumes for this film,' he says, 'or, rather, her costume. For she had only one style to wear—the abbess's habit. It was made of the same material that goes into oven gloves, rough and stiff, and Yvonne had been at pains to give it a medieval look, rather than a couture finish, by sewing it together with bone needles. I watched Audrey slip it on and stand in front of the mirror and then, with hope that it could be improved, ever so slightly, into something that a twelfth-century Givenchy might have blessed with his scissors, she twitched and tugged and tucked it this way and that. She finally resigned herself to its unyielding form. She really was a good sport. After topping all the lists of the best-dressed women in her career, here she was in her comeback film dressed in an over-large oven glove.'

Audrey was much more nervous about how she would be photographed. She always had been; but there were so many things she knew nothing about now—things that had changed the way stars looked when the camera gazed at them, now not always in awe of them. She spoke to Denis O'Dell, the producer of the film, who in turn spoke to David Watkin, the lighting photographer, who was sympathetic to Audrey's anxiety—but she would have to take her chances, like everyone else, she was told.

Next to how she looked, Audrey worried about how long the film would take to shoot. She couldn't bear to be separated from her children: a symptom of the distance she felt was opening up between Dotti and herself. 'She'd heard I was a quick worker,' Lester says, 'and that helped make up her mind to do the film. In fact, we shot it in just under six weeks.' When Sean and Luca arrived on the Spanish location, they were not noticeably impressed by the sight of their mother in her abbess's stiff, heavy robes. Luca was more excited by the bows and arrows and the twelfth-century Spanish castle transformed by fake plaster crenellations into a replica of the sheriff's stronghold in Nottingham. 'Why doesn't Daddy play Robin Hood?' Luca asked. Audrey replied, 'Because he doesn't have the right suit.'

In fact, Andrea Dotti at that moment would have been happy to have had a posse of Merry Men around him. Audrey had hardly started the film when shocking news reached her about her husband in Rome. Now that Dotti lived alone there most of the week, he was not spared the fears of many prominent Romans. One day, when her 'dear Doctor Kildare', as Audrey had nicknamed him, was a few hundred yards from their apartment, four men wearing balaclavas tried to drag him into their parked Mercedes. He resisted. After inflicting cuts and bruises on him as he lay on the sidewalk, protecting his face and head, the assailants were beaten off by security guards from the nearby Egyptian Embassy. After medical treatment, Dotti passed an anxious evening trying to contact Audrey by telephone before the media alarmed her with their stories of his misadventure. This episode strengthened Audrey's resolve to make Tolochenaz the centre of family life.

If *Robin and Marian* held a special poignancy for Audrey over and above the chance it gave her to make a comeback, that lay in its story of middle-aged people whom fate had separated resuming life where they had left off—this time with the resolve to make a better job of it and deny the years their victory. She felt that such a film was a sort of watershed in her own life. Grey streaks were starting to show in her dark brown hair. Beauty still inhabited her face, but the skin seemed drawn tightly over that superlative bone structure. There were reports that she had undergone some minor cosmetic remodelling, but she never admitted to this. She had changed her hairstyle for the role of Marian. Gone were both the gamine cut and the layered style that had followed it. In their place was a ringlet style devised by Sergio of Rome. 'A love story about mature people', was how she summed up the film to any interviewer permitted on the set. At Lester's request, she had relaxed her once inflexible rule about meeting the media while working: that, too, was a sign of how times had changed. Now films often lived or died by their publicity—or lack of it.

She stressed the word 'mature', as if she had no regrets about the roles in which 'immaturity' had been part of her fetching image. How she looked now was how she felt. Happy—she said. Privately, she was relieved to discover that Sean Connery didn't give a hoot about how old he looked. Though at forty-six he was only a year younger than Audrey, he looked ten years older. 'The bones creak a bit in the film and in my legs,' Connery confessed. 'This Robin is trying to be a young revolutionary at the age of fifty, and it doesn't work.' Audrey's stamina was expended on resisting the heat, rather than the Sheriff of Nottingham. She sat patiently in the shade, waiting to be called for her scene, with the rough fabric of her convent robes folded up above her knees. 'I perspire. It comes from my days as a dancer.'

The reconciliation of Audrey's approach to acting with Connery's was a problem that only the latter's good grace resolved. 'He loves the work to go quickly,' Lester recalls, 'he'd be happy to play the scene without rehearsal. Audrey liked to check it out well in advance and then knock it off on the first take or two. We had to strike a balance. Sean was very gentlemanly. We rehearsed.' Once shooting began, progress was swift. One reason was the multiple cameras used by Lester, almost alone at the time. One took the master shot, another at a different angle took the medium shot favouring one or other player, a third took the close-up. Audrey should have been pleased by Lester's pioneering of a technique that helped her spontaneity. She was, up to a point. But it meant that the lighting stayed put—which the greater sensitivity of film stock now facilitated—and Audrey wistfully recalled how they had used to fuss over her in days gone by. 'Of course it meant she no longer got the attention she had been used to,' says Lester, 'and her anxiety wasn't surprising. Moreover, we didn't look at the daily rushes. The material was being edited while we shot it and the editor was simply told to get on with it. Audrey wasn't used to that, either.'

The lighting values of the scenes were less precisely harmonized than they would have been in a studio. Lester liked the sense of a sketched sequence that an artist had just that moment dashed off. 'But as a result, some of Audrey's scenes were a little dark—one in particular was dubbed "Robin Hood Meets the Invisible Woman". But her marvellous voice held all the emotion: you hardly needed to see her.' Though she never complained, it cannot have been easy for Audrey to feel so unprotected. Nor was it easy for her to be virtually the only woman in an all-male group including Nicol Williamson as Prince John, Denholm Elliott as Will Scarlet, Robert Shaw as the Sheriff of Nottingham, Ronnie Barker as Friar Tuck and Richard Harris as King Richard. 'I am the only Wendy among the Lost Boys of Sherwood Forest,' Audrey said with amused resignation, turning one legend into another which fitted her own fantasies more comfortably.

She took off for Rome every free weekend. Dotti, according to Lester, found his way to the location just once. In his wife's absence, the doctor had been the object of the paparazzi's intrusiveness to an even more embarrassing extent than before. The tabloids had a field night when they caught him in the company of Florence Grinda, the twenty-nine-year-old estranged wife of the former Davis Cup tennis star Jean-Noël Grinda. Dotti protested that he and his companion shared only a mutual fascination with backgammon. One hopes that Audrey may have seen the funny side of it, too; but the evidence was not reassuring.

It was sadly plain to her that she had married a man who was—although still in love with the Audrey Hepburn he had married—nevertheless highly susceptible to other women. Now that it was public knowledge, her friends were not slow in supplying names. Italian women took their husbands' girlfriends for granted and, in Audrey's circle in Rome, a man who did not have a mistress was considered an oddity. Audrey never reconciled herself to this tradition. 'Beneath the radiance,' said a close friend at this time, 'there was a very upset woman. But of course she never brought it out in public.' The differences with Dotti were put down to the fact that, as she said to Rex Reed, 'I'm not a city person. That's the basic . . . disagreement between Andrea and me . . . I'm very bored by cement.' Then, falling back on a tenet of her mother's, she closed off that avenue of inquiry by saying, 'I take care of my health and the world takes care of my thoughts.' Her only wish? 'Not to be lonely.' Yet she made no mention of a husband by her side to keep loneliness at bay. Other things

21

THE COMFORTERS

*G*ENERALLY speaking, *Robin and Marian* was well received. Critics welcomed Audrey back. '[The film] is at its best,' wrote Vincent Canby in the *New York Times* in March 1976, 'when it plays its love story without smart talk or gags largely through Miss Hepburn's magnificent face, which time has touched just enough to make us aware of the waste that Marian's last twenty years represent'—and, he might have added, Audrey's last ten. Uniting her with Sean Connery worked well, too. Connery's Robin, a rough husk of a warrior, paired off perfectly with Audrey's mellowed, almost matronly Marian. Their final scene together, when she helps him fire the arrow into the greenwood that will determine his grave (and hers), has an operatic fall to it that the players communicate like tenor and soprano in a Verdi opera.

Though she never expressed any dissatisfaction with her appearance to Richard Lester, Audrey was not too happy with the rough texture of the movie. The lighting, she said to a friend, 'makes me look as if I'm ready for the geriatrics ward'. But overall, she was touched by the personal warmth of the notices—at a time when she needed reassurance.

What didn't escape her—or a few friends who were in the know—was the accidental but apt resonance of autobiography in Marian's relationship with Robin. Just as Marian had taken a second chance with love, so Audrey had entered into her second marriage determined that it wouldn't duplicate the falling trajectory of happiness which had been the pattern of her first. It had not worked out. She and Dotti had now discovered they had less in common than each had imagined. Some years later she acknowledged this with more frankness than she was able to muster at the time. 'At first, it was just a romance and considering the age difference—he is nine years younger than I—I didn't think it would go beyond that. Of course, it eventually did. But I determined my second marriage would be my last and that I'd put aside my career to make it work. When we had Luca, that strengthened my resolve . . .' Yet here lay the main cause of breakdown. Dotti would have preferred his wife to keep on with her career. It overlapped with the glamorous world of celebrities that had such a potent appeal for him. When Audrey withdrew into domesticity, she removed a reflecting mirror from her husband's life.

She tried tolerating the lifestyle that he made no secret of enjoying. 'Oh, Andrea's been doing it all his life,' she would say, making light of a husband caught in the flashbulbs with a beauty like Dalia de Lazzano by his side. When she went to Los Angeles early in 1976, to present William Wyler with his Life Achievement Award from the American Film Institute, Dotti accompanied her, ostensibly to observe some of the new psychiatric techniques being practised at the University of California. En route for home, she stopped over in New York for the premiere of *Robin and Marian*. Tears came to her eyes at the greeting given her by thousands of people waiting outside Radio City Music Hall. Fans presented her with orchids and roses, always white ones, her favourite. 'We love you, dear Audrey,' came the cries. She had passed into that rare realm of stardom where people count the passing of their own years by the movies of hers they saw as they grew older.

She was back in Los Angeles before the month of March was out, this time to present Jack Nicholson with his 'Best Actor' Oscar for *One Flew Over the Cuckoo's Nest*. Such a film, she said, held a special interest for her psychiatrist husband, since it dealt with the then fashionable notion of the so-called 'mad' being saner than those who kept them locked up. Actually, Audrey had been more impressed, and disturbed, by another film she had seen privately about a week before its New York opening. This was *Face to Face*, written and directed by Ingmar Bergman and starring Liv Ullmann. It is about the nervous breakdown of a gifted professional woman who presents to the world a face of emotional serenity—a face much like Audrey's—who lives what seems to be a perfectly organized life, but who is inwardly a spiritual desert. Audrey had heard the same sounds of doubt infiltrating the protective wall of her own apparent self-sufficiency.

Significantly, she took the opportunity in interviews she gave then to praise the great Swedish director's film, and also another film of his made for television, *Scenes from a Marriage*, which she had seen in Switzerland a year or so earlier. In that psycho-chronicle of a failing marriage, the Scandinavian actor Erland Josephson plays a professional man, a university professor with a yen for young girls, whose marriage to a seemingly well-organized and self-disciplined woman has reached a plateau. Neither husband nor wife wishes to precipitate the break-up, nor to admit to the

'Even when I was little, what I wanted most was to have a child.' After several miscarriages, she got her wish in January, 1960, with the birth of Sean Ferrer.

On the outside, looking in: with co-star George Peppard in *Breakfast at Tiffany* Though Holly Golightly, the rootless 'kook', was one of her most popular rol Audrey felt she was miscast. 'The part needed an extravert, and that's not me,' she said. Holly's cat was the goodtime gi friend and 'familiar'. Audrey herself preferred small dogs. Henry Mancini's theme song 'Moon River' was Holly's theme song – and Audrey's signature tu It was to follow her through life.

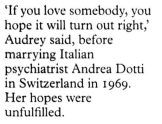

Audrey in a rare moment
of rough treatment, as the
blind woman threatened
by a drugs gang in *Wait
Until Dark*, produced by
her husband Mel Ferrer in
1967. Soon afterwards, the
two parted.

'If you love somebody, you
hope it will turn out right,'
Audrey said, before
marrying Italian
psychiatrist Andrea Dotti
in Switzerland in 1969.
Her hopes were
unfulfilled.

Snapped unawares by a *paparazzo* in Rome, with her second son Luca in the early 1970s. Parisian elegance has given way to the housewife look. Motherhood provides the compensation.

Back on screen with her new leading man Ben Gazzara in Peter Bogdanovich's comedy *They All Laughed*. Playing a woman whose marriage is falling apart, she was trying to stop the same thing happening to her off screen, with less success.

With Robert Wolders, the Dutch-born former actor and widower of Merle Oberon who became Audrey's final companion in Switzerland and on her travels for Unicef. 'He is solid in every way,' she said.

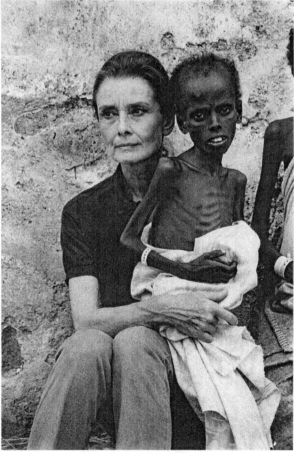

'I have seen famine elsewhere, but nothing like this,' Audrey said in Somalia, in September 1992. She made over fifty trips to Third World crisis spots as a tireless roving ambassador for the United Nations Children's Fund. But the strain now shows shockingly in her own ravaged features: her stamina gave way before her compassion.

The only home Audrey owned: La Paisible ('The Place of Peace') in the village of Tolochenaz, near Lausanne, Switzerland. To this manor house she came back to die in January 1993.

'Like a giant basket of flowers.' The soil under which Audrey Hepburn sleeps in the small village graveyard is continually covered by tributes from visitors from all over the world.

other that they are no longer finding satisfaction in being together. 'Sex isn't everything,' Liv Ullmann, who plays the wife, says at one point: words which Audrey's interviews echo at this time. In the last section of the film, Bergman's characters do get a divorce and the movie casts its eye, with unexpected charity, on their remarriages. '*Scenes from a Marriage* I consider a masterpiece,' Audrey said, 'the epitome of a story about two people. It was as near to an intimate experience as it was possible to have on film.' She was referring not to the characters in the film, but to herself watching them. To friends in Switzerland and Italy, she often talked of this film, leaving some of them with the impression that it had given her an illuminating glimpse of her own predicament.

Around this time, Ingmar Bergman was arrested in Sweden and charged with evading taxes—an allegation later dismissed by the courts as baseless, but only after a lengthy period of interrogation which compelled him to work abroad. Audrey was uncharacteristically passionate in her defence of Bergman. She denounced what she saw as the 'persecution' of a fellow artist, particularly one whose movie had touched the emotional centre of her own life. She offered Bergman a 'refuge' in her house at Tolochenaz. He did not take it up. Had he done so, one wonders what bond might have been formed between them, what kind of film he might have gone on to make if his 'hostess' had been available and willing to enact his psychodramas. Instead he gave that other great Hollywood—or, rather, ex-Hollywood—star, Ingrid Bergman, her chance to appear in a contemporary Swedish film which he directed two years later in Norway. *Autumn Sonata* is generally judged to be one of the best films that either Bergman made. It deals with the strained and ambiguous relationship between a mother and daughter. Audrey may have seen it. If so, the similarity to the tense relationship between her mother and herself could not have escaped her.

No doubt about it: she was in a more self-absorbed and troubled mood at this moment of her life than at any other. She discussed religion with her friends, something she had rarely done before, since she was not an orthodox believer. She took to reading poetry. William Wordsworth's *The Prelude,* the poet's statement of belief in the union of all living things, was one of her favourites. So was T. S. Eliot's *The Waste Land* and his verse drama *The Cocktail Party.* To an English friend, the actor Robert Flemyng, who had appeared in the first production of the play in Edinburgh in 1949, she sometimes quoted words spoken by Eliot's otherworldly psychiatrist, a role played by Alec Guinness just before he had joined Audrey for their tiny scene together in *The Lavender Hill Mob:*

It is a good life. Though you will not know how good
Till you come to the end . . .
The destination cannot be described;
You will know very little until you get there;
You will journey blind. But the way leads towards possession
Of what you have sought for in the wrong place.

Audrey left Hollywood for home feeling very 'down'. 'Once the Oscars were a ceremony,' she said, 'now they are only a ritual.' Disillusionment followed her home to Switzerland. She turned down all the scripts she found waiting for her. One was *A Bridge Too Far,* about the doomed attempt by Allied parachutists to capture the crucial bridge at Arnhem in 1944. Ironically, Liv Ullmann accepted the role Audrey had been offered. One role that would have been perfect for her, she missed because of confusion over the casting. *The Turning Point,* directed by Herbert Ross, was set in Audrey's old world of ballet. Princess Grace of Monaco had been approached to appear in it as her comeback film. Her Serene Highness was tempted but declined: officially she was a good Roman Catholic, and the role called for her character to enjoy an adulterous liaison. An alternative had to be found in a hurry, and Anne Bancroft snapped up the part. With the candour that comes with age—she was almost fifty—Audrey said, 'The older you get, the more you have to resign yourself to not working or taking inconsequential or frightening parts.'

Whether the part she then accepted in a melodrama called *Bloodline* was supposed to be 'inconsequential' or 'frightening', people had the good manners not to ask. Officially known as *Sidney Sheldon's Bloodline,* after its best-selling paperback author, it was a meretricious thriller of a type that would find its most exotic mutation in the next decade when series like *Dallas* and *Dynasty* hooked the viewing multitudes of several continents with the weekly churning of the status quo. Audrey Hepburn playing the twenty-five-year-old heiress to a pharmaceutical empire who becomes the target of a psychotic killer—it had an air of desperation, had it not? It had an even sharper odour of money.

Every year, a great number of German accountants, dentists, doctors, property men and others with very large incomes looked round for a way to lessen their tax liabilities, and ended up throwing money at the several film-making syndicates which had sprung up to take advantage of the Bonn government's generous tax-break laws. In June 1978 one of these syndicates, Geria, released $6m to finance *Bloodline,* with the proviso that the money was spent by the end of the year. No one could lose. Even if the film flopped, everyone would be in profit: the investors, the makers, the stars. It was the perfect agent's deal, and Kurt Frings was well placed to take advantage of it. Terence Young, one of Frings's clients, swiftly agreed to direct it. Audrey Hepburn, almost a founder member of the Frings circle of famous players, agreed to star in it for a million dollars. A fee of that dimension attached to a film of this kind changed its status overnight. It not only ensured that the project would happen, but made it front-page news and had foreign distributors rushing to buy it before even a foot had been shot. 'I'm drawing my pension,' Audrey said.

In fact, she was providing for her children's future. The money was paid into a tax-free account she kept in the Cayman Islands and eventually found its way into a trust fund for Sean and Luca.

Sidney Sheldon was accommodating, too. He agreed to rewrite the role so as to add ten years to it and bring it more plausibly into line with Audrey's age. This was needless: as Audrey Hepburn was playing the role, who gave a damn what age the frightened woman was? Audrey's children were less of a problem to her work schedule now that Luca, nearly eleven, was at school (and well guarded) in Rome and Sean, nineteen, was studying literature at a Swiss university. But Audrey still insisted on being shown a shooting schedule and checking it against an airline schedule for flights between Rome and Munich, where principal photography was to take place. She wanted to be convinced that she could be at her son's side in an emergency. Other locations included London, Zurich, Paris, New York and Sardinia, in order to give Audrey's boardroom tycoon a global background, as well as to use up the investors' money before the tax-break period expired.

Once again she was made aware of the aura that surrounded her—all the stronger since Givenchy was doing her 'power dressing' for her. 'Why is everyone so worshipful?' she asked the crew on the first day. Of all the international cast assembled for the film, Audrey was the one who was shown royal deference. Romy Schneider, Michelle Phillips and Irene Papas: they were like attendant maids-of-honour beside the legendary Hepburn. Omar Sharif knew her well enough to share wry jokes about the roles they were playing. James Mason spoke with tolerant sarcasm of the 'performing animal act' into which everyone was locked. But Ben Gazzara behaved with a forthright ribaldry about the whole risible melodrama that Audrey, in her present mood, found fun. Being with Gazzara soon lightened her spirits.

Gazzara in some ways resembled Mel Ferrer and Albert Finney. He spoke his mind without inhibition. He was openly dismissive of material he judged to be beneath his talent, standing apart from it until called on to perform but then acquitting himself professionally. He had a wide and forceful vocabulary which he didn't moderate just because Miss Audrey Hepburn was within earshot. To put it vulgarly (as he would), he was a man with balls. Audrey took to him at once, rather like a royal personage who finds the candour of *lèse majesté* a refreshing jolt after the smothering predictability of protocol. As Finney had discovered a few years earlier, a slightly brutal and playful approach got Audrey's attention very quickly: she enjoyed Gazzara's sexual chauvinism. He possessed a quality of danger he had brilliantly exploited in his early cinema roles, as a sadistic army cadet in *The Strange One* and as an enigmatic rape suspect in *Anatomy of a Murder*. He had the self-absorbed actor's unpredictability of response, and played on it. The son of an Italian immigrant from Sicily, he liked a good time and living well. Just as Audrey had succumbed to the Latin capacity for open enjoyment when she met Andrea Dotti, she now fell under the spell of Gazzara's more abrasive and ebullient temperament. He took charge at a time when Audrey badly needed cheering. 'It isn't age or even death that one fears,' she told the American reporter Curtis Bill Pepper at this time, 'as much as loneliness and lack of affection . . . I think I'd never worry about age if I knew I could go on being loved or having the possibility of love.' Ben Gazzara supplied that possibility.

To say that *Bloodline* was badly received by the critics would be an understatement: it was slaughtered. 'Ghastly, hackneyed, humourless, grubby and . . . so disjointed as to be a pain to follow', was the opinion of the London *Sunday Express* critic. Despite the licence granted by a melodramatic potboiler, the pace dragged so badly that the director seemed scarcely capable of taking the money and running—limping, more likely. Even Givenchy's fourteen outfits—the classically simple tailored suits, the mousseline chemises, the black dinner suit squandered in only one minute of screen-time, the black evening dress with beaded tulle bodice and one flower worn over the left breast which lasted a little longer in a love scene at Maxim's—all failed to be critic-proof. Audrey caught it with the rest, hot and strong. 'What especially did Miss Hepburn's advisers think she could salvage from a script whose chaos is beyond repair?' asked the London *Evening Standard*'s critic. The answer was as redundant as the question. She had 'salvaged' a fortune, and was content with that. The *Daily Telegraph* was at least well-mannered, if banal: '[*Bloodline*] offers a not unpleasant string of improbabilities set in a number of international locations.' The extent of the 'improbabilities' may be judged from the closing sequence where Audrey clings to the unsound roof of her blazing villa in Sardinia, having to make up her mind before she is irredeemably singed which of the two men waiting below to catch her in his arms (she hopes) is the man who wants to kill her.

Indecisiveness was reflected, with more pain and point, in Audrey's deteriorating relations with her husband. They had a row, as a result of which Dotti moved out of their apartment. Then there was a reconciliation. Declaring her belief in 'a second chance', she set off in the middle of 1979 to have a second honeymoon with Andrea in Hawaii, taking along some of the $200,000 worth of Givenchy clothes from *Bloodline*. By the time they returned, divorce was once more in the offing. The trip had only opened the cracks in their marriage even wider. Audrey turned back to her career. Her situation was now the reverse of that of many movie stars: on discovering that the attention paid to them is diminishing along with the fees they once earned, they find a solution in remarriage, which revives the interest of the media and restores a reassuring sense of prominence, even if it comes without achievement. Though her marriage was within months of breaking up, Audrey was not by nature inclined to retrieve her fortunes this way. A good role in a well-directed and successful film was what she looked for.

Unfortunately, the man who had guided her to so many of these in the past was now entering a period of personal misfortune. Illness and other troubles to do with health and marriage were gradually removing Kurt Frings from the influential mainstream of movie-making. The industry was once again in a financial crisis. Frings's clients, who included Elizabeth Taylor and Richard Burton as well as Audrey, had all suffered very public reverses at the box-office. 'We'll never get a million again,' Burton recorded in his diary. The truth was that the public found the off-screen lives of the Burtons and others like them of more consuming interest than any stories in which they might feature on-screen. As a result, when Audrey needed the very best advice in order to re-establish the momentum of her career, she was deprived of it. She fell back on her own intuition.

When it became clear that her marriage had irretrievably foundered, she flew to Los Angeles for talks with the writer-director Peter Bogdanovich, whom she had got to know and like at the tribute to William Wyler a few years earlier. His last film, *Saint Jack,* had starred the man whose company Audrey had found such agreeable compensation for appearing in *Bloodline,* Ben Gazzara. Audrey's son Sean, fresh out of college, was now working for Bogdanovich as a film editor.

Peter Bogdanovich, then forty, was an ex-actor who had studied with Stella Adler, then become a film critic and protégé of Roger Corman, for whom he directed a B-picture thriller, *Targets,* that brought him critical attention. He had become a front-rank director in 1971 with *The Last Picture Show.* Though several box-office reverses had been suffered by the former wunderkind and ex-partner of Francis Coppola and William Friedkin, Bogdanovich was still bankable, and had the rare gift of unpredictability that promised the possibility of a winning hand of cards in whatever his next venture might be. He was literate, intuitive—and fun. These were all qualities which Audrey needed at this time. 'I met her at the Pierre Hotel, in New York, to discuss doing a picture,' Bogdanovich says. 'She wasn't too sure of what the future held for her, but she wanted to enjoy whatever it was. As well as work, she needed comfort.'

Bogdanovich was a nostalgic. Like Audrey, he missed what was now being called the 'Golden Age' of Hollywood. She had been a part of it just as movie-making slipped away from the studio system that had created such stars as Crawford, Davis, Gable and Garbo, though she had caught up with its perennial survivors like Cooper and Astaire and Grant. Bogdanovich had done the next best thing: he had recreated his affection for vintage Hollywood in his early films. Besides *The Last Picture Show,* a valediction to the cinema's role in the rites of passage of small-town American teenagers, *What's Up, Doc?* resuscitated the screwball comedy style of Howard Hawks, and *Paper Moon* turned back the clock to the pre-war genre in which grown-up stars were paired with precocious moppets. The less successful *At Long Last Love* was a homage to the Astaire and Rogers musical. Audrey understood this kind of cinema and felt safe in the hands of such a talented devotee. Bogdanovich rose to the opportunity.

He proposed a romantic comedy as a cure for her depression: a film he would write with her in mind, as well as direct. It would recall those comedies based on amusingly deceitful relationships, like *Roman Holiday* and *Love in the Afternoon,* in which when one party discovers what's really going on, it no longer matters—both parties have fallen in love with each other. *They All Laughed* became the title of a story about a tycoon's wife who is feeling lovelorn and flies to New York for a brief change of scene. Unknown to her, her husband has hired a private detective to keep an eye on her. They fall in love. It sounded like the sort of film that Wilder or Wyler (or, in an earlier era, Lubitsch) might have concocted. It also came pretty close to what was happening in Audrey's own life at that moment. That was part of the trouble that overtook the film before it was finished.

'The movie we made was not the movie we started out with,' Bogdanovich confesses today, 'which is why David Susskind, who was the executive producer, got so angry when he saw it. It was a movie that was
written as much about the people in it as about the characters they played.
Ben Gazzara, who played the detective who falls in love with Audrey, had
a lot of me in him. Dorothy Stratten'—the blonde *Playboy* model whom
Bogdanovich hoped to make into a star, as he had Cybill Shepherd—'had,
well, a lot of Dorothy in her character. But Audrey, most of all, had the
characteristics that belong to—Audrey Hepburn. As we were shooting
the picture, I was incorporating the cast in the parts. What I think is most
interesting is bringing an actor and character so closely together that you
don't know where one leaves off and the other begins.'

Bogdanovich had long thought that Audrey looked tremendous in the
sort of street clothes that Givenchy did not design. 'When she was "off
duty", so to speak, she invariably wore faded jeans and a sailor's pea-jacket,
with perhaps a headscarf. I told her that was the look I wanted, the clothes
she was most familiar with. She took me upstairs to her suite at the Pierre,
opened the closet and slid all her clothes out on to the bed. And there and
then we selected the ones she would wear in the film.'

When shooting began on the streets of New York, in April 1979, 'Audrey wasn't in the least pretentious or demanding. I warned her there
would be no creature comforts. For one thing, all our trucks were ten
blocks away. For another, we couldn't close anything down—it wasn't
Breakfast at Tiffany's time any longer—and we had to get the shots quickly,
because if people see you shooting in the street, you're dead. And though
Audrey wore big dark glasses in the film—as she did in life—she was,
after all, recognizably Audrey Hepburn. "Go into a store," I'd tell her, "wait
there. When we're ready, the third assistant director will call you." She'd
do just that, then when we'd got the shot, she'd show me what the store had
insisted on giving her—a scarf, a handkerchief, a lipstick—all because it
was Audrey Hepburn who was standing in the store, and they were thrilled.
I said, "When we've done this scene, you can work the other side of the
street." That made her laugh. That kept her happy.' Audrey's looks mattered
less to her now than the comfort of feeling she was a part of the film-
making 'commune' that Bogdanovich ran so well. 'The kind of fragility she
always had was even more noticeable now. She looked at times as if the
wind would blow her over. You wanted to shelter her. But then, somehow,
she marshalled everything with great force and concentration. She was a
soldier of the emotions.'

Her confidence needed continuous attention. To anyone of a less devoted sensitivity to actors' anxieties than Bogdanovich—he had, after all, been one himself for a time—this could have been intensely irritating. 'I recall her continually asking, "Pete, is it all right?"—"Perfect, Audrey."—"Sure you wouldn't like to change a line?"—"No, Audrey, just perfect."—"I didn't exactly say what you wrote."—"No, I noticed, but it's absolutely all right. Great improvement."—"Sure you wouldn't like me to try it the other way?" And so on. Audrey had high spirits, but when they let her down she didn't have any confidence in herself. I got the feeling that as well as needing work, she was looking for love.'

Contrary to stories published at the time, Audrey did not find what she was looking for with Ben Gazzara. 'She had been very close to him in the earlier film they'd made together—*Bloodline*—but not in this one,' Bogdanovich says. Gazzara's own marriage was in difficulties, and he was not prepared to return Audrey's affection with the same intensity as before while he was grappling with the troublesome, and expensive, business of tidying up the pieces of his own marital upset. To cool matters down, or stop tongues wagging, he invited his wife to come and watch the filming of *They All Laughed*. This had the opposite effect to the one intended: it added rather eccentric kindling to the speculation that the gossip columnists were doing their utmost to fan into a love-affair.

On-screen it was a different matter. 'Audrey did some quite surprising things in the scenes when I was directing her,' says Bogdanovich, 'quite carnal, some of them. It's a very sensual moment when she kisses Gazzara—and she is the one doing the kissing, no doubt about that. Another scene when they are in bed together, she astonished me. "Where did you go?" I asked her. "Everywhere," she said. I got the impression she was pretty desperate for love.'

Everything short of love, Audrey could expect and got from Bogdanovich. He was more and more deeply committed to Dorothy Stratten. A few weeks after shooting had finished he returned to Los Angeles from a weekend trip to be met at Los Angeles airport with the news that Dorothy had been murdered by her jealous and psychotic husband. Bogdanovich went into a long period of grief, which eventually expressed itself in a book, *The Death of the Unicorn*, affectionately recalling the dead woman. 'The effect of Dorothy's murder on the film wasn't good,' he says now. 'It placed the accent of prurient interest on her role, which had been very finely balanced against Audrey's, and turned what was conceived as a romantic comedy into something fraught with impending tragedy. Now all you could think of was Dorothy's death. Sean Ferrer was in Vancouver when he heard about it and drove eighteen hours nonstop to be with me and comfort me—Sean was his mother's son all right.'

As *They All Laughed* neared the end of its thirteen-week schedule in New York, Bogdanovich and Audrey discussed future projects. Surprisingly, these centred on her returning to the stage with Bogdanovich directing and, on occasion, playing her leading man. 'We were both keen on Noël Coward. *Hay Fever* was one of his plays Audrey was keen on doing—with Michael Caine, though. Another possibility was *Blithe Spirit,* but she said, "I don't want to play Elvira the spirit wife, if that's what you're thinking of. I want to play the clairvoyante." I said, "But Margaret Rutherford played that." "Yes," she said, "she knew what the best part was." '

For all Audrey's protestations of wanting to work with him again, Peter Bogdanovich couldn't help feeling that she wouldn't be seen on the screen very often in future. 'I don't know what it was, but she seemed to be looking for something in life that movies by their very transient nature couldn't satisfy. She had all these marriage troubles building up back in Italy. I felt she was trying to see them through and wondering what the future held. I really got the feeling it wouldn't be found on the screen. I transferred that feeling to the film we made together. It's there in the ending, when she flies off in a helicopter. The quadruple exposure of Audrey when we reprise the cast at the end of the movie expressed something of this feeling as well—it's a kind of envoi. That's how I intended it, anyhow. Looking back, it is slightly weird.'

Audrey returned to Rome to be with Luca. She moved out of the palazzo apartment and leased a trim, two-bedroomed villa in a quiet neighbourhood of the city. Its flower garden reflected her need now always to have growing things within sight or reach. Luca, who was still at school there, stayed with his mother, which was how Audrey wished it to be. It was for her child's sake—to make a clean break with the past, if possible, yet retain the most precious thing from it—that she now entered into the first stage of what proved to be a long and difficult divorce. It was made all the more tortuous by the fact that the marriage had taken place in a Protestant church in Switzerland while part of the proceedings for dissolving it were undertaken in Italy, a country where a father's rights carry a great deal of legal weight.

Now that the impending divorce was public knowledge, Audrey felt there was no use in denying that her marriage had been unsuccessful. She still maintained a well-mannered discretion, but was candid in admitting that 'My husband and I eventually had what you could call an open relationship'. Then she added, 'It's inevitable, I suppose, when the man is younger.'

Not always. Several months earlier, Audrey had met a man seven years younger than herself; his fidelity to her would be her greatest aid and comfort as she entered on the last and most moving stage of her life.

22

NEW MAN IN HER LIFE

*R*OBERT Wolders was a tall, lean man with deepset eyes and a beard that gave him an air of gravitas beyond his years. Like Audrey, he was Dutch by birth, the son of an airline executive. He had been partly raised and educated in the United States. Quizzed as a student about his future ambitions, he replied soberly, 'To please the ladies.'

Wolders possessed all the charm needed to do so, and some talent as an actor. He had attended drama school in New York, played minor roles in a remake of *Beau Geste* in 1966 and a Second-World-War potboiler called *Tobruk* in 1967, and then, one imagines, thankfully emptied the sand out of his boots to climb into the saddle in the Western TV series *Laredo* where his smooth-chinned, clean-limned appearance was all that the part demanded. He caught Noël Coward's eye at an arts festival where Wolders was appearing in a play of Coward's. The Master remembered his name when asked by Merle Oberon to recommend a suitable leading man for her comeback film. 'He may have great promise, Merle,' Coward said, 'besides which, he struck me as an awfully nice boy.' The film wasn't destined to fulfil the 'promise' Coward had discerned, but the second half of his recommendation quickly bore fruit. Oberon first met Wolders at a Hollywood dinner party. As she described it, 'I asked him what his name was as I was picking up my table napkin, ignoring the name card that was in front of him. "Robert Wolders, ma'am," he said. I then had a second look at him. What an incredible coincidence! Here was the man Noël Coward had mentioned a few weeks earlier.'

They began Merle's film, entitled *Interval,* in February 1972. It was a vanity production paid for by her husband, the Italian millionaire industrialist Bruno Pagliai, with a view to restoring his wife's credibility as a movie star and at the same time relieving the boredom of her life in Acapulco. Oberon was then sixty-one, but had kept her looks, which were part-Asian—a fact that emerged after her death along with the revelation that she had employed her mother all her life as her housekeeper. She had been married to Sir Alexander Korda, the Anglo-Hungarian film mogul, and the photographer Lucien Ballard before wedding the wealthy Pagliai. She cast herself in *Interval* as a rich woman who has killed her husband in a car accident and now falls in love with a penniless young artist, whom she meets among the Mayan ruins of Yucatan. The stranger, played by Wolders, restores her sanity and gives her a reason for living. Life swiftly imitated art (though this is stretching that word to breaking point). Having made Oberon happy in the movie, Wolders proceeded to make her happy in real life by marrying her, though she was almost twenty-five years older than he.

'He has given my life new meaning. Given me my youth back,' she said, sounding as if she were using some leftover dialogue from the film. But Robert Wolders had done just that. They had seven years of happiness together before Oberon's death in 1979. Though married, they behaved like lovers. They strolled hand in hand along the beach at Malibu, where Merle had moved after her divorce from Pagliai. They sailed their yacht together off Catalina Island. They checked into small hotels along the Pacific coast of California, using assumed names, like honeymooners rather than husband and wife. When Oberon had to undergo a triple bypass operation in 1977, Wolders kept sleepless vigil at her bedside. 'My poor, poor Robbie, I'm letting you down,' she was reported to have said to him as she was dying two years later. She left him the beach house and two million dollars, enough to live for the rest of his days without working.

Wolders was inconsolable. His friends rallied round, including Mrs Edgar Bergen, widow of the celebrated ventriloquist and mother of the actress Candice Bergen, and Connie Wald. The latter attempted to pull Wolders out of his depression by inviting him to dinner along with Billy Wilder and his wife and Connie's best friend, Audrey Hepburn, who was about to make *They All Laughed* and suffering from the distress of her broken marriage. The grieving widower was seated beside the film actress, just as he had been seated beside the actress who became his first wife. Audrey, despite her own sorrows, immediately tried to cheer him up. Other people's afflictions brought out the best in her. They took to each other at once, breaking into Dutch while they chatted and sharing memories of childhood in the Netherlands. 'Friendship at first sight,' Audrey later called it, maybe remembering how 'love at first sight' had not proved a very solid basis for her two previous marriages.

Their respective troubles receded for the duration of the dinner and in the few days before Audrey returned to New York to begin work on her film. 'She made me feel better,' Wolders confirmed, adding that, at this stage, 'that was all she had set out to do.' It was some months before they met again, in New York, where Wolders had gone to settle some matters to do with Oberon's estate. Connie Wald called to suggest that Audrey would be glad to see him; her marriage difficulties were multiplying, and she needed companionship. Now it was Wolders's turn to be the comforter. Film commitments prevented their meeting until a night shoot was cancelled at the last minute. Fearing a lonely evening, since her former closeness with Ben Gazzara had cooled into a professional relationship, Audrey asked Wolders to come over. As he remembered it, he made himself two hours late for a dinner engagement by just sitting there with Audrey, talking about her problems. Two weeks later he returned to New York with the intention of seeing her more regularly. Soon they were calling each other several times a day.

If Wolders is to be believed, Audrey was not so much romantically inclined towards him as maternally concerned for him. 'She felt I needed a woman in my life,' he said. He did. But it hadn't struck Audrey yet that the woman was herself. This truth, which scriptwriters know all about, only sank in over the ensuing months. By then, Audrey had returned to Switzerland and set the machinery for her divorce in motion; Wolders was in Malibu. Their daily exchange of confidences by late-night, long-distance telephone only increased their desire to be physically nearer each other. Audrey encouraged him to come to Tolochenaz.

The divorce negotiations were draining her. Her husband was insisting on his custody rights being spelled out, as well as his son's place of residence. The two sets of lawyers, Swiss and Italian, discovered how far apart they were in representing the interests of two people who had little in common except a son. Even given the sincere wish of both parents not to hurt their child, the divorce was clearly going to take some time. Robert Wolders had just the sympathetic temperament to keep Audrey sane over the months ahead. To her, this was what love was really all about: companionship, guardianship in the sense that T. S. Eliot had used the word. In *The Cocktail Party*, a trio of 'guardians' constitute a sort of Salvation Army in miniature to help and counsel their troubled friends and acquaintances.

With nothing to detain him in America, Robert Wolders stayed on at Tolochenaz. His friendship with Audrey was treated discreetly, lest it complicate the already tangled divorce proceedings. In any case, until the divorce was finalized, there could be no talk of marriage. When it did finally come through, in 1982, there was no real need for her and Wolders to get married, as they understood each other so completely. Neither had anything to gain from it financially. Though not as rich as Audrey was, Wolders had invested his inheritance well. He could never be accused of being a fortune-hunter. Both of them had been through enough unhappiness—a death in Wolders's case, two divorces in Audrey's—for them to realize the tenuous nature of a relationship not based on love, and not necessarily made securer by marriage. 'There is no reason why we shouldn't marry,' Audrey explained later, 'but we're just very happy the way we are.'

To the *Vanity Fair* writer Dominick Dunne, she elaborated: 'It was clear that Robbie and I had found each other at a time in our lives when we were both very unhappy. And now we're terribly happy again.' Filling an emotional void seems to have been a talent that came naturally to Wolders. 'Sometimes it is better late than never,' Audrey said. 'If I'd met him when I was eighteen, I wouldn't have appreciated him. I would have thought, 'That's the way everyone is.''' If this sounds simplistic, it is worth remembering that Audrey tended to see things in simple terms, until it was proved otherwise. That natural gift was part of her charm, but also what made her vulnerable to hurt.

Though Wolders had started out as an actor, he did not have the restless, relentless drive of Mel Ferrer. He wasn't an entrepreneur or a wheeler-dealer or a player in the game of film-industry politics. He wasn't committed to a career for himself—or Audrey, for that matter. Unless things changed very much—and sudden change always held fears for Audrey—she wouldn't be making many (or any) more films requiring months of shooting. Tolochenaz suited her and Wolders. Soon they were leading a placid life, made safe by routine, though not ruled by it. The villagers accepted Wolders as 'l'ami de Madame Audrey'. By this time it was possible to keep in touch with the larger world beyond the lakeside canton by means of fax, satellite television and all the other sophisticated methods of communication. Audrey had no intention of becoming a recluse, and there were constant demands on her time and her services, as well as proposals for a 'comeback' film or two, or three . . . This was where Robert Wolders came into his own. He had a gift for drawing up an agenda for Audrey's day (and his own) and seeing that she was protected from people she didn't want to see or things she didn't want to do, all without giving offence. Instead of a cold rebuff, which would expose Audrey to resentment, he could transmit a sense of acceptable disappointment when she had to refuse an offer, or turn down an invitation.

The question of starting a family hardly arose. Audrey was over fifty and probably past child-bearing age, even if her history of miscarriages had not made it unwise for her to try. To a close friend, she confided that such wasn't her wish, anyhow. A new child would scarcely have entered its teens when its mother 'would be an old crone'.

Baroness van Heemstra now lived almost permanently at La Paisible. She was in failing health. Audrey and her mother had had their differences over the years, but when the old Dutchwoman slipped away in her famous daughter's Swiss manor house, Audrey said, 'I was very lucky being able to take care of her. It's so sad when people have to die away from home.' She accompanied her mother's body to the Netherlands for burial.

Audrey's father, the Fascist who had spent the war years interned in a British prison camp and then vanished, would probably never have re-entered this story of his daughter's life had it not been for a slip of the tongue which Audrey made in 1989 during an interview with the journalist Edward Klein.

They were talking in the relaxed atmosphere of the den in a friend's house in Los Angeles, probably Connie Wald's. It was, Audrey had assured Klein, 'my very last magazine interview, ever!' As she had done in many interviews she had given over the last thirty or so years, she related how Joseph Hepburn-Ruston—described by Klein as a 'ne'er-do-well Hungarian [sic] Irish father'—had 'disappeared' from home when Audrey was only six. Then, a little later in the interview, when she was relating how success had enabled her 'to give my mother everything she deserved', Audrey stumbled. She added, 'I was able to help my father.' Klein pounced on this discrepancy. ' "Your father?" I interrupted, "I thought your father disappeared from your life when you were a child." ' Slowly, and with what her interrogator called 'a great deal of pain', Audrey related the rest of the story. She had finally found her 'lost' parent, she explained. The Red Cross had helped her trace him.

This was not true. Audrey's discovery of her father's whereabouts occurred in much more dramatic and touching circumstances. Again it is her Austrian relative, Walter Ruston, who provides the answer. 'Audrey came to Brussels, where I was living, for the premiere there of *The Nun's Story.* This would have been in the middle of 1959. I met her and Mel at a reception after the film. Almost the first sentence Audrey addressed to me was, "Where is my father?" ' It was nearly twenty years since she had last seen the parent she loved so dearly and missed so much, when he had put her aboard the Dutch aircraft that returned her to the Netherlands within weeks of the outbreak of war. 'I had Joe's address in Dublin, where he was living now—I got it from his mother, the woman we called Aunt Anna, who still lived in Vienna. Of course I gave it to Audrey.'

Joseph Hepburn-Ruston had remarried. Almost next to nothing is known of his third wife, except that she was Irish and her first name was Fidelma. In correspondence with his mother, in letters that are discreet yet terribly touching in the pain they conceal, Joseph reveals that he and his new wife had a child, a baby girl who would have been Audrey's half-sister; but she had died immediately after birth. A photograph of Fidelma, taken by her husband, reveals a young woman of spirit with a wide smile and laughing eyes. She carries two tennis racquets, resting one on each shoulder, as if her husband has handed his own to her while he took the picture. A man in love with outdoor sports from his early polo-playing days in the smart set in Java, Hepburn-Ruston had obviously found a sympathetic spouse.

It is likely that he married Fidelma in the early 1950s, though witnesses in Dublin who knew Hepburn-Ruston do not speak of a wife. They do speak of a certain pathetic extravagance that he retained in his personal habits. Pamela Manahan, a Dublin woman teaching underprivileged girls at a club in a poor area near Lower Mount Street, came across evidence of this. 'There were a lot of little huckster shops tucked away among the tenement buildings in this very poor area of Dublin. Imagine my surprise on seeing a selection of tins containing fish fillets in wine and other exotic tidbits of the kind you'd be more likely to find in Fortnum & Mason in London. Quite out of place in this Sean O'Casey-like setting. On my enquiring who the likely purchasers of such delicacies might be, the woman behind the counter said, "Oh, I stock them for a fellow who says he's Audrey Hepburn's father." I saw him in the shop once—but I didn't approach him. He looked a very reserved chap; it didn't seem to me he'd welcome a stranger very easily.'

It is safe to assume that, once she had got her father's address, Audrey lost no time in making arrangements to visit him.

Had her father never contacted her? Klein very reasonably interjected. Audrey's reply sounds a shade disingenuous. 'It might have happened earlier . . . but maybe he didn't want to see me. His sense of discretion . . .' Then, perhaps appreciating that she was venturing into even deeper waters if she amplified the reasons for such 'discretion'—for she had not revealed to anyone her father's past in an internment camp—Audrey broke off: 'Perhaps I don't want to talk about it.'

The story she left untold—if indeed she knew the full details, which is unlikely—would certainly have been painful to relate. For it was Audrey's mother who stubbornly and systematically prevented any contact between her child and her ex-husband. When he heard that Audrey was visiting her grandmother in Vienna in 1954, he sent her a registered letter: no reply was received and he saw Ella van Heemstra's unforgiving hand in this.

Hepburn-Ruston's letters to his mother, written from Dublin in German in the period before Audrey finally caught up with him, make poignant reading. They are those of a penitent father who can only follow his famous child's travels around the world by what he reads about her in the newspapers, or by what his mother might relay to him after she has received a note from Audrey. 'Have you heard from Audrey?' he enquires in a letter of 7 July 1956, adding that he knew she was currently in London with Mel for the premiere of *War and Peace*.

It would appear that Audrey at one time had possessed a contact address for her father, since he speaks of receiving a telegram from her for the Christmas of 1954; but thereafter all personal communication between them mysteriously stopped. He sent recorded-delivery letters to the addresses he had for her in Rome and Paris. None was acknowledged, but the letters were not returned to him, which made him believe that someone in her circle was intercepting them.

He told his mother that he had not been in a position to send Audrey any gifts 'since after my internment for five years I had lost everything and possessed only my clothes'. Occasionally now he saw himself referred to in the newspaper articles about Audrey's career. The context was invariably painful. One journalist described the father who had vanished as 'a pathological anti-Communist' and hinted 'that I am not completely sane. God know what they have told poor Audrey.' In another letter to *'meine liebste Mutter'*, Joseph complained that he could not defend himself against these personal attacks without doing harm to Audrey. In this plaintive correspondence, the baroness is never mentioned directly, by name that is, but it is clear from the context (and Hepburn-Ruston's innuendos) that he believed it was she who was exerting emotional blackmail by using the threat he still represented to his child's career—should his Fascist past become known—to frustrate a meeting between father and daughter, and, additionally, foiling all his attempts to communicate with her.

He told his mother that, should he succeed in contacting Audrey, his former wife would have no hesitation in publishing the most damning account of his sullied political past—perhaps he feared it would include details of his undercover work for the Nazis in London—and this might make it difficult for him to remain in Ireland, his country of refuge. Even allowing for a degree of mania, Hepburn-Ruston's fears were real enough and were heightened by his overriding concern not to be the cause of any harm or unhappiness to Audrey. It was a heart-wrenching impasse for the wretched man. He followed her film career with the loyal attention of a fan; but a father's devotion was cruelly frustrated—until Audrey met Walter Ruston and at long last discovered her father's current whereabouts and circumstances.

At this point in her interview with Edward Klein, Audrey fell silent for a beat or two. Tears clouded her eyes. Then she rallied and told Klein that she had travelled to Dublin with her then husband, Mel Ferrer, and discovered her father at an address she had been given, in a small apartment, only a couple of rooms, though in no way living in an impoverished state. He still, it appears, showed evidence of the slim, handsome man she remembered from her childhood. He had remarried. His wife (unnamed in the interview) was a woman thirty years younger than her husband—'almost my age,' said Audrey.

The reunion of father and daughter can be dated from the interview, for Audrey refers to the film she had recently completed, John Huston's *The Unforgiven*. Allowing for the spinal injury she suffered when her horse threw her in February 1959, Audrey's visit to Dublin must have taken place some time in the second half of that year, probably the end of summer. Hepburn-Ruston, who had been a good horseman in his younger days, had apparently read of his daughter's accident in the papers, for Audrey recalled him saying, 'Of course you were a fool to ride that grey stallion.' She told Klein, 'He was cross with me for riding a horse that was going to throw me.' That is the only recorded evidence of the conversation between Audrey and her father. Of how he had spent the intervening period Audrey said nothing. But she assured Klein that she had taken care of her father's every need for the two decades following their reunion. 'It helped me lay the ghost.'

The circumstances of Hepburn-Ruston's death remain as vague as so much else in his life. Audrey is on record as saying that he died in his nineties. On one occasion, she was specific and said he had died aged ninety-four. The register of deaths in the Irish Republic for 1980 (and the years before and after) contains only an 'Anthony Hepburn', who died in Dublin at that age. This is almost certainly Audrey's father, even in death carrying on his lifelong habit of changing his name—dropping one element of his family name and switching from one to another of his given names— to suit his circumstances or a need for concealment. The deceased is described on the death certificate as a 'civil servant'. It is a suitably anonymous description, and possibly not too far from the truth. This writer believes that Hepburn-Ruston, entering his sixties when he left Britain for Eire and clearly too old to seek official entry into the Irish Civil Service, occupied himself in some semi-official capacity in a department of the Irish government or on the fringe of academia. There is a story, whose truth it has not been possible to establish, that he did some work, cataloguing or indexing, for Trinity College, Dublin. But there is a more intriguing possibility still.

During his internment on the Isle of Man he held himself apart from the other prisoners, immersed in 'textbooks'. No one can recall what these were, but one likelihood is that he was making a study of the Irish language and that when he settled in Ireland he worked for one or other of the organizations established to revive and promote its use. Such an embrace of the nationalist aspirations of the Irish Republic ties in with his anti-British stance. The address given for 'Anthony Hepburn, deceased' is a house in Merrion Square which was occupied between 1970 and 1988 by an organization known as Gaelleagras na Seirbhisi Poibli, loosely translated as the Irish Language Organization for the Public Service. It had previously been the American Embassy; nowadays it is occupied by MSF, Ireland's leading union for skilled and professional people. Neither the US Embassy nor the Irish Language Organization has any official record of employing a 'Hepburn' or a 'Hepburn-Ruston'. But considering his age, it is unlikely that Audrey's father would have been employed in a capacity that found its way onto the payroll. The probabilities point to a casual, part-time involvement, and the use of the address (for whatever reason) as one of convenience on the death certificate.

Tony Moriarty, research officer at MSF, points out that there used to be a private mews at the back of the Merrion Square building, which was demolished at the end of the 1960s as it was full of dry rot. Perhaps it was in one of those small mews 'cottages' that Hepburn-Ruston received his daughter: Audrey's emphasis on her father's cramped accommodation, yet on its not being in an impoverished area, supports this theory. Merrion Square was—and remains—one of Dublin's most prestigious addresses. From what one knows of his liking for the good things of life, it would be in keeping with Hepburn-Ruston, in his diminished circumstances, that he should have chosen to live in genteel poverty. His daughter's arrival improved the quality of his remaining twenty years, although what connection he subsequently maintained with her is unknown: he makes no other recorded appearance in her life. The full story of his relationship with the child who became a world-famous film star, and with her strong-willed but erratic mother, remains tantalizingly just out of sight. The research that might tell more is inhibited both by understandable family silence and the fact that detailed records of Hepburn-Ruston's career have not been made public. It is probable that material which would have been useful was destroyed in the post-war years, along with official papers concerning internment, by a British government by then guiltily aware of its shameful wartime record on imprisonment without charge or trial. It is difficult, if not impossible, to hide a secret completely from the world. But Audrey Hepburn, compassionate as well as prudent, managed to conceal most of the secrets surrounding her father for almost all of her life.

'What is your life like in Switzerland?' Dominick Dunne asked her in 1991. In reply, she used the word she had always used when asked a question about her private life; one that deflected curiosity without giving offence. Dunne recorded the word in a way that likened it to a note of music. ' "Divine," she said, pouncing on the word, elongating it, pronouncing it in capital letters, and shutting her eyes to experience it.'

In her life with Robert Wolders, Audrey's day hardly varied. Still an early riser, up at 6 a.m., she was out in the garden before the dew was off the plants, cutting fresh flowers for the vases; then indoors to her kitchen for herbal tea and a light breakfast, then a tête-à-tête with her Sardinian housekeeper to put together a shopping list for the open-air market in Lausanne on Saturday morning. Her servant frequently had a hard job warding off Audrey when it came to cleaning and dusting La Paisible. She and Wolders kept several dogs. Jack Russell terriers had now succeeded the line of spoilt little Yorkies that had all been called Famous. She had given Wolders a terrier after he confessed that, as a boy, he had never had a dog of his own. With dogs, Audrey felt as she did with children—safest. They were totally trusting, completely vulnerable, and this encouraged her to open her feelings to them in faith and without reservation—which, she said with a hint of wry experience when the subject arose, one seldom did with human beings. 'Who thinks you're as fantastic as your dog does?'

Obviously Robert Wolders did. Those who saw them together noted the ease they had acquired with each other almost from the first time they met. Both were unfussy about the food they ate; but then they ate so little of it: mostly vegetables, though they were not rigidly vegetarian. Audrey did not drink wine but was still partial to a glass of whisky. 'Would you be very shocked if I poured myself a small whisky?' she would ask the rare guest she did not know well. 'It's awfully early, I know, but it must be six o'clock somewhere in the world.' She still smoked, though a brand a cut above her favourite Gold Flakes which had long ago been taken off the market because of their high tar content.

Her dress sense remained classic and simple. She had never collected jewellery. The simplest piece, no matter what it cost, looked good on Audrey. Alongside a more flamboyant star like Elizabeth Taylor, Audrey stood out like royalty: she didn't need to compete. Indeed, she retained an odd unworldliness about things that others took for granted. Dominick Dunne recalls that he once saw her and Taylor arriving together at some film function. Audrey sensed the frenzied excitement of the ambience that Taylor moved in and, after embracing her contemporary and seeking to make small talk, she pointed to the largest jewel in the collection on Taylor's gown and asked 'Kenneth Lane?' (Lane was a top costume jeweller so the remark may just have been double-edged, but it is unlikely.) Taylor replied, 'No, Richard Burton.' One star thought of such a magnificent jewel simply in terms of its commercial provenance; the other, in terms of the marital tribute it represented. For Audrey, no man had to express his affection in carats.

Audrey had often been approached to write her memoirs but had always refused. Privacy remained her inflexible rule. She weakened only to write the text for a coffee-table book, *Gardens of the World*.

Though her life was now one that nourished contentment, the marks of age were beginning to appear. Her face showed the strain she had been through over her most recent divorce. The skin appeared thin and tight-stretched, though considering the wonderful foundation beneath it, this only amounted to the patina that gathers on a work of art and enhances it. She made no pretence at concealing the light network of lines around the corners of her lips and eyes. 'My laugh lines', she called them, adding that laughter was the greatest gift anyone could bring her. A few of her close friends felt that the years of enforced dieting, and short spells of anorexia, were taking their toll, as her constitution searched for the resources to withstand the ageing process. Still, her energy seemed to belie any need for greater concern. All Audrey's life had been passed in an effort to conceal struggle and she was not going to admit to it now.

She wore her hair in the simplest and least fussy style when she was at home—a ponytail secured with a broad white band. As ever, the muscles in her thighs and torso that ballet training had put in place fifty years before served her superbly. She moved around her home with a grace that made it look as if the domestic chores had been choreographed for her. Wherever she went outside her own tight little enclave, she was recognized and drew small crowds as if she had rung a dinner bell for hungry people. She was surprised—or pretended to be—that people still knew who she was: 'Well, I must still look like myself.' Wisely, she never tried doing that dangerous thing: competing with her old image. She paid her fans the most graceful compliment in her power. She grew old along with them.

Only one thing depressed her and took a temporary toll on her spirits:

the deaths of friends. She called it 'the gathering in'. David Niven, who had lived in Switzerland at Château d'Oex, and with whom she had shared 'the gift of laughter' when they had met during the early out-of-town opening of *Gigi,* over thirty years earlier, died slowly and painfully of motor neurone disease. Little by little, this buoyant and debonair man grew incapable of responding to the sights and sounds that counted for so much in his world and Audrey's: good friends, lovely homes, cheerful talk, companionship at the supper table. Audrey wept openly as she sat well to the side of the small Swiss chapel where the congregation offered thanks for Niven's life on earth.

Perhaps it was an emotional resistance to the loss of such rare talents as Niven that now caused her to accept most of the invitations that arrived at Tolochenaz to pay tribute to stars she had known and worked with. Audrey Hepburn suddenly began turning up with surprising frequency at memorial dinners, galas and award ceremonies. She enjoyed herself, but there was no mistaking her deeper instinct: she recognized how fleeting fame was. It should be celebrated while one was here to do so.

She consented immediately when she was asked in 1986 to contribute to a television documentary about William Wyler, who had died five years earlier. She appeared in the hour-long film with Gregory Peck, Laurence Olivier and Barbra Streisand—'a class reunion', she called it. Crowds waited on tiptoe outside her hotel, and at any other public engagement, for a glimpse of her. When she signed copies of *Gardens of the World* in Ralph Lauren's new store on Madison Avenue, itself a facsimile of field-sport kits and English country-house living as they might have appeared in a Billy Wilder or Stanley Donen comedy, the line of waiting people reached round the block to Park Avenue. To leave, she had to slip out by the back door.

Celebrity is a virus that is hard to kill. Despite her love of the reclusive life, Audrey was probably bitten again by it on occasions like these. When a television film was offered to her in 1986, she accepted 'for the fun of it'. It was called *Love Among Thieves*—a title that made her laugh when she read it first—and was very much a rehash of ingredients she knew well and had no need to strain herself over. Romance, mystery and murder set against lush backgrounds and given a gloss to make its old-fashioned provenance acceptable to modern tastes—very much a Ralph Lauren sort of reproduction. She played a concert pianist who steals a Fabergé egg in order to ransom her kidnapped fiancé. Robert Wagner was the art dealer on her trail from Paris to Mexico. It was a trifle, barely an intermission in what she called 'the perfect peace of my life today'.

Yet 'peace' for Audrey always had to involve more than mere passivity.

The scripts started to come in again after she had appeared in *Love Among Thieves* and she was amazed to see how much she was still considered to be worth. 'It's not that I've got more valuable, it's inflation that's got higher,' she said to Billy Wilder, perhaps unconsciously and in a more modest fashion echoing Gloria Swanson in Wilder's *Sunset Boulevard:* 'I am big. It's the pictures that got small.' But Audrey knew that to resume film-making on a regular basis would be to seek a false assurance. Love was always vital to her sense of well-being. It felt good to be the star again, to be the magnet for waiting crowds; but it was all the more satisfying because, like so many intense pleasures, it was of brief duration: a day trip, not a vacation, over and done with before it staled. Besides, as well as being loved, she needed to feel useful. Film-making, she was only too aware, would not provide that. She was not a nostalgic person: the past was a country she only entered when invited and whose gate she shut, often thankfully, when she left. She was an energetic person: she lived in the present. How best could she use her energies? Where was the work that would engage her sympathies? The answer came far sooner than she anticipated and in a form that would consume the store of years remaining to her—far fewer than Audrey or anyone else then imagined.

23

THE MISSIONARY'S STORY

'W E didn't go to her,' says Christa Roth, the German-born co-ordinator of Unicef's 'goodwill ambassadors' at the organization's Geneva office, 'she came to us.' The statement is simple and factual, but Christa Roth gives it an inflection of almost divine guidance.

Audrey and Robert Wolders had decided to make a tour of the Far East in October 1987, stopping at Macao, the Portuguese enclave on the Chinese mainland, for the final night of its first international music festival. Audrey had been invited to dedicate the gala concert, which was to be televised live to several countries in Europe and Asia, 'to all the world's children'. All the artists had waived their fees for the night, and the money raised would go to Unicef. After the concert, Audrey wondered aloud: Dedications took little effort—wasn't there something more she could be doing for Unicef?

Unicef's field representative in the Hong Kong area passed on her inquiry. A working lunch was arranged when she returned home and a date swiftly fixed to let Audrey see what working for the charity might involve her in. 'At that time the World Philharmonic Orchestra was embarking on an enormous global tour,' Christa Roth recalls, 'some sixty to seventy concerts.' One was planned for Tokyo in March 1988. 'We knew Audrey had a huge following among the Japanese. We all decided she should appear there on our behalf, introducing the orchestra and speaking about our work. The numbers who attended exceeded our wildest expectations. It was like a national event. I think that experience decided Audrey: if she could lend her name and fame to Unicef in such a way that it would help our work with children, she would. That was the beginning; that was how it all started. No one could have foreseen what it led to.'

Unicef was then in very urgent need of funds—'It always is,' Christa Roth says resignedly. Contrary to what many believe, it has to raise all its money by its own efforts. Its funds do not come out of the general United Nations budget. At that time it had to find over $20 million for relief work among five million people, half of them children stricken with famine in northern Ethiopia. Audrey was a welcome addition to the roster of celebrities who could convert their star power into the financial currency which is the lifeblood of charities. When Unicef saw the strength of her commitment, as well as the special talents she brought to promoting its work around the world, she joined a small, very valued group of 'goodwill ambassadors'. They included Peter Ustinov, Richard Attenborough, Roger Moore, the Japanese writer and actress Tetsuko Kuroyanagi, Liv Ullmann, the cricketer Imran Khan, the singer Julio Iglesias and the explorer Edmund Hillary. Danny Kaye had been one of the most active ambassadors for Unicef but had died shortly before Audrey was 'signed up'. Unicef strongly emphasizes that in no way was Audrey Hepburn a replacement for the American actor and comedian. 'She was an addition,' says Christa Roth. Besides her humanitarian impulse, Audrey commended herself to Unicef because of something more prosaic but almost as important: she had had a long and successful career that did not need any extra limelight that Unicef might flatteringly shed upon her. 'She was dedicated to us, not to herself,' says Christa Roth, adding with a smile, 'We could be sure we wouldn't be bothered with artists' agents.'

The announcement of Audrey's appointment was made on 8 March 1988. Beyond a token dollar a year, the job carried no salary. Moreover, all expenses other than official travel and accommodation were to be met by Audrey out of her own purse. Hardship was almost guaranteed on some of the tours she would be expected to undertake in the impoverished Third World. Physical peril from civil wars, never mind medical risks in countries where disease was endemic, were always a clear and sometimes a present danger. There were next to no diplomatic privileges. Unicef accorded Audrey what it calls 'a UN laissez-passer'. It is the highest category of travel, ensuring the bearer a speedy passage as well as the customary courtesies enjoyed by those on official visits. But that was the limit of it— no gifts, no featherbedding. 'And Audrey Hepburn never claimed customs-free privileges,' says Roth.

Every programme of travel she was to undertake over the next few years was financed by public subscriptions, charity events and private donations. Audrey was tremendously conscientious in saving Unicef money. She used to jot down her expenses in a little notebook in exactly the same way that, when a fledgling film star, she wrote down how much of the per diems allowed her by the film studio had actually been spent by her, and then at the end of shooting handed back what was left over. An unheard-of accountancy practice in Hollywood.

Her first Unicef assignment was undertaken within a fortnight of her appointment being announced. She would go to the famine-hit regions of Ethiopia. She made only one stipulation: that Robert Wolders travel with her wherever Unicef despatched her. The two of them boarded a Swissair flight to Addis Ababa. Though she had never been the sort of film star who trailed a caravanserai of porters and baggage, Audrey's preparations for this trip looked particularly spartan: one carry-on bag and two suitcases. All too soon, the luxury of Swissair was to be exchanged for bumpy journeys seated on rice sacks in the backs of trucks, or clinging to Wolders's arm in alarmingly dilapidated helicopters clattering over the dry cracked plains to tented villages and makeshift medical camps. It was a far cry from ordering a bidet to be in place when she arrived in the Congo to film *The Nun's Story,* or having an air conditioner flown all the way from Hollywood. During her trips, she gave interviews in conditions that were a million miles from the protected environment of a film studio or the security of a hotel suite.

She wore the simplest of travelling costumes: usually chino pants, a Lacoste shirt, perhaps a headscarf and, when the sun had dipped and the night chill was descending, one of her famous pastel-coloured rollneck sweaters. 'I am not here to be seen,' she said, 'but so that the rest of the world can see others.' She made good that statement a thousand times over.

She held babies in her arms and brushed away the flies crawling on their eyelids. She went to places where there was no electricity, no water, no heating, no sanitation. She saw people bathing in rivers running with sewage and then drinking from the water. She was greeted in wonderment and silence at an orphanage in Mekele, in Northern Ethiopia, until she spoke the two simple words in the local tongue that she had practised as assiduously as when she was learning a Hollywood script: 'Thank you.' Then the staring eyes of hundreds of blank-faced children suddenly broke into life 'and positively twinkled before me'. She reflected: 'It's ironic that it was because of children that I stayed at home all these years. Now it is for the sake of the children that I'm travelling all over the world.'

She visited food distribution centres, hospitals, dam construction sites where people laboured in such numbers that they reminded her of some epic scene in the Old Testament. It struck her that the people of Ethiopia needed spades to dig wells, not just graves for their dead. It was an unbelievably different world to any she had ever known—'like walking on the moon'. In one camp she saw a child standing alone. The video record of the moment shows Audrey asking the little girl what she wants to be when she grows up. In her native language the child replies, 'Alive.' A screenwriter would hesitate to invent that sort of thing and risk the accusation of maudlin sentimentality. Here, the reality of a land in which five-year-olds looked like helpless babies banished any thoughts of that kind. The horror was palpable. In compensation, Audrey found herself dwelling on the physical grace and poise that even starvation could not erode. The women literally bore the human burdens of their children with dignity and fortitude. Who knows: perhaps they felt a kind of basic kinship with this graceful woman whose name and fame were unknown to all but the Unicef field officers shepherding her through the crowds. One interviewer asked her if she thought more social workers were needed, and she replied, 'Mothers are the best social workers of all.'

Some of Audrey's replies, recorded by Unicef's cameras, are so concise, almost epigrammatic, that they run the risk of being thought too neat, too snappy, almost scripted. But what removes that taint is the tone in which she utters them. That famous warm voice, not pitched to the emotions alone now, but wanting to persuade and command the understanding of her listeners, carries with it conviction as well as concern.

'There were very, very few film stars who could match Audrey for total sincerity,' says Christa Roth, 'or discharge their duties without making you suspect they were in it for their own gain. But Audrey, you see, did so much hard work—before, as well as after. She called for all the information we could supply her with about a particular crisis spot. She not only went on her mission well briefed, but she could speak of particular problems—not just Unicef ones—with a detail that convinced her listeners she had used her time well, and wasn't simply bringing back a sincere but rather superficial view of a country. She wanted, above all else, to be credible.' She spent hours with Robert Wolders writing speeches for the press conferences on her return. Christa Roth says, 'We would occasionally send her over a schema—suggestions for points. She invariably rewrote them her own way, like a good actress given the okay to put a scriptwriter's words into her own natural flow. Her professionalism was terrific. She knew how a sentiment had to be boiled down into a phrase, a "soundbite". She was able to deliver it with all the force of her art.' Such was one of the observations of Audrey's that was to find its way into headlines in every language in the world: 'To save one child is a blessing. To save a million children is a God-given opportunity.' It might have been trite were it not, in her case, so abundantly true.

She sometimes spoke with a frankness few politicians could afford. When she returned from Ethiopia, after about a week's hard travelling, she reported how government officials had admitted making 'a terrible mistake' over the whole resettlement policy. Their soldiers had been 'over-zealous', even 'brutal'. She called for a 'corridor of peace' between the government forces and the rebels: she herself was a 'corridor of reason'.

In Unicef's video record of her journeys, Robert Wolders can frequently be glimpsed near her, but not noticeably escorting her, usually a couple of yards behind, vigilant but not attempting to share the limelight—only the burden.

She was very careful in her public appearances on her return, rejecting any she thought inappropriate, like invitations from television shows which had more to do with entertainment than she thought proper for her task—such as game shows. Of course, interviewers often asked her questions about herself and her films. But why not? That was part of the power to attract publicity for the organization. If one looks at some of the appearances on network TV that Unicef recorded, one has to admire the way Audrey balances the glamorous nostalgia for the fans with the far from glamorous facts of famine for the charitably minded.

On her return from Ethiopia she gave press conferences in Britain, Canada, Switzerland, Finland, Germany and the United States. Many of these tours were undertaken at her own expense. This was where Robert Wolders's talents came in most handy. For days before she arrived in some continent, country or city, Wolders would be manning the telephones and faxes at La Paisible, negotiating special rates for Audrey with hotels, wheedling first-class seats out of airlines, balancing the delicate operation of 'paying' for such amenities by allowing those who provided them to reap the benefits of the publicity that Audrey brought, while at the same time tactfully ensuring that the integrity of her mission wasn't compromised by what might seem like a 'personal appearance' tour. She who had shunned interviews in her film-star heyday now gave them round the clock. She rose before dawn to be made up for segments on breakfast television shows boosting Unicef's work. She took the podium in conference rooms filled with media reporters and the merciless cameramen whom she had spent half a lifetime avoiding. 'I scarcely slept or ate,' she recalled after that first baptism in the wide waters of Unicef's charity, 'there simply wasn't time.' In Washington DC she did fifteen interviews a day and somehow squeezed in a working breakfast with twenty-five Congressmen and women, appealing to them to increase their country's aid to Ethiopia. They did.

After the European and North American tours came one to Turkey for World Children's Day. Wherever she went, Audrey showed videos of the heartbreak she had witnessed. Once she felt compelled to apologize for her own well-kempt looks and apparent good health as the camera followed her through multitudes of huddled and derelict men, women and children. 'Yes, of course I was made up for the Camcorder,' she replied to a questioner, not at all thrown by the implications of his inquiry. 'Call it vanity if you like. I just believed I could do a better job for the children if I looked good for the camera.'

Inevitably, some of the publicity she attracted upset her. There were occasions when Audrey's fame shone brighter than the burden of need. One glossy magazine dutifully ran a story of Audrey's 'scrounging'—her own word: no complaint there—for Unicef donations, but then coupled it with a picture-spread of her in Givenchy fashions and a 'recipe' for 'the Hepburn look' that reduced her to a list of brand-name cosmetics, few of which she used. 'I didn't come here to make Givenchy look good,' she said. 'He doesn't need me to do that.'

It was the same story almost everywhere. Journalists who came to listen in sceptical mood, suspicious of the 'set-up'—a former film star dressed by Givenchy talking about starving children—felt their doubts crumble and fall away once Audrey started speaking. 'Celebrity', she told Lynn Barber, was simply 'this piece of luggage left over from my years of movie-making'. The journalist wrote, 'I said something about "sacrificing her time" and she jumped at me. "It's not a sacrifice. Because a sacrifice means you give up something you want for something you don't want. This is no sacrifice: it's a gift I'm receiving." ' Yet the film-star instinct could not be altogether repressed. 'Almost automatically, when our photographer asked her to sit by the window, she said, "But the other way round, eh? Because this is my best side." '

Again and again, her childhood and the mothering she had received from a parent who alternated concern with strict discipline comes to the surface in these question-and-answer sessions. One realizes how Audrey's descriptions of mothers and children she met on her missions reflect on her own childhood. Her mother, like the African mothers with their ailing babies, had had to confront her own child's wartime illnesses. 'During the war I had bronchitis and [my mother] said, "Oh, I wish I could get you some orange juice . . . I wish I could get some milk . . . I wish I could get you eggs." And I thought, Very nice, she wants to spoil me a bit. But today I see what it must have been like to go to bed at night not knowing how you are going to feed your children the next day.' Subtly and ironically, mother and child—often so independent of each other when the baroness was alive—had changed places in Audrey's recall and she had uncovered a fuller, deeper understanding of her parent.

In April 1989 she was off again, this time to Sudan for the start of 'Operation Lifeline'. She travelled over dangerous, land-mined roads in the south and met rebel leaders to plead for safe passage for food and medicines. It was just one trip among some fifty that she was to undertake for Unicef, including visits to El Salvador, Bangladesh, Vietnam, Guatemala, Thailand, Kenya and Somalia. She survived, she said, because there was always La Paisible to return to and recuperate at. On her sixtieth birthday, in 1989, sixty pure white rosebushes were delivered to her there—from Hubert de Givenchy, who then proceeded to plant just as many among the severe topiary of Le Jonchet, his seventeenth-century manor house near Tours in France.

The Unicef videos of these errands of mercy are a kaleidoscope of heart-rending scenes. Always at their centre is this slim woman in the simple shirt, calm in appearance, yet purposeful in everything she does. 'I know all about you,' she assures a local relief worker in Somalia, and the man's face splits like a ripe melon into a grin of pleasure. She tenderly spoons food into the mouths of other women's babies. She suffers a dozen tiny hands to pluck at her ponytail, to pinch her arms—how fat you are, their eyes seem to be saying. Children in a classroom repeat some simple sentence she has spoken to them, applaud her and get her applause in return—and it clearly makes their day. Safety seems to mean nothing to her. She walks among barren palms and scraggy corn stalks long stripped of grain, and the chatter of automatic gunfire can be heard distinctly from not far away. She meets and comforts Caroline Turner, a nutritionist whose Unicef co-worker, Sean Devereux, died in her arms after being shot. Words fail Audrey, but an embrace says what cannot be said. Her approach is always built on simple trust. Tennessee Williams's wonderful line about 'the kindness of strangers' is implicit in every meeting. Her pastel-coloured field-wear contrasts bizarrely with the jazzy colours and rainbow patterns of the native fabrics. At times Audrey looks like an extra-terrestrial, an alien on a benign mission from another planet. Eyes follow her—eyes are everywhere. Eyes like black cherries rolling in cups of milk . . . eyes set in faces that might have been cut out of smooth stone or carved out of wax . . . the eyes of twenty thousand people at a time, all fixed on her.

She cannot ever have been the object of such fascination, not even in the days when fans gathered to see her step from limousine to Oscar ceremony.

But there is a difference this time: half the owners of these eyes are dying. They will never see Audrey Hepburn again.

One day a helicopter drops her on the flight deck of a US aircraft carrier and she is handed a cheque for $4000, collected by the officers and crew in the ninety minutes that was all the warning they had of her impending arrival. She stands on the deck, surrounded by over a thousand servicemen, many of whom were not yet born when she first drove a Vespa through the streets of Rome with Gregory Peck riding pillion. She can hardly contain her tears and stands blinking in the harsh sunlight. 'It can't be any worse than making movies,' one officer says to her, unaware of how immeasurably more fulfilling it is.

Back on dry land—'dry' is the word that can be used almost everywhere she sets foot, a T. S. Eliot wasteland filled with hollow children—she visits hospitals and hears words that are painfully familiar to her: 'edema', 'anaemia', 'congestion'. Her own debilitated state at the end of the war passes in front of her eyes, only it is African children now who exhibit her symptoms of long ago. She goes into a school where—mercifully—the children look reasonably well fed and healthy and their teacher has just finished writing 'A B C D' on the blackboard. Audrey picks up the chalk and to the children's huge delight writes '. . . and love' on the board and then, impulsively, adds the outline of a heart.

Back in the United States, she appears on *Larry King Live* on CNN and hears the shirtsleeved inquisitor say to her, 'Why don't you work?' Her self-control never wavers. Without a flicker of irony she protests, 'But I am working, Larry . . . for Unicef . . . Some do more than others. All do more than I do. But it makes me happy to know that what I do is important, too.' Happier, certainly, than when she was working for those non-charitable organizations called Paramount and Warner Bros. and MGM.

The occasional patness comes, perhaps, from answering the same question too often. Sometimes she sounds as glib as any politician making a pitch for re-election: her journeys aren't political, she says, they represent 'a humanization of politics, not a politicization of humanitarian aid'. She would have asked to rewrite that script had she been making a movie. But then her face clears wonderfully and the next few words come more easily to her tongue because they come so naturally from her heart. 'How strange there isn't a science of peace,' she says, 'since there is a science of war.'

'One of the natural assets Audrey brought to her work was languages,' says Christa Roth. 'She spoke French, Italian, German and some Spanish and, of course, Dutch. When a TV spot was needed urgently to support some Unicef activity, she could deliver it instantly in any of the main languages. We hadn't far to send for her. She lived just down the road, so to speak.'

Was she doing too much, overtaxing herself to danger point? The notion is strongly refuted. 'She had regular health checks. Unless her agenda was filled with work, she was unhappy—feeling underemployed.' It wasn't just field trips and media appearances that absorbed her surplus energy. Many letters addressed to her arrived daily at Unicef's Geneva offices. Most of them were monitored by Christa Roth; many she passed on to Audrey with a suggested reply. Often Audrey drafted her own replies, inevitably identifying with the wretched condition of the writer. Other letters contained banknotes of all imaginable denominations and nationalities, signifying that Audrey's television appeals inspired such trust that donations were sent straight to her from the senders' hearts and wallets. Requests for autographs were without number. Audrey signed thousands of postcard-sized photos of herself, feeling an obligation which stardom had never fired in her to the same degree. When the UN created a special issue of stamps based on children's drawings and paintings, she designed the first-day envelope.

Robert Wolders was inevitably, but willingly, caught up in Audrey's toil. Her passport was British and frequently expedited any formalities that Unicef's laissez-passer didn't regulate. Wolders, being Dutch, sometimes had to go through the tedious business of acquiring special visas for the countries they entered. It was tiresome, but bearable because of the object of their travels. Wherever Audrey stopped overnight on her media tours, Wolders would go ahead, check out their accommodation, the security, the technical qualities of the microphones and the conditions for photo-calls. Sometimes he would listen to Audrey rehearse a speech. She was still a bag of nerves until she started speaking. He would tell her if she was making the script sound like 'hers'.

More than once she was asked by a journalist, giving a meaningful glance at the bearded Dutchman, whether remarriage was on her agenda. 'We have no need,' she would reply, 'because the ceremony wouldn't add anything to what we already possess of each other. We never think of it as living in sin, only living in love.'

Movie-makers still ritually made their pitch for her services. But the notion of committing herself to a major role held fewer attractions now that she had the world stage on which to do her work. One film script slipped under her guard, perhaps because its theme had such a special resonance

for her. The title of the film was *Always*. A love story with spiritual undertones to be directed by Steven Spielberg, it was a remake of a wartime success, *A Guy Named Joe,* about an airman who died in battle and 'returned'
to earth in an angelic form to watch over his fiancée and selflessly steer her
into marriage and happiness with an earthly lover. Such stories were the
consolation that popular entertainment provided for those who had lost
husbands and sons in the war. Not only does love defy death, but the dear
departed are present in spirit, if not in the flesh, to guard and guide us.
Films and plays like these are apt to appear in the aftermath of conflicts: J.
M. Barrie's play *Mary Rose* is a classic example of one that brought comfort
to those who had suffered loss in the First World War. *Always,* though set
in peacetime among the airborne firefighters in one of America's national
parks, had its emotional counterpoint in the casualties of Vietnam.

Audrey's role was only a cameo one, that of the angel who welcomes
Richard Dreyfuss's aviator to heaven after his aircraft has crashed in an attempt to douse a forest fire. Despite the size of the role, Spielberg thought
it vital to find a star whose reputation had an almost mythic dimension:
someone who could play a transcendental being with a, well, heavenly
simplicity. Audrey of course. No one else was approached. Much of her
fee—reputedly more than a million dollars—she turned over to Unicef.

The casting had an eerie echo in something she had said a few years
before when asked—as she so frequently was—about her wartime experiences. 'I saw so many things during the war which made a lasting impression. But out of it all has come the fact that I am basically optimistic
and not pessimistic. What would be awful would be to die and look back
miserably—seeing only the bad things, the opportunities missed, or what
could have been.' 'Hap', the name of Audrey's angel, is the very essence of
these sentiments. 'Hello, Pete', is how she greets the pilot on his arrival in
heaven, so warmly natural a welcome that the poor sap doesn't realize he
has died. When it dawns on him, Audrey reacts as if this were no big deal.
'That's right,' she says, with tender matter-of-factness.

Wearing white slacks and her trademark white rollneck sweater, slim
as ever—though advancing age has sharpened her features, making her
eyes seem unnaturally large in consequence—Audrey creates a feeling almost of weightlessness as she eases Dreyfuss into the hereafter and makes
him presentable for his return to earth, even though he'll be invisible to the
girl he once held in his arms. Her last words of advice were ones that had
been in Audrey's own mind long before the part came along. Don't waste
your spirit by doing things for yourself, she tells him, but only for others.

24

'THE BEST CHRISTMAS OF MY LIFE'

THE toll that Audrey's travels were taking on her health, if not her spirit, was visible and disturbing. Her friends pleaded with her to ease up. It was useless. She drove herself without mercy.

Ian MacLeod, a Unicef field officer, met her on one of her trips to Africa. It had taken her to a feeding and medical centre where many children had died. The sight that greeted her when she arrived was that of the bodies of some twenty children who had died only hours before being loaded into trucks, each one in its tiny sack—'like a shopping bag', Audrey said later. She swayed slightly on her feet, looked as if she were about to faint, then recovered and went on—to see the other children who would soon die, too. 'You could see her emotions change,' MacLeod recalled. 'At first she didn't want to see the worst. But then she said, "That's what I have to see." It seemed to give her more strength to go away and tell the world.'

She rarely took time to relax on her field trips. It was as if she could not be inactive. In consequence, she slept badly. She saw tragedy in the mass, but worried about individuals she met: thus she exposed herself to the worst of both nightmares. The job had taken her over. The enormity of the suffering filled her mind, just as its reality filled the horizon. MacLeod commented on the way the 'infection' of suffering gripped her like a fever, even when she was back in the well-organized West. The personal cost was now apparent and shocking. 'She sits there and her hands are literally shaking,' MacLeod noted. Friends knew that a prime cause of Audrey's determination to 'do my job', whatever the personal cost, was repayment of her childhood debt to the relief charities that had succoured her in illness and probably saved her life. The sense of a circle being closed was inescapable. Every emotion was magnified by memories of her own near-starvation and wartime oppression.

Thus when she came to London in May 1991, it was to join Michael Tilson Thomas, the composer and orchestra conductor, in a concert of words and music based on the diary of Anne Frank. It was a way of raising money for Unicef, paying tribute to the collective spirit of children in distress by recalling the tragedy of the single child who had recorded events and emotions with such resilient matter-of-factness. Tilson Thomas wrote the music and conducted the London Symphony Orchestra; Audrey acted as narrator. In past years she had twice refused to play Anne Frank in a movie, disliking the idea of turning one person's tragedy into personal artifice and mass entertainment, however movingly it might be done. Now there was a cause to be served. And she had seen so much misery, hardened herself by the sight of so much suffering, that she felt purged and ready to present in person this story of certain death and eternal optimism. She was no longer a film star playing a role. She was a participant in a contemporary tragedy that echoed the wartime one. Emotion was in her gift, and now there was no guilt in using it. The concert was a kind of catharsis. A writer who interviewed her beforehand said, 'There is an emotional as well as physical cost to what she does, meeting hunger and distress at first hand . . . Her way of dealing with emotion is the same now as it was forty years ago. She limits its damage and maximizes its power by communicating it.' Fred Zinnemann, who had directed her in *The Nun's Story,* said, 'She has gone way beyond being an actress. I would say she has achieved a kind of wisdom.' It was the 'wisdom' that came from love as well as duty. She had freed herself from the sternness of her Calvinist upbringing and now put to practical use the inspirational faith that her mother's Christian Science had passed on to her. 'I do Anne Frank on pure feeling,' she confessed. As she spoke the words of the diary in front of the orchestra and an overflow audience, she no longer had any fear of breaking down and crying: she had spent all her tears for the children she had seen on her travels. The concert raised a record £30,000 for Unicef.

But the fact remained that Audrey's commitment was consuming her. For all her protests that her life was no longer an ode to duty, but to joy, she denied herself rest and relief. Robert Wolders, the person closest to her, saw the symptoms. But like everybody else, he was incapable of doing anything. Audrey was taking on herself the sufferings of others, not merely narrating them.

One London journalist, James Roberts, who interviewed her about her work for Unicef, reported her telling him the story of ' "a little girl standing, leaning against a sort of wooden door, motionless. There was this tiny white cotton thing that someone had tied around her. I couldn't stand it. I tried to get a flicker of reaction . . . And then this boy who was sitting heaving for air"—[Audrey] gasped and panted as he had done—

"and finally he pulled the blanket around him"—she curled her arms into herself, as he had done. And her voice became fainter, her words indistinct, till she was silent.' It was, in the most dedicated sense of the word, a performance. But it was one whose intensity of remembered emotion simply could not be sustained without doing harm to the instrument which reproduced it. That instrument—Audrey—was bound to shatter.

What was to be her final mission was undertaken when her emotional commitment was highest, but her physical resilience was weaker than she knew, or would admit. On 19 September 1992, in her sixty-third year, she set out on a five-day visit to Somalia and Kenya.

She had her customary checkup before leaving. Her doctor expressed concern at the way she would be physically affected by the rough conditions in Somalia, a country split by rival warlords whose internecine struggles had contributed to the worst outbreaks of famine, disease and human wretchedness on the face of Africa. He asked her if she felt that the journey was really necessary this time. What could *she* do when all the efforts of politicians to achieve a peace, or at least a truce, had failed? The question seemed to discompose her. She refused all further tests, almost as if she feared to learn anything that might disrupt the punishing schedule planned for her. It was to be a dreadful journey, one that fully justified that overworked phrase 'the heart of darkness'. Here is the itinerary:

Sunday, September 20: Arrival at Kismayo, Somalia. Visit Unicef feeding shelter, accompanied by Unicef staff. Move on to inspect camps for people left homeless by drought and war. A light lunch and rest. Then an expedition over rough terrain and through dangerous countryside, preceded by an armed scout vehicle, 30 kilometres north to see the integrated programme of health care, water and sanitation, nutritional support, household security. Continue to Mogadishu. Meetings with UN special envoy. military advisers. humanitarian aid co-ordinators. Finish with press-TV conference.

Monday, September 21: Programmes in and around Mogadishu. First stop, a child-care centre to see maternal welfare advice centre and clinic. Visit to hospital to meet representative of Médecins sans Frontières. Lunch. Visit the port area to meet representatives of world Food Programme, Care agency and International Red Cross. Across-town trip, again with armed outriders, to look at food kitchens. Visit on foot to nearby Swedrelief/Unicef feeding centre for families and children. Evening spent in meetings with media people and reception for Unicef field workers.

Tuesday, September 22: Overland journey to Bardhere with armed escort to visit Unicef feeding centre, plus maternal and child-health programmes. Visit to local hospital. In afternoon, return to Mogadishu to catch flight to Kenya.

Wednesday, September 23: Overland journey to Northern Kenya to visit refugee camps and see emergency programmes.

Thursday, September 24: Fly back to Geneva.

September 24–28: Rest, then report to Unicef headquarters, Geneva, for debriefing.

Thursday, September 29: Press conference at Foreign Press Association, London.

On paper it looks a tight schedule, exhausting for anyone. To experience it was beyond belief. Even given the experiences Audrey had registered elsewhere, it was 'unspeakable'. She had her first sight of the apocalypse to come when she and Wolders flew from Nairobi, where the Swissair jet had landed, across endless tracts of red desert to Kismayo. They looked straight down on the displacement camps around which terracotta-coloured dust dunes rippled like waves, greedy to invade the compounds. Later she discovered that the 'waves' were actually the humps of thousands of graves. Those still alive were like walking shadows—'phantoms', Audrey called them in an interview with *Newsweek's* Christopher Dickey.

Another horrifying discovery that took time to sink in was the almost complete absence of small children in the child-care camps she visited. 'They had all been snuffed out, just like candles . . . It's the ten- and twelve-year-olds you can resuscitate, if they are not too ill . . . But not these tiny ones.' Audrey said she could remember seeing wartime cities where many buildings had been bombed or shelled. But until she visited Mogadishu, she hadn't seen a city in which there wasn't a single building without a shell hole in it or with a roof. 'The place was a total battleground.' She again saw the bodies of the smallest children being loaded in sacks onto trucks. The Irish girls from the charity Concern had the slightly older children laid out in a courtyard and were virtually force-feeding them, for they were too weak to feed themselves. 'They are totally silent . . . Silent children. The silence is something you never forget. You really wonder if God hasn't entirely forgotten Mogadishu.'

The photographs that were taken of Audrey during this visit are startling. They show a woman who has aged suddenly and shockingly. Having looked all her life ten or more years younger than she was, she now looked ten years older. In one picture she carries an emaciated child whose arms and legs are like the stick figures healthier, happier children draw in primary school classrooms. Audrey's face is set and grim. Lines of work, worry and ill health are cut deeply into it. Her mouth is a straight line. Her eyes look sunken, shadowed and pouched with sleeplessness. Her hair, scraped tight against her scalp into the familiar ponytail, now gives the effect of a skullcap. She could be said to have taken on a matriarchal beauty, the stance and stature of a Mother Courage, very different from the still elfin-looking woman who had started her work for Unicef four years earlier. It could also be said that she had passed the point where she could bear no more. She is transfigured. But it is impossible not to feel she is also traumatized.

It was now that her body began to insist on what her mind had resolutely ignored. It told her to stop. On the second day of her visit, she began feeling a spasmodic series of pains in her lower stomach. Local doctors were consulted quickly. But without sophisticated equipment there was little they could do to diagnose her condition. They thought it might be a touch of amoebic dysentery, and advised her to curtail her programme. She refused. 'This isn't the time to rest.' She insisted on going on, though the pain it was costing her was evident in the way she frequently held her stomach and massaged it, trying to smooth away the returning pain. She dismissed it as of little consequence beside the greater distress all around her. She got some relief from painkillers, and that saw her through until she returned to Geneva.

Even then she did not rest or go into hospital. 'It's that wonderful old-fashioned idea: others come first,' she said, and kept her date with the Foreign Press Association in London. In retrospect, this was folly. Audrey was a very sick woman, and must have known it. The most benign reading of her condition would have attributed it to a post-traumatic stress disorder induced by the unbearable amount of human suffering she had witnessed. But she still resisted clinical diagnosis. Perhaps there remained a strong attraction to the notion that the mind can cure what the body surrenders to. Without access to confidential medical advice, one cannot tell for sure.

Audrey appeared in London for her Unicef press conference early in October 1992. James Roberts, present for the *Independent on Sunday,* wrote: 'The smile of this sixty-two-year-old woman had lit up the room [when she entered] as powerfully as the smile of the same woman had lifted the spirits of a generation in cinemas in the 1950s and 1960s. Now, unsmiling, she wrapped the assembled journalists in her sorrow. From the back of the room, there was even a sob.' The stress that showed in her features was attributed to the agonies she had recently witnessed. Possibly only Robert Wolders knew that her appearance was due to anxiety that lay closer to home. He stood by attentively, but helpless to mitigate what he guessed the effort was costing her in reserves which she needed to bear her illness. She was now on twenty-four-hour painkillers. She took no refreshment when she later met individual journalists but for her customary glass of well-watered whisky.

She returned to rest in Tolochenaz. By now, surgical examination was essential. She was still reluctant to commit herself to hospital. In the middle of October she and Wolders flew to Los Angeles, where Connie Wald was waiting to receive them. Audrey was treated at Cedars Sinai Medical Center, at first as an out-patient while tests were done and X-rays taken. The diagnosis was not good. Examination showed a tumour of the colon: an operation was essential to determine if it was malignant or not.

The pictures of Audrey entering the medical facility are stark. She looks racked with pain. She was stooped and shrunken, as if the delayed effect of dehydration and exhaustion had caught up with her and overwhelmed her resistance. The bone structure that had maintained her fragile beauty through thick and thin now stood out through the skin of her face. She had begun to take on the physiognomy of the very victims she had spent the last few years ministering to on her Unicef tours.

An emergency operation was performed on the morning of 1 November 1992. The tumour was removed and a partial colon reconstruction carried out, and she entered the intensive care unit of the hospital while further tests were done. To everyone's relief, the prognosis appeared hopeful. The tumour had a 'low-grade malignancy' rating. 'We think we've caught it in time,' a medical spokesman said. Soon she was able to walk about her private suite and receive friends, Gregory Peck and Elizabeth Taylor among them. Her status became that of an out-patient again and she rested with Connie Wald, painfully in suspense, if not physically in pain, awaiting the results of more tests. She said that she believed she had been 'lucky'. If anyone ever deserved to be that, it was Audrey Hepburn.

The shock, when it came, was all the more cruel because of the remission that had preceded it. Severe stomach pains some three weeks later caused her to be rushed back to hospital. The tests this time were devastating. They showed a severe intestinal blockage and doctors feared the malignant cancer tissue might have spread. By mid-December, the prognosis was chilling. She would have, at most, three more months of life.

Robert Wolders was at her bedside all the permitted hours, and watched over her while she slept a drugged sleep that at least restrained her from constant concern about her unfinished Unicef work. Only a few very close friends from the Hollywood community were admitted: Connie Wald, Gregory Peck and Elizabeth Taylor, herself no stranger to physical suffering. Taylor held Audrey's hands in her own. Besides their stardom, the two women shared a belief in the power of the spirit to master the weakness of the body. Both their mothers had been Christian Scientists, and the proximity of death now returned them to that faith.

Audrey was given drugs and everything else necessary to alleviate her suffering. But she who had seen death a thousand times over in the faces of others could not have been deceived. They told her bluntly that the cancer was winning. 'She is a valiant fighter,' said a close friend, 'but she didn't want to be a party to any deception—especially not self-deception. She had lots of things to do, and very little time left to do them in.'

One piece of good news was broken to her. In one respect at least, her prayers had been answered. Her dream of seeing the starving children of Somalia being fed and cared for looked as if it were coming true when, in the second week of December 1992, American troops landed on the Somali coast as representatives of the United Nations, with the mission of restoring peace to the war-torn land and making sure food supplies reached its starving people, young and old. 'She is happy to know she has done her part', a medical spokesman said of Audrey's reaction to the news. Her eloquence had made Somalia's famine front-page news. Now, with ghastly irony, her own dwindling health shared the same pages.

If it is not tasteless to say so, the knowledge that Audrey Hepburn was not long for this world probably made a sharper, more personal impact on the feelings of the millions of people to whom she had appealed on behalf of the dying of other nations.

As she lay in hospital, her career was being recalled again and again, in all languages, in print and on television. It is impossible not to think of such media concern as a kind of premature obituary. But if it was a memorial, it was built on love. The writer and critic Sheridan Morley, in New York at the time, passed a video store and noticed its windows 'stacked from floor to ceiling [with] boxes and boxes of her films already neatly arranged as some kind of memorial tribute, the way that photographs of mortally ill or nearly deceased or newly deceased royalty used to be placed in the windows of Viennese pastry shops. Struck at first by what seemed to me to be appalling taste, I stood in the rain to stare at the videos and realized that it was in fact a wonderful celebration of a great career.'

It was typical of Audrey's well-graded sense of priorities that as soon as she understood that medicine could do no more for her, she should not wish to stay any longer in Los Angeles. For her, that city had always meant one thing only: work. Now she had a more pressing agenda even than the schedule of a film. She must get back home to her beloved La Paisible— as quickly as possible. She wanted to 'see the snow again' sparkling on the Swiss mountains the way she remembered the crystal lustres on the chandelier in her parents' house holding her gaze as she looked up at them in wonderment from the cradle of her father's arms. She was so weak that flying to Geneva by a commercial airliner was out of the question. A friend came to her rescue—two friends, actually. Bunny Mellon, the socialite and philanthropist, had once been the only woman whom young Hubert de Givenchy had considered elegant enough to take with him when he left Balenciaga to open his own couture house. The couturier now got in touch with her, and she placed her private jet at Audrey's disposal, along with a doctor and nurse, for the long flight home.

When the Gulfstream jet landed at Geneva airport on 21 December 1992, Audrey was met by her housekeeper and two of her Jack Russell terriers. Robert Wolders helped her down the steps of the aircraft. She took an age to descend them, looking dreadfully pale and leaning heavily on his arm. When they got home, the first thing to greet her in the hall of La Paisible was a huge bouquet of lilies of the valley. She did not need to look at the card. It was Givenchy's flower.

Her son Sean was already there. The house was filled with the white flowers she loved. She was not bedridden all the time. She rested in the mornings, then had a light meal and, if the weather wasn't too cold, managed a short walk around that part of the terrace and garden from which Giovanni the gardener had brushed the snow. 'Signora,' he said to her, 'when you get better, will you come and help me plant and trim again?' Audrey answered that of course she would . . . 'but not like before'. Two nurses, day and night, were given a room in the house.

Audrey's Christmas cards were sent out as usual. This year she had chosen a quotation from the Indian writer and philosopher, Rabindranath Tagore: 'Each child is a reminder that God has not lost hope in man.'

On 25 December, she came downstairs and lay on a sofa in the reception room, covered with a camel-hair rug, while her family grouped themselves around her. According to Sean, she was in good spirits, calm and enjoying every moment of the reunion. At the end of the day, when it was time for her to be carried upstairs to bed again, she looked at everyone and said, 'I've had the best Christmas of my life.'

As the first weeks of the new year, 1993, passed, a sort of attendant hush descended over the manor house and the village. The news from outside seemed to come from far away. Even the events meant to pay tribute to Audrey took on a kind of unreality. She was told she had been given a Life Achievement Award by the Screen Actors Guild of America. It had been accepted on her behalf by Julia Roberts, the star of *Pretty Woman,* a Hollywood fairy tale of a very different kind, harder and franker, than the one which had made Audrey a star. She was also to be given the Jean Hersholt Humanitarian Award for her Unicef work. It would be presented at the Oscar ceremonies in March. She must have smiled, thinking how Jean Hersholt in person had presented her with her 'Best Actress' Oscar for *Roman Holiday* nearly forty years before. It was unlikely that she would be able to keep this appointment.

Around the middle of the month, Audrey's residual strength began to trickle away. Further expeditions to the garden were out of the question. She lay in her bed, or on the sofa in the long living room, partially sedated but refusing to be drugged into unconsciousness. Thus she heard that Mother Teresa of Calcutta had commanded a twenty-four-hour prayer vigil for 'my good Christian sister Audrey Hepburn'.

According to one of her friends, she thought of marriage to Robert Wolders in the time left to her. Then turning towards him, she said, 'No, Robbie, it's not necessary . . . you're closer than any husband.' She was never in the least downhearted. She exemplified exactly what she had once told the London journalist David Lewin: 'If my world were to cave in tomorrow, I would look back on all the pleasures, excitements and worthwhilenesses I have been lucky enough to have had. Not the sadnesses, miscarriages, or my father leaving home, but the joy of everything else. It will have been enough.'

At seven o'clock on the evening of 20 January 1993, surrounded by her family and her companion, Audrey slipped into final unconsciousness. Death came soon afterwards. Before the night was out, candles began appearing in the village windows. The bell of the small Protestant church a few hundred yards away started to toll the passing of 'Madame Audrey', confirming the news to all within earshot. Neighbours arrived early the next day to place flowers around the front steps of La Paisible.

The rest of the world heard of her death as it went to bed or woke up, when radio and television programmes led their news with it and the daily papers rushed the obituaries they had prepared into print and measured up the life of Audrey Hepburn. Soon the Tolochenaz post office was hard put to handle the grieving communiqués that flowed in by fax and telex. Few outside Audrey's immediate family were as stunned as Christa Roth. The Unicef executive had enjoyed a very close bond with Audrey that went far beyond their official duties. They were both wartime children who had grown up in privation and seen unimaginable suffering. 'She had been like a sister to me,' Christa Roth recalls. 'I had kept saying to myself, "I know how strong her will is . . . she will pull through." The BBC had telephoned me and asked me to pre-record an obituary for them. With the best will in the world, I simply couldn't do so—not while there was still hope.

'I would have asked Audrey's advice on any matter, however personal to me. She had that rare capacity to listen to people and to come up with the right advice, by instinct as much as anything. She gave you her whole attention. Such people you miss.'

Unicef was swamped with messages of condolence from the famous and the unknown, so many that there was no room for them in Christa Roth's office suite and they had to be stacked along the corridor in plastic sacks. Over the following months, every one was opened and read. Sean Ferrer went through them himself, sending formal responses in most cases, but in others dictating personal notes of thanks, especially if the letters had come from people who had worked in the Third World countries his mother had visited. Soon the television people would descend and ask to see 'the office where Audrey worked at Unicef'. And then Christa Roth would tell them with a smile, 'An office . . . ? Audrey never had an office. I always went to her, and she went to wherever she was needed.'

Doris Brynner, Audrey's near neighbour and her closest friend in Switzerland, felt the same personal pang—one of guilt, almost—to know she would never see her again. 'We had a pact, Audrey and I, that we would go together. Now I'm left living without her, and I feel utterly bereft.'

Epilogue: The Passing
of a Fair Lady

T RIBUTES to Audrey began to come in, wave upon wave of them, as the people who had been her friends, or her famous contemporaries, heard the news.

The strength of feeling when a beautiful and well-loved woman is taken prematurely from the world was evident in many of these and purged them of the unctuousness that frequently anoints the clichés of celebrities. Even Elizabeth Taylor's slightly over-rich statement that 'God has a most beautiful new angel now' redeemed itself by hinting at Audrey's earthly practicality when she added, 'who will know just what to do in heaven'. Sophia Loren declared, 'She enriched the lives of millions'—which evoked the more sober thought that she had saved the lives of some, though not as many as she would have wished. 'I absolutely adored her,' said Sean Connery, looking back on their autumnal union in *Robin and Marian*, 'and so did everyone else.' Banal, but just. Ex-President Reagan described her as 'a true great who will be greatly missed'. Roger Moore, her near neighbour in Switzerland and fellow Unicef ambassador, avoided the language of publicists (and presidents), and managed a nudge of well-earned rebuke at the same time: 'She was that rare thing in Hollywood, a star who genuinely cared for others before herself.'

The obituaries filled columns. Martha Sherrill, in the *International Herald Tribune*, wrote: '[She] had enchantment in her, and an effortless grace. In every role . . . she transcended gloom and everydayness with a rare combination of fragility and abandon and ancient European wisdom.' That might have been pitching it a little solemnly, but Audrey was certainly a wise child. Anthony Lane, in the *Independent on Sunday*, caught Audrey's gift of contagious optimism: 'She heightened the spirits of those around her, or made them behave with uncontrollable gallantry. When Audrey Hepburn walked into the movies, all heaven broke loose.' Speaking of her work for Unicef, Sheridan Morley wrote: '. . . while all other real-life princesses seem on these occasions to be acting, Hepburn, the only actress among them, did it for real and with no theatricality at all.' And Gregory Peck linked the present sadness with that wonderful first, fresh moment when a new star swims into view: 'No doubt. The princess did become a queen—not only on the screen.'

Peter Ustinov, another Swiss neighbour and co-worker for Unicef, published his tribute in *The European*. It seemed to many the one that best addressed the strange transcendency that Audrey achieved at the very end of her life, when her stardom assumed a missionary quality that was without fear or reproach: the charity worker became sincerely inseparable from the celebrity figure. 'There is a rampant cynicism in that part of the world which describes itself as developed,' Ustinov wrote. 'It would be quite prepared to understand the motives of a star willing to go to places such as Somalia in order to advertise milk powder for a fee; but it doubts the sincerity of the same star for going there without financial advantage in the service of a humanitarian impulse . . . It goes without saying that entertaining the merest thought along such well-worn lines about Audrey Hepburn would be unjust and ugly beyond measure. She knew better than anyone else that the recompense for such work lies in the eyes of those in need of succour.'

Audrey was incapable of taint. Yet there is a feeling of mystery about her last years that good deeds do not entirely explain. Audrey carried some secrets to the grave, on which it has been possible to shed a little light—particularly where her unhappy parentage is concerned. But the currents of charity and mercy that carried her through to the end have a self-willed momentum that suggests a sense of desperation as well as commitment. Undoubtedly, the terrifying landscape of inhumanity she travelled through as a Unicef worker, seeing its breadth and infinitude, is part of the explanation. Today, some people believe that Audrey drove herself too hard—that 'compassion overload' eventually overwhelmed her and caused her delicate constitution to collapse in such a sudden and irreversible way. The psychological impact of aid work on the scale she attempted is not well documented and it would be impertinent, as well as in bad taste, to speculate further on whether her early death might have been avoided had her concern been expressed with less self-sacrificing intensity and had she been able to relax the pace she set herself, which is by no means certain.

There is an affinity—though whether it is an elective affinity, it's impossible to say—between Audrey's way and the hard and terrifying way to enlightenment that is chosen by Celia, the heroine in T. S. Eliot's *The Cock-*

tail Party, which Audrey was fond of quoting. Celia, the girl who wanted to 'get into films', works out her own salvation by choosing to join an austere order of nursing sisters, going to a desolate land and there meeting an end that is almost saintly:

> In fear and pain and loathing—all these together—
> And reluctance of the body to become a *thing*.
> I'd say she suffered more, because more conscious
> Than the rest of us. She paid the highest price
> In suffering. That is part of the design.

One cannot say whether, consciously or not, this was ever part of Audrey's 'design'. But the stoicism and peacefulness and eventual joy that blessed her at the end of her life seem to have led, as Eliot put it,

> towards possession
> Of what you have sought for in the wrong place.

Bleak comfort, perhaps, for most of us, if it means a cruel premature death. But for Audrey Hepburn, who can doubt that despite death she felt she had achieved her vocation?

Audrey died on a Wednesday. The funeral was planned for the following Sunday in the little peach-coloured Evangelical church. The service was to be conducted by Tolochenaz's Protestant minister, Pastor André Monnier. Pastor Maurice Eindiguer, now in his eighties, who had married Audrey and Mel Ferrer in 1954, and baptized Sean, came out of retirement to deliver the eulogy. The church held only about a hundred people comfortably and, with the evidence of the coverage that the event would attract, Audrey's family were justifiably anxious lest it, and indeed the village, be overwhelmed by the media, not to mention the hundreds of ordinary mourners and sympathetic sightseers. Their fears were unfounded. The respect that Audrey earned in life attended her in death. It was visible in the discipline of the crowds thronging the streets, silent for the most part save for stifled weeping. Even the dozens of hefty men with TV cameras on their shoulders attended by microphone-bearing acolytes seemed unaccustomedly respectful of the living as well as the deceased, and apologized for pushing their way to the front.

The day was cold. There was a biting wind that added tears to eyes already brimming. By 10.15 a.m. the flower arrangements sent by the Dutch royal family, by Elizabeth Taylor and Gregory Peck, by Unicef, and by dozens of others close to Audrey or related to her only by ties of feeling and admiration, had been delivered to the church.

Shortly before noon, the side gate of La Paisible opened and Audrey's blond oak coffin was borne towards the church on the shoulders of some of the men she had held dearest: Sean Ferrer and Luca Dotti, Jan van Ufford, Robert Wolders and Hubert de Givenchy. The sixth pall-bearer was one of Audrey's neighbours, manifesting the grief felt by the villagers of Tolochenaz. Mel Ferrer followed in the cortège with his wife Elizabeth. He looked much aged, white-haired, and under strong emotion. At first he appeared to hold back as he entered the church with the invited guests who numbered around a hundred and twenty. Then, as the coffin was rested on the flower-decked catafalque, Sean Ferrer detached himself from the pall-bearers and, embracing his father, drew him in among the intimates. Andrea Dotti, drawing close to his own son, wiped tears away from behind his thick glasses.

Just as the church doors were being shut, a figure in a flapping trench coat arrived: Alain Delon. 'Even the first time I dated Audrey, I was late,' he gasped as the ushers seated him. 'Sorry, sorry.'

Organ music filled the church with the strains of a Bach prelude, valiant rather than sombre. As it swelled, the voices of children filled the air with song. Sean Ferrer, knowing his mother would have wished children to be to the fore on the day that thanks were offered for her life and work among them, had invited the choir of St George's International School in Montreux to render 'The Lord is my Shepherd'. Pastor Eindiguer, his voice breaking under the strain of emotion, spoke of the light of Audrey's visit to Somalia being reflected in the faces of the ailing children. The rather clichéd address was matched at this very moment by the winter sunshine, which up to then had been concealed by clouds, breaking through and flooding the church. If not a divine omen, at least it was a gratifying coincidence.

Prince Sadruddin Aga Khan, a UN commissioner, spoke next, observing humbly that Audrey had endured more hardship and hazards in her work than most diplomats would be prepared to accept. Then came the service's most touching moment.

Sean spoke of that last Christmas Eve, 'when Mummy read a letter to us written by a writer she admired . . . "Remember," it said, "if you ever need a helping hand, it's at the end of your arm. As you get older, you must remember that you have a second hand. The first one is to help yourself, the second one is to help others." ' He ended on a quiet note. 'Mummy believed in love . . . that it could heal, fix, mend and make everything all right in the end.'

The wreaths and floral tributes, masses of lilies, carnations entwined with pink and white marguerites, banks of white and red roses, stretched along an entire wall of the church. By the end of the service, the air was warm with the pungent smell of burning candles mixing with the sweeter fragrance of blossoms opening in the heat. Audrey's coffin was lifted up by its bearers: no great weight, it seemed. The mourners lined up behind it outside, their faces cooling quickly in the crisp Swiss air. There was a shuffling on of coats, adjusting of gloves and scarves, and then the group moved the couple of hundred yards to the tiny sloping burial ground on the other side of the arterial road on which all traffic was halted.

Audrey's grave backed on to a drystone wall at the very top of the incline. It looked west over the adjacent vineyard, directly towards her home. It was to be marked by a simple cross in newly varnished brown wood. The crosspiece carried her name 'Audrey . . . Hepburn', on each side of the upright, and on the upright itself were the dates of her birth and death '1929 . . . 1993' above and below it. Hers appeared to be the only Anglo-Saxon name in a graveyard filled with such family names as 'Dufour', 'Morel', 'Angeloz' and 'Jacot'.

About seven hundred people followed the official guests, but stood respectfully outside the walls of the cemetery. In the nearby ploughed field, seagulls from Lac Leman swooped and settled and rose again, undisturbed in their feeding by the little assembly. One by one the guests filed past the open grave and looked down on the coffin on which there now lay a single white tulip. Each dropped a rose, a lily or a white carnation into the burial hollow, some murmuring a brief prayer, a last goodbye, before passing on. Mel Ferrer wept openly at the graveside and was embraced by the grey-bearded Robert Wolders. Whatever acrimony Audrey's failed marriages evoked at the time was dissolved in the grief at her premature and cruel passing.

Then, their tribute paid and their emotions spent, the guests regrouped and walked back to La Paisible for the reception. Through the small iron gate of the cemetery, the other mourners began to enter and place their own less kempt but no less sincere bouquets on the newly turned earth, now covering the place where Audrey Hepburn had come to rest. Soon it looked as if she were not lying in the ground at all, but cradled in a giant basket of flowers.

Filmography

Films

Dutch in 7 Lessons (Nederlands in 7 Lessen) (1948). Producer: H.M. Josephson. Director: Charles van der Linden. AH played a KLM air stewardess.

One Wild Oat: Eros-Coronet (1951). Director/producer: Charles Saunders. Screenwriters: Veronon Sylvaine, Laurence Huntington. AH was an uncredited extra.

Young Wives' Tale: Associated British/Allied Artists (1952). Director/producer: Henry Cass. Screenwriter: Anne Burnaby. AH played a lodger in a household of warring couples. Stars: Joan Greenwood, Nigel Patrick, Derek Farr, Guy Middleton.

Laughter in Paradise: Associated British/Pathé (1951). Director/producer: Mario Zampi. Screenwriters: Michael Pertwee, Jack Davies. Photography: William McLeod. Music: Stanley Black. AH played a cigarette girl briefly glimpsed in a nightclub. Stars: Alastair Sim, Fay Compton, Guy Middleton, George Cole, Hugh Griffith.

The Lavender Hill Mob: Ealing Studios/Rank/Universal (1951). Director: Charles Crichton. Producer: Michael Truman. Screenwriter: T. E. B. Clark. Photography: Douglas Slocombe. Music: Georges Auric. AH played a cigarette girl. Stars: Alec Guinness, Stanley Holloway.

The Secret People: Ealing/Lippert (1952). Director: Thorold Dickinson. Producer: Sidney Cole. Screenwriters: Thorold Dickinson, Joyce Cary. Photography: Gordon Dines. Music: Roberto Gerhard. AH played a ballet dancer caught up in an assassination plot. Stars: Valentina Cortese, Serge Reggiani.

We Go to Monte Carlo (a.k.a. *Monte Carlo Baby*): Ventura Filmmakers (1952). Directors: Jean Boyer, Jean Jerrold. Producer: Ray Ventura. Screenwriters: Jean Jerrold, Jean Boyer, Alex Jaffe. AH played a film star. Co-stars: Cara Williams, Philippe LeMaire, Marcel Dalio.

Roman Holiday: Paramount (1953). Director/producer: William Wyler. Screenwriters: Ian McLellan Hunter, John Dighton, Dalton Trumbo. Photographers: Franz Planer, Henri Alekan. Music: Georges Auric. AH played a runaway princess in Rome: Academy Award. Co-stars: Gregory Peck, Eddie Albert.

Sabrina: Paramount (1954). Director/producer: Billy Wilder. Screenwriters: Billy Wilder, Ernest Lehman, Samuel Taylor. Photography: Charles Lang Jr. Music: Frederick Hollander. AH played a chauffeur's daughter who falls in love with the sons of a millionaire. Co-stars: Humphrey Bogart, William Holden.

War and Peace: Ponti/De Laurentiis/Paramount (1956). Director: King Vidor. Producers: Carlo Ponti, Dino de Laurentiis. Screenwriters: King Vidor, Bridget Boland, Robert Westerby, Mario Camerini, Ennio de Concini, Ivo Perrili. Photography: Jack Cardiff. Music: Nino Rota. AH played Tolstoy's heroine Natasha. Co-stars: Henry Fonda, Mel Ferrer, Vittorio Gassman, Herbert Lom, Oskar Homolka.

Funny Face: Paramount (1957). Director: Stanley Donen. Producer: Roger Edens. Screenwriter: Leonard Gershe. Photography: Ray June. Music: George and Ira Gershwin, Roger Edens, Leonard Gershe. AH played a bookshop assistant transformed by a fashion photographer. Co-stars: Fred Astaire, Kay Thompson, Michel Auclair, Robert Flemyng.

Love in the Afternoon: Allied Artists (1957). Director/producer: Billy Wilder. Screenwriters: Billy Wilder, I. A. L. Diamond. Photography: William Mellor. Music: Franz Waxman. AH played a private eye's daughter romanced by a millionaire playboy. Co-stars: Gary Cooper, Maurice Chevalier.

Green Mansions: MGM/Avon (1959). Director: Mel Ferrer. Producer: Edmund Grainger. Screenwriters: Dorothy Kingsley, Mel Ferrer. Photography: Joseph Ruttenberg. Music: Bronislau Kaper, Villa-Lobos. AH played Rima, W.H. Hudson's child of nature. Co-star: Anthony Perkins.

The Nun's Story: Warner Bros. (1959). Director: Fred Zinnemann. Producer: Henry Blanke. Screenwriter: Robert Anderson. Photography:

Franz Planer. Music: Franz Waxman. AH played a nursing nun in the Belgian Congo. Co-stars: Peter Finch, Edith Evans, Peggy Ashcroft.

The Unforgiven: United Artists/James Productions/Hecht-Hill-Lancaster (1960). Director: John Huston. Producer: James Hill. Screenwriter: Ben Maddow. Photography: Franz Planer. Music: Dmitri Tiomkin. AH played a half-breed. Co-stars: Burt Lancaster, Audie Murphy, Lillian Gish.

Breakfast at Tiffany's: Paramount/Jurrow-Shepherd (1961). Director: Blake Edwards. Producer: Martin Jurrow, Richard Shepherd. Screenwriter: George Axelrod. Photography: Franz Planer. Music: Henry Mancini. AH played the call-girl Holly Golightly. Co-stars: George Peppard, Patricia Neal.

The Children's Hour (a.k.a. *The Loudest Whisper*): United Artists/Mirisch (1962). Director/producer: William Wyler. Screenwriter: John Michael Hayes. Photography: Franz Planer. Music: Alex North. AH played a schoolteacher accused of lesbian love. Co-stars: Shirley MacLaine, James Garner.

Charade: Universal (1963). Director/producer: Stanley Donen. Screenwriter: Peter Stone. Photography: Charles Lang Jr. Music: Henry Mancini. AH played a widow caught up in international crime. Co-stars: Cary Grant, Walter Matthau.

Paris When It Sizzles: Paramount (1964). Director: Richard Quine. Producers: Richard Quine, George Axelrod. Screenwriters: Richard Quine, Julien Duvivier. Photography: Charles Lang Jr. Music: Nelson Riddle. AH played the assistant of a blocked screenwriter. Co-star: William Holden.

My Fair Lady: Warner Bros. (1964). Director: George Cukor. Producer: Jack L. Warner. Screenwriter: Alan Jay Lerner. Photography: Harry Stradling. Music: Frederick Loewe. AH played Eliza Doolittle, the flower girl who is transformed into a lady. Co-stars: Rex Harrison, Stanley Holloway, Wilfred Hyde White, Gladys Cooper.

How to Steal a Million: 20th Century-Fox/World Wide (1966). Director: William Wyler. Producer: Fred Kohlmar. Screenwriter: Harry Kurnitz. Photography: Charles Lang Jr. Music: Johnny Williams. AH played an art forger's daughter. Co-stars: Peter O'Toole, Charles Boyer, Hugh Griffith.

Two for the Road: 20th Century-Fox (1967). Director/producer: Stanley Donen. Screenwriter: Frederic Raphael. Photography: Christopher Challis. Music: Henry Mancini. AH played a young married woman at odds with her husband. Co-star: Albert Finney.

Wait Until Dark: Warner Bros. (1967). Director: Terence Young. Producer: Mel Ferrer. Screenwriters: Robert and Jane Howard Carrington. Photography: Charles Lang Jr. Music: Henry Mancini. AH played a blind woman terrorized by a drugs gang. Co-stars: Alan Arkin, Richard Crenna.

Robin and Marian: Columbia/Rastar (1976). Director: Richard Lester. Producer: Denis O'Dell. Screenwriter: James Goldman. Photography: David Watkin. Music: John Barry. AH played the middle-aged Maid Marian. Co-stars: Sean Connery, Robert Shaw, Nicol Williamson, Richard Harris, Denholm Elliott, Ronnie Barker.

Sidney Sheldon's Bloodline: Paramount/Geria (1979). Director: Terence Young. Producers: David Picker, Sidney Beckerman. Screenwriter: Laird Koenig. Photography: Freddie Young. Music: Ennio Morricone. AH played a pharmaceutical heiress threatened by a killer. Co-stars: Ben Gazzara, James Mason, Irene Papas, Michelle Phillips, Maurice Ronet, Romy Schneider, Omar Sharif.

They All Laughed: PSO/Moon Pictures/Time-Life (1982). Director: Peter Bogdanovich. Producer: George Morfogen. Screenwriter: Peter Bogdanovich. Photography: Robby Miller. AH played a tycoon's estranged wife who falls in love with a private eye. Co-stars: Ben Gazzara, John Ritter, Dorothy Stratten.

Always: Universal/United Artists/Amblin Entertainment (1989). Director: Steven Spielberg. Producers: Frank Marshall, Steven Spielberg. Screenwriters: Jerry Belson, Dalton Trumbo. Photography: Mikael Salomon. Music: John Williams. AH played an angel. Co-stars: Richard Dreyfuss, Holly Hunter, Brad Johnson.

Theatrical Performances

Gigi (1951). Director: Raymond Rouleau. Producer: Gilbert Miller. Writer: Anita Loos from Colette's novel. AH played a girl raised to be a cocotte. Co-stars: Josephine Brown, Cathleen Nesbitt.

Ondine (1954). Director: Alfred Lunt. Producers: The Producers Company. Writer: Maurice Valency from Jean Giraudoux's play. AH played the water nymph Ondine. Co-star: Mel Ferrer.

Television Roles

Mayerling: NBC TV (1957). Director: Anatole Litvak. AH played the mistress of the heir to the Austro-Hungarian throne who dies in their suicide pact. Co-star: Mel Ferrer.

Love Among Thieves: ABC TV (1987). Director: Roger Young. AH played a concert pianist turned jewel thief. Co-star: Robert Wagner.

Television Commercials

Four one-minute commercials made in 1971 for a Japanese wig manufacturer.

A NOTE ON SOURCES

PROLOGUE: THE ROAD TO CHILDHOOD

On her return from Ethiopia, Audrey Hepburn gave a very moving press conference in London at the end of March 1988. This chapter is a conflation of what she said then about her first field trip, supplemented by information given to me personally, as well as my viewing of videos screened for me by Angela Hawke at Unicef's London offices: an overwhelming experience.

I FAMILY SECRETS

To Audrey's cousin, Walter Ruston, a man of great charm, archival diligence and distinction in the world of engineering who lives in retirement in Belgium, I owe the elucidation of the name 'Hepburn', along with the fullest account yet of Joseph Hepburn-Ruston's upbringing, character and post-war relationship—or lack of it—with his ex-wife and daughter. A friend of Mr Ruston, Gino Wimmers, a former film critic resident in Vienna, also obtained for me much information about the Ruston family that underlined how desperately Audrey missed her father.

Joan Ford (née Hawkins) got in touch with me shortly after the original publication of this book with her personal recollections (and other memorabilia) of Audrey's year or two in Kent before the war. It is significant that the absence of Audrey's father went unremarked at the time in this small Kent village: but then the status of a divorced woman, like Audrey's mother, still carried a certain stigma in the 1930s, and, of course there were plenty of other reasons for keeping quiet about Hepburn-Ruston.

As mentioned in the Acknowledgments, the chief source of information about Hepburn-Ruston's early years is Brian Simpson who discovered what appears to be an extraordinarily chequered career, worthy of a modern Corvo, while researching his book on wartime internment in Britain, *In the Highest Degree Odious*. Not surprisingly, Professor Simpson's written request to Audrey for additional information about her father went unanswered. The Foreign and Commonwealth Office was 'unable to help' me unravel further his short-lived consular career. My own inquiries at the Bank of England's Museum and Historical Research section produced a firm denial that he had ever been employed by the bank in any capacity at home or abroad. The bank spokeswoman's comment, 'Hopefully, your proposed book will lay this misconception finally to rest', suggests a certain 'information fatigue' to do with a story whose source is unknown.

295

Although there is no possibility of the Hepburn-Rustons having any blood ties with the Far East, Audrey's appearance and the sympathy which this part of the world always held for her contributed to her huge fan following in the Pacific Rim countries. Her looks, singularly 'un-Dutch', have the exquisite fineness of feature characteristic of many young women in the region. On my visit in October 1993 to Tolochenaz, the Swiss village where Audrey lived and died, I met a Japanese mother and two teenage daughters, both with gamine haircuts, replicas in miniature of young Audrey—beating their way determinedly through heavy rain from the Tolochenaz railway halt to her grave. It was already covered with bouquets of flowers, several with messages in Japanese script. Unicef's Christa Roth confirms that people from the Far East probably outnumber other pilgrims. Audrey's affinity with that part of the world found expression in the commercials she made for a Tokyo wig manufacturer—the only TV advertisements to which she lent her name and looks in later years—and also in her friendship with Setsuko Ideta, the Japanese-born second wife of the painter Balthus, who lived at Rossinière, near Château d'Oex, not far from Audrey. Audrey owned several paintings by Setsuko.

The photograph of Audrey's father in London, as head of the Nazi-financed press agency, was discovered by the picture researcher Tomás Graves, and the history of Hepburn-Ruston during the immediate pre-war years was confirmed to me by Adrian Weale, author of *Renegades: Hitler's Englishmen*. I am most grateful to these two individuals.

To John Warburton, I owe the discovery of the article 'The Call of Fascism' which Audrey's mother contributed to Sir Oswald Mosley's party publication *Blackshirt*. Warburton wrote to me: 'I have a feeling from memory that [Baroness van Heemstra] also had a few other pieces published, but this is the only one I have been able to quickly pin down in my files.' Warburton subsequently photocopied wartime letters from interned members of the British Union of Fascists confirming Hepburn-Ruston's lengthy detention without trial, discussed in chapter 3; but as Audrey's father was understandably bitter and a far from sociable type, very little else about him in the various jails and prison camps he occupied has so far emerged.

2 THE GIRL WITH DEATH IN HER SHOES

For obvious reasons, friends and contemporaries of Audrey's mother and father are scarce today. I was lucky to be put in touch with Mrs Pauline Everts, who still lives in the vicinity of Arnhem. This well-connected and knowledgeable Dutchwoman knew the baroness in the 1930s, saw her virtues and could pardon her faults, and testified to the domestic upsets in the Hepburn-Ruston family. Mrs Everts, as mentioned, remains sceptical about the privations suffered before the autumn of 1944 and the undoubted savagery of German reprisals. For a child of her age, Audrey behaved well during the war, but apart from the encounter with the German soldier while carrying a message to the parachutist, there is no evidence to suggest that she (or her mother) could claim to be 'heroines'. The biographical myth that has begun to accrete around Audrey's wartime 'exploits' was fostered in particular by publicity articles by Anita Loos when Audrey was cast in *Gigi* and a wartime CV was needed for the American press. One hopes that the statue of Audrey, which Arnhem proposes to erect shortly, will not attempt to make her out a wartime heroine. I believe she would have hated that. Small, slightly faded grey photos exist of Audrey in the Arnhem ballet performance she gave in February 1944, taken by a friend of Mrs Everts. Though unsuitable for reproduction, their existence testifies to her reasonably good health at that date and gives the lie to more sensational accounts. Her genuine illness and severe debilitation appear to have happened after the forced evacuation of Arnhem in the last winter of the war. Even so, according to Mrs Everts, she was soon well enough to enjoy dancing at the Brass Hat officers' club.

3 DANCE LITTLE LADY

The writer Michael Burn first broke the extraordinary story of the part he played in saving Audrey's life in an addendum to her obituary published in *The Independent* on 27 January 1993, and subsequently elaborated in a telephone interview with me. It sounds like sheer fiction, but, as he said, war produces many similar coincidences.

Professor Brian Simpson generously gave me leads to Hepburn-Ruston's wartime captivity. Thanks to Nigel Steel and Stephen Walton of the Imperial War Museum, I was able to document the conditions he had to endure on the Isle of Man and elsewhere. John Warburton photocopied letters written by fellow inmates referring to Audrey's father and also contacted at least one survivor of the period who remembered him, though in rather unflattering terms.

Paul Rykens, head of the Anglo-Dutch conglomerate Unilever and a post-war friend of Ella van Heemstra, enters the story thanks to Jeffrey Frost who recalled dining with him and the baroness in London. He goes some way towards solving the mystery of how Ella van Heemstra was able to pick up the pieces of her life so quickly, and so comfortably. The discovery of Rykens gives the lie to the story that Audrey had to leave the Ballet Rambert because she lacked money for the tuition fees. She simply wasn't able to meet Madame Rambert's exacting standards and had the good sense—a quality she never lacked—to start looking, while still a pupil, for the next best thing, which was nightclub cabaret and the West End chorus line.

Audrey's early show-business life is recounted by her in unpublished transcripts of interviews in the Hedda Hopper collection at the Academy of Motion Picture Arts and Sciences Library. (I have often wondered if Hopper used a concealed wire recorder.) For reasons indicated in the text, these papers are an invaluable research tool if used with proper discretion. Hopper's transcripts contain admissions—especially about the early years of stars—that were later overlaid by publicists' fictions. The Jack Oliphant letter is part of the same collection. The late Kay Kendall told me of Cecil Landeau's unreciprocated affair with Audrey, which would account for the tone of his reply to Oliphant.

Angus McBean's account of Audrey's early photo-session for the Lacto-Calamine advertisement comes from an interview Audrey did many years later on *The Eamonn Andrews Show* where the aged but still lucid and articulate photographer was a fellow guest. The video is part of Unicef's information archives.

4 THE BEST ADVICE IN THE WORLD

I knew most of the heads of Associated British and the Elstree film studios—Robert Clark, C.J. Latta, Jack Goodlatte, Alan Thompson and, especially, the publicity director David Jones—and can testify to their mixed feelings over having one of the biggest stars of the day under contract, but not knowing how to make use of her and preferring to make sure of the money she represented to them as a corporate asset rather than risk their own energy and skill—both dubious commodities—in promoting her themselves. Even though Associated British Picture Corporation has now been extinguished as a corporate entity by consecutive and disastrous takeover deals in the 1970s and 1980s, its archives remain closed to researchers, possibly with good reason. If or when they are opened, much may emerge about Audrey's happily successful efforts in eluding the fate they would have prepared for her.

Sidney Cole and Lindsay Anderson are now the best witnesses to Audrey's early co-starring role in *The Secret People*. Both were interviewed at length. I think Audrey's post-*Gigi* note to Cole, reminding him of her role in the film as 'Nora' (in case he had forgotten her!), is one of the truest indicators of her natural modesty and sweetness of character. A few years after *The Secret People*, I asked Thorold Dickinson some personal question about Audrey (I have forgotten what). 'That's not strictly your business,' the tetchy director replied. I have wondered since if his fatherly advice to Audrey, added to Valentina Cortese's recorded dislike of publicity, helped confirm her very early determination to keep her 'private' life to herself.

5 'VOILÀ MA GIGI!'

There are various versions of how Audrey came to be 'spotted' by Colette. This one was given to me by Audrey herself, *circa* 1954–5, a few years after her Broadway success, and was supplemented some years later in a conversation I had with the great French film actor Marcel Dalio at the Cannes festival. Audrey remained conspicuously loyal to those who helped her in her early days—Ustinov, Guinness, Dalio et al., and used her contractual power (not always successfully) to find room for them in the casts of her films. Anita Loos embroidered the account of the meeting when employed by Gilbert Miller to promote the stage adaptation of *Gigi*. During a visit to Cecil Beaton's home, after his stroke and not long before his death, I heard Cathleen Nesbitt, a fellow lunch guest, speak of coaching Audrey: it was a hard task.

The Paramount archives in Hollywood contain the originals of the cables regarding Audrey's engagement for *Roman Holiday:* Other material in London, I am told, 'cannot be found after so long an interval'.

Audrey's screen test exists and has been shown in memorial programmes; it seems to bear out the story of the 'deception' that Wyler had Dickinson practise on her. Her last wink at the camera, as she exits Peck's bachelor apartment, would have clinched anyone's employment chances.

The Paramount attempt to buy Audrey out of her British contract was the subject of several news reports in the British press, commenting with chauvinist approval on Associated British's refusal to give in to Hollywood. Quite soon, the British studio was the target of criticism for not making use of the asset it had hoarded.

6 HER ROYAL HIGHNESS

It comes as a shock to see the original *Gigi* programme with a moderately plump Audrey Hepburn, instead of the finely chiselled features of the later gamine. I have been unable to establish why Gilbert Miller allowed such unflattering pictures to be used. Her appearance shows the strain she was under.

The quotation from Raymond Rouleau's widow about directing Audrey in *Gigi* comes from correspondence conducted with Madame Rouleau by the biographer Charles Higham and published in *Audrey: The Life of Audrey Hepburn* (Macmillan Inc., 1984).

There is still some mystery regarding the newspaper announcement of James Hanson's engagement to Audrey. My speculative suggestion is based on private information. It is certain that, contrary to many subsequent reports, the baroness did not oppose the marriage of her daughter to this handsome and rich young industrialist.

7 MEN IN HER LIFE

Photoplay's interview, intimating that Audrey's enthusiasm for Gregory Peck may have been the cause of gossip about a romantic liaison, is interesting evidence of a star actually learning something new about herself from a journalist. In my experience, however, this is commoner than imagined. Many stars, especially at the start of their careers, have an uncertain grasp of their own image or personality until they read a commentary on it: then it is sometimes co-opted very quickly into the public identity of the star.

8 LOVES AND HATES

The almost total absence of press comment about the Fascist antecedents in Audrey's family is remarkable, even granted the tight grip that Hollywood studios were still able to exercise over the media (cf., my account in *Fatal Charm: The Life of Rex Harrison*, of the successful efforts of Twentieth Century-Fox to keep the studio's name out of the Carole Landis suicide scandal in 1949). Of over a dozen press interviews with Audrey in 1954, I found that only Phyllis Battelle of the International News Service had done her homework. No other newspaper apparently followed up her disclosure.

Ernest Lehman was interviewed by me in his Brentwood home in July 1993 and proved an engaging commentator on 'young' Audrey, though he provides a useful correction to her screen innocence by his recall of the episode with Holden—and corroborates Holden's later account in his memoirs, which might otherwise have been attributed to male vanity.

Lehman's account of how badly Humphrey Bogart behaved amplifies what is known of the star's off-screen personality: despite which, Bogart's personal character, veering disturbingly between macho posturing and crippling self-denigration, continues to be salvaged by his public image as a fearless Hollywood 'outsider'.

9 HUSBAND AND WIFE

The Hedda Hopper files at the Academy of Motion Picture Arts and Sciences (AMPAS) were drawn on for the columnist's early interview with Audrey. An associate of Mel Ferrer's—who wishes to remain anonymous—confirms the close relationship Mel forged with Audrey, as well as Audrey's alarming decline in health. Ned Comstock, at the University of Southern California (USC), provided me with a wide cross section of contemporary newspaper columns, mostly by Louella Parsons, containing the gossip writer's waspish comments but also quite well-based insights into the change taking place in Audrey as her professional relationship with Mel turned into emotional dependence on him. Though Hopper, Parsons and their sorority of gossips are often mocked, sometimes justly, my research among their files for several books suggests that they were more often than not ahead of events that concerned their celebrity subjects. Their network of informants was wide and frequently reliable. Their usefulness to the studios, in keeping stars on their best behaviour by veiled threats or open cajolery, was considerable and valued. Their power merits more scholarly study than the few books about them have so far provided. It is obvious that Audrey and Mel treated Hedda, Louella et al. with kid gloves.

Henry Rogers, who became Audrey's public relations adviser, is the source for much information about Kurt Frings; also Dana Wynter, the film actress who now lives in Ireland and writes. She recalls the amazing self-control Audrey exercised. 'I remember when she was making *Breakfast at Tiffany's* at Paramount and we were doing *On the Double* with Danny Kaye, sitting side by side in the make-up department . . . Audrey's horror over my guzzling the hot donut my hairdresser brought to the studio at crack of dawn, while she broke out one tragic bran muffin and the thermos of Tiger's Milk Mel had concocted for her . . . then Audrey instantly giving up her muffin to reform a fallen sister. An act of the utmost sweetness because it deprived her of—and heaven knows, she needed it!—even mini-nourishment. Problem resolved the following morning by my claiming to have downed a gigantic breakfast before leaving the house. Which luckily she believed . . . while I dismissed wistful thoughts about hot, disgustingly junky donuts. The self-control probably came from dancing days.

'Kurt Frings, who used to stay with us in Palm Springs to play gin rummy with Greg [Bautzer, Dana Wynter's husband] would come back from visiting Audrey in Switzerland, or somewhere, and tell of giving her a box of super-chocolates which she loved, but would take only one, then close the box for that day. There's will-power for you!' (Letter written to me by Dana Wynter, 19 September 1993).

10 SUMMIT CONFERENCES

The description of life at the Italian villa is a conflation of accounts by several US columnists graciously permitted to pay visits. Very shortly Audrey would place all her 'private' homes—rented villas, hotel suites and so on—strictly out of bounds to the media. I have met only one journalist, Robert Osborne, the *Hollywood Reporter*'s senior writer, who was ever invited by Audrey into her home: this was much later, in her Unicef years. She was expressing her gratitude to him for help in publicising her fund-raising. She cooked him pasta: he considered himself well rewarded.

Michael Powell's last book, *Million-Dollar Movie* (Heinemann, 1992) contains an invaluable account of the intrigue over a film version of *Ondine*. Powell's widow, the editor Thelma Schoonmaker, told me, in 1993, that she thought her late husband had been 'a bit hard' on Mel; but I think he spotted the ambitious producer inside the actor very clearly: it takes one to know one.

As mentioned in the text, I was present on the Elstree Studios set of the ill-fated *Oh . . . Rosalinda!!* as Audrey watched Mel performing his tipsy loose-limbed dance routine in and out of a hotel elevator. Very attractively, I thought: his stylized charm fitted this somewhat camp movie—now a cult classic with gay filmgoers—better than more 'solid' performers like Michael Redgrave. He was not ill-mannered in hustling Audrey into the safety zone, away from visiting press people, but took her in his arms and waltzed off the set with her. A week later I was a supper guest along with Audrey and Laurence Harvey at the home of the producer James Woolf: there was little Mel Ferrer could do about it this time.

The description of the *War and Peace* negotiations as the cars drove around Lake Como comes from an unsourced article in the Constance McCormick scrapbooks at USC. Henry Rogers confirms it.

11   PRETTY FACE

Irwin Shaw, a fellow juror at Cannes in 1974, told me then he had warned Audrey that *War and Peace* would be 'a high-priced dud . . . King's past it'. According to Shaw, she said that perhaps Mel could direct it. Shaw said he had replied, 'King's not *that* past it.'

Vidor's assiduous note-making in the margin of every page of his two-volume edition of *War and Peace* makes depressing reading. Painting by numbers is bad enough; but filming by pages is desperate.

Audrey was very disappointed with her Natasha. But Prince Andrei was—and remained—one of Mel Ferrer's favourite performances. 'He took unflagging pleasure in seeing himself in *War and Peace* . . . even though he'd been dubbed into German,' says one informant who watched the film with Mel in Berlin many years later. '[He] was also the only person I'd seen laugh at his own joke-lines during rushes . . . but all in all, he was civilized and educated, which was a novelty in the business.'

12   FUNNY FACE

Stanley Donen was interviewed by me over a lunch that lasted several hours in Beverly Hills in July 1993. Donen is a gift to biographers; his recollections go beyond recalling what happened and invariably ponder why it happened. His affection for Audrey and admiration for her disciplined yet tender nature is apparent in the three films he made with her—and in the very touching tribute he paid her in American *Vogue* in April 1993: from which article some of the quotations come.

The description of the origins of *Funny Face*, and the painstaking rehearsals Audrey suffered so gladly, comes from Roger Edens's account in *Film and TV Music*, Spring 1957.

The entirely unexpected interview with Ella van Heemstra is to be found in the *Christian Science Monitor* of 4 July 1956.

13   STRAINS AND STRESSES

Audrey's coolness regarding another film with Maurice Chevalier was reported to me by Simone Signoret in 1978 during an interview about her recent autobiography, *Nostalgia Isn't What It Used to Be*. Signoret, a left-winger though never a Communist Party member, had no reason to be fond of her famous compatriot, who had been accused of being too close for comfort to the Germans in the war years: the glancing reference to him that she makes in her memoirs is one of withering contempt. But it would have been against Signoret's nature to impute an antipathy of this kind to Audrey Hepburn, whom she liked very much, if it were untrue. Equally, it was contrary to Audrey's nature to speak ill of a fellow artist in public; but she had inquired if Chevalier was going to be cast in the film musical of *Gigi*.

The letter to Roger Edens expressing Audrey's relief at the *Time* magazine review of *Funny Face* is in the Hepburn files at USC.

14   A GOLDEN VEIL

The Nun's Story is one of the best-documented movies in the Warner Bros. production files at USC. The insights offered by contracts, memoranda, cables, etc. were supplemented by conversations in London with Fred Zinnemann at the end of the 1980s when I was assisting him with his *Autobiography* (Bloomsbury, 1992). It was obvious he had a very special place in his heart for Audrey; we sat through *The Nun's Story* together, and I can still hear the sigh from this perfectionist craftsman when Audrey shakes out her hair at the end before opening the door on her new life in the world outside: 'Oh, how I wish I'd put a little grey in it!' I am only surprised it did not occur to Audrey at the time of shooting.

The Hedda Hopper files at AMPAS contain the interview notes in which Hopper gives her advice to Audrey to play the role of Rima before she accepts the role of mother. The fact that Hopper mentions motherhood at all suggests that a small ripple of gossip had begun to spread about Audrey's not having yet started a family.

15   RIDING FOR A FALL

The production history of *Green Mansions,* including several versions of the script used in Mel Ferrer's production, is in the files at USC.

The John Huston papers are in the Margaret Herrick Library at AMPAS. Those dealing with *The Unforgiven* contain a hint—no stronger—that Huston was reluctant to accept Audrey as the Indian girl: perhaps he had had a look at some of the assembly of *Green Mansions*. Perhaps Elia Kazan's protégée, Molly McCarthy, had made an impression on him. As usual, Huston's remark about Audrey's being as good as her namesake in *The African Queen* is a double-edged compliment. Katharine Hepburn had given him his share of trouble: to the ultimate advantage, it may be said, of the film.

Hitchcock's failure to snare Audrey for *No Bail for the Judge* was told me by Ernest Lehman (who, at the time, was writing one of the best ever Hitchcock screenplays, *North by Northwest*) and confirmed by Dana Wynter in a telephone interview with me.

16   THE GIRL WHO CAME TO BREAKFAST

Claude Renoir spoke feelingly of the difficulties he had encountered shooting *Paris When It Sizzles* during a lunchtime meeting with him in 1968 at the Victorine Studios, Nice, where he was filming Bryan Forbes's *The Madwoman of Chaillot* 'avec l'autre Hepburn' (Katharine).

Holden's increasingly eccentric behaviour, due to alcohol abuse, 'à désaxé complètement le rhythme du film', according to Renoir, Audrey's unhappiness with the way her marriage was going was apparent and it is possible that her frustration was taken out on the hapless Renoir. I myself cannot quite credit that this superlative colour photographer should have been unable to adapt to the opportunities Audrey offered him. Certainly his work on the Forbes film is among the best cinematography of its period.

Stanley Donen related the amusing episode of Audrey and Cary Grant during our conversation in Beverly Hills in July 1993. He does not recall the intrusion of the line from *My Fair Lady* as anything more than accidental: it is odd, all the same.

17   MILLION-DOLLAR LADY

The contracts of Audrey and Rex Harrison are in the Warner Bros. collection at USC; along with the memoranda concerning contractual demands by Keep Films, Peter O'Toole's company, which appear to have cost him the role. For further details, see my biography of Rex Harrison, *Fatal Charm* (1992).

My editor, Allegra Huston, daughter of the film director John Huston, picked up the extremely damning fact—which I had forgotten—that it must have been the actor-members of the Academy of Motion Picture Arts and Sciences who denied Audrey a nomination for *My Fair Lady*. Each section of the Academy nominates its own candidates—except for the 'Best Film'. Only when it comes to the actual vote, do all Academy members participate. Thus the resentment against Warner Bros., if not Audrey, must have been well entrenched (or orchestrated?) when the actors and actresses of the Academy withheld her name from the five eligible nominees. I prefer to think the animus was directed at Jack L. Warner rather than at Audrey; but the result was the same. It certainly hurt Audrey personally. Later, in researching the Warner Bros. production files of *Wait Until Dark*, I was struck by her early insistence on an announcement being made that she would play the film role even before it had been finally decided who would play it on Broadway. She clearly didn't want to suffer again the same kind of cold-shouldering from her peers.

Conversations I had with Henry and Roz Rogers over dinner at their Brentwood home in July 1993, and a month later in London, are the source for the evidence of Audrey's extreme annoyance at the approach made to Givenchy and Cannes. Rogers preserves nothing but respect and admiration for his former client.

18   OF FASHION AND AFFAIRS

It is essential for a biographer to visit a place associated with his or her subject. So much is revealed—and sometimes explained—just by sensing the spirit of the place. When writing my biography of Rex Harrison, several days spent in the vicinity of his magnificent mountainside villa at Portofino revealed, better than any witness to his last three months there, the hidden hostility of the local peasantry to the very rich who had built their homes where the rough grass of the vineyards ended and the manicured lawns of the incomers began. The backcloth of the animosity that drove Rex out of Portofino, and ultimately Italy, was apparent. My visit to Tolochenaz, Audrey's domicile, took place in mid-September

1993, and revealed a 'retreat' of the kind that Audrey's increasingly reclusive nature must have immediately felt at home in, but which would have sorely tried the patience of her wheeling-dealing, sun-loving husband. The ominous containment of the place must have got to Mel Ferrer early on. There were few people—and next to no shops—in the couple of streets that form the village. Only when children poured out of school around 12.30 p.m. in their bright anoraks and trousers, did the place look as if it hadn't been visited by a Pied Piper. Even they quickly vanished behind high hedges and gates. Fortunately, the few residents I met all remembered details of 'Madame Audrey' and the day of her funeral with touching clarity and regret (see the Epilogue).

Frederic Raphael provided the revealing details of the filming of *Two for the Road* during a long telephone conversation with him at his home in France. Although Audrey knew what an important transition this film would be for her image and career, Raphael says she was extremely wary. 'Some years later,' he says, 'I sent her the screenplay I had written of a novel called *Richard's Things*. It was returned promptly and politely with the message that she couldn't begin to think of playing a woman who fell in love with another woman.' She had once played such a role—in *The Loudest Whisper*—and it had proved so unrewarding in every sense except the most literal that she appears to have put the experience completely out of her mind: at times the power of positive thinking includes that of totally forgetting. *Richard's Things* was eventually made as a television film. Ironically, the role offered to Audrey was played by Liv Ullmann, whose performance in two later films by Swedish director Ingmar Bergman was to reflect some of the traumas then being experienced by Audrey in her married life (see chapter 21).

Stanley Donen is the source for the story of Finney's 'camping it up'.

19   THE END OF THE ROAD

The Warner Bros. production files at USC contain a plethora of material about *Wait Until Dark*. I am grateful to Sandra Archer for transcribing the memoranda quoted here. The attempts to have the film made in Europe suggest how unwelcome the idea of returning to Hollywood was to Audrey after her rebuff over *My Fair Lady*. The film's box-office success appears to have taken many by surprise. It probably made more money for Audrey, in terms of profit participation, than any other film she made apart from *The Nun's Story*. She even got an Academy Award nomination on the strength of it—or of Hollywood's guilt at denying her one for *My Fair Lady*.

Princess Pignatelli assisted me with the background of life in Rome, though I should emphasize that the conclusions I reached about Audrey's second marriage to Andrea Dotti are mine alone.

20   THE DOCTOR'S WIFE

The quotes from Audrey at this period, early in her marriage to Dotti, come mainly from an interview by Henry Gris, which appeared in *Woman's Own*, among other English- and foreign-language magazines, on 4 March 1972.

Richard Lester's recollections of directing Audrey in *Robin and Marian* were given to me in an interview in London in September 1993.

Audrey's despondency is vouched for by an Italian woman friend who wishes to remain anonymous. The same friend comments on how even Audrey's personal sense of style seemed to be adversely affected by her marital difficulties. 'Now that she was living in Rome, and seeing much less of Givenchy', the same woman wrote to me, 'she dressed like a middle-class Roman matron: rather too fussily and, at times, even commonplace. The elegance that she had been very conscious of didn't seem to matter now. Interestingly, it returned pretty quickly after her marriage was dissolved and she went back to the splendid simplicity of turtle-neck sweaters and white trousers.'

21 THE COMFORTERS

The number of times Audrey refers to the Bergman films she had recently seen in interviews given to North American journalists indicates the strong impression that the two in question, *Face to Face* and *Scenes from a Marriage,* had made on her. Rex Reed, the New York critic, drew my attention to this. Nicolas Freeling, sent by the *Sunday Telegraph* to interview Audrey while she was making *Bloodline,* witnessed the same close identification with the problems of the characters played by Liv Ullmann. See *Sunday Telegraph,* 20 May 1979.

An entertaining account of how *Bloodline* was financed, so that no one could lose, appears in the *Guardian,* 28 March 1979, written by Bart Mills. Information about Audrey's tax affairs derives from a private source.

Peter Bogdanovich's description of Audrey's role in *They All Laughed,* and her mood while making the film, was obtained during a lengthy telephone interview with the writer-director in Los Angeles in November 1993. Bogdanovich is such a perceptive film-maker and historian of Hollywood—his recent book about Orson Welles, the best to date, combines both talents—that one awaits with hope the account of working with Audrey Hepburn that he must write some day.

My comments on Audrey and Ben Gazzara are the outcome of conversations with Gazzara shortly after the release of *They All Laughed* and my personal knowledge of Gazzara, a brilliant actor who does not do enough, over the years.

22 NEW MAN IN HER LIFE

The quotes from Dominick Dunne's interview with Audrey appear in *Vanity Fair*'s issue for May 1991.

The revelations about her father's fate caused by Audrey's slip of the tongue during an interview with Edward Klein are to be found in the 5 March 1989 issue of the magazine *Parade.* I have been unable to discover any other reference by her to the strange conclusion of a story which she had kept from the world all her adult life.

23 THE MISSIONARY'S STORY

I owe a great debt to Unicef for providing me with such a full account of Audrey's work for the international children's charity. Thanks to Sir Peter Ustinov's generous interest in this book, doors were opened that had hitherto been kept shut, or ajar, where the media were concerned in the shocked aftermath of Audrey's death.

In London, during July 1993, I viewed video and television material of some of the most hazardous and heart-breaking tours Audrey had undertaken in Africa. This was screened for me by Angela Hawke, Unicef's press officer in Britain. Though nothing could ever represent the enormous emotional investment Audrey made in Unicef, a contribution was subsequently made by me to the funds on which Unicef is totally dependent for its work.

In Geneva, Christa Roth, who liaises with Unicef's team of goodwill ambassadors, granted me a long interview in September 1993, and answered my questions frankly and intimately. It is one of the rare byproducts of biography-writing to meet people so totally devoted to the welfare of others.

24 'THE BEST CHRISTMAS OF MY LIFE'

Once again, the detailed programme of Audrey's visits, as well as much supplementary information, came from the Unicef offices in London and Geneva.

Audrey's three or four very close women friends—among them Connie Wald and Doris Brynner—as well as Robert Wolders are still too shocked by her abrupt death to feel they can talk about her last days. Mrs Brynner, however, agreed to answer questions of fact. During several telephone conversations with her, she kept me on the right track—I hope—regarding the errors that inadvertently appeared in other reports of Audrey's last months. Details of Audrey's treatment in Los Angeles and final illness in Tolochenaz come from a variety of other trustworthy sources in the United States, Switzerland and the Netherlands.

Lord Weidenfeld was—not for the first time—invaluable in making contact with some of my informants.

EPILOGUE: THE PASSING OF A FAIR LADY

Many of the details of Audrey's funeral were made accessible to me through video film, magazine photos—particularly those copied for me by Maggi Goodman, formerly British editor of *Hello*—and the memories of the Tolochenaz villagers I talked to during my visit in September 1993, all of which also helped to convey the atmosphere of the occasion.

Those who wish to visit Audrey's burial place may find that the best way is by train from Lausanne, a journey of some ten minutes or so, which avoids the slightly nondescript feel of the motorway. Alight at the tiny halt—hardly bigger than two telephone kiosks put together. Ignore the box-like model factories and flats constituting Tolochenaz's industrial sector and instead take the road that runs between apple orchards for about half a mile, turning to the right past some good-class flats and semidetached modern houses. One enters old Tolochenaz almost before realizing it. The wall of Audrey's garden and orchard is on the left and by following the road round to the left one comes upon La Paisible. To get to the tiny graveyard, cross the main road—watching out for constant traffic—and it can be seen on the right after a hundred yards or so. The iron gate is always open and Audrey's grave backs on to the drystone wall.

INDEX

CPSIA information can be obtained at www.ICGtesting.com
Printed in the USA
LVOW10s1803130614

389987LV00001B/1/P